The Roots
of Liberty

The Roots
of Liberty

Magna Carta, Ancient Constitution, and the Anglo-American Tradition of Rule of Law

Edited and with an

Introduction by Ellis Sandoz

amagi®

an imprint of Liberty Fund, Inc.

Liberty Fund

Indianapolis

Amagi books are published by Liberty Fund, Inc.,
a foundation established to encourage study of the
ideal of a society of free and responsible individuals.

𒂼𒄄

The cuneiform inscription that appears in the logo and serves as a
design element in all Liberty Fund books is the earliest-known written
appearance of the word "freedom" (*amagi*), or "liberty." It is taken from
a clay document written about 2300 B.C. in the Sumerian city-state of
Lagash.

Originally published in 1993 by the Curators of the University of Missouri,
University of Missouri Press, Columbia, Missouri, 65201.
All rights reserved
Printed in the United States of America

P   2   3   4   5   6   7   8   9   10

Library of Congress Cataloging-in-Publication Data

The roots of liberty: Magna Carta, ancient constitution, and the Anglo-
American tradition of rule of law/edited and with an introduction by
Ellis Sandoz.
    p. cm.
  Originally published: Columbia: University of Missouri Press, c1993.
  Includes bibliographical references and index.
  ISBN 978-0-86597-709-9 (pbk.: alk. paper)
1. Rule of law—England—History.   2. Constitutional history—
England.   I. Sandoz, Ellis, 1931–
  KD3995 .R66   2008
  342.4202'9—dc22   2007039507

Liberty Fund, Inc.
8335 Allison Pointe Trail, Suite 300
Indianapolis, Indiana 46250-1684

The editor offers grateful acknowledgment to Liberty Fund, Inc., for support of the symposium which occasioned the inquiry precipitating the contents of this book in initial draft. The editor also acknowledges with thanks permission to quote from Sir John Fortescue, *De Laudibus Legum Angliae,* translated and edited by S. B. Chrimes, © 1942 Cambridge University Press. Excerpts from the English translation reprinted by permission of the publisher.

Salus populi suprema lex est, et libertas popula summa salus populi
(The welfare of the people is the supreme law and the liberty
of the people the greatest welfare of the people).
—John Selden

It is an undoubted and fundamental point of this so ancient
common law of England, that the subject hath a true property in
his goods and possessions, which doth preserve as sacred that *meum
et tuum* that is the nurse of industry, and mother of courage, and
without which there can be no justice, of which *meum et tuum* is the
proper object.
—Sir Dudley Digges

There is one nation in the world whose Constitution has political
Liberty for its direct purpose.
—Montesquieu

The Rights of Magna Charta depend not on the Will of the Prince,
or the Will of the Legislature; but they are inherent natural Rights of
Englishmen: secured and confirmed they may be by the Legislature,
but not derived from nor dependent on their Will.
—Philalethes [Elisha Williams]

Contents

Preface to the Liberty Fund Edition

It is with pleasure that I write a few prefatory lines for Liberty Fund's reissue of *The Roots of Liberty* just twenty years after the symposium at Windsor Castle, which first elicited the scholarly studies the book contains. The devotion to liberty under law that is a hallmark of Anglo-American civilization and free government is nowhere symbolized with greater authority than in Magna Carta and the ancient constitution of which it is the noblest monument. The American constitutional tradition of which we so admiringly speak is grounded in the words and deeds brought together in this abiding centerpiece of our heritage as free men, the very *liber homo* announced by Magna Carta.

As conference director, discussion leader, contributor, and editor of the book, I take satisfaction in seeing a new edition appear. Furthermore, the conference itself spurred participants to renewed examination of the complex subject matter we addressed.

The impetus of our discussions can be traced in numerous publications since we deliberated at Windsor in 1988. Representative among these is Sir James Holt's new edition of *Magna Carta* (2d edition; Cambridge University Press, 1992), with its sustained attention to the meaning of *nullus liber homo,* a point of our puzzlement in discussion; and there is John Phillip Reid's *The Ancient Constitution and the Origins of Anglo-American Liberty* (Northern Illinois University Press, 2005), which expands chapter four of the present volume. My own efforts in the meanwhile directly continue the analysis begun then in chapters six and seven of *The Politics of Truth* (University of Missouri Press, 1999), which deal with Sir John Fortescue and with American religion and higher law.

This new edition is both valuable in itself and timely. With our millennial institutions of freedom and unique devotion to individual human worth and dignity under unremitting assault, we face an ideological and international conflict whose end and outcome lie nowhere in sight, beyond a horizon bounded by the iron curtain of the future. *The Roots of Liberty* can be one small help in guiding our passage through the perplexities of these treacherous times.

Ellis Sandoz

September 11, 2007

The Roots
of Liberty

Editor's Introduction: Fortescue, Coke, and Anglo-American Constitutionalism

The law of liberty as it rose to maturity in the British seventeenth and American eighteenth centuries forms the great theme and subject matter of the present volume, with Magna Carta and the ancient constitution the focal symbolisms under consideration. It is a study in history, constitutionalism, and political theory.

I

The emphasis of our study lies in disclosing the roots of liberty, not as some vague ideal, but as it endures into the present as the pulse of effective governing institutions. Such liberty is inseparable from rule of law, and its rise must be sought particularly in patterns and traditions of medieval and Renaissance England's public order. The great chronological remoteness of this period from our late-twentieth-century world belies the sense in which an ancient cause may yet be our own—if love of liberty under law and resistance to despotism can still be found among us as compelling convictions. The gist of the matter, to enlarge upon the metaphor of the "Tree of liberty," was given by the earl of Bolingbroke in reflecting on the periodic rise and fall of liberty in British experience since Saxon times through such minor episodes as the arrival of a Norman king in 1066 and the pretensions of the Stuart kings in the 1600s:

> Tho' the Branches were lopped, and the Tree lost its Beauty for a Time, yet the Root remain'd untouch'd, was set in a good Soil, and had taken strong Hold in it; so that Care and Culture, and Time were indeed required, and our Ancestors were forced to water it, if I may use such an Expression, with their Blood; but with this Care, and Culture, and Time and Blood, it shot again with greater Strength than ever, that we might sit quiet and happy under the Shade of it; for if the same Form was not exactly restored in every Part, a Tree

of the same Kind, and as beautiful, and as luxuriant as the former, grew up from the same root.[1]

The passage evidently impressed Thomas Jefferson, who echoed it in the familiar maxim that "the tree of liberty must be refreshed from time to time with the blood of patriots & tyrants. It is it's [*sic*] natural manure."[2] And the old figure of the Tree of liberty also brings to mind a favorite Bible verse of eighteenth-century Americans asserting liberty and evoking *salus populi*, the security of person and property claimed by free men: "And Judah and Israel dwelt safely, every man under his vine and under his fig tree, from Dan even to Beersheba, all the days of Solomon."[3]

The genesis of this book was a conference on the subject conducted in St. George's House, Windsor Castle, in June 1988, in observation of the 773d anniversary of the signing of Magna Carta. The inspiration of the exchange joined there and resumed here is a thesis that can be stated roughly as follows: Anglo-American liberty and constitutionalism rest essentially on a continuity with the Lancastrian con-

1. [Henry Saint John, viscount Bolingbroke], *A Dissertation Upon Parties: In Several Letters to Caleb D'Anvers, Esq.* 2d ed. (London, 1735), 194–95; as quoted by John Phillip Reid, herein, 284–85.

2. Letter of Thomas Jefferson to William S. Smith, from Paris, November 13, 1787, in Thomas Jefferson, *Writings: Autobiography, A Summary View of the Rights of British America, Notes on the State of Virginia, Public Papers, Addresses, Messages, and Replies, Miscellany, Letters,* ed. Merrill D. Peterson, Library of America (New York, 1984), 911.

3. 1 Kings 4:25 (King James Version). Thus, William Henry Drayton of Charleston, S.C., in 1769: "And I hope, in every circumstance of my life, that I shall act with consistency, with loyalty to my king, reverence to this my native country, and with charity to all men; and, that all the inhabitants of this colony, may not only possess these sentiments, but live always in the *practice* of them.—Then shall every man sit in peace under the cool shade of his fig-tree; possess his wanted liberty; enjoy the blessings of his vine; and in the gladness and thankfulness of his heart, sing—TE DEUM LAUDAMUS!" Quoted from *The Letters of a Freeman, Etc.: Essays on the Nonimportation Movement in South Carolina, Collected by William Henry Drayton,* ed. Robert M. Weir (Columbia, S.C., 1977), 32–33. For the "Tree of Liberty" see also Hugh Alison, *Spiritual Liberty: A Sermon* (Charleston, S.C., 1769), 5–6, and innumerable related references in Ellis Sandoz, ed., *Political Sermons of the American Founding Era, 1730–1805* (Indianapolis, 1991).

stitution propounded by Sir John Fortescue in the fifteenth century as that was revived and enlarged upon by the common law lawyers led by Sir Edward Coke (1552–1634) in the seventeenth-century struggle with the early Stuart kings, James I and Charles I. This ancient constitution (also called Gothic and Saxon) of Edward the Confessor, Magna Carta, Petition of Right, and Glorious Revolution, then, was substantially eclipsed and modified in Britain during the course of the eighteenth century only to be powerfully reasserted in America as part of the struggle leading up to independence, the American Founding culminating in the Declaration of Independence, the framing of the Constitution, and the ratification of the Bill of Rights.

Hence, the tenor of the book is to explore Magna Carta and ancient constitution in context but with an eye on the rise of liberty and rule of law as these came to maturity and their issues sharpened during the eighteenth-century conflict leading to American independence, the framing of the Constitution, and ratification of the Bill of Rights in 1791. One effect of this study will be to further illuminate the groundwork of modern politics by demonstrating the central place of the common lawyers, and the common law tradition as herein delineated, in the fabric of politics over several centuries, especially its powerful presence in the debates leading to the founding of the American republic. Room will have to be made, not merely for a new voice in the historiographic choir, but for a new soloist at center stage in the drama of the rise of free government.

It may be said that the core of the underlying thesis has been advanced by such earlier students of the subject as Frederic W. Maitland, William S. Holdsworth, and Edward S. Corwin. Thus, to indicate matters briefly, Holdsworth writes: "Coke preserved the medieval idea of the supremacy of the law, at a time when political speculation was tending to assert the necessity of a sovereign person or body, which was above the law." Maitland is quoted by Holdsworth as saying, "Coke's books are the great dividing line, and we are hardly out of the Middle Age till he has dogmatized its results." The latter then continues to explain that, in the seventeenth century, Parliament helped Coke to maintain the "medieval conception of the supremacy of law, and to apply it to the government of a modern state. In this matter also England became a model both to the framers of the Constitution of the United States and to the framers of the constitutions in continental states. The Supreme Court of the United States is a body which safeguards, more effectively than any other tribunal in the world, Coke's idea of the supremacy of the law."[4] Holdsworth further states, "It is largely owing to the influence of [Coke's] writings that these medieval conceptions have become part of our modern law . . . *they preserved for England and the world the constitutional doctrine of the rule of law.*"[5] Edward S. Corwin summarizes "Coke's contributions to the beginnings of American constitutional law" in part as follows:

> Coke came forward with . . . the doctrine of a law fundamental, binding Parliament and king alike, a law, moreover, embodied to great extent in a customary procedure of everyday institutions. From his version of Magna Carta, through the English Declaration and Bill of Rights of 1688 and 1689, to the Bills of Rights of our early American constitutions the line of descent is direct. . . . Lastly, Coke contributed the notion of Parliamentary supremacy *under* the law, which in time, with the differentiation of legislation and adjudication, became transmutable into the notion of *legislative* supremacy within a law subject to construction by the processes of adjudication.[6]

While it was neither Holdsworth nor Corwin who directly stirred more recent scholarly interest in these matters, it is worth pausing as we quote them to reflect that our subject matter relates to more than mere antiquarian and academic debate. Rather, it goes in certain vital aspects to the core of the political order concretely present in Britain and America and called by such familiar names as free government, rule of law, liberty under law, constitutional and representative government, republicanism, and the like. This is to suggest that, behind and, one must suppose, through the veil of symbols, modes of discourse, legalistic and historiographic collisions, distinctions, and

---

4. Sir William Holdsworth, *Some Makers of English Law: Tagore Lectures of 1937–38* (Cambridge, England, 1938), 113, 126–32.

5. Sir William S. Holdsworth, *History of English Law*, 13 vols. (London, 1923–1952), 5:493, italics added; cf. Ellis Sandoz, *A Government of Laws: Political Theory, Religion, and the American Founding* (Baton Rouge, 1990), chap. 7.

6. Edward S. Corwin, *The "Higher Law" Background of American Constitutional Law* (1928–1929; rpt., Ithaca, N.Y., 1955), 56–57.

polemics, a living tradition of personal, social, and historical reality finds articulate embodiment. To some unascertainable degree, while we are indeed considering words, often they are more than merely words or rhetorical configurations and linguistic patterns. They are winged words that at least some representative men of our civilization over a millennium or more have lived and died by as articulating basic truth. They have been taken as expressing the heart of the matter in evocative and meaningful symbols.

If language is the way to truth, it may be remembered that truth not only provides intelligibility and knowledge but conveys reality, or luminous *Being* in the comprehensive sense of that term as used by the old philosophers influential throughout the period under study here. Put otherwise, speech partakes of being no less than of thought.[7] This is to raise the possibility that the self-interpretation of existence in a substantial strand of Anglo-American historical reality unfolds in the materials we are considering, whatever else they may signify. Perhaps this may even be a part of their attraction. Why else one may wonder would they command such determined interest and, sometimes, fascination in the late twentieth century among solid historians and lawyers, as well as among such airy speculators as political philosophers?

To universalize the claims of fundamental law is the very essence of the matter when justice and truth are at issue, as they ever are in politi-

---

7. In the words of Étienne Gilson: "The most tempting of all the false first principles is: that *thought,* not *being,* is involved in my representations" (*The Unity of Philosophical Experience* [New York, 1937], 316). The philosophical issues can only be hinted here. They are pertinently discussed from the perspective of medieval scholasticism in Étienne Gilson, *The Spirit of Medieval Philosophy,* trans. A. H. C. Downes (New York, 1940), chaps. 3, 9, 10, 11; and from the equally pertinent perspective of fifteenth-century Platonism of Ficino in Paul Oskar Kristeller, *The Philosophy of Marsilio Ficino,* trans. Virginia Conant (New York, 1943), chaps. 3–7, thus (quoting Ficino): "'The most common of all things . . . seems to be Being itself. It is divided into two classes: the one exists by itself; the other is inherent in something else. The former is substance; the latter, attribute. Substance, again, is either corporeal or incorporeal. In like manner, attribute is either quality or quantity'" (p. 37). And Kristeller writes a bit later on: "In the act of thinking the mind is . . . united with the object through its inherent form, and in so far as the object as being in itself precedes the act of knowing, it follows that through this act the mind is formed by the object" (p. 50).

cal philosophy. Thus, the premier authority on the subject, Sir James Holt, has written of Magna Carta and its career in America that there natural law and ancient constitution became so mingled as to embody "two streams of thought" that, by contrast, in "England . . . had been inimical."

The Charter only survived alongside natural law by being raised to the same universal terms. Cap. 29 [guaranteeing due process of law and carried over into the Bill of Rights of state after state] had become a convenient formulation of a natural right. This was as far removed from Coke's thoughts as Coke had been from the Great Charter itself.

The history of Magna Carta is the history not only of a document but also of an argument. The history of the document is a history of repeated re-interpretation. But the history of the argument is a history of a continuous element of political thinking. In this light there is no inherent reason why an assertion of law originally conceived in aristocratic interests should not be applied on a wider scale. If we can seek truth in Aristotle, we can seek it also in Magna Carta. The class and political interests involved in each stage of the Charter's history are one aspect of it; the principles it asserted, implied or assumed are another. Approached as political theory it sought to establish the rights of subjects against authority and maintained the principle that authority was subject to law. If the matter is left in broad terms of sovereign authority on the one hand and the subject's rights on the other, this was the legal issue at stake in the fight against John, against Charles I and in the resistance of the American colonists to George III.[8]

II

Some sense of the horizon of experience and thought that inspired especially Sir Edward Coke's resistance to royal excesses and his revival of Magna Carta and ancient constitution in the seventeenth century may usefully be recalled in this introduction. Perhaps this can best be done through a glance at Coke's master in the law of the constitution, Sir John Fortescue (ca. 1385–ca. 1479). Thomas Littleton and

8. J. C. Holt, *Magna Carta,* 2d ed. (Cambridge, England, 1992), 18–19.

Fortescue were major figures in the fifteenth-century revival of native English law, the former by his treatise on land law, the latter by his exposition of the constitution, both of them different from Roman law, with which depreciating comparison is made. If, for Coke, Littleton's *Tenures* is "the ornament of the common law, and the most perfect and absolute work that ever was written in any human science," Fortescue's *De Laudibus Legum Angliae* (written during 1468–1471) he finds to be of such "weight and worthiness" that it should be "written in letters of gold."[9]

Fortescue was admitted to Lincoln's Inn before 1420, served in parliament from 1421 for several terms over the next fifteen years, became Chief Justice of the King's Bench in 1442 under Henry VI, and was knighted in the following year. During the War of the Roses (1455 onward), Fortescue adhered to the House of Lancaster against the Yorkists and fled to Scotland with the king and queen in or after 1461, which was also the time of his appointment as Lord Chancellor. In 1463 he was exiled to France (Bar) with Queen Margaret and returned with her to England in 1471. He submitted to Edward IV after his capture and the final defeat of the Lancastrians at the battle of Tewkesbury and served as a member of the king's council until 1473. Fortescue died after May 1479.[10]

Cast as a dialogue between the "Chancellor" and a young "Prince" (Edward, only son of King Henry VI), *De Laudibus* has as a central point the supremacy of law: "all human laws are sacred, inasmuch as law is defined by the words, *Law is a sacred sanction commanding what is honest and forbidding the contrary.* . . . Law may also be described as that which is the Art of the Good and the Just. . . . Moreover, all laws that are promulgated by man are decreed by God."[11] "The laws . . . not only invite

---

9. Sir Edward Coke, *Coke on Littleton* [1628], *The First Part of the Institutes of the Laws of England* (1628), Preface (n.p.). Sir John Fortescue, *De Laudibus Legum Angliae,* ed. and trans. S. B. Chrimes, General Preface by Harold D. Hazeltine (Cambridge, England, 1942), xlix; for the date of composition see lxxxviii. *De Laudibus* was first printed ca. 1546 and became a legal classic with the publication of John Selden's edition in 1616 (see xcix, cvii).

10. A detailed chronology is given by Chrimes in Fortescue, *De Laudibus,* lix–lxvii.

11. Ibid., 7–9 (chap. 3); italics as in original.

you to fear God and thereby be wise . . . , but invite you also to their study, that you may obtain happiness and blessedness so far as that is obtainable in this life . . . the *Summum Bonum.*"

> Human laws are none other than rules by which perfect justice is manifested. But . . . the Justice which the laws disclose is not the kind that is called commutative or distributive or any other sort of virtue, but is itself the Perfect Virtue that is called by the name of Legal Justice, which . . . is perfect because it eliminates all vice and teaches every virtue, so that it is in itself justly called [the whole of excellence or] Virtue. . . . This justice, indeed, is the object of all royal administration, because without it a king judges unjustly and is unable to fight rightfully. But this justice attained and truly observed, the whole office of king is fairly discharged. Therefore, since happiness is the perfect exercise of virtues, and human justice, which is not perfectly revealed except by the law, is not merely the effect of virtue, but of all virtue, it follows that he who is in enjoyment of justice is made happy by the law. Thereby he becomes blessed, for blessedness and happiness are the same in this fleeting life, and through justice he attains the *Summum Bonum* of this world. Not, indeed, that law can do this without grace, nor will you [as king] be able to learn or to strive after law or virtue, without grace.[12]

This striking passage equating law and perfect justice, and distinguishing the latter from commutative and distributive justice, while obviously referring to a distinction given in book V of Aristotle's *Nicomachean Ethics,* may plausibly be read as going considerably beyond that rather cryptic text to imply Plato's cardinal teaching in the *Republic* that Justice (*Dike*) is the perfection of all virtue in a man no less than in a polity. This, by Plato's account, is the condition of the soul of a man who lives a well-ordered life, so that a man can be said to be just in himself. Indeed, it is the characterological embodiment of such

---

12. Ibid., 11–13 (chap. 4). The bracketed words in the second sentence interpolate a translation of Aristotle, *Nicomachean Ethics* V.1.19–20 1130a8–9, evidently the place in the ultimate text paraphrased by Fortescue; cf. Aristotle, *Nicomachean Ethics* VI.8.1–2 1141b23–30 where a parallel discussion of *phronesis* occurs. For Fortescue's sources see Chrimes's notes and cautions in *De Laudibus,* 148–49, and the more general discussion, lxxxix–xcv.

transcendent justice that forms the order of excellence to be imparted to the best polis through the rule of philosopher-kings or by the inspired lawgivers through the rule of true law.[13] However this may be, it is evident that Fortescue's argument equates ancient English law as it structures the living constitution of the realm with Justice and divine and natural law, at least as far as grace permits this to be concretely

---

13. Cf. Aristotle, *Nicomachean Ethics* V.11.9 1138b6; Plato, *Republic* III–IV culminating in the great passage at 443c–444a. Paul Shorey remarks of this passage, "Aristotle . . . would regard all this as mere metaphor," in Plato, *Republic,* ed. Shorey, 2 vols. (Loeb Classical Library Edition; Cambridge, Mass., & London, 1930), 2:415n. Fortescue and his sources need not have thought so, however, and the suggested conflation is not implausible on the ground suggested by Shorey. See also Plato, *Laws* IV.714a–716c where the understanding of rule of true law as divine reason is given; cf. Aristotle, *Politics* III.11., esp. 1287a35–b7.

The surge of interest in and translation of Plato's dialogues during Fortescue's lifetime is a prominent part of the backdrop of the work under consideration and possibly inspired the form of *De Laudibus* as a dialogue. The rediscovery of Plato was led by Florentines, Leonardo Bruni Aretino (1369–1444) among the earliest of them and with important English contacts, anticipating Marsilio Ficino in that respect. The "Leonardus" of *De Laudibus,* Bruni's *Introduction to Moral Philosophy* (dated 1421–1424) is, after the Bible, which is quoted fifty-two times, one of Fortescue's more prominent literary sources, as Chrimes shows (xc–xci). Ficino began the translation of Plato into Latin under the aegis of Cosimo de' Medici's Platonic Academy nearly twenty years after Bruni's death, in 1463 (having completed translation of the *Corpus Hermeticum* in the same year), and completed translation of the dialogues in about 1468 (see Kristeller, *The Philosophy of Ficino,* 16–17). And Platonism was widely available to Fortescue otherwise, including from such other sources as Boethius and a compilation from which most of his classical quotations are believed to have come entitled *Auctoritates Aristotelis, Senece, Boecii, Platonis* (see *De Laudibus,* lxxxix).

No detailed tracing of sources is possible here, of course, but a general point may be suggested. This is that the work of Fortescue is imbued with the understanding of reality reflected in Aristotle and Plato as presented by Renaissance scholars recovering the writings of these Greek philosophers in an atmosphere *pervaded* by the Christian faith experience and assumptions and by scholastic theology; hence the importance of placing Fortescue's work in this rather than in some other primary context. See the remarks of Charles Plummer in Sir John Fortescue, *The Governance of England: Otherwise Called The Difference between an Absolute and a Limited Monarchy,* ed. Plummer (Oxford, 1885), 102–5. Cf. Étienne Gilson, *La philosophie au moyen âge* (Paris, 1944), 736–38; also Gilson's *History of Christian Philosophy in the Middle Ages* (New York, 1955), 541–42, 803–4.

achieved on earth by human laws promulgated and administered by human magistrates. Thus, the historically *ancient* and the ontologically *higher* law—eternal, divine, natural—are woven together to compose a single harmonious texture in Fortescue's account of English law.[14]

To his noble medieval Christian synthesis of jurisprudence and philosophy, resting theoretically especially upon Plato, Aristotle, and Thomas Aquinas, Fortescue adds the authority of "Holy Scripture," citing two maxims: "Be instructed, ye who judge the earth" and "Love justice, ye who judge the earth."[15] He thereby brings together from Revelation the knowing of truth and the love of Justice whose combination enables the courageous king to act justly in ruling. The result is equivalent to Aristotle's insistence that the ethical and political philosophical science of human affairs is not so much concerned with knowing as with doing, thereby evoking by implication the potential-actualization theory central to classical and medieval philosophical anthropology.[16]

The great merit and distinction of the ancient constitution of England, Fortescue continues, is that

14. This line of analysis is borne out by Fortescue's earlier work, *A Treatise Concerning the Nature of the Law of Nature,* where the debts to Aristotle, Augustine, Boethius, and, most especially, Thomas Aquinas are much more explicit than in *De Laudibus.* See Thomas (Fortescue) Lord Clermont, ed., *The Works of Sir John Fortescue, Knight,* . . . (London, 1869), 194, 205–6, 215–16, 219–22, and *passim.* It may be stressed that it would be odd in the fifteenth century if this were *not* so. The kinds of law mentioned are those, in addition to human law, identified and analyzed by Thomas Aquinas in the *Treatise on Law* of the *Summa Theologica* I–II.Qq.90–108. Thus, in answer to whether there is eternal law, Thomas writes: "a law is nothing else but a dictate of practical reason emanating from the ruler who governs a perfect community. Now it is evident, granted that the world is ruled by divine providence . . . that the whole community of the universe is governed by divine reason. Wherefore the very Idea of the government of things in God the Ruler of the universe has the nature of a law. . . . [T]he end of the divine government is God Himself, and His law is not distinct from Himself" (Q.91.A.1 [trans. D. Bigongiari]).

15. Fortescue, *De Laudibus,* 13–15 (chap. 4), quoting from the Vulgate, Psalms 2:10 and Wisdom 1:1.

16. Cf. Aristotle, *Nicomachean Ethics* I.3.6: "the end of this science is not knowledge but action [*praxis*]." For *peri ta anthropina philosophia* see X.9.22. 1181b15–16.

the king of England is not able to change the laws of his kingdom at pleasure, for he rules his people with a government not only regal but also political. If he were to preside over them with a power entirely regal, he would be able to change the laws of his realm, and also impose on them tallages and other burdens without consulting them; this is the sort of dominion which the civil laws indicate when they state [in *lex regia*] that *What pleased the prince has the force of law* [*Quod principi placuit legis habet vigorem*]. But the case is far otherwise with the king ruling his people politically, because he is not able himself to change the laws without the assent of his subjects nor burden an unwilling people with strange imposts, so that, ruled by laws that they themselves desire, they freely enjoy their properties, and are despoiled neither by their own king nor any other.[17]

This constitution of double majesty, of a political people represented in parliament and of a kingship bounded by law, in something more than merely a directive sense (*dominium politicum et regale*), is the heart of England's ancient constitution.[18] Its emphasis lies in secur-

17. Fortescue, *De Laudibus,* 25–27 (chap. 9); italics as in original.

18. The Thomasic distinction between coercive and directive senses of being bound by law may be a useful starting point for understanding Fortescue's conception of the ambiguous relationship of king to law of the realm, since the king seems to be above law in certain discretionary and prerogative respects by the account given in *De Laudibus* (e.g., pp. 86–87 [chap. 36], 136–37 [chap. 54]). With a full cognizance of the realities of medieval political power that would certainly be matched in Fortescue, Thomas writes to this effect: "The sovereign is said to be 'exempt from the law,' as to its coercive power, since, properly speaking, no man is coerced by himself, and law has no coercive power save from the authority of the sovereign. . . . But as to the directive force of law, the sovereign is subject to the law by his own will. . . . Hence, in the judgment of God, the sovereign is not exempt from the law as to its directive force, but he should fulfill it of his own free will and not of constraint.—Again the sovereign is above the law in so far as, when it is expedient, he can change the law and dispense in it according to time and place" (*Summa Theologica* I–II.Q.96.A.5. *ad* 3 [trans. D. Bigongiari]). This position softens the force of Roman law doctrines that Fortescue himself largely rejects, *viz.,* "Whatever pleases the prince has the force of law [*Quod principi placuit legis habet vigorem*]" (*Digest* I.4.1) and "The prince is above the law [*Princeps legibus solutus*]" (I.3.31).

Especially in the English background of these matters, of course, lies not only a reliance on the *conscience* of the monarch to direct him by reason to obedience

ing through the consent of the realm laws protecting the immemorial liberty of free men, serving the well-being of the whole community, and assuring a balance between parliament and king that will foster effective no less than just rule. Fortescue's account, whatever the differences, is patently indebted to the mixed regime favored in a range of forms by Aristotle, Polybius, Cicero, and, in a most interesting way, by Thomas Aquinas, who associates it with the Mosaic commonwealth of ancient Israel. It foreshadows the mixed and balanced constitution of king, lords, and commons that appears full-blown so unexpectedly with Charles I's *Answer to the XIX Propositions of Both Houses of Parliament* in June 1642. Moreover, something on the order of this institutional arrangement delineates the generic essentials of *free government* itself. It remains a cardinal component of constitutional development and theory from *De Laudibus* to John Adams's *Defence of the Constitutions* and Publius's *Federalist No. 51*, not to claim more.[19] S. B. Chrimes's judgment

---

to law but also the political balance of the baronage and constitutional check of parliament grounded in custom. Nor should the *diffidatio* provision in the original, 1215 Magna Carta (chap. 61) be forgotten whereby the customary principle is invoked of coercing a faithless lord, even including the king, to keep within law and agreement. It is there memorably affirmed in detail by the establishment, among other things, of the twenty-five barons of the realm as *fidejussores* who would renounce liegeance and justifiably make war under feudal custom should the king in his natural capacity violate the solemn promises given in the Charter. The great near-contemporary jurist Henry de Bracton (d. 1268) succinctly drew the lesson in words that later came to haunt Charles I: "The king has a superior, namely, God. Also the law by which he is made king. Also his *curia*, namely, the earls and barons, because if he is without bridle, that is without law, they ought to put the bridle on him" (*De legibus et consuetudinibus Angliae* in *Bracton on the Laws and Customs of England,* ed. Samuel E. Thorne, 4 vols. [Cambridge, Mass., 1968–1977], 2:110; cf. 33, 305). On diffidation and related matters see J. E. A. Joliffe, *The Constitutional History of Medieval England: From the English Settlement to 1485,* 4th Ed. (1961, rpt. New York, 1967), 258–60, 285.

19. See the discussion in Holdsworth, *History of English Law,* 6:83–84; Corinne Comstock Weston and Janelle Renfrow Greenberg, *Subjects and Sovereigns: The Grand Controversy over Legal Sovereignty in Stuart England* (Cambridge, England, 1981), chap. 3; Donald W. Hanson, *From Kingdom to Commonwealth: The Development of Civic Consciousness in English Thought* (Cambridge, Mass., 1970), 217–52; James M. Blythe, *Ideal Government and the Mixed Constitution in the Middle Ages* (Princeton, 1992), 8, 10, 42, 45, 260–66, 304, 307. Also Corinne C. Weston,

that literary sources may have supplied "the inspiration" for Fortescue's mixed dominion while observation and ingenuity supplied the substance of his account of the government of England may be as close to the fact as we are likely to get. His further judgment of exactly what that observation and ingenuity produced is stated as follows:

> [Fortescue] was not content to say merely that the English king was limited by divine law, moral rule, and the law and custom of the realm. He says that, but he also says, quite clearly and definitely, that the limitation on the king of England is a *parliamentary* limitation; and in saying that he was saying something that nobody, so far as we know, had said before, certainly not with such distinctness and insistence. Fortescue was the first writer to abandon merely feudal

---

English Constitutional Theory and the House of Lords, 1556–1832 (New York, 1965); Weston, "Beginnings of the Classical Theory of the English Constitution," *Proceedings of the American Philosophical Society* 100 (1956): 133–44, where key excerpts from Charles I's *Answer* are given as an appendix; Weston, "The Theory of the Mixed Monarchy under Charles I and After," *English Historical Review* 75 (1960): 426–43; J. G. A. Pocock, *The Machiavellian Moment: Florentine Political Thought and the Atlantic Republican Tradition* (Princeton, 1975), chap. 11. Also, the critique of earlier interpretations in Michael Mendle, *Dangerous Positions: Mixed Government, the Estates of the Realm, and the Making of the "Answer to the XIX Propositions"* (University, Ala., 1985), esp. chap. 3 where the place of Fortescue is assessed.

For the mixed regime see Aristotle *Politics* IV.6.1–7. 1293b34–1294b42; Polybius *Histories* VI.1.3, 3.8–9; Cicero *Republic* I.29.45, 32.56, 35.54–56. Also Thomas Aquinas *Summa Theologica* I–II Q.105.A.1 where, perhaps for the first time (at least since Philo), the authority of the Bible is invoked for the mixed regime as the primordial form of human government ordained of God, the rule of judges established by Moses that Thomas sketches on the basis of Deut. 1:13, 15 and Exod. 18:21 as the prototype of constitutional monarchy. See the insightful discussion in Brian Tierney, *Religion, Law, and the Growth of Constitutional Thought, 1150–1650* (Cambridge, England, 1982), 87–90. The original Mosaic "republic" is a commonplace of American preachers of the period of the American Revolution; e.g., see the 1775 Massachusetts election sermon of Harvard College president Dr. Samuel Langdon, reprinted in John Wingate Thornton, ed., *Pulpit of the American Revolution; or Political Sermons of the Period of 1776* (Boston, 1860), 227–57, and the analysis in Sandoz, *A Government of Laws*, chap. 5. For John Adams see *The Works of John Adams, Second President of the United States: With a Life of the Author, Notes and Illustrations,* ed. Charles Francis Adams, 10 vols. (Boston, 1850–1856), 4:285, 294–98, 435–43, 540–41, and *passim.*

and pre-feudal notions of the monarchy, and to affirm boldly that it was not only limited, but parliamentary in character. . . . Parliament [itself] has become customary; its assent in taxation and legislation has become customary; and no earthly bond was so binding on Englishmen as custom—unless and until that very parliament accustomed were to unloosen it. The clear expression of these assumptions, fundamental to the whole subsequent course of English government, places Fortescue, if not exactly among the great original thinkers of the English constitution, at least among its immortals.[20]

Fortescue stresses that the rule of law is the same as *true* kingly rule of the kind enjoined by God and supported by Thomas Aquinas no less than by Aristotle; and it is an indispensable prophylaxis against tyranny. A kingdom should be so constituted, he argues, "that the king may not be free to govern his people tyrannically, which only comes to pass when the regal power is restrained by political law. Rejoice, therefore, good prince, that such is the law of the kingdom to which you are to succeed, because it will provide no small security and comfort for you and for the people." Merely regal rule is founded in coercion, on the pattern of Nimrod [Nembroth], and such ruling of a subject people only occurred when men "usurped to themselves the name of king, from the word 'regendo,' . . . [and] as a hunter compels beasts enjoying their liberty to obey him, so [do they] compel men."[21]

Fortescue explains the meaning of *political rule* in chapter 13. It begins from Augustine's definition of "a people [as] a body of men united by consent of law and by community of interest."[22] But this definition is inadequate, because it suggests a body without a head to govern

20. Chrimes in Fortescue, *De Laudibus*, xciv–xcv and ci–cii. In the former place it is pointed out that the words *regimen regale et politicum* occur in the later part of Thomas Aquinas's *De Regimine Principum*, attributed to Ptolemy of Lucca (III.20), and may have contributed to the "inspiration" mentioned.

21. Fortescue, *De Laudibus*, 24–29 (chaps. 9 and 12); Fortescue, *Treatise Concerning the Nature of the Law of Nature*, part 1, chaps. 26 and 34. For Nimrod see Gen. 10:8–9. Cf. Fortescue, *Governance of England*, ed. Plummer, 110–12.

22. Fortescue, *De Laudibus*, 31 (chap. 13), quoting Augustine, *City of God* 19.23.

it. Fortescue next turns to Aristotle, whom he quotes from book I of the *Politics* to the effect that "whenever one body is constituted out of many, one will rule, and the others be ruled." Such a ruler will be called a king and be set up by the people for government of that body. He then elaborates from the analogy suggested by Aristotle: "As in this way the physical body grows out of the embryo, regulated by one head, so the kingdom issues from the people, and exists as a body mystical, governed by one man as head. . . . The law, indeed, by which a group of men is made into a people, resembles the nerves of the body physical." The figure of the realm that articulates itself as a mystical body, animated by the intention of the people (*intencio populi*) and governed by its representative the king, brilliantly conveys the meaning of the order of a society organized for action in history as the newly emergent nation-state of England. Fortescue summarizes:

> You have here, prince, the form of the institution of the political kingdom, whence you can estimate the power that the king can exercise in respect of the law and the subjects of such a realm; for a king of this sort is obliged to protect the law, the subjects, and their bodies and goods, and he has power to this end issuing from the people, so that it is not permissible for him to rule his people with any other power. . . . [T]hus the kingdom of England blossomed forth into a dominion regal and political out of Brutus's band of Trojans, whom he led out of the territories of Italy and of the Greeks.[23]

The interrelationship of the community formed by the people and its ruler, in the anthropomorphic analogy of the body and its head,

---

23. Ibid., 31–33. By Coke's accounting, after Brutus arrived with the Trojan remnant to become the first king of England, he "wrote a book in the Greek tongue, calling it the Laws of the Britons, and he collected the same out of the Laws of the Trojans: this King, say they, died after the Creation of the World 2860 years, and before the Incarnation of Christ 1103 years, Samuel then being Judge of Israel" (*The Reports of Sir Edward Coke, Knt., in English, In Thirteen Parts Complete* . . . , revised and edited by George Wilson, Serjeant At Law, 7 vols. [London, 1776–1777]; quoted from Coke's *Third Reports*, vi–viii). For a fuller statement of the political theory of the referenced passage in *De Laudibus* and related passages in Fortescue's *Governance of England*, chaps. 1 and 2, see Eric Voegelin, *The New Science of Politics: An Introduction* (Chicago, 1952), 42–46, 50.

assumes the Christianized version of Aristotle's notions of men as naturally political and of political or true rule as grounded in consent and concern for the well-being of the whole community. More than this, however, it adapts the New Testament notion (1 Cor. 12) of the invisible church as the mystical body of Christ in whom all the faithful are united and applies it to the *state*, with the new head now being the monarch. The symbolism of community and king as the political *corpus mysticum* is revived and transformed in the later contractual language of Thomas Hobbes, who echoes this passage.[24]

All human law is "law of nature, customs, or statutes, which are also called constitutions [*constituciones*]," Fortescue next explains. When the rules laid down by the law of nature and by customs have been reduced to writing, promulgated by the prince's authority, and commanded to be kept, they are "then changed into a constitution or something of the nature of statutes." They "thereupon oblige the prince's subjects to keep them under greater penalty than before, by reason of the strictness of that command."[25] The law of nature is universal, as Aristotle and Thomas Aquinas teach, and the customs of England are very ancient, states Fortescue with a nod to the Great Migrations and distant myth before them. His dating begins from the first inhabitants, who were Britons who arrived after the fall of Troy led by the eponymous Brutus, son of Aeneas. After this mythic founding, the realm survived subsequent rule by Romans, again Britons, Saxons, Danes, again Saxons, and

> finally by Normans, whose posterity hold the realm at the present time. And throughout the period of these nations and their kings, the realm has been continuously ruled by the same customs as it is now, customs which, if they had not been the best, some of those kings would have changed for the sake of justice or by the impulse of caprice, and totally abolished them, especially the Romans, who judged almost the whole of the rest of the world by their laws.

24. Thomas Hobbes, *Leviathan,* chap. 17; cf. John Locke, *Second Treatise of Government,* secs. 105–12. Cf. John of Salisbury's elaborate use of the organic analogy in *Politicraticus,* ed. and trans. C. J. Nederman (Cambridge, England, 1990), 2:65–67 and *passim.*

25. Fortescue, *De Laudibus,* 37 (chap. 15).

That this was not done to English law, Fortescue argues, proves that no other nation's laws nor any Christian kingdom's laws are so rooted in antiquity. "Hence there is no gainsaying nor legitimate doubt but that the customs of the English are not only good but the best [*optimas esse Anglorum consuetudines*]."[26] His reason for so concluding is primarily that English laws now and always emanate from the entire community, not merely from the will of the king as in the France of Louis XI, where defective regal rule alone prevails (*dominium tantum regale*) and produces the equivalent of a tyranny. Thus, English laws "do not emanate from the will of the prince alone, . . . where so often statutes secure the advantage of their maker only, thereby redounding to the loss and undoing of the subjects." Rather they

> are made not only by the prince's will, but also by the assent of the whole realm, so they cannot be injurious to the people. . . . Furthermore, it must be supposed that they are necessarily replete with prudence and wisdom, since they are promulgated by the prudence of . . . more than three hundred chosen men . . . of parliament. . . . And if statutes ordained with such solemnity and care happen not to give full effect to the intention of the makers, they can speedily be revised, and yet not without the assent of the commons and nobles of the realm, in the manner in which they first originated [*et non sine communitatis et procerum regni illius assensu, quali ipsa primitus emanarunt*].[27]

The superiority of English laws is especially marked by the rejection of torture, by the utilization of pluralities of witnesses, and by the use of juries to render judgments. Fortescue takes care to prove the conformity of jury trial with divine law as disclosed in scripture and as a superior means of arriving at truth and justice.[28]

Rule in accordance with law is not a burden but a liberty and blessing for English kings, Fortescue maintains. For this enables them to serve goodness and justice and curbs their human tendencies to serve selfish purposes, thereby perverting kingship into tyranny, understood

26. Ibid., 39–41 (chaps. 16 and 17).
27. Ibid., 41 (chap. 18).
28. Ibid., 75–77 (chap. 32).

as coercive rule of the community as well as enslavement of the man to his own base passions. This line of analysis is a major theme in Fortescue and closes a gap in classical and medieval political theory between the notions that a good kingship is the best form of government simply while the mixed regime governed by laws is best practicably: the good kingship *is* the mixed dominion of *De Laudibus*.[29]

As to why some kings of England nonetheless sought to change the laws and introduce the Roman civil law, Fortescue again quotes *lex regia* (*Institutes* I.2.6.; *Digest* I.4.1) in explanation: "What pleased the prince has the force of law [*Quod principi placuit legis habet vigorem*]." But, he emphasizes, the

> laws of England do not sanction any such maxim, since the king of that land rules his people not only regally but also politically, and so he is bound by oath at his coronation to the observance of his law. This certain kings of England bore hardly, thinking themselves therefore not free to rule over their subjects as the kings ruling merely regally do, who rule their people by the civil law, and especially by the aforesaid maxim of that law, so that they change laws at their pleasure, make new ones, inflict punishments, and impose burdens on their subjects, and also determine suits of parties at their own will and when they wish. Hence [certain earlier English kings] endeavored to throw off this political yoke, in order thus to rule merely regally over their subject people, or rather to rage unchecked, not heeding that the power of the two kings [i.e., in the purely regal regime and in the mixed dominion] is equal, . . . nor heeding that it is not a yoke but a liberty to rule a people politically,

29. Ibid., 35 (chap. 14): "For, as Boethius said, *There is no power unless for good,* so that to do evil, as the king reigning regally can more freely do than the king ruling his people politically, diminishes rather than increases his power." Cf. Romans 13:1. That the *dominium politicum et regale* is the very teaching of Thomas Aquinas regarding the best form of government as kingship is argued in Fortescue's *Treatise Concerning the Nature of the Law of Nature,* part 1, chap. 16: "that there is a third kind of government . . . we are not only taught by experience and ancient history, but we know hath been taught by . . . St. Thomas. For in the kingdom of England the kings make not laws, nor impose subsidies on their subjects, without the consent of the Three Estates of the Realm" (ibid., 206).

and the greatest security not only to the people but also to the king himself, and no small alleviation of his care.[30]

The distinction between liberty and license drawn in this passage is familiar from antiquity no less than from such later writers as John Locke. The correlation of liberty with law and true (or just) rule is a major theme in political and constitutional theory. It draws sustenance from all of the sources cited by Fortescue (divine law, natural law, customs and ancient laws of England) and is protected by the institutions of mixed dominion that form the hallmark of the ancient constitution sketched and celebrated in *De Laudibus,* points not lost on Coke in a later time.

The liberties enjoyed by Englishmen include, Fortescue writes, security against billeting in private houses against the master's will, compensation for lodging in public establishments, and security of property against arbitrary invasion or uncompensated taking. "Nor can the king . . . , by himself or by his ministers, impose tallages, subsidies, or any other burdens whatever on his subjects, nor change their laws, nor make new ones, without the concession or assent of his whole realm expressed in his parliament."[31] Thomas Aquinas's great maxim, itself adapted from Mark 2:27, is quoted: "The king is given for the sake of the kingdom, and not the kingdom for the sake of the king." The meaning, Fortescue tells the prince, is that "all the power of a king ought to be applied to the good of his realm, which in effect consists in the defence of it against invasions by foreigners, and in the protection of the inhabitants of the realm and their goods from injuries and rapine by natives." Any ostensible king who cannot do these things is termed "impotent" and, even worse than this, "impotence itself," if he is so overcome by his base passions or poverty as to be unable to keep his hands off the property of his subjects or abuses them otherwise. So far from being free, such a supposed king is enslaved and contemptible. On the other hand, a king who defends his own people and their possessions and protects them not only from alien and native enemies but "against his own oppression and plunder, even though his own

30. Ibid., 79–81 (chap. 34).
31. Ibid., 87 (chap. 36).

passions and necessities tempt him otherwise," is truly free and powerful. "For who can be more powerful and freer than he who is able to restrain not only others but also himself? The king ruling his people politically can and always does do this." For these reasons, then, "St. Thomas . . . is deemed to wish that all realms of the earth were ruled politically," just as is England.[32]

Last, among Fortescue's golden words of pertinence here are those on natural liberty:

> A law is . . . necessarily adjudged cruel, if it increases servitude and diminishes freedom, for which human nature always craves. . . . [For] freedom was instilled into human nature by God. Hence freedom taken away from man always desires to return, as is always the case when natural liberty is denied. So he who does not favor liberty is to be deemed impious and cruel. In considering these matters the laws of England favor liberty in every case.[33]

III

The salient contours of the ancient constitution of England as invoked by Sir Edward Coke in the first third of the seventeenth century appear in the foregoing consideration of *De Laudibus*. This body of law and reason accords with the political and constitutional practices and principles of medieval Christianity and, so, is intended by Fortescue, and presumably by Coke as well, to be taken as empirically informed and philosophically acute. Thus, it sets a historically and theoretically attested standard to be approximated if just rule is to be sustained; and it does not accept instances of injustice and abuse as precedents to be followed in the spirit of proto-positivistic crude or de facto Hobbism.[34] It appeals to all the sources of law with the understanding that the ancient laws of England accord with eternal and natural law no less than with immemorial precedent, as befits all human law but is uniquely

---

32. Ibid., 89–91 (chap. 37). Fortescue quotes Thomas Aquinas from *De Regimine Principis* III.11, i.e., a portion of the treatise attributed to Ptolemy of Lucca rather than to Thomas himself.

33. Ibid., 105 (chap. 42).

34. See Charles M. Gray, "Editor's Introduction" to Sir Matthew Hale, *The History of the Common Law of England,* ed. Charles M. Gray (Chicago, 1971), xiv.

achieved in England where norm and fact tend to converge, at least in the patriotic conceits of Fortescue and Coke.

Yet it is just at this rather nebulous point that Coke and his contemporary as well as latter-day adversaries seem to part company. The point is illustrated by Coke's great parliamentary ally John Selden in his critical notes to his 1616 edition of *De Laudibus,* where he writes:

> In truth, and to speak without perverse affection, all laws in general are originally equally antient. All were grounded upon nature, and no nation was, that out of it took not their grounds; and nature being the same in all, the beginning of all laws must be same. . . . [But] although the law of nature be truly said immutable, yet it is as true, that it is limitable, and limited law of nature is the law now used in every state. . . . And hence it is, that those customs which have come all out of one fountain, *nature,* thus vary from and cross one another in several commonwealths. . . . [Thus] were natural laws limited for the conveniency of civil society here, and those limitations have been from thence, increased, altered, interpreted, and brought to what now they are; although perhaps saving the meerly immutable part of nature, now, in regard to their first being, they are not otherwise than a ship, that by often mending had no piece of the first materials, or as the house that's so often repaired, *ut nihil ex pristina materia supersit,* which yet, by the civil law, is to be accounted the same still.[35]

35. John Selden, *Opera,* III, cols. 1891–92, as quoted by Richard Tuck, *Natural Rights Theories: Their Origin and Development* (Cambridge, England, 1979), 84. "This was in fact already the Burkean theory of English law, and its influence . . . can be traced directly on to Matthew Hale . . . and thence to Blackstone and the mainstream of eighteenth-century English legal thinking" (Tuck, ibid.). The year 1616 was a fateful one for Sir Edward Coke. Already removed three years earlier as Chief Justice of Common Pleas by James I and with Bacon's connivance appointed Chief Justice of King's Bench where it was thought he might be less troublesome, Coke in 1616 was ousted from that office after three major conflicts with the king. As was said by one John Castle: "A thunderbolt hath fallen on the Lord Coke, which hath overthrown him from the very roots." Quoted by Catherine Drinker Bowen, *The Lion and the Throne: The Life and Times of Sir Edward Coke (1552–1634)* (Boston, 1956), 390.

The famous metaphor of the unchanging laws of England as the Argonauts' Ship is given by Sir Matthew Hale (1609–1676), Selden's executor, as follows:

The "meerly immutable" core of natural law can, by this analogy, be whittled down to a mere nothing while yet pretending in all appearances to be the same as it always had been by the simple expedient of being called the same, and meaning is lost through the social amnesia of a post-Christian civilization forgetful of the center that no longer holds. More narrowly, the pivotal change lies in subtle shifts of language, changes in the meaning of *nature* itself and of *human nature* as these occur apace in the work of such leading lights of the seventeenth century as Sir Francis Bacon and Thomas Hobbes. For these writers launch a sustained attack on the tradition of thought exemplified by Augustine, Thomas Aquinas, and Richard Hooker that is wholly at odds with the fundamental convictions of Fortescue, Coke, and Sir Matthew Hale. Fortescue conserves the liberty and justice of the ancient constitution by appeal to the sameness of the English laws as these are undergirded by the philosophical truth and theological doctrine of medieval jurisprudence, Thomas Aquinas, and Christianity. Coke actively, even fiercely, combats the slide into enlightened arbitrary modernity, which he confronts in the paradoxical form of the Stuarts' attempted expansion of the prerogative powers of the crown as divine right so as to achieve unfettered absolute rule. He eagerly embraces the teaching of earlier expositors of the law, including Fortescue's noble vision as that is solidly grounded in a theory of law generally (if not precisely) informed by Thomas Aquinas's *Treatise on Law* and the differentiated

---

"But tho' . . . particular Variations and Accessions have happened in the Laws, yet they being only partial and successive, we may with just Reason say, They are the same English Laws now, that they were 600 Years since in the general. As the Argonauts Ship was the same when it returned home, as it was when it went out, tho' in that long Voyage it had successive Amendments, and scarce came back with any of its former Materials; and as Titius is the same Man he was 40 Years since, tho' the Physicians tells [*sic*] us, That in a Tract of seven Years, the Body has scarce any of the same Material Substance it had before" (*History of the Common Law*, 40).

Many of the issues of pertinence here come to light in the exchange between Thomas Hobbes and Sir Matthew Hale as given in Hobbes's *A Dialogue Between a Philosopher & A Student of the Common Laws of England* in Sir William Molesworth, ed., *The English Works of Thomas Hobbes* (London, 1840), 6:1–160, and Hale's *Reflections by the Lrd. Cheife Justice Hale on Mr. Hobbes His Dialogue on the Lawe* in Sir William Holdsworth, *A History of English Law*, 2d ed., rev. (London, 1937), 5:500–513.

structure of reality, including the divine Ground, adumbrated therein. Thus—and the point is crucial—it is not just any "natural law" that Fortescue and Coke have in mind but the natural law and related theoretical structures underlying and substantively informing the medieval constitution of Christian England that thereby make it *fundamental law*. This aspect of our subject has been widely neglected and assertion of it here may sound a bit strange. But something of the kind was intended by Maitland in saying that Coke had dogmatized the Middle Age before England was barely out of it. And Brian Tierney powerfully underscores the point to generally observe that "seventeenth-century writers were often thinking medieval thoughts even when they clothed them in classical dress."[36] Coke resolutely adheres to the precious particularities of the common law as these bear (sometimes in obscure and minuscule ways) on English liberty and on the fundamental law of the realm—the ancient constitution of our discussion. Coke's and the parliamentarians' victory as achieved on *this ground* Holdsworth designates as "the turning-point in English constitutional history."[37]

36. Tierney, *Religion, Law, and the Growth of Constitutional Thought,* 105. The "absolute medievalism" of Coke, which so exasperated Hobbes (Holdsworth, *History of English Law,* 2d ed., rev., 5:480) can only be grasped through an appreciation of the pertinent medieval *substantive* teachings. This is not a mere matter of process—although procedure is vitally important—but it is preeminently one of content. On the neglect and misunderstanding of the medieval components of modern free government see Brian Tierney, "Hierarchy, Consent, and the 'Western Tradition,'" *Political Theory* 15 (1987): 646–52; also his "Religion and Rights: A Medieval Perspective," *The Journal of Law and Religion* 5 (1987): 163–75. (Professor Tierney, it may be mentioned, participated in the Windsor Castle symposium on which this volume is based.) On the revised understanding of the relationship between medieval and modern constitutionalism and law see also Harold J. Berman, *Law and Revolution: The Formation of the Western Legal Tradition* (Cambridge, Mass., 1983), chaps. 2 and 4 and *passim;* cf. Charles H. McIlwain, *Constitutionalism: Ancient and Modern,* rev. ed. (1947; rpt. Ithaca, N.Y., 1958).

37. Holdsworth, *History of English Law,* 2d ed., rev., 6:66. This "because it was then that it was decided that the government of England was to be by the king and parliament, and not, as in most other continental countries, by the king alone." "Both the king and parliament were well aware that in other European countries the medieval representative assemblies had gone under" (6:70). For the symbol *fundamental law* see J. W. Gough, *Fundamental Law in English Constitutional History,* cor. ed. (Oxford, 1961).

The particularities and technicalities of the common law, pregnant as they often are with universalist implications, Coke thought, must be guarded against needless change lest immemorial liberty and justice be lost. What has been said of Hale's attitude might as readily be said of Coke's, whose veneration of the law obviously was as great: "regimes come and go, the common law abides."[38] And details count. Thus, Coke writes: "In troth, reading, hearing, conference, meditation, and recordation, are necessary I confess to the knowledge of the common law, because it consisteth upon so many, and almost infinite particulars."[39] The attitude is represented in the celebrated cry of the barons of the Merton parliament (1236) who refused to alter the bastardy law, a matter recounted with relish by Coke. Whereunto, he tells us, they concurred in "the wisdom of the law abhorring clandestine contracts," hence

> saith the statute, *omne Comites & Barones una voce responderunt, nolumus leges Angliae mutare que hucusque usitatae sunt & approbatae:* in which few words is observable; first the absolute concord and unity, *una voce,* of all the Peers and Lords of Parliament: secondly the denial, *nolumus leges Angliae,* . . . [of] the common law of England: and thirdly, the reason of their denial: *quae bactenus usitatae sunt & approbatae,* as if they would have said, we will not change the laws of England, for that they have been anciently used and approved from time to time by men of most singular wisdom, understanding and experience.[40]

The evocative power of this sentiment of devotion to the immemorial law of England was sufficiently potent so that Charles I, on the eve of civil war, used the very quotation from the Merton barons in concluding his *Answer to the XIX Propositions of Both Houses of Parliament.*[41]

---

38. Charles M. Gray in Hale, *History of the Common Law,* xiv. Holdsworth writes of Coke's "fanatical reverence for the common law" (*Some Makers of the English Law,* 116).

39. Coke, *First Reports,* preface (n.p.).

40. Coke, *Fourth Reports,* vii–viii.

41. See Weston, "Beginnings of the Classical Theory of the English Constitution," 144: "For all these reasons to all these demands our answer is, *Nolumus Leges Angliae mutar[e].*"

The *Second Institute* includes Coke's exposition of Magna Carta. By all accounts the central passage of the Charter is chapter 39, augmented in the second reissue (1217), and then becoming chapter 29 in the Third Great Charter of King Henry III (1225), the version of Coke's exposition and called the *Magna Charta ae libertatum Angliae*. Chapter 29 therein in translation reads: "No free man shall be taken, or imprisoned, or dispossessed, of his free tenement, or liberties, or free customs, or outlawed, or exiled, or in any way destroyed; nor will we condemn him, nor will we commit him to prison, excepting by the legal judgment of his peers, or by the law of the land. To none will we sell, to none will we deny, to none will we delay right or justice."[42] Coke defines the phrase "by the law of the land [*per legem terrae*]" as meaning "by the Common Law, Statute Law, or Custome of England." The sense of these words he gives on the basis of the statute 37 Edward III. chapter 8 as being "without due process of law," thereby prohibiting arbitrary arrest and imprisonment, or deprivation of property or liberty except by the legal processes of indictment or presentment "of good and lawfull men, where such deeds be done in due manner, or by writ originall of the Common law. No man be put to answer without presentment before Justices, or thing of record, or by due process, or by writ originall, according to the old law of the land. Wherein it is to be observed, that this Chapter is but declaratory of the old law of England."[43] In further commenting on the phrase *per legem Angliae*,

---

42. Quoted from Richard Thomson, *An Historical Essay on the Magna Charta of King John: To Which are Added, the Great Charter in Latin and English: The Charters of Liberties and Confirmations, Granted by Henry III. and Edward I., [etc.]* (London, 1829), 139–40. The text of the 1225 document is provided below as an Appendix.

43. Sir Edward Coke, *The Second Part of the Institutes of the Laws of England . . .* ([1641]; London, 1642), 46, 50. The *Institutes* began to appear in 1628 with *Coke on Littleton, First Institute* (cited in note 9, above). The second and third *Institutes* were finished at the same time but remained unpublished until 1641. The fourth *Institute* was written in Coke's later years and also first published in 1641. Delay of publication was due partly to the confiscation of Coke's papers ordered by the king at his death in 1634; delay in publication also related, evidently, to their contents and to Coke's understandable reluctance to spend his declining years again imprisoned in the Tower. As Holdsworth writes: "When [the final three volumes of the *Institutes*] were published in 1641, it was the hour of the victory of the

Coke remarks that all commissions are grounded upon it; that it does not read *legem & consuetudinem Regis Angliae* so as to bind only the king, nor *populi Angliae* so as to bind only the people, but it extends to all as "ancient and fundamental Law." In the Proeme he states that Magna Carta is "for the most part declaratory of the principall grounds of the fundamentall Law of *England,* and for the resideue it is additional to supply some defects of the Common Law."[44]

As to the meaning of liberties [*libertates*] in the text, Coke explains that the term has three meanings:

> 1. First, as it hath been said, it signifieth the Laws of the Realme, in which respect this Charter is called, *Charta libertatum.* 2. It Signifieth the freedomes, that the Subjects of England have. . . . 3. Liberties signifieth the franchises, and priviledges, which the Subject have of the gift of the King, as goods, and Chattels of felons, outlawes, and the like or which the Subject claim by prescription. . . . Generally all monopolies are against this great Charter, because they are against the liberty and freedome of the Subject, and against the Law of the Land.[45]

The bits and pieces of English liberty are expounded in this fashion by Coke. But the supremacy of law as declared in Magna Carta is his noblest theme as he strives to proclaim Magna Carta and ancient constitution as embodying the perfect virtue and justice glimpsed in *De Laudibus.* Thus, he writes in the Proeme that, although the judgments of the king's courts are of high regard in law, parliament has decreed that any such judgment contrary to the Great Charter made by judges

---

common law and the Parliament. Men did not stop to consider the accuracy or the validity of the arguments upon which Coke based his claim that the common law and Parliament were supreme in the state, they simply accepted them, and made his writings the basis, not only of our modern constitutional law, but also of the whole of that large part of our modern English law which is comprised under the general term 'common law'" (*History of English Law,* 2d ed., rev., 5:471–72; cf. 359, 461–66).

44. Coke, *Second Institute,* 51 and Proeme, [2].

45. Ibid., 47; the "hath been said" refers to chap. 1: "*Libertates* are here taken in two senses. 1. For the Laws of England so called. . . . 2. [F]or priviledges held by Parliament, Charter or prescription more then ordinary" (p. 3).

or any of the king's other ministers that conflict with it "shall be undone, and holden for nought." Such a rule, he asserts, applies even to parliamentary enactments.

> The highest and most binding Laws are the Statutes which are established by Parliament; and by Authority of that highest Court it is enacted (onely to shew their tender care of *Magna Charta,* and *Charta de Foresta*) *That if any Statute be made contrary to the great Charter, or the Charter of the Forest, that shall be holden for none:* By which words all former Statutes made against either of those Charters are now repealed; and the Nobles and great Officers were to be sworn to the observation of *Magna Charta* and *Charta de Foresta.*[46]

All of this rests on the solid foundation of the ancient constitution whose antiquity extends back long before Norman times, back to the Saxon laws of King Inas (translated by William Lambarde), whose reign began in 689 A.D., to King Arthur and the knights of the round table, and to many other sources which Coke identifies for the first time, "to the end [that] the prudent Reader may discerne what the Common Law was before the making of every of those Statutes, which we handle in this work and thereby know whether the Statute be introductory of new Law, or declaratory of the old."[47]

From the welter of particularities of time and jurisdiction, Coke finds the common law a sublime harmony whose distant source lies in the wisdom of God himself.

> For as in nature we see the infinite distinction of things proceed from some unity, as many flowers from one root, many rivers from one fountain, many arteries in the body of man from one heart, many veins from one liver, and many sinews from the brain: so without question *Lex orta est cum mente divina,* and this admirable unity and consent in such diversity of things, proceeds only from God the fountain and founder of all good laws and constitutions.[48]

46. Ibid., Proeme, [3].

47. Ibid., [3–5].

48. Coke, *Third Reports,* 3. Cf. the discussion in James R. Stoner, Jr., *Common Law and Liberal Theory: Coke, Hobbes, and the Origins of American Constitutionalism*

IV

It has been especially through J. G. A. Pocock's publication in 1957 of a book entitled *The Ancient Constitution and the Feudal Law* that something called the "common-law mind" has come prominently to view in contemporary scholarship and, with it, a quickened attention to the old and much neglected subject of the ancient constitution. Thus, Pocock writes of a "paradox":

> If the idea that law is custom implies anything, it is that law is in constant change and adaptation, altered to meet each new experience in the life of the people. . . . Yet the fact is that the common lawyers, holding that law was custom, came to believe that the common law, and with it the constitution, had always been exactly what they were now, that they were immemorial: not merely that they were very old, or that they were the work of remote and mythical legislators, but that they were immemorial in the precise legal sense of dating from time beyond memory—beyond, in this case, the earliest historical record that could be found. This is the doctrine or myth of the ancient constitution, which bulked so large in the political thought of the seventeenth century and furnishes this book with half of its title.[49]

Two pages later Pocock further states:

> The belief in the ancient constitution . . . rested on assumptions which were fundamental to the practice of the common law, and it had very great influence in a society whose political and social thinking were so largely dominated by this one law. It cannot be regarded as the creation of any single mind. But Coke did more than any other man to summarize it and make it authoritative; at the same time he reveals the patterns of thought on which it was based with the clarity of truly representative genius. . . . Coke and his con-

---

(Lawrence, Kans., 1992), 13–68. Stoner also participated in the Windsor Castle conference.

49. J. G. A. Pocock, *The Ancient Constitution and the Feudal Law: A Study of English Historical Thought in the Seventeenth Century* (1957; rpt. New York, 1967), 36.

temporaries were indeed only continuing and developing a habit of mind as old as the common law itself.[50]

It is the confluence of the currents of earlier scholarly interests and the convictions regarding the common lawyers led by Coke and Selden with the currents of Pocock's and others recent energetic explorations of seventeenth and eighteenth century historiography that lends impetus to the present symposium and the debate it continues.[51] The extent of quickened interest in this subject matter is thoroughly considered in the reissue of Pocock's book, now augmented by some 130 pages of new material from the author in response to commentary and criticisms published during the three decades since *The Ancient Constitution and the Feudal Law* first saw the light.[52]

In clarification of the passages quoted above from *The Ancient Constitution and the Feudal Law,* Pocock writes in the 1986 *Retrospect* as follows: "I submit it is not a proper reading [of my book to say] that Coke held the whole body of English law to be immemorial, static and unchanging. His notion of custom (and usage) was more flexible than that. . . . But I stressed incessantly that the notion of custom was ambiguous in that it implied both preservation and adaptation." Rather, the word *paradox* is to be stressed, "meaning that the notion of custom, which could imply adaptation, was employed to imply preservation. . . . Yet my intention seems to me now (and has long seemed) to have been to state less that the whole body of the law was held to be immemorial than that any element in it could be held immemorial at will." Thus,

50. Ibid., 38, 39.

51. The range of historiographic attention to the subject of the ancient constitution is concisely summarized in R. J. Smith, *The Gothic Bequest: Medieval Institutions in British Thought, 1688–1863* (Cambridge, England, 1987), 1–10. Cf. Corinne Comstock Weston, "Ancient Constitution and Common Law," in *The Cambridge History of Political Thought, 1450–1700,* ed. J. H. Burns with the assistance of Mark Goldie (Cambridge, England, 1991), 364–411.

52. J. G. A. Pocock, *The Ancient Constitution and the Feudal Law: A Study of English Historical Thought in the Seventeenth Century; a Reissue with a Retrospect* (Cambridge, England, 1987). The "Retrospect" covers pp. 253–387. It should be observed that the ancient constitution is only a part of the author's interest in this volume.

Pocock argues with respect to his own original understanding of matters, that it was less

> the content of the law than the juridical process itself—usage, judgment and statute—that was immemorial; that the reform of obsolete laws and the making of new ones were perfectly compatible with the view that common law rested in ancient usage. . . . I have never quite understood (though the reader must judge) why I have been taken as saying there that Coke thought the law had always been the same, Hale that it had always been in adaptation.

And with a bow to Edward Lear's Pelican Chorus, Pocock ends the page with the flourish, "We think so then and we thought so still."[53] Just how this leaves things is hard to say, but the chapters ahead may clarify matters. For myself, I see Fortescue and Coke more devoted to structure than to process, to the substantive than the formalistic. There is the ring of conviction, a devotion to the truth, in what they wrote as I read their words. However things may be with the Argonauts' Ship, on the matter of liberty, which Fortescue believed infused into human nature by God, the Declaration of Independence's insistence on unalienability gets it right.

The essays that follow deal at large with the documents touched upon in this introduction and in very considerable detail with Pocock's books and many of the problems raised by his perspectives and analysis. The initial question posed by J. C. Holt is whether any such thing as the ancient constitution really existed in the early Middle Ages, and he responds with a straightforward *no* that then, however, opens into a masterful discussion of the setting and significance of Magna Carta for English constitutionalism that ends up sounding very much like *yes.* Christopher W. Brooks next explores the further Pocockian question of the reality of the common law mind, the continuity of the ancient constitution in the sixteenth century, and the sources of Coke's jurisprudence arising in that period. Brooks pays particular attention to religious and Continental influences on the Tudor renaissance and upon Coke's thought. In the third essay, Paul Christianson carefully

---

53. Ibid., 274–75.

examines the seventeenth-century struggle between parliament and crown in England by focusing on the years 1610 and 1628. In these debates he finds the models of not one but three contending versions of the ancient constitution: those of King James VI become James I, of Thomas Hedley, and of John Selden and Edward Coke. He traces the traditions of constitutional discourse associated with each and notes that Magna Carta is the starting point for both king and parliament in arguing their positions. John Phillip Reid's discursive presentation then addresses the manifestations of the common law mind and use of ancient constitutionalism in the language of lawyers and in legal thought more generally during the century from the Glorious Revolution to the American Founding. His persistent critique of Pocock centers on the latter's discerned neglect of what Reid calls "forensic history," or of the mode of lawyerly polemical discourse exhibited in the vast literature of constitutional debate during the seventeenth and eighteenth centuries. However it may be with this line of criticism, there can be no doubt after Reid's richly documented presentation that the common law mind is alive and well in this period, which persuasively suggests that it must also have existed before then.

In the critical Epilogue to our volume, Corinne C. Weston (also one of the original conference participants at Windsor Castle), takes stock of the strengths and weaknesses of the symposiasts' presentations and fills the gaps of some of our arguments. At the same time, it is important to notice, she demonstrates the presence of an alternative understanding of the ancient constitution to the one portrayed by J. G. A. Pocock. Weston makes a powerful case (buttressed by Holt's analysis herein) for a *Saxon ancient constitution* which was widely subscribed to from the seventeenth century through the American Revolution and whose "founding father and patron saint" was Edward the Confessor (d. 1066), last of the Saxon kings. To elucidate the meaning and significance of these salients of the Anglo-American tradition of liberty through rule of law as it comes full circle in our volume, we first turn to Sir James Holt's presentation.

1. The Ancient Constitution in Medieval England

Was there an ancient constitution? The answer is "no." It is and was a figment. Professor J. G. A. Pocock agrees as much:

> It may be conceded here that the term "constitution," as used throughout this book, has not been systematically cleared of anachronism. There will have been a time when it was more usual to speak of "the laws" as "ancient," after which a practice of speaking about "the constitution of government" became one of using "constitution" and "government" as interchangeable terms, hardening finally into the more modern practice in which "the constitution" (unwritten rather than written) could be spoken of as "ancient." The chronology of such a process has not been attempted here.[1]

But a preliminary shy is easy enough: the *Oxford English Dictionary* can provide as strong a dose of skepticism for the modern historian as Ducange does for the medieval. The first example it gives of the use of the word referring to "the mode in which a state is constituted" is from 1610 and comes from Bishop Hall's *Apology against the Brownists;* it refers to Israel, not England;[2] the second is from Clarendon in 1647.[3] As for "the fundamental constitution of the kingdom," much closer to our "ancient constitution," that comes from Scotland in 1689.[4] Sir Edward Coke, it should be noted, did not use the term in this sense.

1. J. G. A. Pocock, *The Ancient Constitution and the Feudal Law: A Study of English Historical Thought in the Seventeenth Century; a Reissue with a Retrospect* (Cambridge, England, 1987), 261, n. 8.
2. "The Constitution of the Common-wealth of Israel."
3. "Who exactly knew the frame and constitution of the kingdom."
4. "Whereas King James the Seventh did by the advice of wicked and evil counsellers invade the fundamental constitution of the Kingdom and altered it from a legal limited monarchy, to an arbitrary despotick power" (Declaration of the Estates of Scotland, April 11, 1689).

So in seeking the element of ancient precedent in Coke's arguments and assumptions and in those of other antiquaries and lawyers of the sixteenth and seventeenth centuries we shall be looking for something else. And the word itself points to the route we must follow, for it leads us immediately into the realm of authority—"a decree, ordinance, law, regulation; usually one made by a superior authority, civil or ecclesiastical, especially in Roman Law an enactment of the Emperor"; the earliest authority quoted in the *Dictionary* is none other than Wycliff.[5] So constitutions had an ordaining *constitutive* ring to them. This was still so in the sixteenth and seventeenth centuries as the newer prescriptive sense was added to the word.[6] If then in the ancient constitution we are pursuing an anachronism it is ours, not Coke's or Selden's.

How it came about that the word *constitution* acquired this new prescriptive sense in the course of the seventeenth century and—a more interesting matter—how it was that Coke, Selden, and other lawyers and antiquaries of the early seventeenth century did not themselves resort to it, are questions I leave to others.[7] I am concerned rather

5. "They studien faste and techen here owene constitucions." The Apostolic Constitutions and the Constitutions of Clarendon are also noted in *OED;* on the latter see below.

6. "The statutys of kyngys, also be over-many, even as constytutyonys of the emperors were" (Starkey, 1538); "All this while our Kings and Bishops called Councels—made Ecclesiastical Lawes and constitutions in their Synods and Parliaments" (Bramhall, 1661).

7. A very useful indication of what the answers are likely to be is provided by Corinne C. Weston, "The Theory of Mixed Monarchy under Charles I and After," *English Historical Review* 75 (1960): 426–43, esp. 428–29; and *English Constitutional Theory and the House of Lords, 1556–1832* (London, 1965), 26–28, esp. n. 34. She points out that under Charles I the term *constitution,* as good and ancient, was appropriated to the royalist cause by Falkland, Culpeper, and Hyde. See Charles's response, drafted by Falkland and Culpeper, to the Nineteen Propositions of June 1642 in which he refers to "the antient, happy, well-poysed, and never enough commended Constitution of the Government of this Kingdom" (William Rushworth, *Historical Collections* [London, 1692], vol. 3, pt. I, 731) and claims that acceptance of the Propositions "would be a total subversion of the Fundamental Laws, and that excellent Constitution of this Kingdom, which hath made this Nation so many Years, both famous and happy to a great degree of envy" (ibid., 732). Compare his reference to the "glorious Frame and Constitution of this Kingdom" in his proclamation of September 27, 1642 (ibid., vol. 3,

with the ideas and assumptions which they inherited from an earlier period, with the material and building blocks which lay to their hand at the end of the Middle Ages for the fashioning of their own scheme of things. That seems simple. Yet it is not so, for the medieval material embodies a blend of law and legend, fact and fiction, statute, its interpretation and misinterpretation, similar to that which modern scholarship has exposed in the seventeenth century. The matter is important. For one thing we need to decide when and how, within what sort of intellectual framework, we can assert that a statute, or indeed anything else, was "misinterpreted." For another, until the medieval foundations are properly delineated, the seventeenth-century superstructure cannot be accurately drawn or its novelty properly assessed. Such an assessment has been based only too frequently on ignorance of much that happened before 1500. It was not an error of which Coke or Selden was guilty.

Yet what they knew and absorbed from the past was of varying authenticity. In reexamining it, uncertainties, dilemmas, and questions, like those raised by the history of the word *constitution* sketched above, are ever present. One last illustration may be added — the constitutions of Clarendon of 1164. This, too, is noted in the *Oxford English Dictionary*, but it was not a contemporary title. It seems to be derived from a marginal entry in the earliest known manuscript version written in 1176. These "constitutions" were in fact a "record" and "recognition" made in the presence of the king of the "customs, liberties and dignities" enjoyed by his ancestors. Throughout the document "customs," *consuetudines,* and *dignitates,* not "constitutions," are the dominant words.[8] The

---

pt. II, 10). The change to the newer prescriptive sense of the word occurred under Charles II and drew the comment from Roger North that it was now "commonly brought forward with a Republican Face" (Weston, *English Constitutional Theory*, 99–100).

8. *Councils and Synods with Other Documents Relating to the English Church* (Oxford, 1981), ed. D. Whitelock, M. Brett, and C. N. L. Brooke, vol. 1, pt. II, 855–85. "[F]acta est recordatio et recognitio cuiusdam partis consuetudinum et libertatum et dignitatum antecessorum suorum" (877). For the marginal entry see 883, n. h. It may be that "constitutions" had too canonical a flavor in the circumstances at Clarendon. However, the word was not used exclusively in a papal or

decrees which Henry II imposed on the English church in 1169 were a different matter. These were "constitutions" properly speaking and were so described.⁹ Such usage was considered and deliberate. When, seven years later, the marginal scribe referred to the customs declared in 1164 as constitutions, he was tarring them with the brush of authoritarian novelty. The stain has faded partly because we have lost the verbal precision of his age and with it his intent. Henry II himself gave the *consuetudines* of 1164 an extra ring of authority *after* they had been promulgated. In the 1169 decrees they appear as *statuta de Clarendune* and *statuta regni.*¹⁰ Customs, once agreed, recorded, and promulgated, acquired force as statute.

Language matters. We have to puzzle out what it means and meant. More important, our materials are the work of men who were themselves puzzling it out, using it to fit context and circumstance, to convey intentions and impressions, to define, to stake out claims, to defeat and counter arguments. Language enhanced disputes; one man's *auxilium* was another's *tallagium.* Above all language was malleable. It demanded interpretation and reinterpretation. It allowed misinterpretation. It lasted. It is this world that we enter with Magna Carta.

In Magna Carta, also, the language is deliberate and precise. The so-called Articles of the Barons, the armistice agreement as it were, comprised *capitula* which embodied *conventiones;* they were Heads of Proposals, to borrow a phrase from a later political crisis. The intention in 1215 was to bring to an end a state of civil war. The *capitula* were therefore also articles of peace, *articuli pacis.* And they contained customs, *consuetudines.*¹¹ But the context was different from that of 1164. In the Articles it is not customs but the keeping of the peace and liber-

---

ecclesiastical context, and the main point must surely be that Henry was aiming, not at a statute or "constitution," but at a declaration of his customary rights.

Lanfranc's "Constitutions" seem not to deserve the title any more than the Clarendon "recognition" of 1164. See *The Monastic Constitutions of Lanfranc,* ed. D. Knowles (London, 1951), 1–3.

9. *Councils and Synods,* 926–39.

10. Ibid., 937.

11. On the title see J. C. Holt, *Magna Carta,* 2d ed. (Cambridge, England, 1992), 429.

ties between the king and the realm which is guaranteed by the form of security.[12] And in Magna Carta, even more, it is liberties, not customs, that are predominant. The Charter was a Charter of Liberties in strict contemporary parlance: in the treaty between King John and the barons concerning the custody of London,[13] and in the Letters Testimonial in which Archbishop Stephen Langton and the bishops certified the text of the "charter of liberty of Holy Church and of the liberties and free customs" which King John had conceded.[14] It was thus that it was seen by the magnates and the bishops. So also was it described by the officials of King John.[15]

At this point the word *consuetudo* demands further comment. In its prime sense it did not necessarily denote antiquity, still less unwritten, ancient law. It was used rather to describe the jurisdictional, legal, and financial relationships between lord and vassal. Customs, in this sense, could be either good or bad, ancient or novel, unwritten or newly promulgated. But they were, or were to be, habitual practice—the classical sense of the word tended always to drive them in that direction.[16] It is from this generalized sense that the constitutions of Clarendon and Magna Carta diverged, the constitutions toward the royal dignities enjoyed by King Henry's ancestors, the Charter toward the liberties which it itself conveyed. The *consuetudines* of 1164 are associated with *dignitates*;[17] those of 1215 with *libertates*. Indeed *consuetudines* scarcely

12. "Hec est forma securitatis ad observandum pacem et libertates inter regem et regnum."

13. Holt, *Magna Carta*, 490.

14. "Cartam—de libertate sancte ecclesie et libertatibus et liberis consuetudinibus."

15. See the letters of June 27, 1215 in Holt, *Magna Carta*, 496. The phrase does not occur in the letters of June 19 where John was more concerned with the restoration of peace; here Magna Carta is simply described as *carta* (ibid., 493).

16. For some general discussion of this matter see J.-F. Lemarignier, "La dislocation du 'pagus' et le problème des 'consuetudines' (xe-xie siecles)," *Mélanges Louis Halphen* (Paris, 1951), 401–10; also J. C. Holt, "The Origins of the Constitutional Tradition in England," in J. C. Holt, *Magna Carta and Medieval Government* (London, 1985), 19–20; and Susan Reynolds, *Kingdoms and Communities in Western Europe, 900–1300* (Oxford, 1984), 13–21.

17. In the Constitutions of Clarendon the king also enjoys liberties (*Councils*

appear in the documents of 1215 except in association with liberties or when qualified by "free." Only once, in confirming the privileges of the Londoners, is the word associated with antiquity.[18] Only once, in condemning the conduct of foresters and other officials is it qualified as evil,[19] this a timely reminder that the prime, generalized sense of the word had not been lost or entirely overlain. Throughout, therefore, customs are subsidiary to liberties. Indeed they are being established and conveyed as liberties. They figure because the liberties concern practices which were commonly described as *consuetudines*. This was no linguistic aberration induced by political crisis. The same emphasis on liberties and the same subordination of customs to liberties is apparent in the reissues of Magna Carta in 1216, 1217, and 1225, in the Charter of the Forest of 1217 and 1225, and in the *parva carta* of 1237, which brought the series to an end.[20]

These were official documents; the emphasis reflected curial attitudes as well as the minds of barons and bishops. No one could have argued in 1215 or even in 1217 that the charters were no more than a definition of ancient custom. Of course, precedent mattered. Existing procedures, long-established principles, or ancient liberties certainly underlay particular chapters.[21] The movement against King John had begun with a cry for the confirmation of the Charter of Liberties of Henry I and the restoration of the laws of Edward the Confessor. A distorted, idealized past was fabricated to set against alleged present ills; and to this we shall return, for ancient custom was part of the argument and well worth having on your side. But it cut both ways. The commissioners appointed by Pope Innocent III to impose his settlement of the dispute — Peter des Roches, bishop of Winchester; Simon, abbot of

---

and Synods, 877), but this is a solitary occurrence of the word; compare chap. 17, *Councils and Synods,* 883.

18. *Articles,* chap. 32; *Magna Carta,* chap. 13.

19. *Articles,* chap. 39; *Magna Carta,* chap. 48.

20. W. Blackstone, *The Great Charter and Charter of the Forest* (Oxford, 1759), 68–69.

21. For existing procedures, *judicium parium;* for long-established principles, the prohibition of the sale of justice; for ancient liberties, the privileges of London.

Reading; and the papal "familiar" Pandulf—in their letters of September 5, 1215, in which they denounced the king's opponents asserted, "The dignity of the king has been filched, since they grant out land, a thing unheard of, and nullify the approved customs of the realm, and establish new laws, and destroy or alter all that has been prudently ordained by the King their lord with the advice of the magnates who were then his familiars—they have gone as far as they could in despoiling the King of his royal dignity."[22] For them approved customs and royal dignity went hand in hand, just as they had for Henry II in 1164. So, whatever the pretenses from whichever party in the dispute, no one could seriously maintain that the concessions of 1215 were validated by substantive coincidence with ancient custom. Validation came, not from substance, but from procedure and form: from the personal oath of the king that he would abide by the terms agreed, by similar oaths of those present at Runnymede and of men throughout the land, oaths to terms embodied in exemplars of the newly issued charter, each under the great seal. And the crucial attack on the agreement in the papal bull of annulment was that the oath had been exacted by compulsion and that the charter was therefore null and void.[23] That verdict was reversed when the papal legate, Guala, set his seal to the reissues of 1216 and 1217, but the threat to the charters' validity remained until in the *parva carta* of 1237 Henry III confirmed them for the first time in full majority. This success story owed something to luck, to Henry's minority, and to the complexities of papal diplomacy.[24] No matter. By design or accident, a conveyance of liberties was brought to the forefront of public life.

It is worth dwelling for a moment on why the settlement took this form. It had to. It could not be embodied in a treaty because king and vassals were not on a par. It was only as warring parties that they could

22. F. M. Powicke, "The bull 'Miramur plurimum' and a letter to Archbishop Stephen Langton, 5 September, 1215," *English Historical Review* 44 (1929): 92.

23. *Selected Letters of Pope Innocent III,* ed. C. R. Cheney and W. H. Semple (London, 1953), 212–16.

24. See especially V. H. Galbraith, "Runnymede Revisited," *Proceedings of the American Philosophical Society* 110 (1966): 307–17; "A Draft of Magna Carta," *Proceedings of the British Academy* 53 (1967): 345–60.

treat as equals; to do that would be to admit the compulsion which lay behind the settlement and lay it open to annulment. It could not take the form of a simple statement of *consuetudines* because other matters, the restoration of hostages and the reversal of unjust judgments, for example, were included. In any case how could the king be bound except by oath and solemn concession made in as near a standard form as the circumstances allowed? And how were liberties usually conveyed publicly and permanently unless by charter? Such considerations left any other solution unthinkable. A charter, whether confirming the earlier grant of Henry I or in some new form, was envisaged at the start of and throughout the crisis. There was no alternative: a charter it had to be. But if men turned to the charter as the only vehicle available, it was not necessarily going to be the most convenient in the long run. It was bound to be restricted to well-worn tracks. Charters provided validation, certainly, but they also brought complications and imposed conditions of their own.

A charter was freely given. It could not be otherwise. Magna Carta was granted "from reverence for God and for the salvation of our soul and those of all our ancestors and heirs, for the honour of God and the exaltation of Holy Church and the reform of our realm"; *spontanea et bona voluntate nostra* was added for the first time in 1225 because by then the young King Henry could be said to have a will of his own. It was a royal act. It followed that the liberties conceded derived from the crown. They could be corroborated only by reissues or further confirmations, by measures which themselves reiterated the crown's authority. So the beneficiaries of 1215 were locked into a circular logic which was not broken by the humiliating circumstances which forced King John to the first great surrender and his successors from time to time to renewed acts of contrition. Royal authority may have seemed to be diminished by a confirmation of the charters, but it was also exercised. The ultimate validation of the Great Charter was the Great Seal, nothing else, and that bore the impression of the king in majesty. There was no escaping that.

Nevertheless men tried. Already in 1215 the king's opponents claimed the moral high ground for themselves. The Charter specified that dispossessions had occurred without lawful judgment of peers, that fines had been agreed and penalties imposed unjustly and contrary to the law of the land.[25] What the Charter granted to the freemen of the land were not just *consuetudines* or even liberties, but rights or laws, *jura*.[26] This was rhetoric, and not less so because it was drawn from the common distinction between law and will. By itself it did not cut a lot of ice.

However, it was linked to a more practical tactic of external compulsion. By his submission to Pope Innocent III in 1213 King John became a *feodatarius*.[27] This opened the traditional action of tolt to the court of a feudal superior. Both the king and his opponents used it in 1215. In the end the process gave the reissues of 1216 and 1217 the seal of papal approval but not a lot besides. From 1225, to be sure, the charters were reinforced by sentences of excommunication against infringers. But the sentences were the work of archbishops and bishops themselves vulnerable as tenants-in-chief of the crown; the popes almost always backed the king. Episcopal insistence on the charters was far from disinterested. It was aimed at extending the privileges of the *anglicana ecclesia* confirmed in general in chapter 1; this provoked baronial as well as royal resistance. The king was careful to except royal rights and exclude new ecclesiastical pretensions from the traditional confirmations and the associated sentences of excommunication. In any case such sentences required the secular arm and ultimately royal approval to become effective.[28] Indeed the best known of such sentences, the *sententia lata* of 1253, was promulgated with the consent of king and magnates.[29] So this route led through a tangled undergrowth

25. Chaps. 52, 55.

26. Chap. 63.

27. This is the word in his own charter of submission. See W. Stubbs, *Select Charters,* ed. H. W. C. Davis (Oxford, 1921), 279–81.

28. Faith Thompson, "The First Century of Magna Carta: Why It Persisted as a Document," *University of Minnesota, Studies in the Social Sciences* 16 (1925): 97–102. For an illuminating and suggestive examination of the problem see J. W. Gray, "The Church and Magna Carta in the Century after Runnymede," *Historical Studies* 6 (1968): 23–38, and for a detailed study of a particular crisis see J. H. Denton, *Robert Winchelsey and the Crown, 1294–1313* (Cambridge, 1980), 136–76.

29. *Statutes of the Realm,* I, 6. C. Bémont, *Chartes des Libertés Anglaises* (Paris, 1892), 71–75. The exceptions and exclusions are stated with considerable precision in letters patent of May 13 promulgating the *sententia.*

of conflicting interests and attitudes to a dead end guarded once more by royal authority.

There were vociferous demands and demonstrations along the way. Reinforce the charters by the threat of excommunication; promulgate the penalty in the most solemn assemblies of king, bishops, and nobles, as in 1237 and 1253; reinforce the threat by papal confirmation, as in 1245 and 1256, have both charters and sentence published in Latin, French, and English as in 1253, or read twice a year in cathedral churches as in 1297; display the Charter of Liberties in church, renewing it annually at Easter, as Archbishop Pecham laid down in 1279; embrace the king himself within the sentence of excommunication, as Archbishop Boniface did by implication in 1234. To modern eyes it is all repetitive and futile. In reality it was a prolonged attempt to bring the enforcement of the Charter within the range of canon law, to attach the ecclesiastical penalties for breach of faith to infringements of promises made "for reverence for God," as the Charter put it, promises repeatedly reinforced by the most solemn oaths to observe and execute the Charter's terms. This was perhaps the best the thirteenth century could do to introduce some countervailing force to royal authority. But the crown remained resilient, its authority unimpaired. These ritual occasions were as evanescent as party conventions. All they left in the end was the *sententia lata* embedded, apparently so incongruously, in the manuscript collections of statutes of the late thirteenth and early fourteenth centuries and subsequently in the *Statutes of the Realm.* But at the time the effort must have seemed worthwhile. To "liberal" bishops, to some of the barons, certainly to the chronicler Matthew Paris, each royal renewal of the oath to the Charter, each promulgation of the sentence, must have seemed a signal achievement, a triumph, yet one more step on the road to an enlightened society governed by royal self-control. It all helped to keep the Charter alive. And it spread knowledge of it wide within and outside the church. Bishop Grosseteste of Lincoln returned home from the great council of 1253 and promptly ordered that the sentence should be promulgated in every church in his diocese.[30] The *sententia lata* was entered

---

30. J. R. Maddicott, "Magna Carta and the Local Community, 1215–1259," *Past and Present* 102 (1984): 35.

immediately following the Charter of the Forest in various editions of the Sherwood Forest Book.[31] To this day the fourteenth-century graffiti in Ashwell (Herts) parish church include the inscription, now very faint, *anglicana ecclesia libera sit.*[32]

Yet this is not the whole story. The charters were not just expressions of royal authority. Certainly, such liberties were derived from royal concession and nowhere else. But the king *had* conceded them. Moreover he had conceded them in a form which located them squarely within contemporary conveyancing. This prosaic, everyday mold was essential; it provided authenticity; anything else risked challenge or annulment. The Charter of 1215 followed the strict letter of such a grant: "We have also granted to all the free men of our realm for ourselves and our heirs for ever, all the liberties written below, to have and to hold, them and their heirs from us and our heirs." This formula was largely repeated in the reissues culminating in 1225, although not in the Charter of the Forest. Still in the thirteenth century men were conscious enough of the importance of livery of seisin and aware that no grant was so secure that it did not benefit from repeated confirmation by the grantor and his successors and from corroboration by a superior lord and other interested parties. In the case of the charters this need was met by the repeated reissues, confirmations, oaths of observance, and threat of ecclesiastical penalties. But conveyancing had moved far beyond the primitive notion that rights conveyed reverted to the lord on the death of the recipient or that homage rendered should be renewed on the death of either party. Where in any case in the concessions of 1215–1225 was the element of service which underlay such insecurity? It was there certainly, but in a residual form, in the concession of the fifteenth on moveables in the final clause of the Charters of 1225. Here it was turned to the beneficiaries' advantage: it was linked to the king's promise that nothing would be sought that would weaken or infringe the liberties and that if it were it should be counted null and void. It was used to reinforce the certainty and permanence of the

31. *The Sherwood Forest Book,* ed. Helen E. Boulton (Nottingham, 1964), 12–28, 33.

32. *Medieval Drawings and Writings in Ashwell Church, Hertfordshire* (Ashwell, 1978).

transaction. And how could the beneficiary die when defined as all free tenants or everybody in the realm? The answer to both these questions was to lead or drive men to the idea that the liberties were conceded to the *regnum*.[33]

But if that was the theory, practice was somewhat different. In the case of a private grant the beneficiary, whether an individual or an institution, retained a charter and/or a letter patent as evidence. There was probably no clear precedent for the grant of 1215. Whether men could discover what had happened in 1100 with the coronation charter of Henry I it is impossible to say; in any case Henry's charter could well have been despatched to the sheriffs. If precedent there were, it is likely to be found in grants and charters to cities and boroughs, especially to London, where charters recording privileges became part of the community's archives available for pleadings, confirmations, and other purposes. At all events it seems certain for 1215 and is absolutely certain for 1225 that the charters were sent to the counties, that is to the county courts, and were held there by responsible knights of the shire or were deposited for future reference in some suitable repository. It is reasonable to suppose that it was through such a procedure that an original of 1215 still survives at Lincoln,[34] and less certainly at Salisbury.[35] Charters of Liberties of 1216 and 1225 and a Charter of the Forest of 1217 still remain at Durham, the center at one and the same time of the bishop's liberty and the court of the knights of St. Cuthbert.[36] A contemporary endorsement establishes that the Charter sent to Wiltshire in 1225 was deposited in Lacock abbey by the knights of the county.[37] The copy sent to Buckinghamshire in 1297 remained in the hands of one of the knightly families of this county and Northamptonshire, the Brudenels, whence it was put on the market in 1981, ultimately finding its way to the United States. The best evidence of all comes from Nottinghamshire, where the Sherwood Forest Book of circa 1400 tells us: "the Charter of the Forest is under patent in the

33. Holt, *Medieval Government*, 203–15.
34. The endorsement, *Lincolnia*, is contemporary.
35. For Salisbury, see Holt, *Medieval Government*, 259–64.
36. Holt, *Magna Carta*, 380, n. 7.
37. Blackstone, *Great Charter*, xlvii.

hands and custody of Ralph Lord Cromwell junior, and the Charter
of Liberties is under patent in the hands and custody of Nicholas of
Strelley and the perambulation of Sherwood Forest of the time of King
Henry III is under patent in the hands of William Jorse of Burton."[38]
This was the third item in the book, following immediately on the
Charter of the Forest and the *sententia lata*. Peter le Neve, who worked
on the book in 1700, developed this memorandum further. "Whence
it is to be understood," he noted, "that each county had two custodians
of the aforesaid charters and if there is forest in the county another
kept that charter."[39] Cumulatively the evidence leaves no real doubt
that the responsible beneficiaries of the charters were the suitors of
the county court. That is where the charters were available. It was up
to the knights of the shire to exploit them.

This opportunity was not entirely novel. In the decade or so before
1215 local communities, including counties, had come to purchase
privileges, guaranteed by charter, which gave them some control over
the office of sheriff, or the conduct of local government, or complete
or partial exemption from the forest law.[40] In one instance, Devon in
1214, the knights of the shire fought a determined case before the justices of the bench, claiming that shrieval excesses, as they presented
them, in demanding suit of court, were in contravention of the liberty
which the king had given them by his charter. Unerringly they put
their finger on the crucial point: "the knights came and denied all sur-
sises and defaults and all offences against the crown of the lord king;
and they stated that they appeared before [the sheriff] as they ought
to do and according to their liberty which the lord king gave them by
his charter which they produced in court."[41] They had their charter to
hand. Against the rights of the crown they set the liberty granted by
the king.

A closely similar argument was presented by the knights of Lincolnshire in 1226. Their action too lay against the sheriff and concerned
his demands for suit of court in the wapentake of Ancaster. The liberty

38. *Sherwood Forest Book*, ed. Boulton, 33.
39. Ibid., 32.
40. Holt, *Magna Carta*, 50–72.
41. *Curia Regis Rolls*, 7, pp. 158–59.

alleged in defense was the Charter of Liberties and in particular chapter 35 of the 1225 reissue, which dealt with the session of local courts. The actions of the sheriff, they claimed, were "contrary to their liberty which they ought to have by the charter of the lord king." This time, however, the argument spread wider. It also concerned suit at the shire court, and here the knights alleged:

> The county court of Lincoln always used to sit at intervals of forty days; and the lord king has conceded to all men of his realm their liberties and ancient customs which are in use; and the custom was always such; and this sheriff has fixed the courts contrary to that custom at intervals of five weeks and sometimes less. Moreover the court used to meet for one day only. And because they held the aforesaid liberties through the lord king it did not seem to them that they ought to change the state of the county court without the lord king and the magnates of the realm.[42]

This brought into the debate the savings clause protecting existing liberties and free customs which had been introduced into the 1225 version of the Charter. And it pointed to the contradictory position into which the crown had got itself: on the one hand the sheriff, seeking to perform his office in holding pleas in shire and wapentake, arguing that his appointment as a sheriff and bailiff of the king was sufficient warrant for his actions; on the other hand the knights, insisting upon and quoting the liberties so recently confirmed. Both sides of the argument stemmed from the king.

However, one side of the argument, the Charter, came direct from the king, while the other side came at one remove, as it were, through the sheriff. This was crucial. It must have been obvious to all that there were grave difficulties in the way of using the charters as a direct counter to the personal actions and immediate policies of the king. The security clause of the 1215 Charter had sought to do just that. It had led the country into civil war and had been abandoned. Further experience soon showed that further pressure in this direction was unlikely to lead to anything more than the charade of a great council, a confirmation of the charters, and a promulgation of ecclesiastical

42. Ibid., 12, nos. 2142, 2312.

penalties. The charters provided no solution to the problem of how to manage a willful king: hence the increasing interest in schemes for conciliar control. But the charters did provide a splendidly effective weapon against the king's agents, against the sheriffs especially, and in the case of the Charter of the Forest against the foresters and those responsible for forest perambulations. For, if knights of the shire could not bring an action against the king in his own court for contravention of the charters, they could certainly do so against his local officers. The king, in short, could be put on the spot: which actions did he really intend—those imposed or demanded by his local agents or those conveyed as liberties in the charters? and who held to the better interpretation of those liberties, his local agents or the local knights? These were questions which only the king and his court could answer. In 1226 the knights of Lincolnshire had a sure hold on the point: they were unwilling to alter the state of the county court "without the lord king and the magnates of the realm."

These issues soon became general. A meeting of representatives from eight counties summoned to Lincoln was prorogued in September 1226. It was followed by a summons of representatives from all except two counties to a meeting at Westminster in October 1227; for this four knights were to be elected in each county to present complaints against their sheriffs "on the articles contained in the charter of liberty."[43] Meanwhile parallel complaints were arising over the execution of the disafforestations envisaged in the Charter of the Forest. By intention or otherwise, chapter 1 of that Charter, which provided for perambulations, was not clearly drafted. Its execution remained a bone of contention between the crown and local communities to the end of the century and beyond.[44] In the confusion of the second round of perambulations of 1225 some of the great northern lords retained what the crown abandoned. The knights of Westmorland made plaint against William of Lancaster, lord of Kendal, that he had kept some woods and moors afforested "to the damage of the knights and other

43. *Rotuli Litterarum Clausarum*, 2, pp. 154b, 212b–13. There is no apparent reason for the omission of Cornwall and Westmorland.

44. Holt, *Magna Carta*, 385–86, 394–95; Maddicott, "Local Community," 36–40.

honest men of the neighbourhood"; similar complaints were brought in Westmorland, Lancashire, and Yorkshire against Robert de Vieuxpont, William de Warenne, earl of Surrey, John de Lacy, constable of Chester, and Robert Grelley. Three of these had participated in the rebellion of 1215; one, John de Lacy, had been a member of the Twenty Five. The plaint against them was based on the final chapter of the Forest Charter, which laid down that all those who received these liberties from the king were to grant the same to their men.[45] Both the forests and county administration required royal action. Henry intervened in each case to emphasize the principle laid down in all versions of both charters that what the king was granting to his men they were to grant to theirs. Moreover in letters of August and October 1234 he addressed the specific point raised by the knights of Lincolnshire and gave rulings on the session of local courts. The second of these was drafted after chapter 35 had been read before archbishops, bishops, earls, and barons and was based on their advice. It was annotated in the Close Roll—"concerning the interpretation of a clause contained in the liberties, how it ought to be understood."[46] But royal intervention did not solve these problems. In Lincolnshire, Bishop Grosseteste subsequently intervened, yet again, in support of the knights; throughout the shires both local government and the extent of the forests remained raw issues.[47]

Nothing in all these arguments and events should be read with an eye on the future. Men were quite accustomed to making and receiving grants of liberties. They were used to confirming them or to demanding their renewal. In the ordinary course of events such grants were marked by some form of livery or were corroborated on oath. No one was surprised when liberties had to be sustained or defended in the courts. Men accepted that they might have to resort to passive resistance or even to private warfare in defending their rights. It was perhaps only in its universality, as a grant to all in the land, that the Charter of Liberties would have seemed at all novel to the casual observer of the political scene in the 1220s and 1230s. And liberties wore

45. *Patent Rolls 1216–25*, pp. 575–76; Holt, *Magna Carta*, 395.
46. *Close Rolls 1231–34*, pp. 588–89.
47. Maddicott, "Local Community," 35–36, 40–48.

old, became meaningless, and were forgotten. Already by the middle years of the century men were turning to other political remedies for their ills—conciliar control at the center, election of local officials in the provinces—and these too had an earlier history going back before 1215.[48] So it would have been difficult for such an observer to predict that the charters would be extraordinarily durable. Where, after all, was the Charter of Henry I?

Yet there were signs: two indications perhaps that the charters were unusual. First, they were granted *in perpetuum*. This insistence on perpetuity was included in all versions and reissues of both charters. Now a grant in perpetuity was unusual between laymen. To go beyond a transfer from a donor and his heirs to a recipient and his heirs was unnecessary and seemingly nonsensical. Nevertheless, a layman might occasionally make a grant in perpetuity to another, especially when it took the form of a sale or quitclaim. Moreover *in perpetuum* became pervasive in the warranty clauses which were common in conveyances of the thirteenth century. The words also occur occasionally in charters granted to lay communities or to boroughs, especially where free borough status or the borough farm was concerned, and in grants of markets and fairs. Perpetuity is likewise the term in almost all charters of disafforestation and in the much rarer grants of jurisdictional or administrative privileges to local communities, counties, or county subdivisions. But the most generalized, and most probably the first, use of the words was in grants in free and perpetual alms to monasteries and other ecclesiastical bodies. More immediately in 1215 there was a precedent in King John's grant of freedom of election to the church of November 21, 1214. This too was to be enjoyed *in perpetuum*.[49] From there the phrase was transferred into the Charter of 1215 where it was first deployed to protect the liberties of the church, with special reference to freedom of election. But it was not restricted to that. The phrase was reintroduced into the usual formulas of a gift from grantor and heirs to recipients and heirs which prefaced the whole of the re-

48. For the choice of local officials see Holt, *Magna Carta*, 61–62; Maddicott, "Local Community," 29, 44–45; D. A. Carpenter, "The Decline of the Curial Sheriff, 1194–1258," *English Historical Review* 91 (1976): 1–32.

49. Stubbs, *Select Charters*, 284. For further comment on *in perpetuum* see Holt, *Magna Carta*, 518–22.

mainder of the Charter. All the liberties conceded were to be held forever. By 1217 the phrase was so distanced from its origin that it was now introduced into the Charter of the Forest. All these concessions too were to be held forever. With the reissues of 1225 the words were embedded in the received text of both charters. Not even King Stephen had conceded as much.

There is no need to attribute personal responsibility for the intrusion of these words into the charters. After all they were common enough. And they were not yet the source of any precise political theory, although the occasional use of *finabiliter* rather than *in perpetuum* in grants between individuals suggests that the incongruity of perpetuity in such a context might well have been appreciated. No one as yet was arguing that the charters were irrepealable fundamental statute, although clearly the words conceded that the liberties were to be permanent. No one was suggesting that the community of laymen was exactly analogous to a community of religious or even to the whole body of the church, although equally obviously the possession of liberties contributed to the emergence of the *communitas regni* both as a concept and as a political phenomenon. It is more probable that the repetition of the phrase reflected a determination that there was to be no going back, a feeling that these were once and for all concessions which at last put a wide range of matters to right. *In perpetuum* served that purpose very well.

A second feature of the charters had more to do with government. They originated in rebellion, but they were drafted in the royal chancery. They are official documents. They are remarkable in the textual improvement which they underwent and in the additional material which they accumulated between the initial Articles of 1215 and the final versions of 1225. Two features of this are particularly striking. First, by 1217 new material was being introduced that went beyond the clarification of earlier provisions. Chapter 32 forbade the alienation of land that resulted in the loss of services to the giver's/vendor's lord. Chapter 35 introduced new arrangements for the sessions of the courts of shire, hundred, and wapentake; we have seen that these immediately became contentious. Chapter 36 forbade collusive alienation in free alms. Most striking of all, the Charter of the Forest, now issued for the first time, settled matters raised inconclusively in 1215 and also dealt with many matters of forest administration which had not been covered at all in the earlier document. Second, it seems beyond doubt that these new provisions were a response to evidence accumulated by enquiries into local government initiated under chapter 48 of Magna Carta in the summer of 1215. No returns to this inquest survive, but it certainly took place. Moreover the new material which appears in the Charters of 1217 bears all the marks of an enquiry characteristic of the operations of Angevin government. Whence else could the new material have come? So in effect the final version of the Charter was used as a vehicle for legislation, legislation drafted by royal officials on the basis of public enquiry. Magna Carta then became the origin of much subsequent legislation; the next in the series, the Provisions of Merton of 1236, acknowledged the debt in many of its provisions which elucidated matters first raised in the Charter. By the end of the century the manuscript collections of statutes, the *Antiqua Statuta*, gave Magna Carta pride of place. It became the first statute. It was kept in being as a source of law as well as a conveyance of liberties.[50]

This dual function was entirely pragmatic. Later generations, especially later generations of lawyers, might wonder how a document could be both statute and privilege at one and the same time; for statute, in one way or another, governed or directed the operations of the courts, while charters were subject to their jurisdiction. Hence Littleton argued that Magna Carta was "not a statute at the beginning until it was confirmed by the Statute of Marlborough cap. 5 and that was the time at which it was made."[51] But in the thirteenth century men were not asking such precise legal questions or making such fine distinctions; statute itself had yet to be defined. Indeed, they could treat the texts themselves in a manner which now seems cavalier. It is well known that the St. Albans chroniclers, Roger Wendover and Matthew Paris, made a mess of Magna Carta. Roger attributed both the Charter of Liberties and the Charter of the Forest of Henry III to King John by the simple

---

50. Holt, *Medieval Government*, 289–307. In the above paragraph and throughout the numeration of the 1225 chapters is also used for 1217.

51. S. B. Chrimes, *English Constitutional Ideas of the Fifteenth Century* (Cambridge, 1936), 43–44 and appendix 61; Faith Thompson, *Magna Carta: Its Role in the Making of the English Constitution, 1300–1629* (Minneapolis, 1948), 66–67.

process of changing the name of the grantor. He excused himself by saying that the charters of the two kings were alike. To compound his error he tacked on to the text a variant version of the *forma securitatis* which is found only at St. Albans. Matthew Paris subsequently obtained a correct version of the 1215 text and simply added the supplementary material in the margins of Wendover's text, which he had already transcribed into his *Chronica Majora*.[52] And this came from two men who were more conscious than many that the charters were a major advance in restricting monarchical excess. The truth was not simply that they lacked the knowledge and expertise to criticize the texts before them, but that all their instincts and training led them to treat variants as glosses. They were not alone in their documentary inexactitude. The so-called Statute or Provisions of Merton was not so much a statute, a product of a single time and place, as Littleton would have required, as an assemblage of material agreed and promulgated on different occasions and over several months between 1234 and 1236.[53] And these confusions perhaps provide a clue, for it was the charters themselves, distributed throughout the shires, which provided the prime examples of clearly defined liberties and exact legislation as it could be understood in the context of the common law.

To summarize, by 1225 Magna Carta embodied two elements and lines of thought, or, if we prefer, could be viewed in two ways. On the one hand it was a grant of liberties; on the other it was a legislative act. On the one hand men and communities could appeal to it against acts of government. On the other it laid down governmental procedures and established points of law which the courts would follow and enforce. In one of its functions a widow could seek her due forty days' residence in her husband's house, a tenant could appeal against prerogative wardship, another claim rights *ut de honore,* or a city seeks free access to local riverbanks. In the other the Exchequer would follow the new rulings concerning baronial reliefs, or the provision concerning the collection of debt, and the justices the rule that common pleas should be held in a certain place. These two functions met where the

52. Holt, *Medieval Government*, 265–87.

53. H. G. Richardson and G. O. Sayles, "The Early Statutes," *Law Quarterly Review* 50 (1934): 204.

interests of the crown and local communities ebbed and flowed in the provisions which concerned local government and the sessions of the local courts.[54]

Probably no one at the time recognized these hybrid characteristics in the documents of 1215 to 1225. But they soon came to react to them, perhaps even to understand the consequences. At least from 1285 to 1290, in the *Mirror of Justices,* there survives a hard-line insistence on the Charter as a grant of liberties, made in perpetuity.[55] The writer's argument is well summarized by Faith Thompson:

> The author of the *Mirror of Justices* attempts a sort of complete commentary, article by article. He begins with an emphatic statement of his motives: "Whereas the law of this realm founded upon the forty articles of the Great Charter of Liberties is damnably disregarded by the governors of the law and by subsequent statutes, which are contrary to some of these articles, and the errors of certain statutes, I have put on record this chapter concerning the defects and reprehensions of statutes." He then proceeds to point out certain defects (usually in the nature of too great brevity or incompleteness of statement) in articles 2, 3, 4, 6, 7, 17, and 26; interprets articles 9, 11, 18, 28, 29, 30, 32, 33, and 34, sometimes correctly, sometimes with embellishments of his own devising; and emphasizes the violation of articles 10, 12, 14, 16, 22, 24, 25, 29, and 35, through the practices of the king's courts and officials, and the tenor of later statutes. In his discussion of the statutes of Merton, Westminster II and others, he points to provisions repugnant to articles of the Great Charter. He reveals himself as a staunch advocate of the "liberties of the Church," and seignorial justice; he is conscious of the lack of adequate machinery to enforce the "liberties" and proposes a novel method for doing so.[56]

His method was not in fact so very novel, given that he was regarding the Charter primarily as a grant of liberties made in perpetuity: it was

---

54. Thompson, *The First Century,* 37–65 and the useful table, 66–67.

55. *The Mirror of Justices,* ed. W. J. Whittaker, intro. F. W. Maitland (London, 1893).

56. Thompson, *The First Century,* 58–59.

that any free man could pursue his free tenement in the liberties of the Charter by an action of novel disseisin.[57] How else, in the first instance, would one pursue such a loss? He was more logical than his critics have allowed.

He was also trying to be more logical than either common sense or circumstances required. Whether or not he was Andrew Horn, chamberlain of the city of London, it is likely that he was a Londoner,[58] and it may be that concern for London's ancient liberties led him into such an approach. At all events he was still vulnerable in confronting the critical difficulty posed by the Charter's content and format. How could law be founded in a grant of liberties? Especially one granted in perpetuity? Was each and every statute liable to be repugnant ever afterward? Was the Charter never likely to become out-of-date? Were its concessions to remain fossilized, never to be adjusted to changing ideas and social circumstances? Or, to put the same question in a contemporary context, was the Charter to be immune from glossing? Willy-nilly our author answered the question by glossing it himself. It was only thus that it could achieve the perpetuity it proclaimed.

The establishment view was looser and less contentious. Bracton simply drew on three chapters in dealing with reliefs, the writ *praecipe*, and the writ of life and limb.[59] He made no special comment; for him, on these issues, the Charter simply embodied law. In 1267 chapter 5 of the Statute of Marlborough, the first coherently drafted statute, provided the first statutory confirmation, as Littleton later appreciated:

> The Great Charter shall be observed in all its articles, both in such as pertain to the King as in others. And enquiry shall be made before the justices in eyre in their circuits and before the sheriffs in the county courts when necessary; and writs shall be granted freely

57. *Mirror of Justices,* ed. Whittaker, 176. On Magna Carta as a property right compare Coke's argument in the debate on the Commons' Protestation in the parliament of 1621 (Stephen D. White, *Sir Edward Coke and the Grievances of the Commonwealth* [Manchester, 1979], 176).

58. H. G. Reuschlein, "Who wrote the Mirror of Justices?," *Law Quarterly Review* 58 (1942): 265–79.

59. *Bracton on the Laws and Customs of England,* ed. S. E. Thorne, 4 vols. (Cambridge, Mass., 1968–1977), 1:244, 343; 2:300.

against offenders, before the King or the justices of the Bench or before the justices in eyre when they come into those parts. Likewise the Charter of the Forest shall be observed in all its articles, and convicted offenders shall be punished by our sovereign lord the king.[60]

That seemed to accept that enforcement of the charters was part of the ordinary judicial process. Nevertheless it did not include enforcement as part of the general eyre and only two chapters, 5 and 35 of the Great Charter, came to be included in the articles of the eyre.[61] The matter was further clarified in 1297. By then men were clearly arguing that the two charters should be treated as integral parts of their respective laws. The *Confirmatio Cartarum* laid down that "our justices, sheriffs, mayors, and other officials which under us have to administer the laws of our land, shall allow the said charters in pleas before them and in judgments in all their points; that is to wit, the Great Charter as the common law and the Charter of the Forest according to the Assize of the Forest, for the relief of our people."[62]

This was repeated in the *Articuli super Cartas* of 1300. Chapter 1 provided that three knights appointed in each county to hear plaints of breaches of the charters were to have the power to impose penalties "ou remedie ne fust avant par commune ley."[63] Magna Carta was now enrolled as statute. It must have seemed quite incongruous that a document which was the origin of so much subsequent legislation and which figured so prominently in the proliferating collections of *Antiqua Statuta* had not hitherto been enrolled as such. That it spoke with the voice of a charter, not a statute, became a minor difficulty which could be reconciled. Littleton did it by reference to the Statute of Marlborough. Other lines were possible. A contemporary of Littleton, delivering a law reading on Magna Carta circa 1450, argued:

> Bifore the makying of this statuet, that is to seie the great chartoure, there was certein lawes used, by the whiche men hade profit and also moche harme. And therfore the kyng, seyng this mischief, or-

60. *Statutes of the Realm*, I, 19.
61. H. M. Cam, *The Hundred and the Hundred Rolls* (London, 1930), 251, 253.
62. Stubbs, *Select Charters*, 492–93.
63. Bémont, *Chartes des Libertés Anglaises*, 100–101.

deyned the greet charter, wherin is contened alle the fruyt of lawes bifore used turnyng to the people profit and al other put away. Yet notwithstondyng that it is called a charter, it is a positif lawe, for it was used that what statuet that the kyng and his counseille made, it was ever set in the kynges comfermyng, so that, the kyng beyng chief of his counseille, spake in his owen name and his conseillz, seiyng "Concessimus et hac presenti carte etc."[64]

The reader's sense of history was inexact; he substituted King Edward for King Henry as the grantor of the Charter. But he was clear enough that the Charter was statute "ever set in the king's confirming." It is an open question who would have been the more surprised if confronted by that—Sir Edward Coke or King John.

A document which lay at the origin of statute and was at one and the same time a grant of liberties in perpetuity called for a recurring gloss: confirmation, interpretation, and commentary. It began as early as 1234 with the "interpretation" by the king and magnates of the disputed chapter 35.[65] It continued at a spate. Beginning with the *parva carta* of 1237 Magna Carta was confirmed in at least fifty-six great councils or parliaments by 1422.[66] By the beginning of the fourteenth century any lawyer of standing, whether judge or attorney, would have access to the Charter of Liberties in his copy of the *Antiqua Statuta*. Particular chapters figure in judgments, exceptions, pleadings, and processes; the evidence proliferates in plea rolls, yearbooks, and the Register of Writs. These developments have been well treated by Faith Thompson and require no further survey here.[67] Yet they require three comments.

First, interest in the charters tended to concentrate on particular

---

64. G. O. Sayles, "A Fifteenth-century Law Reading in English," *Law Quarterly Review* 96 (1980): 569–80. See also H. G. Richardson, "The Commons and Medieval Politics," *Transactions of the Royal Historical Society*, 4th. ser. 28 (1946): 21–45.

65. See above, p. 47.

66. Thompson, *The First Century*, appendix C, and *Magna Carta*, 10, n. 4, 11–12. The count is difficult for the reign of Edward II because of the varying status of the Ordinances of 1311.

67. Thompson, *Magna Carta*, 33–67, on which the information in the following paragraph is based.

sections. This was very obviously so in the case of the Charter of the Forest where chapters 1 and 3 and the consequent perambulations underlay the prolonged dispute over the bounds of the forest which divided the crown and local communities on into the fourteenth century. There were also local disputes about chapter 2 dealing with summonses to the forest courts and about private rights within the forest covered in chapter 17, but these did not generate quite the same heat. The remainder of the Charter was not particularly contentious within the context of the forest law. It was the same with Magna Carta. As we have seen, chapter 35, dealing with the session of the local courts, was of immediate concern. Chapter 29, *nullus liber homo*, was given great prominence by internecine aristocratic conflict under Edward II. Individual litigants made good use of all the chapters which dealt with jurisdiction and penalties: the session of common pleas, the petty assizes, the affeering of amercements, prosecution by royal officials.[68] Rights of wardship and dower still provoked appeals to chapters 4, 5, and 7. The collection of debt still kept chapter 18 very much alive. The Londoners were still ardent in maintaining their liberties and in pursuing the destruction of fish weirs on the Thames.[69] Three chapters—14 on amercements, 18 on distraint for debts, and 24 on the writ *Praecipe*—appear in the Register of Writs. But there were also many chapters which attracted little or no attention. The crown had accepted and continued to execute some of the provisions: chapters 2 and 3, for example, largely settled the questions of reliefs and the succession of heirs; as a result appeals were few and far between. Other chapters seem to have lost the urgency they had in 1215. Disparagement of heirs was apparently a dead issue if, indeed, it had ever been very much alive (6). Sheriffs and other bailiffs were no longer holding pleas of the crown (17). Chapters dealing with demands for varied services (15, 20, 21) provoked little if any active interest, probably because the services were long since commuted. Legislative measures introduced into the Charter in 1217 to deal with loss of services through gift or sale (32), with patronage of abbeys (32), and with alienation in free alms (36) had been overtaken by circumstances or subsequent legislation. By the

68. Chaps. 11, 12, 13, 14, 28.
69. Chaps. 9, 23.

middle of the fourteenth century half the chapters of the Charter were uncontroversial, or dead, or moribund.

Second, the charters seem to have come to play a less obvious political role. In the case of the Charter of the Forest there may have been a real decline of interest as the central forest administration weakened in the course of the fourteenth century. The last forest eyre was held in Sherwood in 1334. By 1301 forest asserts and wastes were being converted into heritable socage tenures from which forest officials were excluded. The bounds, one of the crucial issues raised by the Charter, declined in importance because the forest was eroded from within. The Sherwood Forest Book preserves fourteenth-century bounds of the king's reserves within the forest, dating probably from the eyre of 1334, but the last perambulation of the whole forest recorded in the book was that of 1300. So the Charter of the Forest lost practical importance. It still deserved pride of place as the first item when the Sherwood Forest Book was composed circa 1400, but it no longer occasioned political crises as it had done at times a century or more earlier.[70] Whether something similar happened in the case of the Charter of Liberties is much more open to question. C. Bémont pronounced long ago that the Great Charter "rested in the shade" during the fifteenth and sixteenth centuries.[71] The habit of counting parliamentary confirmations, which originated with Coke, seems to lend him some support. Of the fifty-six conciliar or parliamentary confirmations between 1327 and 1422, only eight came from the fifteenth century.[72] Reference to specific chapters also apparently diminished. As Faith Thompson puts it, in the fifteenth century the Charter was "neither obsolete nor forgotten," but

> not as many different provisions of Magna Carta figure as in the earlier period. More detailed legislation had altered or superseded the Charter in some points. Pleaders still draw on it to make "frivo-

70. *Sherwood Forest Book*, ed. Boulton, 39–42, 56–59, 98–102, 103–8, 185–93.

71. Bémont, *Chartes des Libertés Anglaises*, xlviii–l.

72. Coke's count was "32 severall Acts of Parliament in all" (Sir Edward Coke, *The Second Part of the Institutes of the Laws of England* [London, 1642], Proeme); Bémont noted fifteen under Edward III, eight under Richard II, six under Henry IV, and one under Henry V (*Chartes des Libertés Anglaises*, xlix–l).

lous exceptions". . . . A few of the old standbys still serve to support a claim or defend against an abuse, notably chapters 9, 11, 12, 14 and 35. Now and then citing of the "statute" by pleaders or judges may be quite incidental, introduced by way of illustration, analogy, or precedent, a mere "academic reference."[73]

However, it is easy to exaggerate this decline. It is true that neither Fortescue nor Littleton gave much space to Magna Carta, but nor had Bracton. Certainly Fortescue made no mention of it in his paean of praise for English law; even so, it underlay some of the main points in his argument. It would have been impossible to find chapter and verse for what he had to say about *lex terrae* as applied to arrest, trial, or threat to possessions without calling in the end on the Charter.[74] Readings at the Inns of Court of 1450–1550 reveal considerable interest in chapter 11, covering the locations of the common pleas, and in due-process interpretations of chapter 29. It is significant that both were turned against non–common law jurisdictions of various kinds. This was quite apart from appeals to the liberty of the church of chapter 1, which were triggered by the Reformation.[75] One Tudor occasion is of especial interest. In the debates and negotiations which led to the new Heresy Act of 1534 the Commons reinforced its opposition to ecclesiastical jurisdiction and the use of the *ex officio* oath in cases of suspected heresy by referring to chapter 29 of Magna Carta, which was noted in a full English translation. Among seven further statutes adduced in support there figured four of the six statutes of Edward III, some in summary, some with fragments given verbatim.[76] Precedents had been searched; the linkages were understood; the whole memo-

73. Thompson, *Magna Carta*, 61.

74. Sir John Fortescue, *De Laudibus Legum Angliae*, ed. and trans. S. B. Chrimes (Cambridge, England, 1942), 86–89.

75. *Spelman's Reports*, ed. J. H. Baker (London 1976–1977), esp. 57–59, 71–72, 346–47.

76. *The Complete Works of St. Thomas More*, ed. John Guy, Ralph Keen, Clarence H. Miller, and Ruth McGugan (New Haven, Conn., 1987), 10:lxii–lxvi. The document in question is PRO, SP 1/82. Magna Carta chap. 29 and the associated statutes are at fos. 57ᵛ–58. All are in English. The translation of chap. 29 (given ibid., lxiv, n. 5) is not drawn from Rastell's *Great Abridgement* of 1627; cp. Thomson, *Magna Carta*, 150. I am obliged to Dr. Guy for drawing my attention to this document.

randum is headed *Magna Carta cap. xxix.* This was at a time not of fragile monarchy but in the midst of the Henrician Reformation. The Heresy Act itself, in final form, gives no hint that Magna Carta had stalked through its origination.[77] The importance of the Charter could no longer be measured by statutory confirmation any more than by its absence in Shakespeare's *King John.* In parliament it was not so much forgotten as overlain.

Third, in this process the Charter of Liberties was glossed, interpreted, changed, pressed into use for objectives not originally intended. True, a famous *addicio* to Bracton laid down that "neither justices nor private persons could or ought to question royal charters and the acts of kings, nor even may they interpret them if doubt arises."[78] But practice was different. Magna Carta drew comment and interpretation like a magnet, ever more so as it acquired the standing of a statute and as the justices of the central courts of the common law took to judicial interpretation of other legislation.[79] It was all the easier because judicial and legal interpretation was all of a piece with the textual gloss derived from biblical and patristic commentaries. In their association of text and commentary the justices shared much the same method and among their varied objectives they had one in common: to appropriate received texts to current circumstances.

It is with the consequences of interpreting and glossing that serious historical difficulties arise. The purist is likely to argue that any departure from the strict or literal sense of the original text amounts to distortion or misinterpretation. Once that is allowed Coke and Selden are condemned out of hand as inventors of a figment which they foisted on seventeenth-century England and thence on half the world. But the

77. *Statutes of the Realm,* III, 454–55.

78. Bracton, *De Legibus et Consuetudinibus Angliae,* fo. 34, ed. S. E. Thorne, 4 vols. (Cambridge, Mass., 1968–1977), 2:109. Cp. fo. 106 where a similar view is taken of fines (2:302).

79. The development of judicial interpretation is summarized by T. F. T. Plucknett, *A Concise History of the Common Law,* 4th ed. (London, 1948), 311–16. It is impossible to summarize within the space of a short note the extensive literature on the subject. For a recent and most valuable discussion, which is comprehensive bibliographically, see Louis A. Knafla, *Law and Politics in Jacobean England: The Tracts of Lord Chancellor Ellesmere* (Cambridge, England, 1977).

argument misses two points. First, it is not always easy to decide what the precise sense of the Charter originally was; the celebrated *vel*, "or" or "and," of chapter 39/29 stands out as the most obvious example, concise but nonetheless subject to much debate. Second, and much more important, how could the intention of the charters as grants *in perpetuum* be met except by glossing, interpretation, and adjustment to new circumstances? It is not a matter here of imposing modern sociological concepts on medieval practice. Royal clerks themselves used the word *interpretatio* in describing the comments made by the king and magnates in 1234 on chapter 35. They and their contemporaries were familiar with the need to interpret common, well-used phrases in legal documents; the crown for example was imposing an increasingly restrictive interpretation on charters that conveyed manors "with their appurtenances." Necessarily and increasingly as the thirteenth century progressed judges had to define procedure and interpret statute; the Charter of Liberties was one of those. And men were aware that much might depend on interpretation. Chapter 1 of the Charter of the Forest laid down that land brought within the forest by Henry II should be disafforested where it included the woods of others and was to their damage; if it was his own demesne it might remain forest. That subsumed a crucial question. Were the afforestations of Henry II to be interpreted narrowly as those which were entirely *de novo*, or were they also to include forests established by Henry I which were subsequently lost to the crown under Stephen? Lack of clarity here, which could have been deliberate, was one of the causes of the prolonged dispute over the bounds of the forest in the thirteenth century.

The resulting interpretations, constructions, or glosses varied in character. Some were plain errors that nonetheless matched the intentions of the Charter. In 1315, for example, Theobald Russell, a minor, petitioned for proper maintenance, quoting chapter 5 of the Charter. Chapter 5 mentioned no such thing; Theobald was simply asserting common practice which antedated 1215.[80] Some were more serious mistakes which stretched the sense of the Charter beyond its original meaning. Chapter 23, which provided for the destruction of weirs on the Thames and Medway, was concerned with navigation. Al-

80. *Rotuli Parliamentorum*, I, 318; Thompson, *Magna Carta*, 40.

ready by 1302 it was applied to fishery protection, and it was given statutory blessing in this form in 1472. Meanwhile chapter 16, which was primarily concerned with hawking, was also extended to fishing rights. The two chapters together provided a notably confused origin to the law of fisheries.[81] One such construction played a notable part in the later history of the Charter. This concerned chapter 30, which was aimed initially against restrictions on the movements of alien merchants. Exploited first by the Bardi in 1320 to claim exemption from the wool staple, it was quickly expanded in 1328 to cover denizens as well. It then figured as a precedent in Bates's case of 1608 and was later interpreted by Coke as prohibiting monopolies of trade.[82] Such "errors" or "mistakes" are not at all difficult to fit into the ordinary pattern of legal history where variant constructions and aberrant pleas are run-of-the-mill material.

Magna Carta also presented quite another problem. What meaning was to be given to words and phrases that intrinsically required construction; so much so that they could not be applied without it? This is the nub of chapter 29 and the much-discussed phrase *per legale judicium parium suorum vel per legem terrae*. For these words lead us through a historiographical progression, roughly as follows:

1. There is little difficulty in understanding how it came about that lawful judgment of peers became trial by peers by the middle of the fourteenth century. Here Magna Carta did little more than assert a principle of procedure integral to feudal jurisdiction as it was practiced throughout western Europe in the twelfth and thirteenth centuries. In England it is presented as an axiom in the *Leges Henrici Primi*.[83] That this should be refined into the precise form of trial by peers by the experience of the internecine strife of the reign of Edward II was a natural and logical progression. Arguably it lay within the intent of 1215.

2. It is also reasonably easy to understand how the *judicium parium* and *lex terrae* of 1215 came to include trial by jury. Magna Carta does nothing to elucidate *per legem terrae;* it is not concerned with the detail

---

81. W. S. McKechnie, *Magna Carta*, 2d ed. (1914), 303–4, 344–45; Thompson, *Magna Carta*, 25; S. A. Moore and H. S. Moore, *The History and Law of Fisheries* (London, 1903), 6–18.

82. Holt, *Magna Carta*, 13–14; Thompson, *Magna Carta*, 111–12, 249–55.

83. Holt, *Magna Carta*, 75–76.

of criminal process. But by the fourteenth century criminal process involved trial by jury; it had become part of *lex terrae*. To include it within the traditional term, to treat trial by jury as if it were a gloss of *lex terrae*, was a natural and logical progression, but one, we may note, which embraced a method of trial that scarcely existed in 1215.

3. These changes were brought together in the six statutes passed by parliament between 1331 and 1368. But in these parliament went further by converting *lex terrae* into due process of law, which meant procedure by original writ or indicting jury. As the second statute of 1352 reveals this move was quite deliberate:

> Whereas it is contained in the Great Charter of Liberties of England, that none shall be imprisoned nor put out of his freehold, nor of his liberties or free customs, unless it be by the law of the land; it is accorded, assented and established, that from henceforth none shall be taken by petition or suggestion made to our lord the king, or to his council, unless it be by indictment of good and lawful people of the same neighbourhood where such deeds be done, in due manner, or by process made by writ original at the common law.[84]

The effect of this was to confine *lex terrae* to the common law and to exclude conciliar or prerogative jurisdiction. In the case of the jury construction *includes* later development. Here it *excludes* later development. How soon this took hold is uncertain. Already in the twelfth century *lex scaccarii* foreshadowed the prerogative jurisdiction of later times, and it may be significant that the limiting effect of chapter 29 was turned against the Exchequer no later than the 1330s.[85] That it would be aimed more generally against non–common law jurisdiction is plain from the *Articuli super Cartas* of 1300, which limit the jurisdiction of the Seneschalsea and Marshalsea as well as that of the Exchequer.[86]

4. There was another development, at first sight the most puzzling of all. In 1215 and 1225 chapter 29 began with *Nullus liber homo*. In the statutes of 1331 and 1352 this became "No man" and then in 1354

---

84. Thompson, *Magna Carta*, 91.
85. Ibid., 89.
86. Chaps. 3, 4.

"No man of whatever estate or condition he may be."[87] How this came about no one has hitherto explained. One thing seems certain: neither the commons in parliament, with whom these words originated, nor the judges were expressing a sudden access of concern for the unfree whom the *liber homo* of Magna Carta deliberately excluded. The real explanation is simpler and has to do with language. The sense of "free man" was changing. In 1215 it was all embracing: there was not need to spell out that the *liber homo* of chapter 39 included all from the greatest in the land down to the simple freeholder; indeed, as the Charter tells us "freemen" still held their courts in jurisdiction over their tenants. By the fourteenth century this broad, inclusive sense of the words no longer held good. The language of social stratification was becoming increasingly diverse and specific. By the end of the century society was seen as a hierarchy of knights, squires, and yeomen, to whom gentlemen were soon to be added. Within these arrangements the free man became the franklin. The term was no longer comprehensive, but increasingly particular; freeborn was one thing, gentle or noble born quite other.[88] Hence if the free man of Magna Carta had been allowed to stand in the six statutes it would have tended to restrict these provisions to a particular social grade, and it was to counter this that the statute of 1354 resorted to "no man of whatever estate or condition he may be." It was not designed to give the unfree expanded access to the courts. It was for Coke later to lay down that it embraced the villein except in actions against his lord.[89]

Now are all these changes "legitimate"? And if we accept that chapter 29 could be made to embrace trial by jury what objection can there be to the attempt made in the debate on the Petition of Right to base the writ of habeas corpus also on Magna Carta? And if it is legitimate to turn due process against the Exchequer or Marshalsea in the four-

87. *Statutes of the Realm,* I, 231, 267, 345; Thompson, *Magna Carta,* 90–92.

88. See especially Nigel Saul, *Knights and Esquires: The Gloucestershire Gentry in the Fourteenth Century* (Oxford, 1981), 6–29. There is further comment in J. C. Holt, *Robin,* 2d ed. (London, 1989), 116–23. The chronology of these linguistic changes is naturally difficult to establish in detail. The amendment to *liber homo* in the six statutes is not discussed in either of the above.

89. Sir Edward Coke, *The Second Part of the Institutes of the Laws of England,* 1662 ed., 45.

teenth century why not against the Star Chamber in the seventeenth century? And does "due process" stand in the way of committal on special mandate of the king, the issue raised in the Five Knights' Case of 1627? And do "liberties" and "free customs" run counter to patents of monopoly as Coke maintained in the *Second Institute?* Plainly such questions allow no answer except perhaps one. The arguments in the Five Knights' Case or in the debate on the Petition of Right were no greater distortion than the fourteenth-century interpretations of due process. If the later arguments were "distortions" and "misinterpretations" so were the earlier. If the earlier arguments grew out of the implications of chapter 29 granted as a perpetual liberty in 1225, so did the later. In this crucial section of the Charter, Coke cannot be separated in our treatment of him from the precedents by which he set so much store.

But there is really no choice of interpretation. If we like we may polarize our approach: "error" on the one hand; an infinite regression of construction on the other. The plain fact is that from the thirteenth to the seventeenth century men saw nothing incongruous in construing Magna Carta any more than in glossing Holy Writ. And it is worth noting that the process was not indiscriminate nor the regression infinite. The six statutes of Edward III provide splendid examples of parliamentary construction, of the gloss. The *Confirmatio Cartarum* of 1297 and the *Articuli super Cartas* of 1300 demonstrate equally clearly that glossing had its limits. Both these documents were intimately related to the charters and immediately concerned with their enforcement. But both distinguished very clearly between the charters and the supplementary provisions they contained concerning taxation and other matters. Edward I's maletote on wool was restricted by a specific regulation, not by any constructive gloss on chapter 30 of the Charter; prises again were treated quite separately without reference to chapter 19. So magnates and knights in parliament knew when to gloss and when to add and, in adding, knew that it made sound sense to associate new demands with old concessions, to secure a restriction of the maletote and prises on the coattails of Magna Carta. Edward I also knew the difference. He was ready enough to confirm the charters: he resisted the additional provisions. This was at a time when both the king and his opponents were locked in dispute on yet another point of interpretation—the provisions on disafforestation in the Charter of the Forest.

So the medieval treatment of Magna Carta was striking in its variety. Some of it was accepted; some of it was disputed; particular chapters were used to defend local communities against royal officials; others provided building blocks for further legislation. It was interpreted by hopeful litigants, slick lawyers, legal commentators, and by parliament itself. Some of these constructions became embedded in its history. For more than a century it was a political force; at its weakest a kind of ritual, the first demand, the easiest concession; at its strongest, powerful enough to tow other demands in its wake. Common to all these varied reactions and uses there was a crucial element not so far discussed: the relationship of present to past, of new concessions to ancient practice, of Magna Carta to what had gone before; in short, a sense of history. "And forasmuch as approved Histories are necessary for a iurisconsult—for hee that hath redd them seemed to have lived in those former ages, Histories shall followe in the next place." Thus Sir Edward Coke's library catalog.[90] The intimate relation between law and history was of a special kind. It was concerned with precedent. It involved selection and encouraged error, but it was something different from the simple anachronism of superimposing the present on the past of which Petit-Dutaillis charged Stubbs, and Butterfield a whole host of Whig historians. It was more deliberate, more precise, and in the case of Magna Carta came to involve a specific objective. This was to circumvent the fact that liberties originated in a royal grant by arguing that they were ancient and preordained: the Charter, as a result, could be reduced to a confirmatory or declaratory role.

This argument was familiar by the seventeenth century. Coke declared that "the Charter was for the most part declaratory of the principal grounds of the fundamental laws of England, and for the residue it is additional to supply some defects of the common law"; again "this statute of Magna Carta is but a confirmation or restitution of the Common Law"; and again, on chapter 29, "this chapter is but declaratory of the old law of England."[91] Similar views were held well before the

90. *A Catalogue of the Library of Sir Edward Coke,* ed. W. O. Hassall, pref. S. E. Thorne (New Haven, Conn., 1950), 42, "where History follows Divinity, Lawes of England and Civill Lawe."

91. Sir Edward Coke, *The First Part of the Institutes of the Laws of England* (1628),

seventeenth century. Fifteenth-century readings, as we have seen, took the line that the king "ordeyned the greet charter, wherein is contened alle the fruyt of lawes bifore used turnyng to the people profit and al other put away."[92] There was a hint of the same approach already in 1226 when the knights of Lincolnshire sustained their argument against the sheriff's muster of the shire court by pointing out that the king had granted to all free men their liberties and *ancient* customs. If that is reported correctly, it was a slight but significant twist to the final chapter of the Charter, which confirmed liberties and *free* customs which they formally held.[93]

This appeal to the past was in our sense uncritical. Men confused the essential documents, so that the Charter of 1215 retained a shadowy importance even though superseded by the later versions. In 1231 an Oxfordshire jury attributed the concession of 1217 on the sheriff's tourn to the "Charter of Runnymede."[94] The provisions of 1215 concerning the assessment of scutages and aids and the taking of common counsel were recalled in various contexts up to 1255.[95] Article 56, concerning the law of the Welsh March, was still raised in a plea in 1291.[96] So Roger Wendover and Matthew Paris were not alone in confusing the various crucial texts. It is difficult to attach a special political significance to some of these instances. They probably reflect little other than the occasional survival of the text of 1215. But they all illustrate a casual treatment of documentary evidence. It is not just that the 1215 version was still used, but that its use passed unchallenged. It is with this in mind that we should approach the earlier documentation.

The rebellion of 1215 began with a demand for the confirmation and reissue of a basic text: the coronation charter of Henry I. It is also obvious that the older charter of Henry had a direct influence on

---

book II, chap. 2, sec. 108; *The Second Part of the Institutes of the Laws of England*, 1669 ed., Proeme and 45–57.

92. See above, p. 55.

93. "Libertates suas et antiquas consuetudines suas usitatas" (*Curia Regis Rolls*, 12, no. 2312); compare Magna Carta: "libertates et libere consuetudines quas prius habuerunt."

94. *Curia Regis Rolls*, 14, no. 1188.

95. Holt, *Magna Carta*, 399–400.

96. Thompson, *The First Century*, 65.

Magna Carta: each begins with the liberties of the church and then proceeds to feudal incidents. It seems probable that the charter of Henry I was retrieved from repositories in or near London; Westminster, Lambeth, and the royal Treasury all contributed early versions. A Treasury version was almost certainly the source of the text used in the so-called unknown charter. Its interest for our present purpose is that notes were added to it summarizing further concessions by, or demands on, King John.[97] A London/Westminster version was used in Harleian MS 458, a bifolium containing texts in both Latin and French of the coronation charters of Henry I, Stephen, and Henry II. In all probability this was the work of someone investigating the precedents available in previous royal grants and preparing them for the attention of an audience more accustomed to French than Latin.[98] The text available at Lambeth, copied into the archiepiscopal register Lambeth MS 1212 circa 1250, was also of this Westminster version.[99] All that is reasonably solid ground. It implies that there was a serious investigation of the available texts; they were transcribed with varying but on the whole fair accuracy; additional material was carefully distinguished. There was no attempt to gloss.

However, historico-legal research did not end there. It also extended to two texts drawn from the first half of the twelfth century, the *Leges Henrici Primi* and the *Leges Edwardi Confessoris.* These were a blend of Anglo-Saxon and Frankish law. The *Leges Henrici Primi* especially contained some genuine Anglo-Norman custom and legislation. Both were spiced with a dash of history. These texts were a different kettle of fish from Henry I's coronation charter, where authenticity mattered. They were miscellaneous collections; compared, for example, with the *Decretum* or the *Institutes* their authority was variable and uncertain; still they were texts and so they were glossed, especially the *Leges Edwardi Confessoris.* Again there is very little doubt that this was done in London, probably early in the reign of John. In the surviving manuscript the gloss takes the form of additional material interpolated in the body of the text. In the specifications about justice, judgment of

97. Holt, *Magna Carta,* 418–28.
98. Holt, *Medieval Government,* 14–16.
99. Holt, *Magna Carta,* 423–24.

peers, baronial counsel, and advice, the inserted material anticipates the program of 1215. And it was associated in the texts with the coronation oath.[100] It was to the renewal of the oath and the reissue of the charter of Henry I that the opposition to King John first turned in 1213 and 1214. This established a pattern. The tactic used to secure the settlement of 1215 and 1225, both then and ever afterward, was based exactly on this earlier tactic which already linked oath and charter.

There can be no doubt that all that was deliberate. Charters are not exhumed from repositories, manuscripts are not copied and interpolated, by accident. This material provides the clearest evidence of a program, the intellectual ammunition for a political movement. The work was centered on London. Here the Chapter of St. Paul's provided some of the most ardent supporters of the baronial movement, and it may not be too fanciful to imagine that one or two of them who later played a prominent role in the rebellion, Simon Langton and Gervase of Howbridge, were already up to their necks in the preliminaries. The mayor of London was one of the Twenty Five. Almost certainly a party in the city connived in admitting the barons at the beginning of May 1215. The Charter itself copied the commune of London in seeking to establish a commune throughout the land.

At first sight the program has the appearance of an artificial confection, of items thrown together for the convenience of the moment. That is probably true of any political program. But, like all attractive political programs, this tapped sources which were rich and deep. The coronation oath, the charter of Henry I, the laws of Henry I and Edward the Confessor, were not an accidental association; they were all expressions of ancient law which was now being used as a standard whereby Angevin government could be weighed, criticized, and corrected. Whether the standard was accurate mattered less than that it was ancient, for antiquity was nine-tenths of the law. The most elementary questions asked in the common law courts concerned the past: Is the tenement free? Did disseisin occur within the term of the assize? Is John the heir of William and was William seized on the day he died? Who presented to the living last? Perhaps especially, Who has the better right? —for here the answer might well lead to family descents

100. Ibid., 93–95.

going back for generations. Memory and record were essential to the ordinary operations of the courts. All litigants, jurymen, and judges required a sense of history. Ancient custom was more than an artifact recorded in old documents and texts. It was the common memory of how society was organized and social relations conducted. It was the expression of stability. In the courts it was refined into precise questions because exact answers were required in order to resolve disputes. Legal action required the explicit. But ancient custom was also implicit outside the courts in the organization and arrangement of men's daily lives.

In England this had a special importance. In the courts of law and also in other circumstances memory might well reach back through the twelfth century to the advent of the Normans and what had gone before. The charter of Henry I, on which men pinned their hopes prior to 1215, confirmed the law of King Edward. In the courts men might claim tenure *a conquestu*, but that was no more than an argument of longevity; conquest was a poor justification of title. So the Conqueror legitimized his title by claiming that he was the lawful heir of the Confessor, and his followers often legitimized their title also by reference to their *antecessores*, who might well be Anglo-Saxon. As a result concern for the *antecessor* was deeply ingrained in English law, determining succession practices from the crown down to the meanest freeholder. It was paralleled in canon law by the insistence on the duty of the incumbent to maintain his benefice as it had been held by his predecessor.[101] All this emphasized the past. It highlighted particular documents: Domesday Book, the single great title-deed which enshrined the principle of antecession; the charter of Henry I, which provided the continuity with the law of Edward; and the *Leges Edwardi Confessoris* and the *Leges Henrici Primi*, which described what that law was. It enhanced the reputation and memory of particular individuals: Edward the Confessor, canonized in 1161; Wulfstan, bishop of Worcester 1062–1095, canonized in 1203. Both were the object of royal take-

101. G. S. Garnett, "Royal Succession in England 1066–1154" (Ph.D. thesis, Cambridge, 1988), for a part of which see "Coronation and Propaganda: Some Implications of the Norman Claim to the Throne of England in 1066," *Transactions of the Royal Historical Society*, 5th ser., 36 (1986): 91–116.

overs. Henry II pressed for the canonization of Edward; Henry III built the noble shrine for him at Westminster. King John adopted Wulfstan as his patron saint; he was buried at Worcester near Wulfstan's tomb with effigies of Wulfstan and St. Oswald either side his own. It did not work. The barons appropriated Edward as the source of good and ancient law. Pandulf, the papal nuncio, told John curtly in 1211 that he had no right to seek precedents in Edward's appointment of Wulfstan to the bishopric of Worcester since he ignored the good laws of King Edward and enforced the evil laws of William the Bastard.[102]

At this point both secular and ecclesiastical law were interwoven with legend. For King John was trying to use the tale that Wulfstan, on being dismissed by the Conqueror, had thrust his staff into the Confessor's tomb, whence only he could withdraw it. It was a tale first told in 1138 by Osbert of Clare, prior of Westminster, as evidence of Edward's sanctity. It was then repeated by Ailred of Rievaulx and became well known, contributing in turn to the Arthurian legend. It was with such material that political arguments were forged. Behind both politics and law were minds filled with a largely legendary history, the tall stories of Geoffrey of Monmouth regurgitated as vernacular romance by Gaimar, Wace, and others. King John himself possessed, and seems to have read, a Romance of the History of the English.[103] Let the title speak for itself.

This literary effervescence of the twelfth century enjoyed royal and aristocratic patronage. Henry II was the patron of both Wace and Benoit. Geoffrey of Monmouth's various manuscripts are dedicated to Robert, earl of Gloucester, Waleran, count of Meulan, and King Stephen. Robert of Gloucester passed a copy of Geoffrey's work to Walter Espec, lord of Helmsley, who passed it on to Ralph fitz Gilbert, whose wife, Constance, passed it in turn to Gaimar, asking that he translate it into Norman French.[104] These men and their de-

102. Holt, *Medieval Government*, 7–8; Emma Mason, "St. Wulfstan's Staff: A Legend and Its Uses," *Medium Aevum* 53 (1984): 157–79.

103. *Rotuli Litterarum Clausarum*, I, 29. Among the vast literature on a topic necessarily in summary form here, see especially, J. S. P. Tatlock, *The Legendary History of Britain* (Berkeley, 1950).

104. Gaimar, *L'Estoire des Engleis*, ed. A. Bell (Oxford, 1960), lines 6430–31, 6447–52.

scendants did not see the past as we see it. They read rather of the Marcher baron, Fulk fitz Warin, a participant in the movement of 1215 who first made his name as an outlaw rebel against King John and as the man who triumphed over sundry giants and evil spirits culled from the myths of the Welsh Marches. So their Edward the Confessor and Henry I were not ours. The Confessor was a canonized saint, a worker of miracles; and Henry I was the "keeper of the bees and the guardian of the flocks" who "did right and justice in the land," he whom Merlin had named the Lion of Justice. Thus the London interpolator of the *Leges Edwardi Confessoris*.[105] It was by that comparison that the Angevins stood condemned.

In one instance this blend of law, history, and legend can be analyzed with some precision. Among the statutes of uncertain date included in the *Statutes of the Realm* is a record of the usages and customs of Kent made before the justices in eyre, headed by John of Berwick, in 1293. It is a lengthy statement of the inheritance practice of gavelkind and of sundry other legal privileges claimed by the Kentish freeholders. It asserts that all Kentish men were free. It maintains the principle of antecession; even the felon's heir shall "hold — by the same services and customs as his ancestors held."[106] In one matter, the replacement of knights by gavelkinders on juries of Grand Assize, the record was based on an earlier concession by Henry III, and it was noted that the charter conferring this was in the custody of Sir John Norwood. The charter undoubtedly existed, for it is mentioned in two associated writs in the Close Rolls,[107] and it is noteworthy that it was in the hands of a knight of the shire, as happened elsewhere with Magna Carta. This one point apart, all the remaining customs derived their authority from antiquity. The record concludes: "These are the Usages of Gavelkinde, and of Gavelkindmen in Kent, which were before the Conquest, and at the Conquest and ever since till now."

That was pointed. Why mention the Conquest at all? The answer lies in a legend first recorded at St. Augustine's, Canterbury, some time

---

105. F. Liebermann, "A Contemporary Manuscript of the Leges Anglorum Londoniis collectae," *English Historical Review* 28 (1913): 739.

106. *Statutes of the Realm*, I, 223–25.

107. *Close Rolls 1231–4*, pp. 32, 163–64.

after 1220, in annals attributed to, or copied by, William Sprott and later repeated by William Thorne. This related how at the time of the Conquest William the Conqueror was ambushed on Swanscombe Down by all the men of Kent, headed by Stigand, archbishop of Canterbury, and Aethelsige, abbot of St. Augustine's. They treated: the men of Kent promised to accept William as their liege lord on condition that they should "enjoy the liberties they had always had and use their ancestral law and customs." This was agreed. As a result, "the ancient liberty of the English and their ancestral laws and customs which, before the arrival of Duke William, were in force equally throughout the whole of England, have remained inviolable up to the present time only in the county of Kent."[108] The St. Augustine's story was quite clear. The result of the Conquest was that the English were reduced to everlasting servitude by the Normans. Only the men of Kent escaped the yoke of slavery.

The tale of Swanscombe Down was fiction. The London interpolations in the *Leges Edwardi Confessoris* were fabricated. The interchanges between King John and Pandulf that contrasted the good laws of the Confessor with the evil laws of the Conqueror were recorded long after the event. Nevertheless all three express a potent train of thought that good law was ancient law, in particular Anglo-Saxon law; that charters confirmed and restored, they did not innovate. These were some of the conceits and notions on which the knights of Lincolnshire could well have drawn when they claimed in 1226 that King Henry had confirmed their ancient liberties. They certainly provided the texts for the theory of the Norman Yoke and the argument that the Charter was restorative as they were developed in the seventeenth century. Sprott's tale of Swanscombe Down was repeated by Holinshed and summarized by Lambarde who, in his *Perambulation of Kent* (1576), preserved the best text of the judicial record of Kentish customs of 1293. Tottell also included it in his *Magna Charta cum Statutis* (1556). In addition Lambarde published the London text of the *Leges Edwardi Confessoris* in his *Archaionomia* (1568). Coke possessed copies of both the *Perambulation* and *Archaionomia*.[109] The latter was his main source of information on

108. Holt, *Medieval Government*, 9–12.
109. *Catalogue*, ed. Hassall, nos. 377, 610.

Anglo-Saxon law. There is a most direct textual link between the thirteenth and the seventeenth centuries.[110]

This textual dependence of Coke and others on the achievement of the medieval period extends across the whole activity of the intellect and the imagination: legend, the logical assumptions and implications of legal actions, interpolations in ancient laws, the promises of long dead kings, the charters themselves, the arguments about them, the construction and interpretation of them in plea and statute. Coke and his contemporaries must not be deprived of all capacity for individual thought. But even when original, in construing the Charter as prohibiting monopolies, for example, Coke was conforming in his method to a medieval pattern. Coke's ideas were old-fashioned. It may not come amiss to recall the words of Namier: "What matters most about political ideas is the underlying emotions, the music to which the ideas are mere libretto, often of very inferior quality."

The most important aspects of the antiquarian movement of the seventeenth century lie in the simple things. First, the antiquaries revived the Charter, looked at it as a whole, took in many of the medieval constructions and glosses, provided some of their own, although not many, and, above all, in truly medieval style, proceeded to apply the great tradition to their own particular circumstances. No one summed it up better than Sir Benjamin Rudyard in the debate on the Petition of Right: "I shall be very glad to see that old, decrepit Law Magna Charta which hath been kept so long, and lien bed-rid, as it were, I shall be glad to see it walk abroad again with new vigour and lustre, attended and followed with the other six statutes; questionless it will be a great heartening to all the people."[111]

Second, this renaissance was in part the work of officials of the Crown like Lambarde and was manifested most powerfully by a chief justice, Sir Edward Coke. Judges are not noted for conducting manifest private warfare within the structure of royal government. Yet Coke did just that and had the intellectual confidence, the indignation, to

110. This is examined more generally by Janelle Greenberg, "The Confessor's Laws and the Radical Face of the Ancient Constitution," *English Historical Review* 104 (1989): 611–37.

111. Thompson, *Magna Carta*, 86.

persist. At the time this seemed important. The *Second Institute* was prohibited and only published posthumously by order of the Long Parliament in 1641. But it was important not because of the contents of the *Second Institute,* which few if any of the members could yet have read, but because they too were now acting in anger, in indignation, and in sympathy with Coke's lifework.

If that is the case it leaves us with a problem. What *were* the intellectual origins of the English Revolution? Or perhaps it might be put differently. Was the so-called English Revolution any different in its origins from the political movements which from time to time had disturbed the tenor of medieval England?[112]

112. The question is framed in yet another context by J. S. A. Adamson, "The Baronial Context of the English Civil War," *Transactions of the Royal Historical Society,* 5th ser., 40 (1990): 93–120.

2. The Place of Magna Carta and the Ancient Constitution in Sixteenth-Century English Legal Thought

Legal thought and questions about the relationship between legal ideas and other strains of political and social theory are important and interesting aspects of sixteenth- and seventeenth-century English history, but they are subjects which have suffered in recent years both from scholarly neglect and from misunderstanding. The neglect can be explained partly by reference to the sociology of knowledge. British universities, which were founded and flourished for much of their history as training grounds for clerics, have recently been much more successful in producing students of ecclesiastical history and religious ideas than of legal history and juristic thought. At the same time much recent writing on the political and social history of the period, such as the so-called revisionist reinterpretations of the causes of the civil wars of the mid-seventeenth century, has tended to discount the role of ideas of any kind, much less legal ideology, in the general history of the period.[1]

This neglect is also, of course, one of the primary reasons for the misunderstandings of English legal thought which have accumulated over the years. In particular, it accounts for a failure to investigate or reinterpret a category of analysis which has for too long exercised a paradigmatic influence on our conceptions about the nature of legal ideas about politics and society—the notion of the common law mind. This concept became an orthodoxy in modern scholarship with the publication in 1957 of Professor J. G. A. Pocock's magisterial study of English historical thought, *The Ancient Constitution and the Feudal Law.* Concerned mainly with the attitudes of lawyers to the past and basing his thesis largely on the works of Sir Edward Coke and his contempo-

---

1. For one of many possible examples see J. S. Morrill, *The Revolt of the Provinces: Conservatives and Radicals in the English Civil War, 1630–1650* (London, 1976).

rary Sir John Davies, Pocock postulated a typical common law view of politics and society which was essentially a forerunner of that made famous by Edmund Burke in *His Reflections on the Revolution in France* (1790). According to Pocock, the key to the common law mind was the assumption that English law had no history, that it had been virtually unchanged by any of the major or minor upheavals in the history of England either before or after the Norman Conquest. English lawyers thought that English laws were the best laws because they represented the product of immemorial custom, a kind of mystical process by which the common law had proven itself to be satisfactory to the English through constant usage from a time beyond the written records or memories of men. In addition, the common lawyers completely denied that the civil law had ever had any influence in their country, and they were also extremely insular in their refusal to consider jurisprudential ideas which were contained within the civil law tradition or to wake up to the advances in historical scholarship which were being made by Continental humanist legal scholars such as Budé, Cujas, and Hotman.

Although Pocock's own study concentrated on the history of historical thought, he also believed that the "common law mind" had a wider application to the political history of the early seventeenth century, and this is a position which he has amplified in a recent restatement of the thesis. Coke and Coke's ideas were part of a mentality which had an important place in the controversies between the early Stuarts and their parliaments. The lawyers' idea of an unchanging legal tradition provided a standard, an "ancient constitution," which could be used as a defense by the subject against the encroachments of the crown.[2]

There is no doubt that parts of this picture demand assent. Pocock's interpretation of Coke's thought is accurate, and "ancient constitutionalism" was put to effective use by lawyers during some of the early Stuart parliaments, perhaps most notably in 1628. However, what is

---

2. J. G. A. Pocock, *The Ancient Constitution and the Feudal Law: A Study of English Historical Thought in the Seventeenth Century* (Cambridge, England, 1957). The new formulation and a very accurate account of the debate which the original interpretation engendered can be found in J. G. A. Pocock, *The Ancient Constitution and the Feudal Law: A Study of English Historical Thought in the Seventeenth Century; a Reissue with a Retrospect* (Cambridge, England, 1987).

in doubt is whether "ancient constitutionalism" had always been the major constituent of English legal thought, whether it was part of a longer tradition within English law. Furthermore, so much of the debate to date has been about legal attitudes toward history that we tend to lose sight of more general legal attitudes toward the law, politics, and society. Consequently it is far from clear how significant the ancient constitution was within the nexus of thought and practice which made up the intellectual environment of the legal profession and which was transmitted by the lawyers to the wider public.

Integral to both questions is the problem of what it was that might have made up the legal mentality of both lawyers and laymen (of different social groups) during the early-modern period, and the ways in which these mentalities may have changed over time. The object of this paper is to approach this problem by looking first at the structure of legal thought in general during the sixteenth century. Then it attempts to find a place for the history of that greatest of documents of the "ancient constitution," Magna Carta, within it. In general, the picture that emerges is quite different from that of the common law mentality we have known for so long. In the first place, English legal thought in this period is best seen as part of the broader European tradition of Renaissance jurisprudence rather than *sui generis,* and for that reason I have perhaps gone overboard in avoiding the term *common law mind*. Second, but perhaps not surprisingly when it is considered that the Tudor state frequently presented itself as an absolute monarchy, sixteenth-century lawyers were as often concerned with order, and indeed the basic problem of political obligation, obedience, as with questions concerning the liberty of the subject. For both of these reasons, neither ancient constitutionalism nor Magna Carta, at least until the 1590s, was a very significant feature of legal thought. There was a distinctive legal mentality during this period, but it contained many branches. Ancient constitutionalism was only one of them, and a relative latecomer at that. Finally, the paper offers an account of the particular circumstances in the late sixteenth century and first decade of the seventeenth which led Coke to express for the first time an ancient constitutionalist account of English law and government. I conclude with some brief remarks on the broader significance of early-modern legal thought in the Anglo-American political tradition.

II

The sixteenth century was a great age for the English legal profession. From the 1530s, but especially from about 1560, there was a spectacular increase in the amount of litigation which came before the central courts, so that by 1600 the rate of litigation in the royal courts per 100,000 of population was about four times greater than it is today. At the same time, the legal profession centered on the Westminster courts grew from a relatively small band of lawyers to a social group with a profile relative to the size of the population as a whole that was little different from that of the early twentieth century. It is not surprising, therefore, that much Tudor social and political thought, and not just that produced by lawyers, was articulated in legalistic terms.[3]

Yet in spite of this, an attempt to identify the most basic attitudes of English lawyers toward their law and its place in society does have to confront problems of evidence. The English legal profession and English legal education had an overwhelmingly vocational orientation. Lawyers learned their craft at the Inns of Court in London rather than in the universities. The inns had a teaching function and some teaching exercises. Indeed, the sixteenth century can be said to have marked a high point in the history of the inns as intellectual centers, and this is important in considering the role of legal ideology in this period. Nevertheless, there were limits on the extent to which English lawyers were free to speculate about jurisprudential matters. The senior members of the inns were primarily active practitioners; no English lawyer earned his living exclusively from teaching or writing about the law.[4] Hence, unlike the Continental university schools of law, the Inns of Court and the English legal profession produced few general works, even fewer which laid out with clarity the theoretical and philosophical foundations of the common law. The legal thought of the period must be pieced together from the examination of the odd textbook, one-off tracts, lectures delivered to students at the Inns of Court, and

3. C. W. Brooks, *Pettyfoggers and Vipers of the Commonwealth: The "Lower Branch" of the Legal Profession in Early Modern England* (Cambridge, England, 1986), chap. 4, pp. 75–79, 133–38.

4. W. R. Prest, *The Inns of Court under Elizabeth I and the Early Stuarts, 1590–1640* (London, 1972).

speeches made at meetings of courts such as quarter sessions and assizes.

English jurisprudence was not highly articulate, but it did consist of a number of identifiable assumptions and ideas. These can be most easily introduced by looking initially at *De Laudibus Legum Angliae,* a classic work written by Chief Justice Sir John Fortescue in the 1470s. Fortescue is frequently linked with Sir Edward Coke as a writer who exemplified the English legal tradition, and *De Laudibus* does contain a number of points which fit well with the stereotype of the "common law mind." Fortescue compares foreign, especially French, legal institutions unfavorably with those of the English, and he does not like the civil law doctrine, "What pleases the prince has the force of law." In addition, he held that, since English kings ruled both politically and regally, no English monarch could introduce new laws without the consent of the people.

These aspects of Fortescue's thought are important, but the fact that they are familiar should not lead to the conclusion that he was writing in exactly the same mode as Coke was to do over one hundred years later. In most respects their approaches were quite dissimilar. Coke filled his works with constant references to the landmarks of the common law past such as the laws of Edward the Confessor, Magna Carta, and Littleton's *Tenures.* By contrast, the writer to whom Fortescue refers most frequently is Aristotle, and *De Laudibus* is in essence an Aristotelian account of the place of law in society filtered through the interpretations of the medieval schoolmen. According to Fortescue, the grounds of English law were the divine laws which permeate throughout the universe, natural law, and human laws in the form of statute and custom. Divine law and natural law were ideally discovered either by revelation or by a kind of divine light which illuminated the intuitions of man. But, for obvious reasons, man's knowledge of these sources of law was bound to be imperfect. Consequently, although human (or positive) laws were supposed to conform to the higher laws of God and nature, there were inevitably going to be some areas in which such guidance was unclear. In these circumstances, Fortescue thought that the maxims of the human law (in England the maxims of the common law) should be used as the basis for judicial decision-making. However, human laws contrary to the laws of nature were invalid, and, if necessary, there was no reason why human laws should not be amendable in order to bring them into line with the higher laws.[5]

Many similar opinions, although much more skillfully elaborated, can be found in another work which became a classic in the canon of sixteenth-century legal thought, Christopher St. German's *Doctor and Student.* First published in Latin in 1523, this treatise aimed to lay down a set of rules about the circumstances in which men should be allowed to seek remedies in cases of conscience from the court of chancery; it is the fundamental early-modern statement about the grounds for equitable relief within the English legal system. But, although the objectives of the tract were in this sense fairly technical, the realization of them involved the use of quite sophisticated philosophical arguments about the nature of law. Furthermore, while much of Fortescue's scholastic learning was culled from a fifteenth-century compendium of quotations, St. German enjoyed a reputation as a thinker with expertise in the common, civil, and canon laws as well as in philosophy and the liberal arts, and his concept of equity was drawn largely from the work of the fourteenth-century Parisian conciliarist Jean Gerson.

Doctor and Student, which is in the form of a dialogue, begins with a doctor of divinity asking a student of the common law about the grounds on which the law of England is based. The reply is that there are six grounds: the laws of God, the laws of nature (which in England are called the laws of reason), diverse general customs of the realm, maxims of the common law, diverse particular customs, and, finally, parliamentary statutes. A discussion then follows about the relationship among God's law, natural law, and the positive laws of men. In general the conclusions are that human laws should agree with the laws of God and the law of nature as far as possible, but that in fact many laws, including some canon laws, are appointed purely for the sake of "political rule," and therefore cannot be shown to be entirely valid according to the higher laws. For example, the student points out that in England the law of property is based only on the authority of a custom of the realm which is not contained in any writing or statute.

5. Sir John Fortescue, *De Laudibus Legum Angliae,* ed. S. B. Chrimes (Cambridge, England, 1942), lxxix, 25, 37–41.

He even wonders whether such a custom can be considered a sufficient authority for any law. The reply of the doctor is that a law grounded on custom is the most certain law, but it must nevertheless be understood that such a custom cannot be allowed if it is contrary to the law of reason or the law of God.[6]

Between the publication of *Doctor and Student* and the early seventeenth century there is no English law book which sets out so systematically an overview of the nature of law. Nevertheless, there is little doubt that the kind of scholastic thought which both Fortescue and St. German espoused survived largely intact into the reign of Elizabeth, which began in 1558. Quite apart from the fact that there were frequent references to both writers, Aristotelian teaching was an important part of the syllabus of the universities, and during this age of rapidly rising admissions, many more common lawyers than ever before prefaced their legal educations with a period of study at Oxford or Cambridge. Sir Thomas Egerton, the future Lord Chancellor Ellesmere, undertook extensive study of Aristotle at Brasenose College, Oxford, in the 1550s, and Sir Edward Coke's library at Holkam was well stocked with the works of the Greek. In addition, Ellesmere and Elizabeth's chief councillor, Lord Treasurer Burghley, were patrons of the leading late Elizabethan Aristotelian, Dr. John Case, whose *Sphaera Civitatis,* a commentary on the *Politics,* became a basic university textbook in the 1590s.[7]

The survival of scholastic jurisprudence can also be illustrated by examples drawn from everyday legal practice. The notion that law had to conform to the English version of the law of nature, right reason, remained fundamental. The decision-making process of the judiciary was discussed in these terms. In an age in which printed law reports

---

6. C. St. German, *Doctor and Student,* ed. T. F. T. Plucknett and J. L. Barton (London, 1974), 1–77. Zofia Rueger, "Gerson's Concept of Equity and Christopher St. German," *History of Political Thought* 3:1 (1982): 1–30. See also J. Guy, *Christopher St. German on Chancery and Statute* (London, 1985).

7. Louis A. Knafla, *Law and Politics in Jacobean England: The Tracts of Lord Chancellor Ellesmere* (Cambridge, England, 1977), 40. *A Catalogue of the Library of Sir Edward Coke,* ed. W. O. Hassall (New Haven, Conn., 1950). C. B. Schmitt, *John Case and Aristotelianism in Renaissance England* (Kingston and Montreal, 1983), 6–9, 43, 87, 104, 136–37.

were still anything but comprehensive, there was as yet no clearly established principle that past precedents should bind current decisions.[8] Furthermore, right reason served as a basic principle for justifying the making of new statute law. For example, *A Treatise Concerning Statutes or Acts of Parliament* referred frequently to *Doctor and Student* in the course of developing an argument that existing laws which were not conformable to the laws of reason should be corrected by statute. In short, the anonymous author of this tract presents a justification for the mass of Elizabethan parliamentary legislation which is perfectly compatible with the views of Fortescue or St. German, but very far from vaunting the perfection of immemorial common law in the manner of Coke.[9]

However, if scholastic Aristotelianism and a fundamental outlook which stressed natural law theory were aspects of English legal thinking which may be said to have been inherited from the medieval past, there were also newer influences, or at least changes in emphasis, which arose out of the specific conditions of the sixteenth century itself. As is well known, the Elizabethan age in particular seems to have been obsessed with general fears of social and political chaos, and this was reflected in common law thought by a striking emphasis on obedience and law enforcement. To a large extent this was a product of the quite real threats posed to the realm by religious heterodoxy, the possibility of invasion by the most powerful country in Europe, Spain, and by the dislocation characteristic of a society in which the number of people was rapidly outpacing the capacity of the economy to employ them. Yet, this new strand in legal thinking also had identifiable roots in the intellectual inheritance of the English Renaissance.

In England, as elsewhere in Europe, the key to the Renaissance was the humanist movement, and humanism can be defined accurately, if rather generally, as simply a revival of interest in the classical literature of ancient Rome. Surprisingly perhaps, this early sixteenth-century classical revival had a considerable influence on the legal profession. In his *De Laudibus,* Fortescue identified lawyers with priests,

---

8. Edmund Plowden, *Commentaries or Reports of Edmund Plowden, of the Middle-Temple, Esq. An Apprentice of the Common Law* (London, 1761 ed.), 9, 13, 27.

9. Sir Christopher Hatton [?], *A Treatise Concerning Statutes or Acts of Parliament and the Exposition Thereof* (London, 1677).

but during the 1520s and 1530s, a new image began to emerge.[10] The first evidence of this appears in one of the most important works of the English humanist movement, Sir Thomas Elyot's *The Boke Named the Governour.* Elyot was the son of a judge, a member of the Middle Temple, and an associate of both Sir Thomas More and Thomas Cromwell. Like some other English humanists, he found the law French of the common law barbarous in comparison with the classical Latin that was his ideal. But the other notable feature of his work was the advocacy of a legal profession which modeled itself on the *prudente* of classical Rome. Elyot wanted a profession in which law and rhetoric were combined to produce men who did not simply grovel for fees, but who combined a knowledge of law with oratorical and rhetorical skills in order to serve their country as both effective lawyers and effective governors. His ideals were the historian Tacitus, the famous politician and jurisconsult Servius Sulpicius, and, of course, Cicero.[11]

To a very large extent, the ideal which was proposed by Elyot does seem to have been adopted by the English profession. It lay behind the evolution of the idea that barristers should be paid by *honoraria* or gratuity rather than set fees, and it is perhaps most convincingly exemplified by the fact that even Sir Edward Coke garnished his works with quotations from Cicero. Indeed, in the preface to the *First Part of the Institutes,* he pointed out to his readers that the fifteenth-century English lawyer Littleton had a coat of arms which contained "escalop shells, which the honourable Senators of Rome wore in bracelets."[12]

Furthermore, English lawyers absorbed jurisprudential ideals from their ancient models, and in this respect they shared an outlook which had much in common with Continental legal thought. In his excellent book on *Natural Rights Theories,* Richard Tuck has suggested that from about the middle of the sixteenth century, the humanist lawyers of Continental Europe were much more interested in humanly constructed law, the law positive (or *jus gentium*) and civil remedies, than in abstract

10. Fortescue, *De Laudibus,* 9.

11. Sir Thomas Elyot, *The Boke Named the Gouernour* (1531), ed. H. H. S. Croft, 2 vols. (London, 1880), 1:154–55, 157.

12. W. R. Prest, *The Rise of the Barristers: A Social History of the English Bar, 1590–1640* (Oxford, 1986), 315–18. Sir Edward Coke, *The First Part of the Institutes of the Lawes of England* (London, 1628 ed.), preface.

discussions of natural law. According to Tuck, the central characteristic of their attitudes toward law was a contrast between civilization and the rude and barbaric life of precivilized peoples. Moreover, the *locus classicus* of this view was contained in the first few pages of Cicero's *De Inventione,* in which he gave an account of the origins of eloquence by comparing a time when men wandered the fields aimlessly and in danger of oppression with the time when a great man had formed them together into a civilized society. In general, eloquence and law came to be seen as the means whereby men moved from a naturally brutish life to one of civility.[13]

In England, these links connecting law, rhetoric, and the civilizing process were similarly emphasized by early-Tudor humanists. Thomas Starkey, one of the leading members of Thomas Cromwell's "think tank" of intellectuals and propagandists, expressly embraced the ideal that law was one of the principal means by which rude nature was transformed,[14] and Elyot's *Governour* devotes many thousands of words to the task of trying to convince the aristocracy and gentry that they should give up their ignorant and warlike ways, acquire some book-learning, and take their proper place in the state as inferior magistrates.[15]

Among the lawyers, also, this notion that positive law was the prime defender of civilized life and a bulwark against its disintegration into a brutish state of nature was a constantly reiterated theme. For example, the preface of the 1572 edition of John Rastell's important legal textbook, *An Exposition of Certaine difficult and obscure wordes,* begins with the general remark: "Like as the univerasall worlde can never have his continuance but only by the order and lawe of nature which compellethe every thing to doe his kinde: so there is no multitude of people in no realme that can continue in unitie and peace without they be thereto compelled by some good order and law."[16]

13. Richard Tuck, *Natural Rights Theories: Their Origin and Development* (Cambridge, England, 1979), 33–34.

14. Thomas Starkey, *A Dialogue between Cardinal Pole and Thomas Lupset, Lecturer in Rhetoric at Oxford,* ed. J. M. Cowper (London, 1878), 50–53.

15. Elyot, *The Gouernour.*

16. John Rastell, *An Exposition of Certaine difficult and obscure wordes* . . . (London, 1572), sig. Aii.

At times, the very expressions used echo quite clearly the words of Cicero. English lawyers were particularly addicted to the formula found in *De Legibus* which postulated that without government and law the household, the city, the nation, and the human race could not survive. An early example occurs in a manuscript treatise written in the 1540s by the humanist, lawyer, and sometime reformer Sir John Hales, which is entitled "An Oration in Commendation of the Laws." According to Hales, "If law be gone farewell love, farewell shame, farewell honestie, farewell truthe, farewell faith and all vertue. And in with deceipte, Crafte, subtiltie, periurye, malice, envie, discorde, debate, murder, manslaughter, tyrannye, sedition, Burnyng of houses, pullinge downe of Cyties and townes, ravishing of virgins, violation of widowes [etc.]." By contrast, law "reteynethe justice, justice causeth love, love contynueth peace, peace causeth quyet, Quyet causeth men to applie their industrie and fall to labour."[17] It is a litany which soon becomes familiar to any reader of Elizabethan law books.

For many English lawyers, the ideal of the rule of law was reified to almost totemistic proportions. In 1589, for instance, Sir Christopher Yelverton told an audience at Gray's Inn, which was assembled to mark his promotion to serjeant-at-law,

> I cannot sufficiently, nor amply enough magnifie the majestie and dignitie of the lawe, for it is the devine gifte and invention of god, and the profound determination of wise men, the most strong synewe of a common wealth *and* the soule w[i]thout w[hi]ch the magistrate cannot stand. . . . The necessitie of lawe is such that as in some nacons, where all learning is forbidden, yet the houses of law be suffred, that thereby the people may the sooner be induced to civilitie and the better provoked to the performance of there [*sic*] duty . . . to live w[i]thout governm[en]t is hellish *and* to governe without Lawe is brutish . . . the Law (saith Tully) containeth all wisdome, and all the rules of philosophie, *and* let them all (saith he) say what they will, if man would search the originall *and* very groundes of the Lawes, they seeme for weight of authoritie, strength of reason, and plenty of profit to excell all the philosophers' Libraries.[18]

17. B[ritish] L[ibrary], Harleian MS 4990, fols. 8–8ᵛ.
18. BL Add[itional] MS 48, 109, fols. 12ᵛ–13ᵛ.

Roman texts became a mine of aphoristic truths.[19] Furthermore, many English barristers appear to have been quite familiar with works of Continental juristic humanism which shared their own assumptions about the importance of law to civilized life and which promoted the ideal that jurisprudence was the queen of all sciences. For example, William Lambarde, Sir John Dodderidge, and Sir Christopher Yelverton were all familiar with the work of Joachim Hopperus, a Flemish civilian who enjoyed a successful career under Philip II of Spain, and they, like many others, knew the works of Jean Bodin.[20] Henry Finch's *Nomotexnia* (The Art of Law), which was composed in the 1580s, followed Continental examples in attempting to apply Ramist logical techniques to English law.[21] Late in the reign of Elizabeth, Dodderidge, who later became a judge, produced a bibliography for a treatise on the royal prerogative which he dedicated to Thomas Sackville, Lord Buckhurst, a major figure in Elizabethan government, who appears to have been at the center of a legal circle which also included Coke, William Fleetwood, and the translator of the *Institutes* of John Calvin, Thomas Norton.[22] Dodderidge's work was, of course, to be based on the records and constitutions of the common law, but he also intended to draw on works of divinity, philosophy, and the law of nations, "Imitatinge heerin a Learned Serjeant and afterward in the tyme of Kyng Edward the fourth a learned Judge who very well said that 'when newe matter was considered whearof no former Lawe is extant, we do, as the

19. The Elizabethan Lord Keeper, Sir Nicholas Bacon, decorated his country house with quotations from Cicero and Seneca. Elizabeth McCutcheon, *Sir Nicholas Bacon's Great House Sententiae* (Claremont, Calif., 1977).

20. Lambarde's copy of *Tractatus De Iuris Arte, Duorum Clarissimorum Iurisconsul . . . Ioannis Corassii et Ioachimi Hopperi . . .* (Cologne, 1582) was purchased in 1583. It is copiously annotated. British Library Department of Printed Books Shelf Mark 516.a.55.

21. For a discussion of Finch see T. K. Shaller, "English Law and the Renaissance: The Common Law and Humanism in the Sixteenth Century" (Ph.D. dissertation, Harvard University, 1979), 310–15.

22. For Coke see BL Harleian MS 443, fol. 1; for Fleetwood, BL Stowe MS 423, fol. 107, and BL Harleian MS 6234, fol. 10ᵛ. Norton and Sackville collaborated on *The Tragedie of Gorboduc: whereof three Actes were wrytten by Thomas Nortone, and the two laste by Thomas Sackvyle . . .* (London, 1565). See also *The Dictionary of National Biography*.

Sorbonists and Civilians, resorte to the Lawe of Nature which is the Grownde of all Lawes and thene drawing that which is most conformable for the Common Wealthe do adjudge hit for Lawe.'" The proposed references range from the Bible and Thomas Aquinas, to Plato, Aristotle, and Aristotle's ancient and modern interpreters. Then there are Machiavelli, Justus Lipsius, and French lawyers including Bodin and François Hotman.[23]

No less important, English lawyers also shared general humanist principles about the way in which law should be administered in any society. First, as John Hales put it in the 1540s, "if lawe be a rule whereunto *every* man shoulde reduce his lyvinge me thinketh it veraie necessarie, to put it in writinge to the intente the People might knowe what they oughte to doe and not hange in one man or in fewe learned mens head*es*."[24] Although many writers did not go this far in calling for the codification of the common law, there is no doubt that the advisability of making the law known to the population at large was a question frequently debated during the course of the later sixteenth century, and on the whole the argument was won decisively by the publicists.[25]

Second, lawyers argued that law was of value to society only if it was a source of justice. Hence they tended to see the rule of law as a system of authority before which all men were equal and which disregarded more traditional and informal bonds that existed in early-modern society such as those between magnate and retainer, those between neighbors, and those of kinship. Since jurists held that political society was founded to protect the weak from the strong, it followed (and this idea was also found in Cicero) that in theory at least lawyers should be no friends of magnate retinues and that they should emphasize equality before the law.[26] According to John Hales, one of the chief virtues of justice was that it had "noe Respecte to nature, kynrede, af-

---

23. BL Harleian MS 5220, fols. 3–21. See also BL Stowe MS 423, fols. 106ff., *Historical Discourse* by William Fleetwood, Recorder of London.

24. BL Harleian MS 4990, fol. 16.

25. See, for example, Ferdinando Pulton, *De Pace Regis et Regni viz. A Treatise declaring which be the great and generall Offences of the Realme and the chiefe impediments of the peace of the King and Kingdome* . . . (London, 1609), preface.

26. See, for example, [Anon.], *A Collection of the Lawes and Statutes of this Realme concerning Liueries of companies and Reteynours* (London, 1571).

fynitie, frendshippe, Envie, malice" or hatred. Similarly, William Lambarde reminded Kentish grand jurymen that they should not let their ties in the local community prevent them from doing their lawful duty in presenting malefactors at quarter sessions. Most lawyers appear at the least to have paid lip service to Sir Edward Coke's declaration at the Norwich assizes in 1606 that if "Justice [were] withheld only the poorer sort are those that smart for it."[27] According to one anonymous seventeenth-century writer, "If we would perfectly execute justice wee must make no difference betweene men for their frends[hi]p, parentage, riches, pov[er]tye, or dignitye. Cicero sayth that wee must leave our pleasures and particular profits to embrace the publick good."[28]

Thus, the ideal of the rule of law and its corollaries became commonplaces for lawyers, and the notion that law was necessary for the maintenance of society in general was doubtless accepted by many laymen as well. The wider political implications of these general truths were, however, subject to a variety of interpretations. On the one hand, the rule of law could become a weapon in the art of statecraft and a principal justification for demanding absolute obedience to the prince. In the 1530s, for instance, Richard Morrison, a propaganda writer for Thomas Cromwell, who has been identified by Felix Raab as an early English Machiavellian, drew up a set of proposals for reforming the laws of England. One part of the scheme suggested that summer holidays, which had traditionally been used by the common people to celebrate Robin Hood and "disobedience also to [the king's] officers," should be made instead into occasions which attacked the bishop of Rome and showed the people "the obedience that yo[u]r subiectes by Goddes and mans Lawes owe unto yo[u]r ma[jes]tie."[29]

Morrison's project was apparently rejected, but a manuscript called "A book of things inquirable at inferior courts," which dates from the

27. Conyers Read, ed., *William Lambarde and Local Government: His 'Ephemeris' and Twenty-nine Charges to Juries and Commissions* (Ithaca, N.Y., 1962), 70, 73, 89. Sir Edward Coke, *The Lord Coke His Speeche and Charge* (London, 1607), sig. Civ. Many other examples could be given.

28. BL Add. MS 12,515, fol. 42.

29. Felix Raab, *The English Face of Machiavelli* (London, 1964), 34. BL Cotton MS Faust. C. II. "A Discours touching the Reformation of the Lawes of England," fols. 18–18ᵛ.

later 1530s, possibly 1538, may well have been concocted for the use of lawyers acting as stewards in town courts, sheriff's tourns, and manorial courts. It explains that in the past only matters within the jurisdiction of such local courts had been given in the charge addressed to the jurors, but now the king was intent that the unlearned and ignorant people should "better knowen and due their dewtie first to God, then to his highness as God*es* vicar." In addition to its use in local courts, the charge was also supposed to be read at least four times a year in the parish church. Among a long list of matters dealing with both the administration of justice and the defense of the Henrician reformation, there was a clear statement that the king had been appointed by God to rule over the commonwealth and that any disobedience to the monarch was a violation of holy ordinances.[30]

In the Elizabethan period, likewise, the necessity of the rule of law was often linked to calls for obedience to established authority. Indeed, some legal publicists, and councillors in the queen's government, began to argue that the maintenance of the rule of law was in itself a sufficient foundation for the obedience a subject owed to his prince. The key precept in this line of thinking was that some government was better than no government. The rule of law protected property and the person. It was a way of keeping the animal passions of men, which colored life in the state of nature, at bay. Consequently, it offered an incentive for accepting the existing government on the grounds of self-interest, even if one had doubts about the issue as a matter of conscience. This was essentially the basis of the accommodation which Elizabethan government offered to English Catholics. For example, in a piece of propaganda addressed to those involved in the 1569 rebellion, Thomas Norton, the translator of Calvin, parliament man, and legal man of business to Lord Treasurer Burghley, wrote, "The common weale is the ship we sayle in, no one can be safe if the whole do perish. To God, *and* then to the realme, the crown, to the law and government . . . we all do owe our selves and all that we have."[31]

30. BL Add. MS 48,047, fols. 59–61ᵛ. The dating is based on internal evidence.

31. Thomas Norton, *To the Quenes Maiesties poore deceyued Subiectes of the Northe Countrey drawen into rebellion by the Earles of Northumberland and Westmerland* (London, 1569), sig. Gi.

Some lawyers extended the connection between the value of the rule of law and the necessity for obedience into a conventional theory of divine right monarchy. For example, in 1587 Richard Crompton, one of the more important Elizabethan legal thinkers, published *A short declaration of the ende of Traytors,* a pamphlet which contained the substance of a speech he had given before a meeting of the Stafford-shire quarter sessions earlier that year. The setting is significant because such orations, or "charges," appear to have been a normal part of the procedures which surrounded the opening ceremonies of most local courts during the period. They were probably the main avenue through which the ideology of the lawyers was professed openly to a public which reached at least as far down the social scale as the lesser gentlemen and yeomen farmers who served on petty and grand juries.

According to Crompton's preface to the printed version, his aims on this particular occasion had been to show the people the good they get by the law, to explain their duty to obey the prince, and to illustrate the fate of traitors. He wanted to warn them about the dangers of treason on the grounds of conscience and to set out a legal justification for the execution of Mary, Queen of Scots. Like many other tracts of the same vintage and purpose, *The Declaration* was filled with cautions about the dangers of the times (in 1587 the Spanish Armada was about to set sail) and stressed the advantages which England was enjoying under the beneficent leadership of Queen Elizabeth, especially in comparison with the bloody murders and discords which were taking place on the Continent.[32]

Although hardly systematic, Crompton's call for obedience to Queen Elizabeth was a classic piece of absolutist jurisprudence. His conception of the foundations of political society was a conflation of pagan ideas about a state of nature ruled by the law of nature and an interpretation of the scriptures which placed the foundation of human society after the "universall flodde," when God had appointed kings

32. Richard Crompton, *A short declaration of the ende of Traytors and false Conspirators against the state, and the duetie of Subjectes to theyr soueraigne Gouernour* . . . (London, 1587).

and magistrates to rule over the people. In addition, he incorporated two fairly straightforward quotations from Cicero's *De Legibus*. Law is the highest reason granted in nature; it commands what things are to be done and forbids those which are not. According to Crompton, it followed from this that there is a need for preeminence and superiority in government, for without government, no house, no city can stand. Kings were ordained by God to govern, and their subjects were commanded to obey. Even in the face of injustice or tyranny subjects had no right to rebel against the prince. Even the Turks (whose government Englishmen always associated with the worst form of oppressive regime) had no right to overthrow the ruler God had put on the throne to govern them. The laws of God, the laws of nature, and the laws of the realm all demanded absolute obedience.[33]

Richard Crompton certainly expressed views which would have pleased the queen's government. It is less certain how far they can be described as typical. Only a tiny minority of the thousands of charges which must have been delivered have survived.[34] Much of what Crompton said in Staffordshire was conventional and commonplace, but other writers may have altered the emphasis. For example, William Lambarde's account of the origins of political life sounds very much like that found in the most popular Ciceronian work in England, *De Officiis*. In the beginning the only political society was the family governed by the patriarch, but as population grew, the weak and helpless began to be oppressed by the strong. Consequently, the people went to the man who was most distinguished for his virtue and established him as their king. He protected the weak, and set up an equitable system of government which united the highest and lowest in equal rights. Lambarde developed this view of the origins of political society further by adding that once the rulers who had been established by the people became corrupted, "then were Lawes and rules of Justice devised, within the which as within certaine Limits, the power of governors should from

33. Ibid. Similar views are also expressed in Crompton's *The Mansion of Magnanimitie. Wherein is Shewed the most high and honorable acts of sundrie English Kings, Princes, Dukes, Earles, Lords, Knights, and Gentlemen* . . . (London, 1599).

34. I have been able to identify about twenty in manuscript for the period from roughly 1550 to 1640.

henceforth be bounded to establish laws by which both governors and governed could be ruled."[35]

An even more detailed insight into an Elizabethan lawyer's attitudes toward government is revealed in a series of "readings," or lectures, on the royal prerogative which were given at the Middle Temple in 1579 by James Morice, a man who was on fairly close business terms with Lord Treasurer Burghley, and who was also associated with the Elizabethan presbyterian movement.[36] Morice started his discourse by explaining that he had selected his subject because he wanted to come to a better understanding of the authority of princes and the duty incumbent on subjects to obey them.[37] He also pointed out that there had long been debate about which was the best form of government—monarchy, aristocracy, or democracy. In general, history, particularly Roman history, taught that monarchy was the most effective. Democracy tended to anarchy; oligarchy, or the rule of the best, to faction. However, monarchy was inclined to slip into tyranny and insolent oppression. Therefore another form of government whereby the prince governed by law had been established.

> And for that good kynges and Prynces are nether by Nature Imortale, nor of them selves being Men, Imutable. An other State of kyngdome and better kynde of Monorchie hathe byne by com-

35. William Lambarde, *Archion or A Commentary upon the High Courts of Justice in England* (first published London, 1635, but the preface is dated 1591, and there are earlier manuscript copies), 1–5.

36. Edmund Lodge, *Illustrations of British History, Biography, and Manners, In the Reigns of Henry VIII, Edward VI, Mary, Elizabeth and James I*, 2d ed., 3 vols. (London, 1838), 2:443–46. J. E. Neale, *Elizabeth I and Her Parliaments, 1584–1601* (London, 1957), 267–79.

37. The reading survives in two versions, BL Add. MS 36,081 fols. 229ff., and BL Egerton MS 3376, a contemporary fair copy with a dedication to Lord Treasurer Burghley. The text on which Morice chose to read was a short "saving clause" in the Statute of Westminster I (1275) in which the king states that none of the previous provisions of the statute should result in prejudice to himself (*Statutes of the Realm*, ed. A. Luders, T. E. Tomlins, S. Raith, 11 vols. [London, 1810–1828], 1, 39, chap. 50). In the course of apologizing for selecting this ancient, short, and rather general clause, Morice explained that he did so largely because it enabled him to discuss more generally questions about the power of the monarch. BL Add. MS 36,081, fols. 230–30ᵛ.

*m*on Assent ordayned and establyshed, wherein the Prince (not by Lycentious will and Imoderate Assertions but by the Law, That is by the prudent Rules *and* Preceptes of Reason agreed vppon *and* made the Covenant of the Comon Wealth) may Justly governe and commande, and the People in due obedience saeflie lyve and quyetly enioye their owne.[38]

Morice then considered the etymology of the word *prerogative* in such a way as to be able to make the point that among "The Romaynes the Consent of the people was requysite to the Establishment of their Lawes." Furthermore, he argued that while it was sovereign kings who actually made laws, this was always done through consultation with the people. Such a system worked because "what cawse agayne haue the Comons to murmor or rebell agaynst the Lawes and Statues by w[hi]ch they are gov[er]ned syns they them selves are of Counsell and consent to *the* makinge of the same." Finally, he came to the question of whether the king be above or below the law. The answer was formulated as follows.

It is a comon Sayinge amonge many that the Kinge by his Prerogatyve is above his laws w[hi]ch rightly understode is not amisse spoken. . . . But to say that the Kinge is so a Emperor over his Lawes and Actes of Parliament (bycawse he hath power to make them), as that he is not bounde to governe by the same but at his will and pleasure, is an Oppinyon altogeather repugn[an]t to the wise and politicke State of gov[er]nment established in this Realme, w[hi]ch placeth the Royall Majestie of The kynge as the Leiutenant of Almightie God in the Reverent Throne of Justice and true Iudgment. [It is] Contrarye to the Rule of Equytie and com*m*on reason w[hi]ch sayeth [that laws] beinge made by so grave a Counsell, uppon so greate deliberacion and by the Co*m*mon Consent of all [should be followed by the king].[39]

The detailed survival of this reading is exceptional; so, too, perhaps, was James Morice's attachment to the radical puritan cause. Yet, the fact that the queen's principal adviser, Lord Treasurer Burghley, re-

38. Ibid., fol. 231.
39. Ibid., fols. 235, 243ᵛ–44ᵛ.

quested that Morice send him a copy of the text may suggest that the ideas it expressed were not outrageously unconventional.[40] It seems safe to conclude that many Elizabethan lawyers would have been aware of Aristotle's divisions of the kinds of government into aristocracy, monarchy, democracy, and the mixtures of these three, and many of them may have supported Morice's defense of mixed monarchy. Thus an anonymous paper delivered to the Society of Antiquaries in the late 1590s or early 1600s stressed that the court of parliament had a double power. One involved consultation by way of deliberation for the good government of the commonwealth, so it is *consilium,* not *curia.* The other power came from parliament's role in the administration of justice.[41] For some these conclusions may have arisen from a consideration of the nature of the origins of the state along the lines laid out by Lambarde. For others it may have been a natural corollary of the kind of legal realism which was imbibed from writers such as Bodin. For example, in the late 1590s, the speaker of the House of Commons, Sir Christopher Yelverton, informed the House that there were many forms of government, but that monarchy was the best, and that the English polity was particularly good because there were practical advantages in allowing the people themselves to be the framers of their own laws.[42]

These views amount to contemporary refutations of Sir Geoffrey Elton's recent attempts to depict the Elizabethan parliament as a court

40. BL Egerton MS 3376, fol. 1.

41. BL Add. MS 48,102. "The Severall opinions of Sundarie Antiquaries touching the Antiquitie power, order, Estate, persons, manner and proceeding of the High Court of Parliament," fol. 12.

42. BL Add. MS 48,109. Speeches and letters of Sir Christopher Yelverton, JKB (1535–1612). In his speech at the beginning of the session in 1597 he said that political society had been founded when "pollicie, springinge of . . . necessitie did force men to submitte theire libertie to the frame of others sovereignty" (fols. 18–19). In his closing speech he argued that "the people" were most likely to be ruled by laws when they "be agents in framing them" (fol. 22). Bodin wrote, "When edicts are ratified by Estates or Parlements, it is for the purpose of securing obedience to them, and not because otherwise a sovereign prince could not validly make law" (*Six Books of the Commonwealth by Jean Bodin,* ed. M. J. Tooley [Oxford, 1967], 32).

which had no significant political or advisory function.[43] Yet it is at the same time important to recognize that much of Elizabethan legal thought also bears a close resemblance to what Continental historians describe as political neo-Stoicism.[44] The rule of law was the greatest benefit of government, one which could be maintained only through absolute obedience to the monarch. However, political obligation was not based entirely on divine injunctions that the subject accept the will of the prince. It also involved a calculation of self-interest. The king was supposed to rule for the good of his people and govern according to law. Hence there was a clear perception of the difference between good government and bad government, between just rule and tyranny. Few lawyers went so far as to share the suspicion of the royal use of the law which is expressed in the poetry of the aristocrat Fulke Greville:

> For though perhaps at first sight laws appear
> Like prisons unto tyrants' soveraign might,
> Yet are they secrets, which Pow'r should hold dear
> Since envyless they make her infinite;
> And set so fair a gloss upon her will,
> As under this veil Pow'r cannot do ill.[45]

But many of them did have a clear perception of the potential danger of tyranny. In a speech to quarter sessions dating from the late 1560s or early 1570s, Sir Christopher Yelverton reminded his listeners "how easilie may the haughtie raigne of the unskillful prince slide into Tirranie."[46] More cautiously, but nonetheless clearly, the anonymous author of *The Laudable Customs of London* (1584) noted:

---

43. G. R. Elton, *The Parliament of England, 1559–1581* (Cambridge, England, 1986).

44. Gerhard Oestreich, *Neostoicism and the Early Modern State* (Cambridge, England, 1982). See also *Two Bookes of Constancie Written in Latine by Iustus Lipsius, Englished by Sir John Stradling*, ed. Rudolf Kirk and C. M. Hall (New Brunswick, N.J., 1939), 3–34 for an account of English neo-Stoicism.

45. *The Works in Verse and Prose . . . of Fulke Greville . . . Lord Brooke*, ed. A. B. Grosart, 4 vols. (London, 1868), 1:94–95.

46. BL Add. MS 48,109, fol. 37.

We find it necessarie in all common wealthes, for subjects to live under the direction of Lawes, constitutions, or customs, publickly knowen and received, and not to depende only upon the command-ment and pleasure of the governor, be the same never so iust or sincere in life and conversation. For that the Law once enacted and established, extendeth his execution towards al men alike without favour or affection: Whereas if the word of a Prince were a lawe, the same being a mortall man must needes bee possessed with those passions, and inclinations of favour or disfavour that other men be: and sometimes decline from the constant *and* unremoveable levell of indifferrencie, to respect the man besides the matter, if not to re-gard the person more than the cause. Wherefore it was wel agreed by the wisest Philosophers and greatest politicks, that a dumme lawes direction is to be preferred before the sole disposition of any living Prince, both for the cause afore touched, and for other rea-sons which I will here omit.[47]

However, although Elizabethan legal writers were well aware of the potential conflicts between the power of princes and the liberty of the subjects, and although they were perfectly capable of discussing such matters in general theoretical terms, they preferred to avoid drawing precise lines between the two, and, given the wartime dangers to po-litical stability which they perceived, it is hardly surprising that the monarch was frequently given the benefit of the doubt. This impor-tant characteristic of the interrelationship between legal theory and political reality is perhaps best summed up in the anonymous *Collec-tion of the Lawes and Statutes of This Realme concerning Liueries of companies and Reteynours* (1571). This author was quite open about the abuses of kings such as Henry I, Richard II, and Richard III, but he also took pains to point out that "the Whole body of our law books" show that at no period in history had questions concerning princes been as often

47. *A Breefe Discourse, declaring and approuing the necessarie and inviolable mainte-nance of the laudable Customes of London: Namely of that one, whereby a reasonable par-tition of the goods of husbands among their wiues and children is prouided* . . . (London, 1584), 3–4.

referred to the determination of the law as during the reign of Queen Elizabeth.[48]

III

As should already have become evident from the previous discussion, neither ancient constitutionalism of the sort associated with Coke nor Magna Carta was a particularly prominent feature in sixteenth-century legal thought. Nor by now should the reasons for this be surprising. It is true that the common law was perceived as a set of rules and procedures which had accumulated over time in the year books, law reports, and registers of writs, but within the jurisprudential framework laid down by, for example, *Doctor and Student,* customary practices were valid only so long as they adhered to the laws of God and reason, and the essence of English law lay, not so much in particular precedents or customs, as in maxims which enshrined its reason. There was no systematically thought-out view that customs were valid simply because long usage had proved their utility and justness. In fact, one of the major characteristics of legal development under Elizabeth and the early Stuarts was the regular testing of the reasonableness of such customs against the common law or equity. Most common lawyers, including Sir Edward Coke, were quite active during this period in subordinating local custom to their notion of the law as administered through the royal jurisdictions at Westminster.[49] Indeed, in the wake of the attack on tradition which accompanied the Reformation, customs themselves were seen to have no intrinsic value. For instance, in 1569, Thomas Norton warned the participants in the Northern Rebellion not to be misled into thinking that they were defending ancient liberties and customs. "Are all customes, without respect of good or bad, to be restored; are not rather the bad to be reformed: and so is it true libertie to be delivered from them, and not remayne thrall and bounde unto them."[50]

---

48. *A Collection of the Lawes and Statutes of This Realme concerning Liueries of companies and Reteynours* (London, 1571). "In aedibus Richardi Tottelli," fols. 13^v–14^v.

49. Brooks, *Pettyfoggers and Vipers*, 198–99.

50. Norton, *To the Quenes Maiesties poor deceyued Subiectes* [sig. Eiii^v–iv].

Within this world view, legal history was certainly of interest, but it was not of vital importance in interpreting the law. Hence the Elizabethan recorder of London, William Fleetwood, was fascinated by antiquities, but had read enough of writers like Bodin to be skeptical of his sources.[51] The first printed edition of Bracton (1569) warned the reader to take into consideration changes in the common and statute law since he wrote.[52] Many legal authors such as Richard Crompton and John Dodderidge found no difficulty in accepting that the Norman Conquest had changed English institutions.[53] There was no reason why these past events should necessarily determine the validity or invalidity of present laws and governmental arrangements.

Against this background, Magna Carta found its place in legal thought not so much as a charter of customary liberties, but as a statute, albeit the first of the collection known as the *statuta antiqua*.[54] Consequently, most detailed discussions of it are found in connection with the readings, or lectures, which senior members of the Inns of Court gave for students, and which were always based on a statute. Even in this context, Magna Carta does not figure so frequently as to suggest that it was considered of extraordinary importance. But it was often employed as a vehicle for describing or discussing major areas of the law of the land, both civil and criminal.[55]

---

51. BL Stowe MS 423, fol. 133, for Fleetwood's references to Bodin's *Methodus ad facilem historiarum cognitionem*. There were editions in 1566, 1572, and 1583.

52. D. E. C. Yale, "'Of No Mean Authority': Some Later Uses of Bracton," in *On the Laws and Customs of England: Essays in Honor of Samuel E. Thorne*, ed. M. S. Arnold, T. A. Green, S. A. Scully, and S. D. White (Chapel Hill, N.C., 1981), 386. As Yale suggests, it seems quite likely that the preface to this edition was written by Thomas Norton, although there is no definitive proof. Also, though it is not a point that has been developed here, there is much evidence that Bracton's popularity in the later sixteenth century was connected with the "Romanising movement" which characterized the legal thought of the period.

53. Crompton, *Mansion of Magnanimitie*, sig. [B]. Dodderidge believed that William the Bastard and William Rufus had ruled by their swords, BL Add. MS 48,102A, fol. 6ᵛ. See also Christopher Brooks and Kevin Sharpe, "History, English Law and the Renaissance: A Comment," *Past and Present* 72 (1976): 133–42.

54. Faith Thompson, *Magna Carta: Its Role in the Making of the English Constitution, 1300–1629* (Minneapolis, 1948), 38.

55. I am very grateful to Professor J. H. Baker for helping me to locate manu-

On the whole, and in the pre-Reformation period in particular, the readings contained little of politics or of political controversy, and authors took it for granted that the Charter was a statute which corrected defects in the common law at the time of its enactment. For example, a mid-fifteenth-century reading, which, unusually, survives in English, begins:

> Before the makyng of this statuet, that is to seie the great chartoure, there was certein lawes used, by the whiche men hade profit and also mouche harme. And therefore the kyng, seyng this mischief, ordeyned the greet charter, wherein is contened alle the fruyt of lawes bifore used turnyng to the people profit and al other put away. Yet notwithstondyng that it is called a chartere, it is a positif lawe.[56]

Similarly, a sixteenth-century reading, which must date from just after the break with Rome in the 1530s, starts with the assertion that before the Charter only the common law was used.[57] Both lectures point out specific chapters which had altered the existing common law.

Comprehensive treatments of the entire Charter appear to have been comparatively rare. In most cases the reader chose to expound on no more than a single chapter. For instance, a late fifteenth-century lecture on chapter 17 ("Nullus, vicecomes, constabularius . . .") involved a consideration of the methods of appointment of local officials, their functions, and a discussion of various headings of the criminal law such as murder, manslaughter, burglary, and so on.[58] On the other hand, lectures on chapter 1 (". . . quod Anglicana ecclesia libera sit . . .") were frequently used to lay out the law of sanctuary, and chapters 1–8 were often read in order to explain aspects of the land law

---

script readings on Magna Carta. In the discussion that follows, I have referred to chapters of the 1225 version of Magna Carta.

56. G. O. Sayles, "A Fifteenth-Century Law Reading in English," *Law Quarterly Review* 96 (1980): 571.

57. C[ambridge] U[niversity] L[ibrary] MS Hh.II.6, fols. 1–27. The manuscript is in an early sixteenth-century hand, but it states that the grants to the church in chap. 1 were "voide."

58. BL Harleian MS 1210, fol. 144. Robert Brook used the Charter for a similar purpose in the mid-sixteenth century. CUL MS Gg.V.9, fols. 56–97.

such as wardship or the rights of widows.[59] Even chapter 29 ("Nullus liber homo capiatur") was put to work on relatively technical matters. In an early sixteenth-century reading it was used to argue against the practice of using the writ of capias, or arrest, as a leading process in civil cases.[60] In 1580 Robert Snagge selected it as a text for a lecture concerned primarily with uses, a form of trust frequently employed by landowners.[61]

Not surprisingly, some parts of the Charter did become more controversial during the course of the English Reformation. Both Robert Aske, the lawyer leader of the Pilgrimage of Grace of 1536, and Sir Thomas More, common lawyer and sometime lord chancellor of England, based part of their resistance to the religious policies of Henry VIII on an interpretation of chapter 1 that took literally the king's promise to protect the liberties of the English church.[62] On the other hand, in 1534, chapter 29 of Magna Carta, along with subsequent statutes on due process of law, were cited in support of a parliamentary attack on an early fifteenth-century statute which gave the English church powers to repress heretical preaching.[63] Similarly, an anonymous reading on chapter 1,[64] which appears to have been given at one of the Inns of Court either in the 1530s or early in the reign of Elizabeth, posits royal, rather than papal, supremacy over the English church and cleverly limits the discussion of the "liberties" of the church to a consider-

59. Sayles, "A Fifteenth-Century Law Reading," 571–80. CUL MS Hh.II.6, fols. 2–27. BL Hargrave MS 87, fols. 195–218.

60. CUL MS Hh.II.6, fol. 23^v. This was also the drift of CUL MS Ee.V.22, fol. 18.

61. BL Add. MS 16,169, fol. 245.

62. Thompson, *Magna Carta*, 140–41.

63. Public Record Office, London, SP 1/82, fols. 55–58. J. P. Cooper, "The Supplication against the Ordinaries Reconsidered," *English Historical Review* 72 (1957): 636–38. S. Lehmberg, *The Reformation Parliament, 1529–1536* (Cambridge, England, 1970), 186–87. I am grateful to Professor John Guy for bringing this incident to my attention. Magna Carta was used again to attack procedures in the ecclesiastical courts during the reign of Elizabeth. See p. 103.

64. BL Harleian MS 4990, fols. 154^{v}ff. Thompson, *Magna Carta*, 192, suggests a date early in the reign of Elizabeth on the basis of style and language. But the reading consistently refers to the "king" and also appears to assume the existence of priors and abbots, evidence which may point to the earlier date.

ation of particular privileges of ecclesiastical personnel, the nature of sanctuary, and the jurisdiction of the church courts.[65]

In addition, this reading is prefaced by some general remarks on the nature of law and the origins of the Charter which illustrate the kinds of polemical use to which Charter history, like the law itself, was put in the Tudor era. The reader reminded his audience that the laws of the land had continued in long use before the making of the Charter, and that some of these laws had been made by Lucius, some by Edward the Confessor, and some by William the Conqueror. However, these remarks were distinctly secondary to the force of the preface in general, which harps primarily on the familiar theme of the necessity of the rule of law for the maintenance of peace and prosperity within the commonwealth. Echoing Fortescue, the author described law as the means by which the "body politique" was bound together. He went on to explain that a body without law was a dead body which could not "move or stirr." This point, he claimed, could be demonstrated from the histories of many foreign countries, but it was not necessary to consider those, because the history "of our own country," and of the making of the Charter, proved it well enough.

> And for yo[u]r better understandinge therein I have thought good to shewe unto you what disorder doth growe by the lacke of lawe and dewe execution of the same. And howe that for lacke of good lawes, great warres and discentions did growe w[i]thin this realme betwext the kinge and his subiectes, which was the onelie cause of the making of the forsaid statute, and therefore as concerninge the lacke of lawes in the Comonaltie yt cannot be denyed but that contrie or Commonwealth that is not ruled by certayne lawes and provisions can never contynewe any tyme in peace and order but shall alwaise remayne from tyme to tyme in disorder and discention. . . . If Law be taken from the Prince, what tormoyle is like to grow amonst the subjects.[66]

65. See fol. 163ᵛ for the intriguing statement that an argument at the commencement of "this vacation" had demonstrated that the king, not the Pope, had always been held supreme governor of the spirituality by the common law.

66. BL Harleian MS 4990, fols. 154–56ᵛ.

The fact that chapter 1 had become controversial must have made it particularly difficult for some time after the break from Rome to see the Charter as a whole as a statement of immemorial law which was still in force. For example, another reading on chapter 1, which dates from the reign of the protestant heir to Henry VIII, King Edward VI, states that grants of liberty to God and the English church were void because God and the church were not the sort of legal entities capable of receiving such grants.[67]

Nevertheless, Magna Carta was the first of the ancient statutes, and it clearly contained within it many of the major principles of the practice of the common law. Its position between circa 1530 and circa 1570 is perhaps best summed up by George Ferrers in the preface to his published English translation. His purpose in undertaking the work, like that of so much Tudor legal publishing, was to make the laws of the realm more widely known to the public. Moreover, Ferrers thought that this was particularly necessary in the case of Magna Carta because "many of the termes aswell frenche as latyn be so fer out of use by reason of theyr antiquyte, that scarcely those that be best studyed in the lawes can understand them." But for Ferrers, the translation also had more than merely antiquarian interest. In these old laws, if "they be well sought, is conteyned a great part of the pryncipples and olde groundys of the lawes. For by searching the great extremites of the common lawes before the makynge of statutes, and the remedyes provyded by them, a good student shall soone attayne a perfect judgement."[68]

By comparison with this evidence of the interest in the Charter which existed in the first half of the sixteenth century, that which survives for most of the Elizabethan period is relatively meager. Magna Carta seems to have figured only infrequently in lectures at the Inns of Court, or, if Faith Thompson is an accurate guide, in the everyday practices of judicial decision-making. As we have seen already, the thrust of Elizabethan juristic thought depended little on ancient constitutionalism, and there is surprisingly little mention of Magna Carta

67. BL Lansdowne MS 1138, fol. 1.
68. [George Ferrers], *The Great Charter Called in latyn Magna Carta, with divers olde statutes whose titles appere in the next leafe* (London, 1542), "To the reader."

in the systematic works which were addressed by the legal profession to the public at large.

However, there are from the 1580s and 1590s several exceptions to this generalization which must be pursued in some detail. First, in the 1590s, two sympathizers of the Elizabethan puritan movement, James Morice and Robert Beale, referred to Magna Carta in the course of their attacks on the legality of the infamous oath *ex officio* which was administered by the ecclesiastical court of High Commission. The point at issue in what became a raging controversy was whether people accused of religious nonconformity could be forced to swear that they would truthfully answer questions even though no specific charges had been laid against them.[69] In his *A brief treatise of Oathes,* for example, Morice cites chapter 29 in his efforts to prove that the use of such oaths was contrary to the common law. Nevertheless, what is more interesting is that Morice's position in fact depends very little either on the Charter or on a more general ancient constitutionalist argument. His treatise proceeds primarily by way of an account of the use of oaths in both the canon and civil law as well as at common law. The main thrust of the case is that the oath *ex officio* was contrary to the laws of God and reason, and he quotes Christopher St. German for the view that laws against the laws of God are void ("neither righteous or obligatorie"). Magna Carta is referred to briefly in a section of the work which examines the common law position on the oath, but chapter 29 is not vital to the case as a whole, and it is not put forward by Morice as if it were. His mode of argument is in fact quite consistent with the kind of thought which we have seen already in his reading on the royal prerogative in 1579, and which was typical of scholastic and humanistic legal discourse rather than ancient constitutionalism.[70] Robert Beale, on the other hand, did appeal more often to the "law of laws" in his contribution to the argument. But, his use of the Charter and other early statutes appears more like the lawyerly citation of legislative authority than a fully developed view that such "olde Lawes" established an in-

---

69. Participants in the Elizabethan controversy referred to that of the Henrician period, which has been mentioned above, p. 100.

70. James Morice, *A brief treatise of Oathes, exacted by Ordinaries and Ecclesiastical Iudges* . . . (London, circa 1592), 33–34, 47.

violable "ancient constitution."[71] In this respect, it is useful to compare
Beale's approach with that of another puritan lawyer, Nicholas Fuller,
whose attack on the oath *ex officio* was published in 1607, sometime
after the appearance of the first of Sir Edward Coke's influential *Reports.* Fuller clearly expresses the classic ancient constitutionalist view
that the authority of laws like Magna Carta rested precisely on the fact
that they were old. Thus the king and subjects of England were guided
by laws, "which . . . by long continuance of time and good indeavor of
many wise men, are so fitted to this people, and this people to them, as
it doth make a sweete harmony in government."[72]

No less interesting are references to Magna Carta by two other
lawyers whose writings have already been examined in some detail,
Richard Crompton and William Lambarde. Crompton's *Short declaration of the ende of Traytors,* it will be remembered, was in the main a glori-
fication of the ideal of the rule of law and a call for absolute obedience
to the monarchy. However, Crompton concluded this tract, which includes quotations from Cicero, Aristotle, and Marsilius of Padua, with
a note that the English were particularly blessed because they had the
law of 9 Henry III (he does not mention Magna Carta by name), which
laid it down that no man shall be taken or imprisoned, nor disseised
of his freehold, nor put out of his liberties, or free customs, but by
the judgment of his peers. In addition, he remarked that although the
queen was above "her lawes" in some respects, she was pleased to be
ordered by the same "as other her noble progenitors have doone."[73]

Magna Carta and the rights which it epitomized were therefore important for Crompton. They provided the basis for the comparisons
he made in this and other works between the "blessed" state of the English and the tyrannies suffered by those who lived in other European
countries, a theme which both echoes Fortescue in *De Laudibus Legum
Angliae* and was to be continued in the political speculations of some
seventeenth-century parliament men. Even so, although Crompton

71. Thompson, *Magna Carta,* 216–22.
72. *The Argument of Master Nicholas Fuller, in the Case of Thomas Lad and Richard
Maunsell* . . . ([London], 1607), 13–14.
73. Crompton, *Short declaration,* sig. E4ᵛ–F.

saw the Charter as a source of exemplary laws, he does not appear to be discussing political obligation or the nature of the English state in terms of an ancient constitution. Indeed, the liberties of Englishmen in his scheme of things are a kind of *quid pro quo* of obedience.

William Lambarde's public remarks on the Charter occur in a charge he delivered at the Michaelmas meeting of the Kentish sessions of the peace in 1586. It is important to stress that Lambarde's utterance on this occasion was even less than Crompton's a statement of any kind of systematic political theory. His primary aim was to convince the grand jurors to whom he was speaking that they should actively participate in what Lambarde saw as the essential purposes of quarter sessions, the encouragement of public virtue and the punishment of vice. Nevertheless, his analysis of the origins of Magna Carta makes interesting reading.

> . . . the times hath been when the nobility and commons of this realm have (with all humility and heart's desire) begged at the hands of their princes the continuation of their country laws and customs; and not prevailing so, they have armed themselves and have sought by force and with the adventure of their honors, goods, and lives to extort it from them. But we (God's name be blessed for it) do live in such a time and under such a prince as we need not to make suit, much less to move war, for our country laws and liberties. We have no cause to strive so much and so long about Magna Charta, the Great Charter of England, as it was called. For our prince hath therein already prevented us, so that not only the parts of the Great Charter but also many other laws and statutes no less fit and profitable for us than they are freely yielded unto us. . . .[74]

In many respects, this speech certainly sails very close to ancient constitutionalism, and such an interpretation might seem all the more justified when it is recalled that Lambarde was a leading Elizabethan antiquarian who published a Latin translation of Anglo-Saxon laws.[75]

74. Read, ed., *William Lambarde and Local Government*, 79–80.
75. W. Lambarde, *Archaionomia: Sive de priscis Anglorum legibus libri. G. Lambardo interprete* (London, 1568).

Nevertheless, he should not be stereotyped too rashly. His heavily annotated copy of *Tractatus De Iuris Arte, Duorum Clarissimorum Iurisconsul . . . Ioannis Corassii et Ioachimi Hopperi,* which was purchased just one year after it was published, shows that he was in fact a follower of Continental legal science of the nonhistorical variety.[76] As we have seen, he had a general theory about the origins of political society which appears to have presupposed a degree of popular participation in the framing of government.[77] Furthermore, Lambarde was well aware that important changes had taken place in the nature of English legal institutions since the Conquest, not to mention before it. For example, he believed that William I had ruled as a conqueror, and that parliament was for a short time discontinued as a consequence of the Norman invasion. In his textbook for justices of the peace, *Eirenarcha,* he equates the creation of royally appointed justices of the peace by Edward III with the time when "the election of the simple Conservators or Wardens of the Peace, was first taken from the people, and translated to the assignment of the king."[78] Thus at the point at which his historical and his legal thought met, Lambarde was seeking in the past for an ideal constitution which embodied a large degree of participation at both the national and the local level and as near a perfect expression of justice as possible. He was not necessarily arguing for particular laws or institutions simply because they had a long history.

Yet, all qualifications notwithstanding, these references to the Charter remain intriguing. In one sense, they undoubtedly reflect a legal and political chauvinism which can be traced back at least as far as Fortescue. In another, they illustrate the way in which the classically inspired ideal of the rule of law paved the way for a notion that such rule should be based on traditional practices and procedures, the native law of the realm. This idea was likely to have been particularly appealing to writers like Lambarde, Morice, and Beale who would have been well aware of simultaneous scholarly efforts to prove that, in spite of papal usurpation, royal supremacy over the English church dated back

76. See note 20 above.

77. Lambarde, *Archion,* 20, 108–110.

78. William Lambarde, *Eirenarcha: or of the Office of The Justices of Peace in two Bookes* (London, 1581), 20–21.

to the days of primitive Christianity. In any case it was a fairly common precept of juristic humanism that laws should be well suited to the people they governed.[79] Magna Carta and other ancient statutes had long been used to illustrate due process of law within the English system. For this reason, if no other, it was bound to be of fundamental interest to English lawyers.

At the same time, the references by Crompton and Lambarde to Magna Carta and the ancient customs of the English in speeches which they were delivering to the ordinary lesser gentry and yeoman farmers who made up the grand juries at quarter sessions raise the question of whether they might not also have been adopting such reference points because they felt that they would have a particularly convincing impact on their audiences. This introduces the problem of how the charter was perceived at the popular level, but it is not, of course, an easy matter to resolve. If reissues of the Charter were read aloud in the county courts of the thirteenth century,[80] it enjoyed no comparable exposure in the sixteenth. On the other hand, the idea that there was a prescriptive process by which customs became law as a result of usage beyond the memory of men may have been relatively well known in the world of truly unwritten law which surrounded the activities of manorial courts. In this sense, the notion that there was an ancient constitution which had proven itself over time might well have been grasped easily by ordinary people. The problem is that there is not much evidence that this was in fact the case. Faith Thompson found that, throughout the sixteenth and the early seventeenth centuries, Magna Carta was much more frequently referred to by lawyers than by laymen,[81] and, as we have seen, although lawyers thought a good deal about law and government, ancient constitutionalism was not in the sixteenth century a major component of the ideology which they exchanged with the public. Instead, they were advocating the rule of law and justice, and were usually willing to allow that any statute, including Magna Carta,

79. *The Six Bookes of A Common-Weale, Written by I. Bodin a famous Lawyer and a man of great Experience in matters of State. Out of the French and Latine Copies, done into English by Richard Knolles* (London, 1606), 469–70.

80. J. C. Holt, *Magna Carta* (Cambridge, England, 1965), 288.

81. Thompson, *Magna Carta*, 279.

could be changed by parliament to bring English law into line with the laws of reason and the laws of God. Nor did they need to believe in immemorial laws in order to define a tyrant.

IV

If ancient constitutionalism and Magna Carta were relatively insignificant in the sixteenth century, then the task remains of trying to explain, briefly, why they became more important in the seventeenth. At this point it is necessary to offer an interpretation of how their leading proponent, Sir Edward Coke, came to employ the concept of "immemorial usage" as a way of discovering the "reason" which Cicero had claimed was inherent in all laws.

Much depended on a set of circumstances which made older modes of common law thought vulnerable at just about the time James I came south from Scotland to sit on the throne of England in 1603. On the one hand, lawyers were facing serious public criticisms because they seemed unable to solve the administrative and professional problems associated with the sixteenth-century increase in litigation and because their system of judge-made law was extremely susceptible to the charge that it was uncertain.[82] "Right reason" as a basis of decision-making raised suspicions that the law was nothing more than what a particular judge willed it to be at any given moment.[83] The writings of many of the leading figures of the first fifteen years of the seventeenth century—Coke, Davies, Bacon, Ellesmere, Selden, for example—display a tremendous defensiveness about the common law and its practitioners.[84]

---

82. Brooks, *Pettyfoggers and Vipers*, chap. 7.

83. See, for example, D. E. C. Yale, ed., *Epieikeia: A Dialogue on Equity in Three Parts* (New Haven, Conn., 1953), 25, and BL Add. MS 41,613, fol. 81ᵛff., "The Course of the Lawes of England and the abuses of the ministers thereof Laid open."

84. Knafla, *Law and Politics*, 274. F. Bacon, "Maxims of the Law," in *Works*, ed. J. Spedding, 14 vols. (London, 1857–1874), 7:315–19. Sir John Davies, "Discourse of the Common Law" (1615) in *The Complete Works of Sir John Davies . . .*, ed. A. B. Grosart, 3 vols. (London, 1869–1876), 2:263–72. J. Selden, "Notes on Sir John Fortescue, *De Laudibus Legum Angliae*," in *Opera Omnia*, 3 vols. (London, 1726), 3:1183.

No less important, lawyers also had to come to terms with the accession of James I. The new king brought with him a sophisticated and clearly articulated argument in favor of absolute monarchy which upheld, but which was essentially unbounded, by law.[85] Even more disturbingly, one of his major political ambitions was the creation of a union between the kingdoms of England and Scotland.[86] Nearly all Englishmen seem to have hated this prospect on purely racial grounds, but many also realized that a "perfect" union of the two kingdoms would require a union of laws. Hence a defense of the uniqueness of the common law became a politic means of opposing the union. At the same time, the possibility of such an amalgamation of laws led some lawyers to contemplate the relationship between systems of laws and the societies in which they worked. For example, Sir John Dodderidge's "A brief consideracon of the unyon of two kingedomes in the handes of one kinge," noted:

> By the unyon of kingedomes, a totall alteracon of lawes of those nacons, or at least of one of them is introduced. But lawes were never in any kingedome totallie altered without great danger [to] the whole State. And therefore it is well said by the Interpreters of Aristotle, that lawes are not to be chaunged but with . . . cautions and circumspectons . . . no Nacon willinglie doth alter theire lawes to the which they have bene borne, and brought upp, as the provinces of Netherland maye well witnes.[87]

The gradual emergence of Coke's view of the ancient constitution in his published *Reports* was influenced by these same factors, although there was yet another, a controversy with the English Jesuit Robert Parsons, which also played a vital part.

The prefaces of the first two of Coke's *Reports,* published in 1600

85. "The Trew Law of Free Monarchies: Or the Reciprock and Mutuall Duetie Betwixt A Free King, and His Natural Subjects," in *The Political Works of James I: Reprinted from the Edition of 1616,* ed. Charles Howard McIlwain (Cambridge, Mass., 1918), esp. 61–64.

86. Bruce Galloway, *The Union of England and Scotland, 1603–1608* (Edinburgh, 1986).

87. BL Sloane MS 3479, fols. 60–61.

and 1602 respectively, offer much in the way of praise for English law, and were primarily concerned with the need to maintain its certainty by establishing better law reporting.[88] But in the *Fourth Reports,* which was published in 1604, Coke began to address the issues which arose in the wake of James I's accession one year earlier. His basic message was that changes in the law were dangerous. Furthermore, he explained clearly his view on the relationship between the law and monarchy. "The King is under no man, but only God and the law; for the law makes the King: Therefore let the King attribute that to the law, which from the law he hath received, to wit, power and dominion; for where will and not law, doth sway, there is no king."[89]

Similarly, in the *Fifth Reports* (1605) Coke expressed a sentiment which was particularly appropriate in the context of the Anglo-Scottish Union: the common law is our birthright, and the best inheritance that the subjects have.[90] However, and somewhat incidentally, in his discussion of Cowdrey's Case, he also claimed that the protestant church in England had existed since the beginning of Christianity, and this assertion brought forth a published attack on the *Fifth Reports* by Parsons, who was one of the most radical of the English Catholics. Parsons's main point was that he did not see how Coke could justify his claim since there was little evidence about the law before the Conquest. He argued instead that the common law had been brought in by William of Normandy, and that if it were the birthright of any, it benefited very few.[91]

In the sixth of the *Reports* (1607), Coke made a point of saying that he was not going to bother to answer the criticisms made by Parsons. But in fact his most strenuous efforts to prove the antiquity of the common laws and to nullify the consequences of the Norman Conquest

88. *Les Reports De Edward Coke, L'attorney generall le Roigne* . . . (London, 1600), "To the Reader." The preface is headed by a quotation from Cicero. "*Lex est certa ratio.* . . ." Edward Coke, *Le Second Part des Reportes* . . . (London, 1602).
89. *Le Quart Part des Reportes* . . . (London, 1604), sig. [B5].
90. *Quinta Pars Relationum* . . . *The Fifth Part* (London, 1605), "To the Reader."
91. [Robert Parsons], *An Answere to the Fifth Part of Reports* . . . *Lately set forth by Syr Edward Cooke, knight, the Kings Attorney generall. Concerning The ancient and moderne Municipall lawes of England which do apperteyne to Spiritual Power et Iurisdiction* . . . *By a Catholic Divine* ([Saint Omer], 1606), preface, 12–16.

began at this point.[92] The *Seventh Reports* (1608) provided a brief interlude from the historical theme, but in the eighth (1611), he returned to criticisms that had been raised against his claim for the antiquity of English law, and joined issue with unnamed historiographers who wanted to see more of his evidence.[93] On the other hand, by the time of the publication of the *Ninth Reports* in 1613, Sir Edward had found that the "light touch" he had given his recent publications by including history in them had been successful with readers, so he churned up some more exhibits "which I am persuaded will add to their satisfaction *and* solace therein, who do reverence and love (as all men ought) the national laws of their native country."[94]

Ancient constitutionalism as formulated by Sir Edward Coke was, therefore, a response to a particular set of political, religious, and legal conditions. It was not the product of a deep-rooted mentality, even though it is easy to see how the idea of the singular importance of the rule of law, even political neo-Stoicism itself, could lead to a view that government in England was defined by a set of ancient legal practices which had proven themselves over time. It was a handy way to argue for the rule of law without having to make commitments about the nature of political obligation. Nevertheless, ancient constitutionalism had so few clear antecedents in sixteenth-century English thought that it is tempting to suggest that its systematic formulation may have owed something to the importation of foreign ideas. In its hatred of popery and in its insistence on the existence of ancient liberties which could be proven by the study of the past, English ancient constitutionalism bears a number of resemblances to the work of the French protestant François Hotman, in particular to his *Francogallia*. Hotman's political radicalism, his disparagement of Coke's hero, Littleton, and his paradoxical hatred of lawyers undoubtedly made his name one with which Coke would not like to have been associated.[95] But Hotman's works were

92. *Le Size Part des Reports* . . . (London, 1607), "To the Reader."
93. *La Huictme Part des Reports* . . . (London, 1611), "To the Reader."
94. *La Neufme Part des Reports* . . . (London, 1613), "To the Reader."
95. *Francogallia by François Hotman,* ed. and trans. R. E. Giesey and J. H. M. Salmon (Cambridge, England, 1972), 497–513 for Hotman on lawyers; Edward Coke, *La Dixme Part des Reports* . . . (London, 1614), preface, for Coke on Hotman.

certainly known in late sixteenth-century England. As we have seen already, John Dodderidge, a member of the legal circle connected with Thomas Sackville, Lord Buckhurst, which also included Coke, ranked Hotman among the most important of authors to be consulted in connection with a treatise on the royal prerogative. Furthermore, Hotman's son and literary executor, Jean, resided in England for a lengthy period during the 1580s. He became a friend of the courtier Sir Philip Sidney and secretary to the queen's favorite, the earl of Leicester, during the latter's military campaign in the Netherlands in 1586.[96]

To reapply a phrase from F. W. Maitland, a Roman reception in sixteenth-century England did lead to something of a Gothic revival in the seventeenth. What must be stressed in addition, however, is that many aspects of sixteenth-century legal thought survived into the seventeenth century as well. Any analysis of the relationship between law and politics in the early Stuart period which depends exclusively on a common law mind whose main component is ancient constitutionalism is doomed to failure.

To argue this is not to deny the importance of the common law mind, but to enrich it. As Professor Judson found some years ago, the ideal of the rule of law was as much a commonplace in the seventeenth century as it was in the sixteenth.[97] But, as in the sixteenth, the political significance of this commonplace could be elaborated by both lawyers and laymen alike in a number of different ways. For those with a puritan cast of mind, the idea that human law should conform to the law of God led to calls that the laws of England should be remodeled in accordance with Mosaic law. For many the logic of the fight against social and political chaos led mainly to an acceptance of the necessity for obedience to the established monarch. For others, it was associated with a state which was ruled by laws made jointly by king and parliament.[98] But this latter view may in fact have been the one which was most often supplanted by the ancient constitutionalist argument. The fact that lawyers found it necessary to employ history in order to secure

96. *Francogallia*, ed. Giesey and Salmon, 109–10.

97. Margaret Judson, *The Crisis of the Constitution: An Essay in Constitutional and Political Thought in England, 1603–1645* (New Brunswick, N.J., 1949).

98. I hope to deal elsewhere with the relationship between legal and political thought in the early seventeenth century.

the liberties of Englishmen in the seventeenth century is a testimony both to the success of the early Stuarts in promoting absolute monarchy and to the fact that by the early seventeenth century contractual arguments had been seriously tainted by popery.[99]

At the same time, the ideal of the rule of law also had a logic of its own which arguably made a significant contribution to the political and social culture of the period. This is not to deny that the idea in some form already had a long history in 1500,[100] but to observe that during the sixteenth century it was quite regularly promoted by a large legal profession, and at times by the state itself, to levels of the population which reached down to the tenants of manorial courts. Furthermore, there were significant differences between the lawyers' idea of a society in which order was maintained through equality before the law and other strands of early-modern political thought such as those which emphasized hierarchy, or those which prescribed deferential obedience based on a patriarchal concept of authority. In this respect legal ideology has been unduly neglected in recent historiography as a factor in shaping the mentalities of governors and governed between the Reformation and the outbreak of civil war in 1642.

Legal thought did not stress that England was a society of orders; ideally law was no respecter of persons. Nor did it very often see political society as a body politic in which all the parts were assigned their proper place and function just as head and feet have their proper roles in the human body. Lawyers certainly advocated obedience to established authority, but they usually argued the case in terms of the self-interest of the individual and rarely in the sixteenth century utilized patriarchal arguments in which the duty to obey the prince or local justice of the peace was derived from the Fifth Commandment injunction that children should obey their parents.[101] It is true that the neces-

99. J. P. Sommerville, *Politics and Ideology in England, 1603–1640* (London, 1986).

100. I have been struck by Professor Holt's emphasis in *Magna Carta* on the extent of an awareness of justice and the rule of law in the county communities of the twelfth and thirteenth centuries.

101. Many early-modern historians see patriarchalism as the dominant social and political mentality of the late sixteenth and early seventeenth centuries. For an account see Gordon J. Schochet, *Patriarchalism in Political Thought: The Authori-*

sity for order was frequently stressed, but this order was an alternative to a Hobbesian state of nature, not the maintenance of any particular social order. Indeed, conflict between the civil society of equals before the law which was advocated in legal thinking and other notions about an ordered society can be seen clearly in connection with reactions to the enormous increase in the number of lawsuits during the second half of the sixteenth century. Among many lay, patrician, social critics, litigation was regarded as a dangerous phenomenon which threatened to allow tenants to vex their landlords and promised generally to upset the social order. Among legal thinkers, on the other hand, although there were critics of vexatious litigation, it was argued simply that lawsuits enabled men to redress the wrongs they thought had been committed against them.[102]

Magna Carta and ancient constitutionalism might have been significant in promoting such ideas, but the evidence suggests that for much of the sixteenth century they were not. Indeed, the importance of both in the seventeenth century depended largely on the existence of classically inspired attitudes toward law. Insofar as the concept of a civil society ruled by law became an important part of Anglo-American political discourse, perhaps even of the Anglo-American mentality, part of the story lies in the Renaissance jurisprudence of the sixteenth century.

---

tarian Family and Political Speculation and Attitudes Especially in Seventeenth-Century England (Oxford, 1975).

102. Brooks, *Pettyfoggers and Vipers*, 132–36.

3. Ancient Constitutions in the Age of Sir Edward Coke and John Selden

Debate over the nature and shape of the constitution became very intense at times in early seventeenth-century England, in part because many viable alternatives jostled for hegemony. Although some historians continued to characterize these disputes as a struggle for sovereignty between the crown and parliament (in reality, between the king and the House of Commons) into the 1950s, Margaret Judson had already softened the edges of confrontation and J. G. A. Pocock had provided a cosmopolitan model for hearing the historical voices of both common and civil lawyers. Other historians of political thought tempered the threats of "divine right" monarchy by placing it within wider intellectual contexts. While accounts of parliaments centering on the clash between the king and the Commons continued to appear into the 1970s, such historians as J. S. Roskell, John Kenyon, and G. R. Elton had begun to question this interpretative pattern in the 1960s. During the later 1970s, a host of revisionist studies, with Conrad Russell's book as the flagship, not only gave greater prominence to the court and the Lords than had other recent accounts, but also replaced the pattern of opposition with one of the search for consensus.[1]

1. Cf. Margaret Judson, *The Crisis of the Constitution: An Essay in Constitutional and Political Thought in England, 1603–1645* (New Brunswick, N.J., 1949), and J. G. A. Pocock, *The Ancient Constitution and the Feudal Law: A Study of English Historical Thought in the Seventeenth Century* (Cambridge, England, 1957), with Williams B. Mitchell, *The Rise of the Revolutionary Party in the English House of Commons, 1603–1629* (New York, 1957), and George Mosse, *Struggle for Sovereignty in England* (New York, 1950). For "divine right" monarchy see Christopher Morris, *English Political Thought from Tyndale to Hooker* (Oxford, 1950), W. H. Greenleaf, *Order, Empiricism and Politics* (Oxford, 1964), and James Daly, *Cosmic Harmony and Political Thinking in Early Stuart England* (Philadelphia, 1979). For parliaments, cf. Thomas L. Moir, *The Addled Parliament* (Oxford, 1958), Robert Ruigh, *The Parliament of 1624* (Cambridge, Mass., 1971), and Robert Zaller, *The Parliament of 1621* (Berkeley, 1971), with J. S. Roskell, "Perspectives in English Parliamentary His-

So far had many historians moved away from the traditional interpretation by 1978 that J. H. Hexter could ask: "Why has the matter of liberty and the rule of law on the one hand and lawless rule and despotism or tyranny on the other slipped out of focus in the cleverest writing of the past fifty years about the causes of the English Revolution?" Questions sometimes obtain unanticipated answers, and recently absolutist versus constitutionalist interpretations have received a good deal of attention from such literary and art historians as Jonathan Goldberg, Stephen Orgel, and Roy Strong, and an even more carefully stated presentation by the historian of political thought Johann Sommerville.² From the works of divines, civil lawyers, and, to a lesser extent, playwrights, Sommerville documented the existence of absolutist political ideas in early Stuart England, stressed their rational coherence, and argued that they vied for dominance with natural law constitutionalist theories and the less coherent interpretations of common lawyers.

Those historians and literary critics who have stressed the conflict between absolute monarchy and parliamentary rule as the key to the constitutional disputes of early Stuart England have taken the publica-

---

tory," *Bulletin of the John Rylands Library* 46 (1963–1964): 448–75; J. P. Kenyon, *The Stuart Constitution, 1603–1688: Documents and Commentary* (Cambridge, 1965; 2d ed., 1986); G. R. Elton, "A High Road to Civil War?" in Charles H. Carter, ed., *From the Renaissance to the Counter-Reformation* (New York, 1965), 325–47, and "Tudor Government: The Points of Contact: Parliament," *Transactions of the Royal Historical Society,* fifth series, 24 (1974): 183–200; Conrad Russell, *Parliaments and English Politics, 1621–1629* (Oxford, 1979); and Paul Christianson, "Politics and Parliaments in England, 1604–1629," *Canadian Journal of History/Annales Canadiennes D'Histoire* 16 (1981): 107–13.

2. J. H. Hexter, "Power Struggle, Parliament, and Liberty in Early Stuart England," *Journal of Modern History* 50 (1978): 48. See Jonathan Goldberg, *James I and the Politics of Literature* (Baltimore, 1983); Stephen Orgel, *The Illusion of Power* (Berkeley, 1975); Stephen Orgel and Roy Strong, *Inigo Jones: The Theatre of the Stuart Court,* 2 vols. (London, 1973); Roy Strong, *Van Dyck: Charles I on Horseback* (London, 1972) and *Britannia Triumphans: Inigo Jones, Rubens and Whitehall Palace* (London, 1980); and J. P. Sommerville, *Politics and Ideology in England, 1603–1640* (London, 1986), "Ideology, Property and the Constitution," in Richard Cust and Ann Hughes, eds., *Conflict in Early Stuart England* (London, 1989), 47–71, and "James I and the Divine Right of Kings: English Politics and Continental Theory," in Linda Levy Peck, ed., *The Mental World of the Jacobean Court* (Cambridge, 1991), chap. 4.

tions of James VI in Scotland as the key to understanding the discourse of James I and Charles I in England. The line from the *Trew Law* and the *Basilikon Doron* to the masques and paintings of the reign of Charles I appeared undeviating. What James wrote in the 1590s governed royal political thought during the first four decades of the seventeenth century. However, during the past decade a number of historians have begun to notice greater nuances of constitutional disagreement, especially during the early part of the reign of Charles I, as seen in the works of Glen Burgess, Thomas Cogswell, Richard Cust, John Reeve, Malcolm Smuts, and myself.[3]

Drawing upon recent studies and a modification of the model of the ancient constitution first articulated by Pocock, this essay will make a chronological analysis of selected portions of the discourse of constitutional dispute in the period before 1630. It will argue that James changed his discourse in 1610 by fashioning an interpretation of "constitutional monarchy created by kings" which vied for hegemony with at least two other versions of the ancient constitution, "constitutional monarchy governed by the common law" and "mixed monarchy," voiced in the same year by Thomas Hedley and John Selden. Although James continued to derive his power from God in arguments against the claims of papal supremacy (as noted by Sommerville), absolutist arguments only began to impinge upon domestic affairs in justifications for the loan of 1627 (as noted by Cust) and became an important

---

3. See Glen Burgess, "Common Law and Political Theory in Early Stuart England," *Political Science* 40 (1988): 4–17; Paul Christianson, "John Selden, the Five Knights' Case, and Discretionary Imprisonment in Early Stuart England," *Criminal Justice History* 6 (1985): 65–87, "Royal and Parliamentary Voices on the Ancient Constitution, c. 1604–1621," in Peck, ed., *Mental World*, chap. 5, "Young John Selden and the Ancient Constitution, ca. 1610–18," *Proceedings of the American Philosophical Society* 128 (1984): 271–315; Thomas Cogswell, *The Blessed Revolution: English Politics and the Coming of War, 1621–1624* (Cambridge, England, 1989); Richard Cust, *The Forced Loan and English Politics, 1626–1628* (Oxford, 1987); L. J. Reeve, *Charles I and the Road to Personal Rule* (Cambridge, England, 1989), "The Arguments in the King's Bench in 1629 Concerning the Imprisonment of John Selden and Other Members of the House of Commons," *Journal of British Studies* 25 (1986): 264–87, and "The Legal Status of the Petition of Right," *Historical Journal* 29 (1986): 257–77; and R. Malcolm Smuts, *Court Culture and the Origins of a Royalist Tradition in Early Stuart England* (Philadelphia, 1987).

stream of discourse only during the 1630s (as noted by Reeve). The first half of the essay will concentrate upon the interpretations fashioned by James, Hedley, and Selden in 1610 and upon treatises written by common lawyers during the following decade. The second half will concentrate upon and illustrate the clash of constitutionalist positions in the parliamentary session of 1628, especially in the debates leading up to the drafting and passage of the Petition of Right. Although covering only a small portion of the debates over the distribution and exercise of power which took place in early seventeenth-century England, such thick descriptions from the second decade and the end of the third decade should provide a plentiful illustration of the rich discourse on the ancient constitution uttered by a wide variety of voices.

Schooled in Reformed theology and practiced in the civil law tradition of Scotland, King James VI published such cogent absolutist works as *The Trew Law of Free Monarchies* (Edinburgh, 1598) and *Basilikon Doron* (Edinburgh, 1599), both reprinted in London in 1603. Written more in theological than in civil law discourse, the *Trew Law* briefly set down "the trew grounds, whereupon I am to build, out of the Scriptures, since *Monarchie* is the trew paterne of Divinitie . . . next from the fundamental Lawes of our owne Kingdome . . . thirdly, from the law of Nature, by divers similitudes drawn out of the same." The scriptures showed that "Kings are called Gods by the propheticall King *David,* because they sit upon GOD his Throne in the earth, and have the count of their administration to give unto him." Kings hold their power from God and account to him alone. Nature reinforces the rule of one through patriarchy: "By the Law of Nature the King becomes a naturall Father to all his Lieges at his Coronation: And as the Father of his fatherly duty is bound to care for the nourishing, education, and vertuous government of his children; even so is the king bound to care for all his subjects." As well as fitting into the assumptions of a patriarchal society, the image of father and children resonated with language commonly used to describe the relationship of God with his people. In the "fundamental laws" of Scotland, kings held both a logical and a historical priority of place. Recounting the establishment of a kingdom in Scotland by Fergus and his successors, James combined a negative blast against the writings of George Buchanan, his tutor, with a positive vision in which wise kings accepted by barbarians created the kingdom of the Scots; "before any Parliaments were holden," the kings of Scotland distributed the land, "devised and established" the "formes of government," and "were the authors and makers of the Lawes."[4] According to James VI, the laws of God, nature, and Scotland combined to place sovereignty in the hands of the king. In return, subjects had the duty to obey. Although a similar theory of absolute monarchy marked his arguments against Catholic divines, it found little public voice in the speeches of James I in his new kingdom.

After ascending the throne of England, the British monarch displayed considerable discretion. In 1604 and 1605, the addresses delivered at the opening of the sessions of parliament contained little constitutional content, while that of 1607 tactfully stressed the positive role of parliaments in making and revising laws. However, in some of the early programs of his reign, such as the union between England and Scotland and Bate's Case on impositions judged in the Exchequer, some of his new subjects perceived a threat to the common law of England. In 1607, James spoke of the union of laws largely from a universalist perspective and tended to interpret the common law as a "municipal law," just one local variation on the universal principles best expressed in the Roman law and capable of improvement if codified, extended, and interpreted according to civil law principles. Although aiming at reconciliation, James made what common lawyers must have perceived as a dangerous attack upon the "obscuritie" and "want of fulnesse" in the unwritten nature and particular principles of English customs. During the next decade, a host of common lawyers would defend the certainty of English judgments; however, the call for a codification of the common law by parliament had the support of such luminaries as Sir Edward Coke. For those who attempted a charitable construction, James tipped his hand by discussing the civil law prerogative of sovereigns to grant citizenship, for "in such a ques-

4. Charles Howard McIlwain, ed., *The Political Works of James I: Reprinted from the Edition of 1616* (Cambridge, Mass., 1918), 54–55, 62. For the early works of James see Jenny Wormald, "James VI and I, *Basilikon Doran* and *The Trew Law of Free Monarchies:* The Scottish Context and the English Translation," in Peck, ed., *Mental World,* chap. 3. For a more lengthy analysis of the constitutional thought of King James see Christianson, "Royal and Parliamentary Voices," 72–78, 85–86, 87–88, 89, 92–93.

tion wherein no positive Law is resolute, *Rex est Judex* [the king is the judge], for he is *Lex loquens* [a speaking law], and is to supply the Law," a privilege which he hastened to decline to put into action.[5] In 1607, James had not yet learned to speak in language appropriate to the common law.

CONSTITUTIONAL MONARCHY CREATED BY KINGS

The discourse of the king changed, however, in a creative speech delivered to both Houses on March 21, 1610, in which James fashioned a case for "constitutional monarchy created by kings." This interpretation clearly echoed one side of the medieval common law legacy, the branch that stressed the creative initiatives of kings. Caught in a dilemma, James sought to dissociate himself from the interpretations of the royal prerogative made in *The Interpreter,* a book recently published by John Cowell, the professor of civil law at Cambridge. In one passage, Cowell had argued that the king of England was "above the Law by his absolute power" and in another that "simply to binde the prince to or by these laws [of England], were repugnant to the nature and constitution of an absolute monarchy." Pushing to an extreme the not entirely dissimilar ideas expressed in the *Trew Law,* Cowell's interpretation of royal power had come under very strong attack in the House of Commons. Attempting to maintain some continuity with his published writings and yet to adapt his theory to the English situation, King James opened his speech by comparing the powers of kings with that of God: "The State of MONARCHIE is the supremest thing upon earth: For Kings are not onely GODS Lieutenants upon earth and sit upon GODS throne, but even by GOD himselfe they are called Gods." Kings derive their authority from God. James needed to maintain this position on the powers of kings in the abstract for his polemics against Roman Catholic writers, but here he also distinguished "betweene the

5. McIlwain, ed., *Political Works of James I,* 292–93, 299; Sir Edward Coke, *Le Quart Part des Reportes* (London, 1604), sig. B3; for the question of law reform in early seventeenth-century England see Louis A. Knafla, *Law and Politics in Jacobean England: The Tracts of Lord Chancellor Ellesmere* (Cambridge, England, 1977), chap. 5. For the relationship of civil to common law see Paul Christianson, "Political Thought in Early Stuart England," *Historical Journal* 30 (1987): 955–71, and Brian P. Levack, *The Civil Lawyers in England, 1603–1641* (Oxford, 1973).

generall power of a King in Divinity, and the settled and established State of this Crowne, and Kingdome."[6] The "divine right" of kings remained a powerful part of the argument throughout the speech, but now took a new historical and covenantal twist.

A transitional sentence in which the British monarch distinguished between the unlimited powers of "Kings in their first originall" and the limited powers of "setled Kings and Monarches, that doe at this time governe in civill Kingdomes" marked the shift. Just as God had come to govern "his people and Church within the bounds of his reveiled will,"

> So in the first originall of Kings, whereof some had their beginning by Conquest, and some by election of the people, their wills at that time served for Law; Yet how soone Kingdomes began to be setled in civilitie and policie, then did Kings set down their minds by Lawes, which are properly made by the King onely; but at the rogation of the people, the Kings grant being obteined thereunto. And so the King became to be *Lex loquens,* after a sort, binding himselfe by a double oath to the observation of the fundamentall Lawes of his kingdom: *Tacitly,* as by being a King, and so bound to protect aswell the people, as the Lawes of the Kingdome; And *Expresely,* by his oath at his Coronation: So as every just King in a setled Kingdome is bound to observe that paction made to his people by his Lawes, in framing his government agreeable thereunto, according to that paction which God made with *Noe* after the deluge, *Here after Seed-time, and Harvest, Cold and Heate, Summer and Winter, and Day and Night shall not cease, so long as the earth remaines.* And therefore a King governing in a setled Kingdome leaves to be a King, and degenerates into a Tyrant, as sone as he leaves off to rule according to his Lawes.[7]

6. John Cowell, *The Interpreter* (Cambridge, 1607), sig. 2Q1^r, 3A3^v; McIlwain, ed., *Political Works of James I,* 307, 308; see Sommerville, *Politics and Ideology,* 121–27 (for Cowell) and 132–34 (for a different reading of the speech of James).

7. McIlwain, ed., *Political Works of James I,* 309; the covenants God made with Noah, Abraham, Moses, and through Christ provided the starting points of the "covenant theology" so favored by early seventeenth-century Reformed preachers.

This passage worked the themes and imagery of earlier speeches and writings into a new mode of discourse in which "Kings set down their minds by Lawes," binding upon themselves and their successors; the coronation oath was a formal "covenant" by the king to observe "the fundamentall Lawes of the Kingdome" and held just as strongly as "that paction which God made with *Noe* after the deluge," which would last until the end of the earth. This looks like a direct contradiction of one of Cowell's contentions.

The stress placed upon the covenant of God and kings changed the relationship of an individual king to the law in a "civil kingdom." Kings ruled by arbitrary will only at the start of societies; in making law they restricted their own freedom of action and that of their successors.[8] Just as God chose to channel his grace through the church, so kings chose to exercise their power through courts of law and parliaments; like God, they could not go back on their word. In one imaginative leap, James had subverted the derivation of political power from the people argued in the standard constitutionalist position, appropriated the strengths of constitutional government (stability and the consent of the community of the realm), and still maintained the creative initiatives of monarchs. The arbitrary power of early kings gave place to the greater stability of established laws and practices.

Although pointedly declaring his faith in the common law in this speech, James also expressed a desire to preserve the study of the civil law at English universities, both as a civilizing influence and as a means of communicating with foreign nations. Here he mirrored the receptionist view of the common lawyers, that is, that the common law had "received" useful portions of the Roman and canon laws and allowed these to operate only within the limits established by custom or statute. To distance himself from Cowell and assuage any fears that he meant to favor the Roman or civil law, James stressed that it should remain "so bounded, (I meane to such Courts and Causes) as have beene in ancient use; As the Ecclesiastical Courts, Court of Admiraltie, Court of

8. Cf. Daly, *Cosmic Harmony*, 25. James may well have built upon the interpretation of Lord Chancellor Ellesmere as outlined in his judgment in Calvin's Case; for Ellesmere's constitutional ideas see Knafla, *Law and Politics*, chap. 2.

Requests, and such like," while "reserving ever to the Common Law" all matters "concerning the Kings Prerogative, or the possessions of Subjects, in any questions, either betweene the King, and any of them, or amongst themselves, in the points of *Meum et tuum* [mine and yours]." Encompassing such "fundamentall Lawes of this Kingdome," the common law provided a firm support for monarchy.[9] This discourse proclaimed that James had set aside both the natural law absolutism and much of the theological mentality displayed in his earlier works.

What some listeners may have perceived as a universalist perspective still intruded into the observation that Scotland, France, and Spain were governed not "meerely by the Civill Law, but every one of them hath their owne municipall Lawes agreeable to their Customes, as this Kingdome hath the Common Law." This seemed to reduce the common law to mere municipal custom. Defensive common lawyers also may have perceived a threat in the king's reiterated plea that aspects of the common law "be purged and cleared" by "the advise of Parliament." James asked for three major reforms: first, the writing of the law in "our vulgar Language: for now it is in an old, mixt, and corrupt Language, onely understood by Lawyers"; second, the production of "a setled Text in all Cases . . . so that the people should not depend upon the bare opinions of Judges, and uncertain Reports"; and third, the review and reconciliation of statutes, reports, and precedents. Such a codification of the common law by act of parliament would have diminished the powers of judges and juries to create customs; on the other hand, it would have enhanced the recognition that the monarch, peers, and representatives of the commons made law: "For the King with his Parliament here [in England] are absolute, (as I understand) in making or forming any sort of Lawes."[10] Emphasizing the crucial role of statute, James proclaimed that absolute lawmaking power in England resided with the king-in-parliament. This marked a significant transformation of his earlier absolutist discourse. Within a few years of becoming king of England, James VI and I tentatively had

9. McIlwain, ed., *Political Works of James I,* 310–11. In the previous sentences the king had defended the continued practice and study of the civil law in England.

10. Ibid., 311, 311–12, 309, 310.

come to understand the affinity of the common law for the initiatives of princes and had fashioned traditional common law discourse into a cogently argued interpretation of constitutional monarchy which retained the initiative for governing in the hands of the crown. Of course, plenty of room still existed for debate over the nature of the ancient constitution of England.

More than hints of civil law discourse continued to trouble relations between King James and members of his first parliament. Despite royal warnings, members of the House of Commons continued to attack the judgment of the Exchequer in Bate's Case, which had upheld the legality of impositions. Informed of this, the king returned from Thetford and on May 21 lectured members of the lower House about the impropriety of such debates. Although defending his right to impositions from English precedents, James could not resist the comparative perspective normally taken by civil lawyers in arguing that "all kings Christian as well elective as successive have power to lay impositions. I myself in Scotland before I came higher, Denmark, Sweden that is but newly successive, France, Spain, all have this power." Specifically refuting three sorts of arguments against impositions, James spent considerable effort in warning against the dangers of limiting the discretionary powers of the crown:

> You must not set such laws as make the shadows of kings and dukes of Venice; no Christians but papists and puritans were ever of that opinion. If you have a good king you are to thank God, if an ill king he is a curse to the people but *preces et lachrimae* [prayers and tears] were ever their arms. But may you therefore bridle him? Shall I turn this upon you, you have many privileges yourselves but because heady and ill-disposed men may abuse them, therefore shall you not have them?

Only "papists and puritans" favored ascending theories of constitutional government. By subverting the reciprocity of trust between prince and people, such attacks upon the prerogatives of kings also weakened the privileges of members of parliament. Having defended his rights against attacks made in the Commons, James ended this portion of the speech by offering a token of peace, the promise that he

would not increase impositions during his lifetime without first consulting parliament.[11] However, this promise came too late to dampen
the fears aroused by what members of the Commons perceived as the
application of civil law discourse to the English constitution.

The interpretations voiced by King James soon engendered replies
from a host of common lawyers sitting in the House of Commons. In
the insular voice of his colleagues, Nicholas Fuller noted that although
"the King were in truth very wise yet is he a stranger to this government" and offered to remedy this situation: "The King speaks of France
and Spain what they may do, I pray let us be true to the King and true
to ourselves and let him know what by the laws of England he may do."
Apparently, the chancellor, justices of the King's Bench and Common
Pleas, attorney general, and solicitor general could not tell the king
what he might do by the common law as well as could the attorneys
sitting in the House of Commons! The dispute over the right of the
Commons to debate the legitimacy of impositions ended with a tactical withdrawal by the king in a conference with members of the House
held on May 24. Concerns over the constitution reached a climax in
the powerful debate over impositions held in committees of the whole
House which lasted from June 23 to July 2 and featured long, learned
speeches by such worthies as Sir Francis Bacon, Sir John Doderidge,
Heneage Finch, Nicholas Fuller, William Hakewill, Sir Henry Hobart,
Thomas Hedley, and James Whitelocke.[12] Supporting their cases with
full lists of precedents, most of these speakers attacked the prerogative
right to levy impositions; centering on the crux of the matter, Hedley
fashioned a compelling interpretation of the common law and its relation to the royal prerogative, the powers of parliament, and the liberties of English freemen.

11. Elizabeth Read Foster, ed., *Proceedings in Parliament 1610*, 2 vols. (New
Haven, 1966), 2:102, 103, 104–5. Although James delivered this speech to both
Houses in Whitehall on May 21, 1610, he pointedly singled out members of the
Commons for criticism.

12. Ibid., 2:109; for the speeches in these debates see 108–10, 114–17, 152–
252. Many of the speakers on both sides later became royal judges in the Chancery, Common Pleas, or King's Bench.

CONSTITUTIONAL MONARCHY GOVERNED
BY THE COMMON LAW

Drawing upon the tradition of Sir John Fortescue, Hedley re-
worked the concept of *dominium politicum et regale* into a more complete,
subtle, and sophisticated model of "constitutional monarchy governed
by the common law" than that available in the writings or speeches
of his contemporaries. In 1610, Fortescue's *De Laudibus Legum Angliae,*
which existed in many manuscripts, several printed Latin editions, and
several English translations, still provided the most lengthy, analytic,
and highly regarded account of the relationship of the crown and the
common law in the governance of England. The prefaces to the early
Reports of Sir Edward Coke, solicitor general (1592–1594), attorney
general (1594–1606), chief justice of the Common Pleas (1606–1613),
and chief justice of the King's Bench (1613–16), provide a contemporary context. In the lengthy preface to the *Third Reports,* Coke made
reference to particular writs and processes having existed "time out of
mind of man in the times of Saint Edmund" and outlined a history of
the common law from the time of Brutus (ob. 1103 B.C.), through the
Druids, Romans, Saxons, and Conquest to the early Norman kings,
which filled in portions of Fortescue's similar sketch with additional
historical evidence. Uneasy in his grasp of early Norman laws, Coke
argued that Domesday Book "was made in the raigne of St. *Edward* the
Confessor" and that "it is verily thought that William the Conquerour
finding the excellencie and equitie of the Lawes of England, did trans-
port some of them into Normandie, and taught the former Lawes written as they say in Greeke, Latine, Brittish, and Saxon tongues (for the
better use of Normans) in the Normane language, and the which are
at this day (though in processe of time much altered) called the *Customes of Normandy.*"[13] In other words, instead of introducing Norman

---

13. Sir Edward Coke, *Le Tierce Part des Reportes* (London, 1602), sigs. C3ᵛ, C4ʳ–
D2ʳ (quoted at length in Pocock, *Ancient Constitution,* 38), C4ʳ, and E1ᵛ; Domesday, of course, dated from the reign of William the Conqueror. Sir Edward Coke,
Le Second Part des Reportes (London, 1602), contained a brief panegyric of the
equality, certainty, and antiquity of the common law. For the debate over British
history see T. D. Kendrick, *British Antiquity* (London, 1950), and for Camden see
especially F. J. Levy, *Tudor Historical Thought* (San Marino, 1967).

law into England, William the Conqueror had introduced British laws into Normandy! Although well read in the English common law from the days of Glanville forward, Coke displayed little grasp of the contemporary debate over the history of the Britons, nor had he picked up the humanist historical method pioneered by the great antiquary William Camden.

In the *Fourth Reports,* however, the attorney general provided a coherent definition of English law which differentiated the common law from customs and statutes without mentioning those laws of God and nature so crucial for Fortescue:

> The Lawes of England consist of three parts, The common Law, Customes, and acts of Parliament: For any fundamentall point of the ancient Common laws and customes of the Realme, it is a Maxime in pollicie, and a triall by experience, that the alteration of any of them is most daungerous; For that which hath beene refined and perfected by all the wisest men in former succession of ages, and proved and approved by continual experience to be good and profitable for the common wealth, cannot without great hazard and danger to be altered or changed.

In the judgment in Calvin's Case printed in the *Seventh Reports,* Coke would develop at length the important theme of experience, the view that the common law had withstood the test of time. In the *Fifth Reports,* he stressed the protection offered to lives and property of English subjects by the common law: "The auntient and excellent Lawes of England are the birth-right and most auntient and best inheritance that the subjects of this realm have, for by them he injoyeth not onely his inheritance and goods in peace and quietnes, but his life and his most deare Countrey in safety." The *Sixth Reports* quoted at length from Fortescue, from two Saxon charters, and from an "Act of Parliament holden in the 10 yeare of King Henry the second" to demonstrate to the most skeptical the antiquity of the common law.[14] In these early

14. Sir Edward Coke, *Le Quart Part des Reportes* (London, 1604), sig. B2ᵛ, *Quinta Pars Relationam* (London, 1605), and *La Size Part des Reports* (London, 1607); see *La Sept Part des Reports* (London, 1608), f. 2–3 (quoted in Pocock, *Ancient Consti-*

works, Coke had touched upon some of the themes which would come together in Hedley's speech, but these scattered remarks did not provide as coherent an interpretation as that fashioned by the less famous attorney.

Hedley opened by stressing the power of parliament to deal with high matters of law: "these which doubt whether the parliament may judge of law, let them read the statute of 25 Edward 3, where they may see many cases formerly adjudged high treason to be declared to be no treason." This led into a discussion of the nature of the common law which explicitly rejected "what judges will," "common reason," "reason approved by the judges," and "the parliament, which is nothing else in effect but the mutual consent of the king and people," as "that which gives matter and form and all complements to the common law." Because a parliament could not change the laws of succession, bind future parliaments, nor abrogate the whole of the common law, Hedley argued, "the parliament hath his power and authority from the common law, and not the common law from the parliament."[15] Common law reigned supreme in the ancient constitution.

The wisdom "strength, honor, and estimation" of the common law sprang from its foundational principle, the test of time: "Time is wiser than the judges, wiser than the parliament, nay wiser than the wit of man." This principle led to a working definition of the common law which embraced both reason and immemorial custom: "the common law is a reasonable usage, throughout the whole realm, approved time out of mind in the king's courts of record which have jurisdiction over

---

tution, 35). Compare Coke's definition of the common law with that of Sir John Fortescue, *De Laudibus Legum Angliae,* ed. John Selden (London, 1616), chaps. 8 and 17, which also gave an account of its antiquity similar to that contained in the *Third Reports.*

15. Foster, *Proceedings in Parliament 1610,* 2:173, 174. The treason statute of 25 Edward III, of course, formed the basis for treason in early Stuart England; see Conrad Russell, "The Theory of Treason in the Trial of Strafford," *English Historical Review* 80 (1965): 30–50. For Hedley, also see J. G. A. Pocock, *The Ancient Constitution and the Feudal Law: A Study of English Historical Thought in the Seventeenth Century; a Reissue with a Retrospect* (Cambridge, England, 1987), retrospect chap. 1, and Sommerville, *Politics and Ideology;* neither credits Hedley with the important role stressed in my interpretation.

the whole kingdom, to be good and profitable for the commonwealth." The local nature of customs, "confined to certain and particular places" in the country, would not suffice alone, nor would reason unaided by experience; the art and wisdom of generations of judges created general laws out of particular cases by applying the principle of "equity, that whatsoever falleth under the same reason will be found the same law," but this took place in an indirect manner in which "many other secondary reasons" intervened until local customs were finally "deduced by degrees . . . to some primitive maxim, depending immediately upon some prescription or custom"; in this complex process, common lawyers displayed "as much art and learning, wisdom and excellency of reason as in any law, art or profession whatsoever."[16]

This subtle interplay of maxims and immemorial custom built continuity and flexibility into the laws. The rationality of maxims assured that "no unreasonable usage will ever make a custom (pleadable in law)," while the ability to overrule judgments assured that the mere "reason or opinion of 3 or 4 judges" could not make law. The continual questioning of judgments did not mean, as King James mistakenly had claimed, that common law lacked certainty; an examination of "all the suits in law" would reveal that for every case "delayed for doubtfulness of the law, there have been 1000, nay 10,000, proceeded and ended without any question or doubt at all in law." Hedley claimed that the unwritten nature of the common law provided greater certainty than statutes and civil law, both of which needed continual interpretation. The "work of time" so "adopted and accommodated this law to this kingdom" as "the skin to the hand, which groweth with it"; "confirmed

16. Foster, *Proceedings in Parliament 1610*, 2:175, 176. Compare the last passage with Sir John Doderidge, *The English Lawyer* (London, 1631), 124–25: "The matter of the Law of England generally taken, *ex qua constituitur* [with respect to its origin], is the law of Nature, the law of God, the generall Customes of the Realm, Maximes drawn out of the Law of Nature, as the Principles of reason, primarily and secondarily deduced, Constitutions and Acts of Parliament. *Materia [material] circa quam*, on which it worketh, are *lites et contentiones* [suits and disputes], cases of debate daily comming into question touching persons, possessions, and injuries done by word or act." On pp. 154–62, Doderidge provided examples of such maxims drawn from logic, natural philosophy, moral philosophy, civil law, and canon law.

by time," immemorial custom far better upheld the liberties of freemen and "establisheth kings and their regal power" than could any law created by "the wisest lawgivers or parliament or council," for such law was not "reversible by that power that made it."[17] Any attempt to replace the refined wisdom of generations with the fallible judgments of one parliament, as in the "reforms" advocated by King James, appeared to threaten the very nature of the common law.

Having established that the common law was founded on good, immemorial usage, Hedley could fairly easily deal with the issue of impositions. He dismissed all arguments from international law; the powers of other princes had nothing to do with the laws of England; all that mattered were English customs and statutes. In support of the right of the king to "lay such impositions without assent of parliament," Hedley could see only "certain precedents and one only judgment now lately given in the Exchequer in Bate, his case." Bate's case represented an exception. The precedents cited in that judgment bore little weight; not only had they come from times of war, they had aroused the opposition of contemporaries. In addition, the crown had not attempted to collect extra-parliamentary impositions "for 180 years together, vizt. sithence the time of King E.3 till the end of Queen Mary"; this cast doubt on any royal right, for "as time maketh a custom, so time will discontinue and dissolve the same." In addition, no writ or authority in the law books existed to support this purported prerogative; although "the common law be no written law, yet there is no principle or maxim of law which is not to be found in some of our books," so their absence here seemed telling. Since "the king without assent of parliament cannot alter" or make "any law," the introduction of impositions by royal prerogative alone broke the common law:

> in this kingdom of England, the laws of the kingdom are the inheritance not only of the king, but also of the subjects, of which

17. Foster, *Proceedings in Parliament 1610*, 2:178–79, 179–80, 180. In *The Speech of the Lord Chancellor of England, in the Eschequer Chamber Touching the "Post-Nati"* (London, 1609), Ellesmere quoted Ranulf de Glanville and Henry de Bracton on this point, but also interpreted the civil law as unwritten law; see Knafla, *Law and Politics*, 217–18. None of Coke's early *Reports* argued that the common law was unwritten.

the king ought not to disseise them or disinherit them. Therefore it followeth consequently and necessarily, that the king cannot alter the property of the lands or goods of any of his free subjects without their consent, for that is to desseise or disinherit them of the fruit and benefit of the law, which is all one as to disinherit them of the law itself.[18]

By enforcing an action which changed the law without the formal consent of the peers and the people, the decision in Bate's case endangered the liberties and property of all English freemen.

Hedley spoke at length about "the ancient freedom and liberty of the subjects of England" as confirmed by Magna Carta and upheld by the judgments of law; Magna Carta emerged as a repairing of the distortions of the ancient constitution wrought by the Norman conquest, "a restoring or confirming of the ancient laws and liberties of the kingdom, which by the Conquest before had been much impeached or obscured." Although the forces opposing King John had countered the force of the conquest, the power of the sword eventually gave way to collective confirmation of the great charter: "This Charter, if it was first gotten in time of war, hath been since confirmed in time of peace at the least 30 times by several parliaments in several kings' times and ages, which Charter (as I said) doth notably confirm the freedom and liberty of the subjects." The nexus between the liberties of free Englishmen and the military power of kings received considerable discussion, including lengthy passages on the superior fighting capacities of the English yeomen: "our infantry which are selected out of the commons and are not only more numerous than their chivalry or gentry of these other states, but better soldiers also, for their courage is equal, because their freedom and liberty is equal with theirs."[19] Because Magna Carta had restored the ancient relationship between the liberties of

18. Foster, *Proceedings in Parliament 1610*, 2:181–82, 182, 188–89; see 189–90; since other speakers had established at length the chronology and contested nature of impositions collected by prerogative, Hedley did not need to recite the precedents.

19. Ibid., 190, 195; without any explicit reference to Machiavelli, the last passage went on to attack the false security of trusting in mercenary soldiers; see p. 196.

freemen and the prerogatives of the crown, threats to this balance also endangered the defense of the realm.

Even this brief analysis should have demonstrated that Hedley fashioned a complex model of the ancient constitution which more than subverted the interpretation of "constitutional monarchy created by kings" advocated by King James some two months earlier. Hedley voiced an interpretation favored by many common lawyers. By reducing all law to local, regional, and national custom refined by reason through the continual trying of cases, it rebutted the universalist claims of civil lawyers. By stressing the superior wisdom of time, it countered the claims of both natural law absolutists and mixed monarchists, both of whom placed the capacity to make law in the hands of a single or collective sovereign. Immemorial custom, common to the realm and induced into maxims, gave the common law its wisdom, strength, flexibility, and continuity. The common law assigned all powers and privileges within the realm.

MIXED MONARCHY

Before the end of 1610, another major interpretation of the ancient constitution appeared in the *Jani Anglorum facies altera* (London, 1610) of John Selden. Covering the laws of southern Britain from the days of the ancient Britons to the death of Henry II, it was the first lengthy history of the English constitution. In contrast to King James and Thomas Hedley, Selden fashioned an image of the ancient constitution as a mixed monarchy in which kings, clergy, nobles, and freemen had shared sovereignty from the very beginning. In the early pages of the *Jani Anglorum,* the ancient constitution emerged as a political structure in which the major marks of sovereignty resided outside the hands of any single monarch. Ruled by petty kings or queens, the Britons met together in assemblies ("per concilium") to discuss public affairs and to decide such crucial matters as foreign relations or war and peace. So small were these kingdoms that southern Britain best fit into the category of an aristocracy, rather than a monarchy. British society gained its unity from a common law and religion, not from any single political authority. Religious leaders, the Druids, acted as the guardians of rituals, morals, and laws. Portrayed as judiciously combining the salient characteristics of priests and judges, the Druids gathered at a central meeting place to make, interpret, and preserve the laws for all of Britain. Not written down, such laws perforce sprang from custom. They owed nothing to the will of a royal law-giver. Indeed, Selden's interpretation of the pre-Roman period left even less room for a powerful monarchy than had his model, François Hotman's account of ancient Gaul.[20] This subtle section of the *Jani Anglorum* subverted any historical claim that kings founded the English portion of the ancient constitution of Britain.

Monarchy and Germanic customs arrived in England with the Saxon invasion and provided a lasting framework for the ancient constitution. Although seven Saxon kingdoms had existed at first, only one king held a recognized position of suzerainty. Unlike ancient Britain, then, Saxon England possessed a true monarchy. "The king was always one amongst the heptarchs or seven rulers, who was accounted (I have *Beda* to vouch it) the *Monarch of all England*." These kings proclaimed law with the advice of the leading men of the realm. Consultation took place within an institutional system which derived from the Germanic *wapentakes* described by Tacitus; these became the *witans* of the Anglo-Saxons and, in turn, were called parliaments under the Normans. "These assemblies were termed by the Saxons, Wittena gemotes, i.e. meetings of the wise men, and Micil sinodes, i.e. the great assemblies. At length we borrowed of the French the name of *parliaments*. . . . An usage, that not without good reason seems to have come from the ancient *Germans*."[21] In addition to making or declaring the law, such bodies chose those who enforced the law locally. The framework of the Saxon constitution, with its royal rule through consultation,

20. John Selden, "The Reverse or Back Face of the English Janus," in his *Tracts*, trans. Redman Westcot [Dr. Adam Littleton] (London, 1683), 17 (see also 17–18, 93); cf. Coke, *Le Tierce Part*, sig. C4^r–D1^r. Since Selden favorably cited Coke's *Reports* on several occasions in this early section, he must have made a deliberate break both in his attack upon Brutus and in his classification of the government of the Britons as an aristocracy; see "English Janus," 17, 56. See François Hotman, *Francogallia*, ed. Ralph E. Giesey and J. H. M. Salmon (Cambridge, 1972), 154–55.

21. Selden, "English Janus," 95, 94, 32, and *Jani Anglorum facies altera* (London, 1610), 43, 124–25. For a fuller account of Selden's early works see Christianson, "Young John Selden."

proved strong and flexible enough to absorb one group of foreign invaders, the Danes, and the potentially disruptive change of religion from paganism to Christianity. The greatest challenge came, however, with the end of the Saxon monarchy.

The undeniable reality of the Norman conquest posed more of an obstacle for Selden than it had for Hedley. Aware of the arguments over the origins of feudal tenure presented by members of the French historical school of legal studies, Selden stood on the brink of applying these insights to England by arguing that the feudal law arrived with the Conqueror. Not only did William I introduce new laws and customs, he employed old procedures and laws in new ways. However, Selden drew back from unequivocal support for this interpretation. The case for a sharp break remained ambiguous, especially since the laws of William the Conqueror appeared to differ little from those of Canute or Edward the Confessor. Indeed, a careful comparison of Norman offices of state and early titles of honor with those of the Saxons led to the conclusion stated in the last sentence of the *Jani Anglorum:* "As to doing justice, as in all other cases, and managing of publick affairs, the *Normans* had almost the same names and titles of officers and offices as the Saxons had."[22] Not much room for innovation here. William the Conqueror, while often acting for expedient reasons, paradoxically preserved not only a large number of Saxon laws but the fundamental shape of the Saxon constitution.

During the following centuries, feudal laws blended with Saxon customs to produce a potent, vital constitution presided over by the three estates of king, magnates, and representatives of the commons, all gathered together in parliaments, the symbol and reality of England's mixed monarchy. The *Jani Anglorum* detailed the development of this pattern up to the death of Henry II. When pondering whether King Stephen had "banished" the Roman civil or Roman Catholic canon law from England, however, the account used the complaints against the

---

22. Selden, "English Janus," 98; see also 52, 55, 57–58, 94–99. For the obstacle of the Norman Conquest, cf. Pocock, *Ancient Constitution*, 42–43, 53–55, 99–102, 149–50, and *passim*, with Johann P. Sommerville, "History and Theory: The Norman Conquest in Early Stuart Political Thought," *Political Studies* 34 (1986): 249–61.

favorites of Richard II, recorded in the *Rotuli Parliamentorum,* to demonstrate that the civil law had never held sway in England.

> But the barons of parliament reply, That they would be tyed up to no rules, nor be led by the punctilioes of the *Roman* law, but would by their own authority pass judgement . . . inasmuch as *the realm of England was not before this time, nor in the intention of our said lord the king and lords of parliament ever shall be ruled or governed by the civil law.* And hereupon the persons impleaded are sentenced to be banished.[23]

This passage showed how the common law towered over its potential rivals within the realm and underlined the sovereign place of the king-in-parliament in the constitution.

COMPETING COMMON LAW VOICES

In 1610, King James VI and I, Thomas Hedley, and John Selden gave public voice to three rival interpretations of the "ancient constitution": "constitutional monarchy created by kings," "constitutional monarchy governed by the common law," and "mixed monarchy." That of James not only received a hearing in parliament but also rapidly appeared in print in three editions, that of Hedley remained in manuscript, while that of Selden received a single printing.[24] As well as providing competing models for understanding the laws, statutes, and legal writings from the past, these interpretations also enabled divergent distributions of power in the present, with "constitutional monarchy created by kings" empowering durable initiatives for the crown, "mixed monarchy" creative powers for parliaments, and "constitutional monarchy governed by the common law" creative jurisdiction for judges and juries. Each interpretation carried practical implications for contemporary understanding of the emergency powers of the crown, the liberties of the people, and the governance of the

23. Selden, "English Janus," 68; see also 58–91.

24. For the editions of the speech by James see A. W. Pollard and G. R. Redgrave, *A Short-Title Catalogue of Books Printed in . . . 1475–1640,* rev. W. A. Jackson, F. S. Ferguson, and Katherine F. Pantzer (London, 1976), nos. 14396, 14396.3, 14396.7. Much of the material in Selden's *Jani Anglorum* would soon appear in his "Illustrations" to Michael Drayton, *Poly-Olbion* (London, 1613); see Christianson, "Young John Selden," 282–86.

realm. Far from remaining static, these interpretations provided the foundations for competing traditions of constitutional discourse in the decades which followed.

Portions of Hedley's model of "constitutional monarchy governed by the common law" received support in the preface of the Irish *Report* of Sir John Davies, attorney general of Ireland, and in the *Eighth, Ninth,* and *Tenth Reports* of Sir Edward Coke. In his preface, Davies stressed the immemorial nature of the common law, while in his prefaces, Coke argued for its antiquity. Both eschewed the violent interpretation of the Norman Conquest put forward by Hedley. Cautiously unwilling to discern a serious break at the Conquest, Davies noted:

> the *Norman Conqueror* found the auncient lawes of England so honorable, and profitable, both for the Prince and people, as that he thought it not fitt to make any alteration in the fundamentall pointes or substance thereof . . . he altered some legall formes of proceeding, and to honor his owne language, and for a marke of Conquest withall, he caused the pleading of divers Actions to be made and entred in *French,* and set forth his publique Ordinances and Acts of Counsell in the same tongue.

In other words, William changed some of the language of the law, but he retained its substance. More firmly, Coke deliberately stressed that King William I "sware to observe" the "good, approved, and auncient" laws of the realm, calling together "*twelve of the most discreete and wise men in everie shire throughout all England*" to declare their laws, the "summe of which, composed by him into a *Magna Charta* (the groundworke of all those that after followed) hee blessed with the seale of securitie and wish of eternitie, closing it up with this generall: *And wee further commaunde that all men keepe and observe duely the Lawes of King Edward.*"[25]

---

25. Sir John Davies, *Le Primer Report des Cases et Matters en Ley Resolves et Adjudges en les Courts del Roy en Ireland* (Dublin, 1615), sig. *3ʳ, and Sir Edward Coke, *La Huictme Part des Reports* (London, 1611), preface; the marginal note for Coke's first section in italics is to "Es. lib. Monast. de Lichfield.," that for the second section in italics to "Ex libro manuscripto de legibus antiquis." The common law side of Davies came through in this preface; ironically, the cases reported drew strongly on the civil law as well; see Hans J. Pawlisch, *Sir John Davies and the Conquest of Ireland: A Study in Legal Imperialism* (Cambridge, 1985).

In other words, the Conqueror formally embraced the laws of Anglo-Saxon England through a charter of confirmation which acted as a model for later charters.

Although William II "corrupted" justice, according to Coke, a "great charter" of Henry I "*restored the Lawe of King Edward,* (such Lawe as was in the time of the holy Confessor) *with those amendments which his father added by the advise of his barons.*" King Stephen, in his "great Charter of Liberties *to the barons and commons of England,*" confirmed: "*All the Liberties and good lawes which* Henry *king of England my Uncle graunted unto them: And I graunt them all the good lawes and good customes which they enjoyed in the raigne of King* Edward,*"* while his successor, Henry II, confirmed the restoration earlier made by his grandfather, Henry I. Within this sequence, the Magna Carta and Charter of the Forests from the reign of King John merely carried forward the pattern of the past; in turn, they were "established and confirmed by the great charter made in 9. *Henry.* 3. which for their excellencie have since that time beene confirmed and commanded to be put in execution by the wisdome and authoritie of 30. several parliaments and above."[26] In other words, a series of Great Charters marked the transition from the Saxon to the medieval constitution, while the treatises of great common lawyers, from Glanville, Bracton, and the author of *Fleta* forward to Fortescue, both testified to the antiquity of the common law and also carried it forward into new situations. Numerous written records demonstrated the continuity of English law from the days of the Saxons to the early seventeenth century.

Similar plentiful ancient sources did not exist for Sir John Davies, whose preface to the *Primer Report* started off by stressing that although the records of English rule in Ireland stretched back to the time of King John,

> during all the time that the lawes of England have had theire course in Ireland, which is nowe full foure hundred yeares, there hath not beene any Report made and published of any Case in lawe, argued, or adjudged in this Kingdome: but all the arguments and reasons of

26. Coke, *La Huictme Part,* preface; Coke cited Roger of Hoveden for the first quotation and relied on Hoveden, William of Malmesbury, and Matthew Paris for the second.

the judgements and resolutions given in the Courts of Ireland, have hitherto beene utterly lost, and buried in oblivion.

With no equivalent of the medieval English law reports and treatises available, it was difficult to explain how the common law could have ruled in Ireland for four centuries without any major writings. Only the preface of the *Primer Report* dealt with the ancient constitution of Ireland; the text provided a detailed account of important cases on what Hans Pawlisch has called "highly sensitive aspects of constitutional and administrative reform at issue in the first twelve years of James I's reign."[27] As solicitor general and attorney general in Ireland, Davies played a key role in this "legal imperialism." At stake was the largely successful attempt of the English protestant officials in Ireland to replace Gaelic laws with English common laws in such important matters as religion, landholding, inheritance, fishery rights, customs, and coinage. How could the legal mind behind these changes provide a justification for the immemorial, and therefore proper, rule of the common law in Ireland?

Davies stressed the unwritten nature of the common law, ever "preserved in the memory of men, though no mans memory can reach to the originall thereof." This, in turn, led to a definition of the common law similar to that offered by Hedley:

> For the *Common lawe* of England is nothing else but the *Common custome* of the Realme: And *a custome* which hath obtained the force of a lawe, is alwayes said to bee *Jus non scriptum* [unwritten law], for it cannot bee made or created, either by Charter, or by Parliament, which are actes reduced to writting, and are alwayes matter of *Record*, but being onely matter of *fact*, and consisting in use and practise; it can be recorded and registred no where, but in the memory of the people.

Custom grew to perfection by continual usage from time out of mind and was more "perfect" and "excellent" than any written law. Davies

---

27. Davies, *Primer Report*, sig. *1ᵛ; Pawlisch, *Sir John Davies*, pp. 34–35. Coke had discussed the medieval English common law reports in the preface to his *Tierce Part*, sig. D3ʳ. Davies dedicated the *Primer Report* to Lord Chancellor Ellesmere.

argued that this meant that no "*Lawegiver*" created the common law: "for neither did the King make his owne *prerogative* nor the Judges make the *Rules* or *Maximes* of the law, nor the common subject pre-scribe and limitt the *liberties* which he enjoyeth by the law. . . . Long experience, and many trialls of what was best for the common good, did make the *Common lawe.*" If no single or collective lawgiver made the law, none could withdraw or change it in any major way. This included parliaments. When statutes had changed "any fundamentall pointes of the Common lawe, those alterations have beene found by experience to bee so inconvenient for the common wealth, as that the common lawe hath in effect beene restored againe, in the same points, by other Actes of Parliament, in succeeding ages."[28] On placing the common law above the king in or out of parliament, Coke, Davies, and Hedley all agreed.

For Davies, however, the supremacy of the common law over assem-blies had immediate practical consequences. It empowered the ser-vants of the crown in Ireland to introduce a "reform" program which had failed to pass in successive Irish parliaments through a series of judicial decisions. As the solicitor general and later the attorney gen-eral of Ireland who presented the arguments recorded in the *Primer Re-port,* Davies had appealed to a historical interpretation of the common laws of England and Ireland and a concurrence with the civil law of nations. These arguments and decisions made it even more necessary for Davies to stress the benign, reasonable certainty of the common law, especially of its rules and maxims.

> England having had a good and happy *Genius* from the beginning, hath bin inhabited alwaies with a vertuous and wise people, who ever embraced honest and good Customes, full of Reason and con-veniencie, which being confirmed by common use and practise, and

28. Davies, *Primer Report,* sig. *1ᵛ–2ʳ, *2ᵛ (Pocock, *Ancient Constitution,* 32–33, quotes this and the following two paragraphs), *3ʳ, *2ʳ. Davies cited Ellesmere's speech in Calvin's Case for his interpretation of the unwritten nature of the law and clearly drew his references to Glanville and Bracton from the same speech as well; see Knafla, *Law and Politics,* 217. Coke had placed the common law above king and parliament in the preface to his *Tierce Part,* sig. D4ʳ, and *Quart Part,* sig. B2ᵛ.

continued time out of minde, became the *common lawe of the Land.* And though this law bee the *peculiar invention* of this Nation, and delivered over from age to age by *Tradition* (for the common lawe of England is a *Tradition,* and learned by *Tradition* as well as by Bookes) yet may wee truly say, That no humane lawe written or unwritten, hath more *certainty* in the *Rules* and *Maximes,* more *coherence* in the parts thereof, or more *harmony of reason* in it: nay, wee may confidently averr, that it doth excell all other lawes in upholding a free *Monarchie,* which is the most excellent forme of government, exalting the prerogative Royall, and being very tender and watchfull to preserve it, and yet maintaining withall, the *ingenuous liberty* of the subject.[29]

Nowhere else in the world could one find such a reasonable law, well tried by time, which carefully balanced the prerogatives of the crown and the liberties of the subject. For Davies, the common law captured the native genius of the English conquerors; only savages could reject such a valuable gift. This praise of the English common law articulated a historical justification for its imposition upon the newly conquered territory of northern Ireland.

Despite the complaints of some "of our Countrimen," Davies argued, the "*Customary unwritten lawe*" of England was "farre more apt and agreeable, then the *Civill* or *Canon lawe,* or any other written lawe in the world besides," a claim often made by English common lawyers in the early-modern period. In the parliament of Merton, "the greate and wise-men of England" had refused to change their law of inheritance, and in the parliament of 11 Richard II, they had declared that "the Realme of England, neither had bin in former times, nor here after should bee Ruled and governed by the *Civill* law." Indeed, Davies devoted the greatest portion of his preface to a defense against such criticisms of the common law as the use of law French in reports, the certainty of judgments, the delay of justice, and the defense by lawyers of bad causes.[30] Ironically, the unwritten subtext of legal imperialism,

29. Davies, *Primer Report,* sig. *2ᵛ.
30. Ibid., sig. *2ᵛ, 3ʳ; see also sig. 3ʳ–11ᵛ; Coke had dealt with the question of the uncertainty of judgments in the preface to his *Second Part* and the use of law French in *Tierce Part,* sig. E1ʳ.

so vigorously argued in the cases in the text of the *Primer Report,* received no discussion in the defense of the common law presented in the preface.

Although Coke also faced questions about the antiquity and provincial nature of the common law, he sought refuge neither in unwritten custom nor in immemoriality. Perhaps uncomfortable about aspects of his earlier arguments for continuity over the Conquest, he returned to this issue in 1613 and 1614. Using the *Mirror of Justices,* characterized as "a very auntient and learned treatise of the Lawes and usages of this kingdome whereby this Realme was governed about 1100. yeares past," he attempted to prove that parliaments, chancery, King's Bench, Common Pleas, Exchequer, itinerant justices, various county and local courts, the court of admiralty, and serjeants-of-law all existed before the Conquest. An analysis of the laws of Kings Ine, Edward, Edgar, Ethelred, Edmund, and Canute supported the argument that the "high Court of Parliament" was "a part of the frame of the common lawes," one that lasted through the Conquest and guided the will of the Conqueror. Additional evidence from the *Modus Tenendi Parliamentum* argued that these assemblies contained "the kings, the lords, and commons, according to the maner continued to this day," while the equating of Anglo-Saxon "burghes" with medieval parliamentary boroughs showed that "divers of the most auntient Burghes, that yet send burgesses to the Parliament, flourished before the Conquest." This strong emphasis upon parliaments marked a new departure for the chief justice. Although the Saxons

> called this court *micel gemott,* the great assemblie, *wittena gemott,* the assemblie of the wise men, the Latin Authors of those times called it *Commune concilium, magna curia, generalis conventus, &c* [common council, great court, general convention]. And let it be granted that *William* the conqueror changed the name of this court, and first called it by the name of Parliament, yet manifest it is by that which hath beene said, that he changed not the frame or jurisdiction of this court in any point.[31]

31. Sir Edward Coke, *La Neufme Part des Reports* (London, 1613), preface, sigs. c1^r-2^r, 2^v-3^r, c3^v. The *Modus* was a fourteenth-century treatise which purported

By 1614, the identification of the witenagemots of the Saxons with
the parliaments of the Normans had become a commonplace. Reliant
upon sources which pretended greater antiquity than they possessed
and not as familiar with the institutions of Anglo-Saxon England as
Selden had become by 1614, Coke could more easily read later institutions back into the past.

Drawing again upon the *Mirror of Justices* in the *Tenth Reports*, Coke
continued to stress the continuity of the ancient constitution over the
Norman Conquest; however, this preface also systematically listed
and briefly discussed such early works on the common law as Glan-
ville, Bracton, Britton, *Fleta*, the *Novae Narrationes*, and the *Old Natura
Brevium* and such fifteenth- and sixteenth-century treatises as those by
Fortescue, Nicholas Statham, Thomas Littleton, Anthony Fitzherbert,
Christopher St. German, William Stamford, John Parkins, William
Rastell, Sir Robert Brooke, Sir James Dyer, and William Lambard.[32]
This systematically strengthened the link of the past to the present.

Throughout the prefaces to his *Reports*, Coke presented an image
of the common law and constitution as ancient, with the major institutions of governance, including the central law courts, parliaments,
and other central and county offices, going back in an unbroken chain
to the days of the Saxons. Placing credence in the *Mirror of Justices* and
the *Modus Tenendi Parliamentum* as reliable evidence for Anglo-Saxon
institutions, long after other leading antiquaries had abandoned these
as early sources, Coke displayed considerable historical naïveté. This
prevented him from building an up-to-date, systematic historical case
for continuity. Presenting a coherent image of the common law as immemorial, unwritten custom, Davies spent even less space on historical
interpretation; he did not have the profusion of medieval treatises that
Coke used to link the laws of twelfth and thirteenth centuries to those
of the present. In the first eleven *Reports*, Coke occasionally argued
that a particular custom reached back beyond human memory, but
he did not follow Hedley or Davies (and through them, Bracton and

---

to come from the reign of Edward the Confessor; Selden had questioned its antiquity and that of the *Mirror* in 1610 and firmly dismissed it in 1614; see Christianson, "Young John Selden," 278, 312 nn. 47, 48.

32. Sir Edward Coke, *La Dixme Part des Reports* (London, 1614), sigs. d3 and
d3ᵛ–[e2ʳ].

Glanville) to characterize the entire common law as immemorial, unwritten custom. Lumping Coke and Davies together into one model of the "common-law mind" presents some serious distortion of their positions.[33] Although interesting and not without influence, the prefaces of these *Reports* did not add up to a systematic interpretation of the ancient constitution that matched the completeness and coherence of those presented by Hedley and Selden.

Within the context of the prefaces of Coke and Davies, the eminence of John Selden's annotated critical edition of Sir John Fortescue's *De Laudibus Legum Angliae* in 1616 takes on added significance. Although several editions and translations of this key treatise already existed in print, Selden employed the humanist technique of collating several manuscripts to prepare his Latin text and added an Elizabethan English translation and copious notes, mostly in English. In other words, this fifteenth-century treatise received the respect normally accorded only to the classics.[34] The notes not only brought portions of Fortescue's interpretation more closely in line with recent scholarship, but worked to subvert both the concept of immemorial custom argued by Davies and the anachronistic historical interpretations voiced by Coke. For a confident, learned young man just starting to become known for his *Titles of Honor* (London, 1614), this edition of the most prestigious common law text on governance marked a bold political move.

The historical sophistication and learning which raised Selden's annotations so far above any other contemporary attempt to defend the antiquity of the common law became apparent in the notes upon that long passage quoted by Coke in the preface to the *Sixth Reports*. Fortescue had argued that the Britons, Romans, Saxons, and Normans had ruled England through the same customs and that these represented the most ancient law in the world. Coke took this interpretation more or less at face value; Selden dealt with it in a critical, indepen-

33. These prefaces provide the major primary sources for Pocock, *Ancient Constitution*, chap. 2. As early as 1610, in the *Jani Anglorum*, Selden had used William Lambard, *Archaionomia, sive de Priscis Anglorum Legibus* (London, 1538), as his major source for Anglo-Saxon laws; Coke's major contribution came in the cases discussed in the *Reports*.

34. For a fuller discussion of this edition see Christianson, "Young John Selden," 295–99.

dent manner. He poured the scorn of humanist philology on Fortescue's argument that common law predated the laws of ancient Rome:

> The antiquity which he means of our Laws before the Civill of Rome
> is only upon these conditions. First that the story of *Brute* bee to be
> credited, and then that the same kind of law and policy hath ever
> since continu'd in *Britain*. That Storie supposed him heere CCC.
> yeers and more before *Rome* built. But (with no disparagment to
> our common laws) we have no testimony touching the inhabitants
> of the Isle before *Julius Caesar,* nor any of the name of it till *Polybius,*
> in *Greeke,* nor till *Lucretius* in *Latin.* . . . All testimony of later time,
> made of that which long since must be, if at all it were, is much to
> bee suspected. And though the *Bards* knew divers things by tradi-
> tion . . . yet I see not why any, but one that is too prodigall of his
> faith, should beleeve it more then Poeticall story, which is all one
> (for the most part) with a fiction.[35]

Under the principle of synchronism, scholars should place little credence in evidence for the Trojan origin of the British monarchy because the evidence for this interpretation came from poets who lived
centuries after the event. With the demise of the legend of Brutus went
a defense of the antiquity of the common law treasured by generations
of Englishmen.

Selden's quiet scholarship subverted the whole image of the common law as immemorial custom, unchanged through thousands of
years. Carefully drawing upon a wide range of evidence—including
such ancient authors as Caesar, Tacitus, and Pliny; Justus Lipsius,
the foremost expert of his day; and inscriptions found on ruins from
Roman Britannia—Selden demolished Fortescue's assertion that the
Romans had ruled Britain by the common law. Nor had the same customs survived unscathed through the turmoil of succeeding conquests
by the Saxons, Danes, and Normans:

35. Fortescue, *De Laudibus,* Selden's notes, p. 15; for the passage commented
upon see chap. 17; it was quoted at length in Coke, *Size Part,* sig. ¶3, and Christianson, "Young John Selden," 296. Selden attacked the legend of Brutus in his
notes to *Poly-Olbion* published in 1613; see Christianson, "Young John Selden,"
283–84.

But questionlesse, the *Saxons* made a mixture of the *British* customes with their own; the *Danes* with the old *British,* the *Saxon* and their own; and the *Normans* the like. The old laws of the *Saxons* mencion the *Danish* law (DANELAGE) the *Mercian* law (MERCENLAGE) and the *Westsaxon* law (WESTSAXONLAGE) of which also some Counties were governed by one, and some by another. All these being considered by William I. comparing them with the laws of *Norway.* . . . They were you see called St. *Edwards* laws, and to this day, are. But cleerly, divers Norman customes were in practice first mixt with them, and to these times continue. As succeeding ages, so new nations (coming in by a Conquest, although mixt with a title, as of the *Norman* Conqueror, is to be affirmed) bring alwaies some alteration, by this wel considered, That the laws of this realm being never changed will be better understood.

This passage deliberately deconstructed Fortescue's seamless web of law into a series of distinct customs which kings and conquerors restructured into suitable collections, such as the laws of King Canute, King Edward, and King William. Aware of the distinctions which separated the laws of Wessex, Mercia, and the Danelaw, Selden solved some of the puzzles of Saxon law codes; since Coke had thought that the "*Marchenleg*" was a "Booke of the Lawes of England in the British toong" written by "*Mercia proba,*" the wife of "king Gwintelin," some "356. yeres before the birth of Christ," this represented a considerable scholarly accomplishment.[36] So did the image of law as something changing over time in relation to the changing needs of the community of the realm.

Moving outside the insular perspective which marked the writings of those who defended "constitutional monarchy ruled by the common law," Selden noted that the Roman civil law had not commanded a continuous allegiance in western Europe from the days of ancient Rome, but had passed from usage from 565 to 1125 A.D., and stressed this point to defend the superior antiquity of the common law over the recently revived Roman civil law. In addition, he provided a profoundly

36. Fortescue, *De Laudibus,* Selden's notes, pp. 7–9, and Coke, *Tierce Part,* sig. D1ʳ; see also Selden's notes, pp. 9–14, and Christianson, "Young John Selden," 296–97.

historical model for reducing all laws to a combination of the original "state" or constitution of a particular society, rationally tempered over time by statutes and customs. In response to those who asked "When and how began your common laws?" Selden replied:

> Questionless it's fittest answered by affirming, when in like kind as the laws of all other States, that is, *When there was first a State in that land, which the common law now governs:* then were naturall laws limited for the conveniencie of civill societie here, and those limitations have been from thence, increased, altered, interpreted, and brought to what now they are although perhaps (saving the meerly immutable part of nature) now, in regard of their first being, they are not otherwise then the ship, that by often mending had no piece of the first materialls, or as the house that's so often repaired, *ut nihil ex pristina materia supersit* [that none of the earlier material remains], which yet (by the Civill law) is to be accounted the same still. . . . Little then follows in point of honor or excellency specially to be atributed to the laws of a Nation in generall, by an argument thus drawn from differences of antiquitie, which in substance is alike in all. Neither are laws thus to be compar'd. Those which best fit the state wherein they are, cleerly deserve the name of the best laws.[37]

This answered the slights of the civilians in their own discourse and also provided a historical model for interpreting the laws of England, or any other independent European jurisdiction. Instead of reading late medieval common law back into Saxon England, Selden argued that at their origin societies formed a "State" or distribution of powers which limited the law of nature through the creation of positive laws and customs. Although various individual laws were added or repealed to adjust to the ever-changing needs of society, the shape of the "State," as with the often repaired boat, remained the same. The mutability of laws did not create an impermanent commonwealth. In England the ship of state took the form of a mixed monarchy in which the king, nobility, clergy, and freemen had shared in the ability to make law through custom and statute from the very beginning. Other jurisdictions had different distributions of power and different methods for

37. Fortescue, *De Laudibus,* Selden's notes, pp. 19–20.

making new and repealing old laws. Each of the kingdoms of Europe possessed its own ancient constitution.

In 1610, King James VI and I, Thomas Hedley, and John Selden fashioned three rival interpretations of the ancient constitution, which I have called "constitutional monarchy created by kings," "constitutional monarchy governed by the common law," and "mixed monarchy." Each drew upon aspects of common law discourse and molded these into a reasonably coherent model of governance which dealt with the distribution of power, privileges, liberties, and responsibilities within the society. During the following years, portions of Hedley's "constitutional monarchy governed by the common law" received considerable support from leading legal spokesmen. Although subverting the continuity of English institutions over the Norman Conquest in his first edition of *Titles of Honor,* Selden came to provide a major defense of "mixed monarchy" in his edition of Fortescue and his *Historie of Tithes* (London, 1618). In a speech made in the Star Chamber to the assembled justices of the central common law courts on June 20, 1616, King James I extended his theory of "constitutional monarchy created by kings" to cover all English magistrates and, reminding the judges that they were "no makers of Law, but Interpretours of Law, according to the true sense thereof," chided Coke and his colleagues to "observe the ancient Lawes and customes of *England* . . . within the bound of direct Law, or Presidents; and of those, not every snached President, carped now here, now there, as it were running by the way; but such as have never beene controverted, but by the contrary, approved by common usage, in times of the best Kings, and by most Learned Judges."[38] By the middle of the second decade of the seventeenth century, the seamless discourse of the common law, if it had ever existed as the immemorial *jus non scripta* of Hedley and Davies or the creation by royal actions of James, had become a collection of competing scripts.

Although King James and a number of common lawyers had voiced at least three discrete interpretations of the ancient constitution dur-

38. McIlwain, ed., *Political Works of James I,* 335. For a fuller discussion of this speech see Christianson, "Royal and Parliamentary Voices," 85–86. For *Titles of Honor* and *Historie of Tithes* see Christianson, "Young John Selden," 286–95, 299–307.

ing the second decade of the seventeenth century, neither confrontation nor closure had yet arrived. In practice, Selden's model of "mixed
monarchy" continued to interact and overlap in rather untidy ways
with Hedley's "constitutional monarchy governed by the common law."
Neither directly confronted the royal image of "constitutional monarchy created by kings." Since Coke and Davies held positions as leading
legal servants of the crown at the times they published their treatises
and since prudent people with political ambitions could not directly
challenge the known ideas of the monarch in public, such reticence
hardly seemed surprising. Although Lords Chancellor Ellesmere and
Bacon had worked out interpretations which mirrored (and perhaps
helped to form) that of the king, neither they nor James had openly
challenged the general interpretations voiced by Hedley, Davies, Coke,
and Selden. By the end of that decade, however, such spokesmen as
James, Coke, and Selden had gained considerable experience in drawing upon evidence from the history of England to define and refine
their positions. This, along with more immediate concerns, may help
to account for the alacrity of the constitutional debate which opened
in the parliament of 1621 and reached an early peak in the parliament
of 1628–1629.[39] Rather than providing a survey of those debates, the
rest of this essay will take a more detailed look at the constitutional
discourse used in the session of 1628.

Deliberations about the nature of England's government appeared
very germane in 1626–1627. As the privy council scrambled to find the
soldiers, the sailors, the supplies, and, above all, the money to win wars
against Spain and France, it acted in ways which, while not completely
without precedent, moved well beyond the ordinary methods of governance. A number of these wartime practices stood out as perceived
grievances, namely the billeting of troops in people's homes, the use
of martial law in England to discipline troops, the formal request of

---

39. For example, even Ellesmere's fairly particular observations on the parliament of 1604–1610, in which Hedley's speech was delivered, and his criticisms of
Coke's *Reports* remained in manuscript; see Knafla, *Law and Politics,* chap. 8. For
the debates in the parliament of 1621 see Christianson, "Royal and Parliamentary Voices," 87–94. For differing interpretations of disagreements in the parliaments of the 1620s see Russell, *Parliaments and English Politics;* Cust and Hughes,
eds., *Conflict in Early Stuart England;* and Cogswell, *Blessed Revolution.*

loans for stipulated sums from those subjects who would normally pay parliamentary subsidies, and the imprisonment of those who refused to provide such loans. Billeting and martial law pressed upon scattered communities, but the loan of 1626 touched upon most men of property. The vast majority paid; more than a few brave gentlemen and yeomen refused and faced incarceration. Among those jailed, five knights sought release on bail through a writ of habeas corpus. Seeking to defend its action, the privy council instructed the Warden of the Fleet to enter on the return of these writs that the knights involved were "committed by his majesty's special commandment." This sufficed for one, Sir Thomas Darnel, but not for the others: Sir John Heveningham, Sir Walter Erle, Sir John Corbet, and Sir Edward Hampden. Starting on November 22, 1627, learned counsel for the knights presented their case before the King's Bench; on November 26, the attorney general, Sir Robert Heath, replied with the case for the crown; and on November 27, the Lord Chief Justice, Sir Nicholas Hyde, reported the resolution of the court.[40] Despite the care of the judges to protect both the prerogative of the crown and the liberties of the people in their decision, a great debate over the essence of the common law and the ancient constitution had commenced.

THE FIVE KNIGHTS' CASE

The actions of the council, the defense of prerogative taxation by at least four divines, and the Five Knights' Case of 1627 worked together to precipitate the debates over the prerogatives of the crown and the liberties of the subject which took place in the parliament of 1628. In the search for a consensus, such key spokesmen as Sir Edward Coke, Sir Dudley Digges, Edward Littleton, John Selden, a host of other lawyers in the House of Commons, Attorney General Heath, Solicitor General Sir Richard Shelton, and Sir Francis Ashley, King's Serjeant, articulated and defended rival interpretations of the ancient constitution with practical implications for the everyday relationships between the king's servants and the subjects of the realm. Deriving the

---

40. Quoted in J. A. Guy, "The Origins of the Petition of Right Reconsidered," *Historical Journal* 25 (1982): 291; see also 291–92. Guy has worked out the correct chronology on the basis of the records of the King's Bench.

liberties of subjects from the grants of monarchs, Heath favored "constitutional monarchy created by kings." When "that first stone of sovereignty was . . . laid," he argued in the Five Knights' Case, the sovereign stood alone; kings, having created the law, could "do no wrong" and remained free, especially in times of emergency, to step outside "legal and ordinary" procedures; the imprisoned knights should follow "the right way for their delivery, which is by a petition to the king. Whether it be a petition of right or grace, I know not; it must be, I am sure, to the king," the fount of all law and bounty.[41] This spelled out some of the legal implications of the theory articulated by James VI and I in 1610; by creating institutions of government and legal procedures, kings had limited royal power, but the crown still retained a great deal of initiative and discretion for dealing with matters of state.

The attorneys for the defense in the Five Knights' Case—Selden, Sir John Bramston, William Noy, and Sir Henry Calthorp—argued that the crown must follow recognized procedures or else it would jeopardize the ancient liberties of freeborn Englishmen. This severely diminished the discretionary power of the crown, but need not have refuted the model of "constitutional monarchy created by kings." While his colleagues seemed to advocate "constitutional monarchy governed by the common law," Selden pursued his model of "mixed monarchy"; the refusal of the crown to spell out a specific charge against Sir Edward Hampden when presented with a writ of habeas corpus represented an attempt to establish as customary a procedure which endangered the hereditary liberties of freemen. By attempting to change the law with improper reference to precedent and statute, the collective modes of

41. T. B. Howell, ed., *A Complete Collection of State Trials* (London, 1809), 3:50. Recent accounts of the Five Knights' Case and its bearing upon actions taken in the parliamentary session of 1628 appear in David S. Berkowitz, "Reason of State and the Petition of Right, 1603–1629," in Roman Schnur, ed., *Staatsräson: Studien zur Geschichte eines politischen Begriffs* (Berlin, 1975), 165–212; Linda S. Popofsky, "Habeas Corpus and 'Liberty of the Subject': Legal Arguments for the Petition of Right in the Parliament of 1628," *Historian* 41 (1979): 257–75; Guy, "Petition of Right," 289–312; and Christianson, "Discretionary Imprisonment." For the political context see Cust, *Forced Loan;* for the constitutional debate see Judson, *Crisis of the Constitution;* and for the parliamentary setting see Russell, *Parliaments and English Politics.*

creating law, such actions challenged the mixed nature of the English monarchy. The legal cases presented by Heath, Selden, and the other attorneys applied the rival interpretations of the English constitution articulated by James, Hedley, and Selden to a concrete issue at law.[42]

Of a far different nature, the sermons of Isaac Bargrave, Roger Manwaring, Robert Sibthorpe, and Matthew Wren supported the loan and the punishment of those who refused to provide money to the crown on the basis of civil law arguments. Manwaring, especially, developed the divine right derivation of royal power from God into an absolutist argument that the English monarch had a prerogative power to tax without the consent of parliament:

> If any King shall command that which stands not in any opposition to the originall lawe of God, nature, Nations and the Gospell (though it be not correspondent in every circumstance to laws Nationall and Municipall) no subject may without hazard of his own damnation in rebelling against God, question or disobey the will and pleasure of his soveraigne. For as the father of his country he commands what his pleasure is out of counsell and judgement.[43]

This raised the laws of God, nature, and nations above the common law of England in a very relevant, practical manner and severely weakened the obedience to the common law covenanted by King James. Although some divines had used similar absolutist arguments earlier in the century, especially to defend the powers of the English monarch against claims of papal supremacy, they now served to justify domestic policy. The sermons of the divines raised the specter of transforming England into an absolute monarchy.

THE PARLIAMENTARY SESSION OF 1628

All these issues received considerable attention in the Parliament of 1628–1629. The debates of the House of Lords and the House of Commons provide a rich vein of constitutional discourse which delib-

42. For a fuller discussion see Christianson, "Discretionary Imprisonment," 65–72.

43. Roger Manwaring, *Religion and Allegiance* (London, 1627), as quoted in Cust, *Forced Loan*, 64 (see also 62–67), and Sommerville, *Politics and Ideology,* 127–31.

erately drew upon the *De Laudibus* of Fortescue, the speech of March 21, 1610, of James I, the *Reports* of Coke, the Irish *Report* of Davies, and the research of Selden to uphold both the prerogative of the crown and the liberties of English freemen. Concentrating upon Coke and Selden, but drawing upon the speeches of a range of lawyers and royal servants, the following pages will attempt to give the reader a sense of the many voices involved. Since each of these speeches dealt with particular points in debates on specific topics, some care will be taken to sketch in the context. The attempted impeachment of Manwaring also provided an occasion for a heated contestation of absolutist discourse. Condemnation of the loan and of the billeting of troops raised few problems, but discretionary imprisonment (an issue involving competing interpretations of the common law) and martial law (an issue involving the relationship between the civil and common laws) proved very contentious and demand greater attention. Since both sides tacitly agreed to accept Magna Carta as the practical starting point for the issues at stake, most of their historical discussions covered that portion of the ancient constitution which had existed from 1215 to 1628.

When parliament opened on March 17, 1628, Sir Edward Coke sat in the Commons as a knight for Buckinghamshire and John Selden as a burgess for Ludgershall (Wiltshire), a borough controlled by the earl of Hertford.[44] On March 21, Coke preferred a bill "against long and

---

44. See John K. Gruenfelder, *Influence in Early Stuart Elections, 1604–1640* (Columbus, 1981), 163. In 1628, the Seymour connection also included Sir Francis Seymour and Edward Kirton, Sir Francis's estate manager. For the Petition of Right see Berkowitz, "Reason of State," 190–212; Christianson, "Discretionary Imprisonment"; Jess Stoddart Flemion, "The Struggle for the Petition of Right in the House of Lords: The Study of an Opposition Party Victory," *Journal of Modern History* 45 (1973): 193–210, and "A Savings to Satisfy All: The House of Lords and the Meaning of the Petition of Right," *Parliamentary History* 10 (1991): 27–44; Guy, "Petition of Right," 296–312; Popofsky, "Habeas Corpus," 257–75; Russell, *Parliaments and English Politics*, chap. 6; and Stephen D. White, *Sir Edward Coke and "The Grievances of the Commonwealth," 1621–1628* (Chapel Hill, N.C., 1979), chap. 7. The main body of sources for this parliament is: Robert C. Johnson, Maija Jansson Cole, Mary Frear Keeler, and William B. Bidwell, eds., *Proceedings in Parliament 1628*, 6 vols.; *Commons Debates 1628*, vols. 1–4 (New Haven, 1977–1978); *Lords Debates 1628*, vol. 5, and *Appendices and Indexes*, vol. 6 (New Haven, 1983) [henceforth, *Commons 1628*, vols. 1–4, and *Lords 1628*].

unjust detainment of men in prison." On the next day, the Commons heard rousing, general speeches on the issue of the liberties of subjects from such experienced orators as Sir Francis Seymour, Sir John Eliot, Sir Benjamin Rudyard, Sir Thomas Wentworth, Sir Robert Phelips, and Sir Edward Coke. In the committee on religion, complaints arose against the books of such Arminian divines as John Cosin and Richard Montague and on such sermons preached in support of the recent loan as those by Manwaring and Sibthorp. On March 25, the issue of discretionary imprisonment arose in a committee of the whole House. Selden laid the bait by suggesting that "since the business concerns the King and his privy councillors, I desire therefore a day may be appointed for the King's counsel to come in and defend what was done if they can." On the same day, the committee of the whole voted unanimously that "The subjects of England have such propriety in their goods and estates that they cannot be taken from them, nor subject to any levies without their assent in parliament."[45] This struck a blow against the recent loan and paved the way for further expressions of grievance. The business of Manwaring's sermons would remain in the wings for several months, while the issues of imprisonment, billeting, and martial law dominated center stage.

Extended debate over discretionary imprisonment opened on March 27, with a lengthy speech in a committee of the whole by Richard Cresheld, a future serjeant-at-law. After agreeing that kings "are gods before men," he argued that "the act of power in imprisoning and confining his Majesty's subjects in such manner without any declaration of the cause, is against the fundamentall laws and liberties of this realm." Near the close of his argument, Cresheld noted: "Sir John Davies . . . said in those reports of the tanistry customs: that the kings of England have always had a monarchy royal and not monarchy seignoral, where under the first, saith he, the subjects are freemen, and have propriety in their goods and freehold, and inheritance in their lands; but under the latter they are as villeins and slaves and proprietors of nothing." He also cited Littleton, Brooke, Plowden, Dyer, Coke, and the year books for the reigns of Edward III, Henry VII, and Henry VIII. Near the end

45. *Commons 1628*, 2:42, 109, 135; for the opening speeches see 55–74 and for the committee on religion see 85–87, 89, 92–93.

of his speech, Cresheld asked if any of the "counsel in the late cause adjudged in the King's Bench" would care to show how Magna Carta and the first Statute of Westminster applied to "the letting of people to bail."[46]

Selden obliged immediately with a detailed presentation which listed the "remedies provided by the common law against imprisonment." His reading of the Five Knights' Case did not stand uncontested, however, for Solicitor General Shelton firmly supported the decision made by the King's Bench and pointed out that the case had not dealt with the power of the king and council to commit, but with the granting of bail to people imprisoned on the special command of the king by means of a writ of habeas corpus. He noted that "the judgment was *remittitur quosque, etc.,* which was not to authorize their imprisonment, but that the court would take further time to advise of it," and added that "Sir Edward Coke had in 12 *Jacobus* done the like," that is, refused bail in a similar case.[47]

With both sides engaged, a full-scale debate raged in the committee of the whole House for the next two days. A series of lawyers opposed the right of the crown to imprison without specifying a cause; while some speakers attacked Attorney General Heath's defense of such commitments on the grounds of reason of state and others defended the privy council's reading of the royal prerogative, Shelton prodded Coke into explaining his change of mind since the judgments of 12 and 14 James I. Although denying that the king ordinarily had the power of discretionary imprisonment, Sir Francis Nethersole, the agent for Elizabeth of Bohemia, drew upon the law of nature and a common law maxim to argue that the king needed this power for emergencies:

> It is not my opinion that the King hath or ought to have any legal ordinary power to commit men in an ordinary judicial manner without cause, but in some time and in some rare cases we are to allow the King to commit men without setting down the cause of the com-

---

46. Ibid., 2:147, 150, 149. For Cresheld see Wilfrid R. Prest, *The Rise of the Barristers: A Social History of the English Bar, 1590–1640* (Oxford, 1986), 276–77 and n. 101, 352–53.

47. *Commons 1628,* 2:150–51, 152; see also 150–52, 154–55, 158–59, 161–62, 164–65, and Christianson, "Discretionary Imprisonment," 72–73.

mitment, and that from the law of nature that dispenseth with her laws to preserve things. Want of power in the head is not good for the body, but having been taught that all reasons of foreign laws here are dreams, I will allege only the laws of England. It is a written law in the common law *salus populi suprema lex est.*

The maxim came from Coke's *Tenth Reports.* Selden quipped back with a maxim of his own, "*Salus populi suprema lex, et libertas popula summa salus populi* [The welfare of the people is the supreme law and the liberty of the people the greatest welfare of the people]," and drew upon the case of the Apostle Paul to add, "It was the law of the Empire not to send a prisoner without signifying the crimes laid against him."[48] Those who wished to defend the actions of the crown on civil or natural law principles received a clear warning.

On March 29, the spirit of King James entered into the debate through the mouth of Henry Sherfield, the recorder of Salisbury, who quoted at length from those sections of the speech of March 21, 1610, where James had said that "no law can be more advantageous to extend the King's prerogative than the common law" and "there is a difference between a king in general and in divinity, and the King of England who is bound by his oath to preserve our laws." This centered upon the crux of the speech, the distinction made by James between natural law absolutist and common law constitutionalist interpretations of monarchy. Interpreting the maxim quoted by Nethersole, Sherfield provided a common lawyer's reply: "To rule by law is the King's and the people's security. Also the liberty of the subject is one of the great favorites of the law. . . . The King cannot arrest a man or command one to arrest him. When no cause is set down in the warrant, the law adjudgeth it to be void."[49] The security of the people consisted in following the proper legal procedures.

Shortly thereafter Coke intervened in the debate to attack discre-

48. *Commons 1628,* 2:172, 183; for the full debate see 171–85, 188–209; this maxim appeared in Coke, *Dixme Part,* f. 139.

49. *Commons 1628,* 2:188–89. For Sherfield see Paul Slack, "Religious Protest and Urban Authority: The Case of Henry Sherfield, Iconoclast," in Derek Baker, ed., *Studies in Church History* (Cambridge, 1972), 9:295–302, and Prest, *Barristers,* 390, 414–16.

tionary imprisonment because of "the universality of persons" who could suffer from "this absolute authority that is pretended" and because of the "indefiniteness of the time" that they could suffer in prison without a charge, for had "the law given this prerogative it would have set some time to it." Such a principle went against the reason of the common law. Before making his earlier ruling, Coke also explained, he had only had time to consult one authority; now after having consulted many more precedents, he admitted his earlier mistake. As the debate neared an end, Selden moved: "Let a subcommittee search into those judgments and precedents." Supported by Phelips and Coke, the motion carried. Selden chaired the subcommittee and, on March 29, obtained permission to enlarge its search by obtaining copies of the relevant documents.[50] This marked the conclusion of the opening debate.

During the days and months ahead, this subcommittee proved a formidable body; it reported directly to the committee of the whole without having to pass through the House in session. This brilliant procedural move made it easier for Selden and his colleagues to maintain their initiative. Persistent in their probing, the members unearthed an actual conspiracy on the part of Attorney General Heath to have a judgment in favor of the prerogative of discretionary imprisonment entered on the roll of the King's Bench. This unrecorded draft went beyond the issue of bail to support commitment "generally by mandate of the King" even though "on the aforesaid return no special cause of detention appears." The Commons expressed its increased fear over the actions of the king's servants by unanimously passing through the committee of the whole three strong resolutions against discretionary imprisonment.[51]

Another aspect of the struggle for the liberties of English freemen emerged on April 2, when the committee of the whole discussed "the violation of the propriety of goods by loans, taxing of men's goods,

50. *Commons 1628*, 2:191–92, 173–74; see also 176–77, 181, 193, 202. For Selden's notes from subcommittee meetings see *Proceedings in Parliament 1628*, 6:94, 105.

51. *Commons 1628*, 2:212 n. 3 (a translation of the Latin of the draft judgment); for the resolutions see 231, 239, 240; for the drafting see 236–37.

and billeting of soldiers" in the afternoon. On the next day, the House unanimously passed the resolutions against discretionary imprisonment and, for good measure, added a fourth on the property of the subject. Two days later, Sir Edward Coke carried a motion to request a conference with the Lords "concerning certain ancient and fundamental liberties of England"; Digges would introduce the case of the Commons, and Littleton, Selden, and Coke, each with two able assistants, would present the recently passed resolutions and the arguments in support of their adoption to the Lords.[52]

This conference took place on April 7 and set much of the tone for the first session of this parliament. Digges opened with a learned, composite model of the ancient constitution:

> that the laws of England are grounded on reason more ancient than books, consisting much in unwritten customs . . . so ancient that from the Saxon days, notwithstanding the injuries and ruins of time, they have continued in most parts the same, as may appear in old remaining monuments of the laws of Ethelbert, the first Christian king of Kent; Ina, the king of the West Saxons; Offa, of the Mercians; and of Alfred, the great monarch who united the Saxon Heptarchy, whose laws are yet to be seen published, as some think by parliament. . . . By the blessing of God a good king, Edward, commonly called St. Edward, did awaken those laws . . . which William the Conqueror and all his successors since that time have sworn unto.
>
> And here, my Lords, by many cases frequent in our modern laws strongly concurring with those of the ancient Saxon kings, I might, if time were not more precious, demonstrate that our laws and customs were the same.[53]

Portions of the interpretations of Coke, Davies, Hedley, and Selden infused this speech, but the spirit and scholarship of Selden prevailed. The reference to unwritten custom probably came from Davies and Hedley. Scholarly insights into the Saxon laws, especially to the manuscript of the laws of Alfred in the library of Sir Robert Cotton, bore the

---

52. Ibid., 2:252, 276, 296.

53. Ibid., 2:333–34. For this speech see Popofsky, "Habeas Corpus," 268–70.

mark of Selden; on the other hand, a citation to the Book of Lichfield (not quoted above) could have come from either Coke or Selden. The absence of Trojan origins and of references to the *Mirror of Justices* and *Modus Tenendi Parliamentum* undoubtedly stemmed from the influence of Selden, who also probably provided quotations from the preambles of Saxon law codes, with their reference to the advice of nobles, clergy, and those learned in the laws, although the latter may have come from Coke. No doubt, Digges added his own well-honed sense of rhetorical flourish.

After presenting the background, Digges went on to show how the liberties of English freemen, which stretched back to the days of the Saxons and had received confirmation many times since, had suffered a severe invasion in recent years:

> Be pleased then to know, that it is an undoubted and fundamental point of this so ancient common law of England, that the subject hath a true property in his goods and possessions, which doth preserve as sacred that *meum et tuum* that is the nurse of industry, and mother of courage, and without which there can be no justice, of which *meum et tuum* is the proper object. But the undoubted birthright of free subjects hath lately not a little been invaded and prejudiced by pressures, the more grievous because thy have been pursued by imprisonment contrary to the franchises of this land.

Later in the conference, Coke would take up the theme of industry and courage. The failure of habeas corpus in the Five Knights' Case, Digges went on to explain, had enforced an examination of the relevant "acts of parliaments, precedents and reasons" by the Commons, whose spokesmen now would present the results of their research to the Lords, with Littleton handling the statutes, Selden the precedents, and Coke the reasons.[54]

Littleton sought to establish that the phrase *per legem terrae* (by the law of the land) in Magna Carta and the subsequent statutes meant that the imprisonment of an English freeman must take place through

---

54. *Commons 1628*, 2:334, 333–58. For the speeches at this conference see Christianson, "Discretionary Imprisonment," 74–76, and cf. White, *Sir Edward Coke*, 137–42.

either indictment or presentment, while Selden tried to demonstrate that the precedents showed that those imprisoned upon the mandate of the king or council had received bail upon a writ of habeas corpus. Littleton quoted the relevant portions of the statutes, including the Matthew Paris version of Magna Carta, chapter 29, and gave a lengthy explanation of why the word *repleviable* from the first statute of Westminster did not mean "bailable"; this expanded upon and systematically developed the arguments presented before the King's Bench and the House of Commons by Selden. Selden patiently explained the procedure used when seeking remedy through a writ of habeas corpus and then recited, one by one, some thirty-one precedents, read the full text of draft judgment for the Five Knights' Case drawn up at the command of the attorney general, and provided the resolution of the judges of 34 Elizabeth I as recorded in the book of selected cases compiled by Lord Chief Justice Anderson.[55]

Last came the chance of the former Lord Chief Justice to finish the case of the Commons. After reading the four resolutions passed by the lower House into the record, Coke spent the major part of his time developing nine legal reasons to demonstrate "That these acts of parliament and these judicial precedents in affirmance thereof (recited by my colleagues), are but declarations of the fundamental laws of this kingdom." The first developed the distinction between freemen and villeins, arguing that "if free men of England might be imprisoned at the will and pleasure of the King by his commandment, they were then in worse case than bondmen and villeins; for the lord of a villein cannot command another to imprison his villein without cause, as of disobedience, or refusing to serve, as is agreed in our law books." The second reason argued that, in such matters, the king must act "judicially, by his judges"; the third discussed the remedies to commitment offered by various writs; the fourth opposed "the extent and universality of the pretended power to imprison"; and the fifth stressed the "indefiniteness of time" as stipulated in the return. Selden had used the first and second of these arguments in his presentation before the King's Bench and in his speech in the Commons of March 27. As noted

55. *Commons 1628*, 2:334–56. For Selden's speech of March 27 see 2:150–52, 154–55, 158–59, 161–62, 164–65, and Bodleian, Selden MS, supra 123, f. 244ʳ.

above, Coke had already expressed the third, fourth, and fifth in a debate in the committee of the whole House.[56]

In an eloquent passage, Coke portrayed the dolorous consequences of failing to uphold the distinction between *meum et tuum:*

> The sixth general reason is drawn *a damno et dedecore* [from injury and disgrace], from the loss and dishonor of the English nation, in two respects: 1, for their valor and prowress so famous through the whole world; 2, for their industry, for who will endeavour to employ himself in any profession, either of war, liberal science, or merchandise, etc., if he be but tenant at will of his liberty? And no tenant at will will support or improve anything, because he hath no certain estate; and thus should be both *dedecus* and *damnum* to the English nation and it should be no honor to the King to be king of slaves.

Both the power and riches of the realm sprang from the liberties of English freemen. Readers of Fortescue knew this argument well, and, of course, Hedley had developed it at some length in the parliament of 1610. Coke went on to emphasize that "the pretended power" of discretionary imprisonment "being against the power of the King and of his people can be no part of his prerogative," that an expression of the cause of commitment provided greater safety to the king should a prisoner escape, and, last, that earlier judgments had ruled against similar actions.[57] The Lords observed an impressive performance. The spokesmen of the Commons, guided in many points by the visible and invisible hand of Selden, had delivered a learned lesson on the nature of the ancient constitution and a powerful defense of the liberty of freeborn Englishmen.

DEBATES IN THE COMMONS ON THE MILITARY

While the Lords engaged in their own investigation of the resolutions of the Commons and the draft judgment, the Commons returned to the questions of the billeting and pressing of soldiers. Dur-

56. *Commons 1628,* 2:356, 357–58; for Coke's earlier speech see 2:191–92; for Selden's earlier speeches see 2:150–52, 154–55, 158–59, 161–62, 164–65, and Howell, *State Trials,* 3:16–19.

57. *Commons 1628,* 2:358.

ing a debate on impressment, Selden launched into a long historical account on the raising of troops, showing that "Three courses were used," in the past, "for levying of forces for wars: 1. By calling them together who are bound to serve by tenure. 2. By sending to those who were engaged by covenant to serve the King. 3. By this new way of pressing." The first predated the conquest, grew under William I to provide "60,000 knights and armed men," and still continued in force; the second "was the frequent way" from Edward II to Henry VIII and usually involved the granting of indentures to "barons and great men" who "could raise 1,000 men at any time"; the third became standard only under the Tudors. Citing statutes from the reigns of Richard II, Henry VI, Henry VII, Henry VIII, and Edward VI, Selden drew the radical conclusion that "in all these statutes there is not a word of any soldiers pressed or sent away by compulsion, and so the law then knew no pressing."[58]

For those schooled in any version of the ancient constitution, therefore, the conclusion obviously followed that the crown could not press troops legally. Faced with the collapse of the regular method of raising soldiers and sailors while England was engaged in a war with Spain and France, reformer after reformer, including Phelips, John Pym, Digges, Wentworth, and Eliot, supported the apprehensions expressed by Solicitor Shelton on this issue and not the historical arguments presented by Selden. Coke directed attention away from impressment and back to the crux of the complaints made by constituents, the misuse of power by royal servants: "The prerogative of the King is like a river which men cannot live without, but if it swell it will overflow, and perhaps run out of the course, and that swelling is caused by the misemployment of the power of deputy lieutenants, and this I desire should be examined." Defusing the issue, Coke moved "that there may be a select committee to draw a bill for this business."[59] As one of the few people who had a historical grasp of tenure in 1628, Selden pre-

---

58. Ibid., 2:279–81; cf. 286–87, 290–91, 292. Selden had discovered tenures by knight service, but he still favored a monetary value for a knight's fee at this time. One of the few contemporaries who could have grasped this interpretation readily was Sir Henry Spelman; see Pocock, *Ancient Constitution*, chap. 5.

59. *Commons 1628*, 2:288, 293; see also 287–88, 291, 292–93.

sented an account too accurate and too drastic for the perception of most of his contemporaries; ironically but clearly, he overstepped the bounds of parliamentary propriety!

In order to expedite grievances over the conduct of troops, the Commons divided these into two categories: billeting and martial law. Although debate continued on the contentious issue of martial law, the House expeditiously heard individual complaints on billeting and established a subcommittee to draft a petition to the king on this issue. On April 9, Sir Nathaniel Rich presented a draft petition on billeting; within two days, it passed the final two readings. Accompanied by the Commons, Speaker Finch presented the petition to King Charles on April 14; it pointed to the unprecedented nature of billeting, noted the grave difficulties that this procedure had created in the country, and asked "for the present removal of this unsupportable burden, and that your Majesty would be graciously pleased to secure us from the like pressure in time to come." In his answer, the king promised to examine the petition, but he prodded the Commons to vote supply with greater speed and to spend less energy on worrying about liberties: "I have faithfully declared that I will be as forward for the preservation of your liberties as yourselves; therefore go on without distrust or more apologies."[60] Ironically, the new evidence on the draft judgment revealed in the Lords just two days previously helped to sap the confidence of members of parliament in the "forwardness" of Charles or at least of some of his ministers for the liberties of Englishmen.

INVESTIGATIONS IN THE LORDS ON DISCRETIONARY IMPRISONMENT

While the Commons prepared its petition on billeting, the Lords heard Attorney General Heath offer his interpretation of discretionary imprisonment. Since the papers delivered to the Lords on April 9 for examination by the king's counsel were fourteen acts of parliament copied from records in the Tower of London, eleven "several sheets of precedents out of the King's Bench, etc.," the draft judgment prepared by Attorney General Heath, and reports of the speeches

---

60. Ibid., 2:360–71, 452–53; for Rich's report see 391; for the passage of the petition see 376, 397; and for the text of the petition see 451–52.

made on April 7, with that by Digges running to one sheet of paper, that by Littleton to twelve "sides close written," that by Selden sixty sides, and that by Coke nine sides, he did not lack a target. Opening his testimony on April 12, Heath agreed with the summary of the issues at stake made by the Commons: "The first, that no free man ought to be imprisoned by the King or Council without cause shown. If he be restrained by the King or Council, etc., being returned by *habeas corpus* ought to be delivered."[61] Following, however, came a lengthy, detailed attack upon the interpretation put forward in the resolutions of the Commons and the arguments presented by Littleton, Selden, and Coke.

After discussing Magna Carta and the statutes cited, the attorney general made the telling point that it was "strange that there should be no printed book nor statute that positively says the King cannot commit without showing a cause, being it is a thing so much concerns the liberty of the subject." Turning from statutes to precedents, the experienced common lawyer explained: "When we cannot tell what *lex terrae* [the law of the land] or *consuetudo Angliae* [the custom of England] is, we resor[t] to the usual practice of former times." Each case received a careful interpretation which showed how it did not display the bailing of a prisoner without some direction from the king or privy council; a comment on the last case underlined his differences with the spokesmen of the Commons by noting, "The rules laid down by Mr. Selden [were] utterly mistaken." Heath also defended his "draft of the judgment intended to be entered" in the roll of the King's Bench; carefully, he noted that he had "called upon the clerk often," admitted that he could not "have entered it without acquainting the judges," and explained that, comparing it with "the old precedents," he "found no difference but a few words more and therefore resolved never to enter it." At this point, the duke of Buckingham supported his client by interceding to say, "The Attorney had a check from the King because he had not entered that draft." This intervention, while it took some pressure off Heath, hardly reassured those who feared for their liberties. After debating the issue of allowing the Commons a chance to reply to the presentation made by Heath, the Lords agreed and

61. *Lords 1628,* 186, 208, 203.

ordered "Mr. Attorney to put his arguments in writing so soon as he can" for a full discussion of the issues at a joint conference of both Houses.[62]

To those peers upset by Buckingham's report of the royal command to register a judgment on the controlment roll against all customary practice, the testimony of the judges must have sounded more comforting. On April 14 and 15, the justices spoke individually and established a number of points about the Five Knights' Case. First, in the words of Justice Whitelocke, there "was no judgment, nothing done to derogate from the king or invade" the liberties of the people, only "a rule in court of *advisari vult* [will advise]," that is, the ruling that the prisoners had been remitted until the court should advise on the matter. This meant that the prisoners could seek bail again at any time on a new writ of habeas corpus. In the words of Justice Jones, the judges "all agreed that the next day, or the next term a new *habeas corpus* might have been demanded by the parties, and they must have done justice," while Whitelocke added, "I never did read a record that did make it appear to me that the judges of the King's Bench did deliver a man upon the first return of *per mandatum domini regis* [by command of the lord king]." In regard to the draft judgment, Whitelocke reported the comforting news that the Justices and clerk had followed the old customs: "Mr. Attorney did that which beseemed a good servant. We as judges between the King and people. We gave order to the clerk to enter nothing but that which was accustomed to ancient course."[63] In other words, the justices had deliberately avoided deciding the issue of discretionary imprisonment and had not allowed the clerk to enter on the roll the draft judgment presented by Attorney General Heath. After hearing the justices of the King's Bench and receiving their submission as a written report, many Lords came to see the forthcoming joint conference as a means for reaching some sort of accommodation between the prerogatives of the crown and the liberties of the people.

62. Ibid., 206, 213, 203, 198; for Heath's report see 197–203, 206, 208–13, and for the debates of the Lords over when and whether to hold a conference with the Commons see 204–14, 232–33, 235–37.

63. Ibid., 222, 223, 225; for the report by the Justices of the King's Bench to the Lords see 217, 219–20, 222–26, 228–32, 234–40, and Guy, "Petition of Right," 301.

THE GREAT DEBATE

A dramatic joint conference of both Houses, held on the afternoons of April 16 and 17, gave formal reality to the ideal of the High Court of Parliament and capped the debate between the spokesmen of the Commons and the attorney general. Lord Keeper Coventry opened the proceedings by reading the declaration of the justices which summarized their reports to the Lords. Although acknowledging that Magna Carta in "all parts" and the six "subsequent statutes"—among the many statutes cited by Littleton, the six accepted by both sides as later explanations of Magna Carta, chapter 29, seem to have been 3 Edward I, chapter 15 (the first statute of Westminster); 5 Edward III, chapter 9; 25 Edward III, statute 5, chapter 4; 28 Edward III, number 9; 37 Edward III, chapter 18; and 42 Edward III, chapter 3—still stood in force, Attorney General Heath correctly noted that a "difference in the manner of application" of these laws still remained in dispute, and especially the "great question" of "how far the words of *lex terrae* extend." In reply to the opening orations, Coke explained that the spokesmen of the Commons had "*delegatam potestatem* [delegated power], to hear only," and not to speak to "that which is new," so they would "not meddle with the resolution of the judges, but report it to the House." Littleton next agreed that the seven statutes remained in force, but he reiterated the view expressed during and after the Five Knights' Case that Magna Carta made little sense unless "*per legem terrae*" bestowed greater privileges upon freemen than upon villeins.[64] The spokesmen of the Commons continued to insist that "by the law of the land" meant imprisonment by either indictment or presentment, while Heath argued that the common law demanded only a general cause such as the command of the king or council.

The most profoundly disturbing reading came in an intervention by Sir Francis Ashley who seemed to challenge the supremacy of the common law in England:

> We must consider what is *lex terrae,* which is not so strictly to be taken as if *lex terrae,* were only that part of the municipal law of this

64. *Commons 1628,* 2:500–501; see also *Lords 1628,* 268–71. For a fuller account of this great debate see Christianson, "Discretionary Imprisonment," 77–82.

realm which we call the common law; for there are divers other jurisdictions exercised in this kingdom which are also to be reckoned the law of the land, as in Caudrey's case, in the 5th *Report,* fol. 8. The ecclesiastical law is held the law of the land to punish blasphemies, apostasies, heresies, schisms, simony, incest, and the like, for a good reason there rendered, *vizt.:* that otherwise the King should not have power to do justice to subjects in all cases, nor to punish all crimes within his kingdom.

The admiral jurisdiction is also *lex terrae,* for things done upon the sea. . . .

The martial law likewise, though not to be exercised in times of peace when recourse may be had to the King's courts; yet, in time of invasion or other times of hostility when an army royal is in the field . . . it is then the law of the land, and is *jus gentium* [the law of nations], which ever serves for a supply in defect of the common law when ordinary proceedings cannot be had.

And so it is also in the case of the law merchant . . . where the cause shall be determined by the law of nature. In like manner it is in the law of state: when the necessity of state requires it, they do and may proceed according to natural equity, as in those other cases because, in cases where the law of the land provides not, there the proceedings may be by the law of natural equity; and infinite are the occurrences of state unto which the common law extends not. And, if this proceeding of state should not also be accounted the law of the land, then do we fall in the same inconvenience mentioned in Caudrey's case, that the King should not be able to do justice in all cases within his own dominions.

Not only had Ashley spoken with "no authority nor direction" from the Lords, as Lord President Manchester immediately pointed out, he had asserted a number of highly provocative points.[65]

Most common lawyers held that the canon and civil laws exercised jurisdiction in England only to the degree that the common law had

---

65. *Lords 1628,* 282–83, 284. For an extended account of Ashley's interpretation, which draws more fully upon his reading of 1616 on Magna Carta, chap. 29, at the Middle Temple see Faith Thompson, *Magna Carta: Its Role in the Making of the English Constitution 1300–1629* (Minneapolis, 1948), 286–93, 343–45.

allowed by statute or custom; this meant that the common law was *the* law of the land, while the others were laws only through such a reception. Few common lawyers would have agreed that the law of nations (*jus gentium*) should supply any purported "defect" in the common law; indeed, most would have viewed that assertion, normally forwarded by civil lawyers, as a threat to the supremacy of the common law in England. The "law of state" raised a particularly ominous specter, because of its promised almost infinite possibilities of extension. No doubt, Manwaring would have found the loan of 1627 equitable! An unidentified spokesman of the House of Commons, probably Selden, quickly answered:

> We read of no law of state, and that none of these laws can be meant there [in Magna Carta] save the common law, which is the principal and general law, and is always understood by the way of excellency when mention is of the law of the land generally. And that though each of the other laws which are admitted into this kingdom by custom or act of parliament may justly be called "a law of the land," yet none of them can have the preeminence to be styled "the law of the land." And no statute, law book, or other authority, printed or unprinted, could be shown to prove that the law of the land, being generally mentioned was ever intended of any other than the common law; and yet even by these other laws a man may not be committed without a cause expressed.[66]

Others intervened, as well, to answer the points raised by Ashley, before returning to a point-by-point refutation of the interpretations presented by Heath. Most of the two-day conference centered upon a long, case-by-case dispute over the precedents, in which members from both sides fought valiantly to persuade the Lords to accept their case. Even an attempt by Coke and Heath to end the conference with gentility ended up in a squabble which made accommodation more difficult.

---

66. *Commons 1628,* 2:530. This repeated arguments made at greater length in the notes to Fortescue and the *Historie of Tithes;* see Christianson, "Young John Selden," 297–99, 305–8. Selden had earlier argued in the Commons that "no prince in Christendom" claimed the privilege of discretionary imprisonment; see *Commons 1628,* 2:159.

COMMON LAW AND MARTIAL LAW

Ashley's intervention probably sensitized members of the Commons to an even greater extent about any attempt to detract from the supremacy of the common law. The issue of competition among various jurisdictions erupted in the Commons on April 18 with a heated debate on martial law in a committee of the whole which pitted the civil lawyer, dean of arches, and admiralty judge Sir Henry Marten against such common law worthies as Sir Edward Coke. In a long, learned speech, Marten had suggested, "where the [common] law may be executed with convenience the martial law is not to be executed, as the common law may with conveniency be executed. This reacheth not to soldiers in tenure or covenant, but the soldiers *in actu* [in the line of duty]. Execution of martial law is needful where the sovereign and state hold it needful and it impeacheth not the common law." Although attempting to take into account the sensitivity of common lawyers and noting later in the speech that the "common law permits admiral law," thus mirroring the receptionist model of the common lawyers rather than the universalist perspective of many civil lawyers, Marten's reference to convenience and the discretionary powers of the sovereign created discomfort in the minds of other members. Among other voices, Coke answered: "Sir H. Marten said martial law is to be used in convenient time. Who shall judge of that? It will bring all to an absolute power. He said the laws common and martial may stand together. It is impossible. . . . If the soldier and the judge should sit both of one bench the drum would drown the voice of the crier."[67] Were convenience allowed to rule and courts martial and common law courts to sit at the same time, Coke feared a slide into absolutist practices and a subversion of common law jurisdiction. Let custom continue to rule, he advised. If the courts in Westminster stayed open, England remained at peace. Common law commissions of oyer and terminer could take care of any difficult cases in the countryside.

Silent at first, Selden joined in during the second day of this discussion with an impassioned defense of the ancient constitution against any who would make other laws equal and coordinate with the common law of England:

67. *Commons 1628*, 2:542–43, 558; for the full debate see 541–61.

Our question is whether these commissions for martial law are not against law or no. There was no difference between lawyers yesterday. One civilian differed from us, not as a lawyer but as a statesman. A soldier (said he) is subject to the common law and to martial law for conveniency. Convenience does not make a law, neither does civil law govern as it is studied. By the civil law a soldier is to be ruled only by martial law and not by the civil or common law. Whatsoever civilians discourse, they always thus conclude: *haec omnia constant ad jura Comistabuli et Marescalli Angliae* [all these things belong to the jurisdiction of the Constable and Marshal of England]. Let them then dispute those courts and deliver their opinion. As the canon law, the law of marrying, and the law merchant does stand with the common law, so they say does the martial law. There are but two ways of making laws, custom and act of parliament. Those are laws of custom. Can any man tell me what martial law is, and how to punish men according to the commission only? It hath reference to instructions by the Council, and it was never known in England that any law was made but by custom or act of parliament. . . . I say this is a third way of making laws; and this is a new law, not heard of before. In the state of Rome no other authority made martial law but that that made the common law. The same is done in the Low Countries. As for our definition of time of war, it was said by one that it was for the preparation to war. Why then war is peace, because it is a preparation to peace, and peace to war. It was said that in former times all men of fashion were soldiers, and if they were all subject to martial law, where was this common law. As for martial law to be exercized upon the marching of an army, it may be done by a commission of oyer and terminer, and so it hath been done in former times. Amongst those pleas that do remain, there are very few *placita exercitus* [pleas of the army], and those of one year only, of Edward the 3rd, some thinking them to be martial law, but there was no such plea, but by the verge within the army by common law. As in the King's Household, and within the verge, the Lord Steward is judge, so were those *placita exercitus* before the steward, being all under the verge. I avouch 2 passages out of an old book against Sir H. Marten, H[enry] 7: 1, all belongs to the Constable and Marshal when the battles be ordained; 2ly, in the martial court, and when the King is in war, only the Constable and Marshal ought to hold court.

Probably only those familiar with Selden's earlier writings would have grasped the full import of this speech. It contained two main points. First, that neither the civil nor the common law dealt with such major matters as martial law on the arbitrary principle of convenience; both used established procedures for disciplining soldiers under arms: Roman law placed soldiers under a martial law coordinate with civil jurisdiction, and common law offered three choices, enforcement of order through a royal commission of oyer and terminer, an act of parliament, or the Marshal's court. The rule of law had no place for "convenience." Second, Selden stressed two legitimate methods of making law within the ancient constitution: custom and act of parliament. Since the recent instructions issued by a royal commission upon the mandate of the privy council fulfilled neither of these conditions, they represented a new and dangerous method of creating law. This speech with its complex argument not only addressed the issues at hand, of course, it also summarized that interpretation of the ancient constitution upheld by Selden for the past decade, his vision of England as a mixed monarchy, with the king, the Lords, and the Commons sharing power from the very beginning. No wonder that his colleagues entrusted him with the chair in the subcommittees on discretionary imprisonment and on martial law.[68]

THE PROPOSITIONS OF THE LORDS

After censuring Serjeant Ashley for the "unfitting speeches" which he had made at the conference, the Lords spent two full days of debate on the resolutions of the Commons. Unable to reach agreement in the House, they appointed a committee on April 23 to work out suggestions for an accommodation; it produced the propositions sent to the Commons on April 25, "in writing with liberty for to add, alter, or take away any part of it." In the midst of a lengthy report by Selden on the place of martial law in the ancient constitution, a messenger from

68. Ibid., 2:566, 568, 572; this quotation is a composite text drawing mainly upon the versions found in Proceedings and Debates and in Stowe MSS. 366; for the committee see 569, 573, 577.

the Lords interrupted to request a meeting of a committee of members from both Houses. At this gathering, the peers presented five propositions which asked King Charles (1) to "declare" that Magna Carta and the six subsequent statutes remained in force; (2) to "declare" that "every free subject of this realm has a fundamental propriety in his goods and a fundamental liberty of his person"; (3) to "ratify and confirm" to his subjects "all their ancient several just liberties, privileges, and rights"; (4) to pledge that "his Majesty" would "proceed according to the common law"; and (5) "touching his Majesty's royal prerogative, intrinsical, incident to sovereignty and entrusted him from God," to "resolve" that when he "shall find just cause for reason of state to imprison or restrain any man's person, his Majesty would graciously declare that within a convenient time he shall and will express the cause of the commitment or restraint, either general or special."[69] On the whole and especially in the fifth point, these statements reflected the language and enshrined the interpretation supported by Attorney General Heath. The Lords had devised a clever set of proposals which appeared to present a viable compromise between the royal prerogative and popular liberties but, in reality, upheld a moderate version of the model of "constitutional monarchy created by kings" put forward by spokesmen for the crown.

The Commons opened debates on the five propositions on April 26. Many members, including not a few with connections in the upper House — such as Sir Nathaniel Rich, Sir Dudley Digges, and John Pym — favored some sort of accommodation between the previous resolutions of the Commons and the new suggestions from the Lords.[70] Sir

69. *Lords 1628*, 293, 344–45; *Commons 1628*, 3:74, 81 (see also 72–74, 79, 83–85, 86–87, 88–90). For the disputes in the Lords see *Lords 1628*, 293, 300, 303, 311–18, 330–31, 333–37, 339–41, 344–47; Berkowitz, "Reason of State," 196–98, 204–7; Flemion, "Struggle for the Petition of Right," 199–202, 205–8, and "A Savings to Satisfy All," 33–36.

70. *Commons 1628*, 3:94–119. Rich was a relative of the earl of Warwick, Digges the client of the archbishop of Canterbury, and Pym a client of the earl of Bedford; for Rich see the *D.N.B.*, 16:1005, and Gruenfelder, *Influence in Elections*, 157; for Digges see Thomas Kiffin, "Sir Dudley Digges: A Study in Early Stuart Politics" (Ph.D. diss., New York University, 1972), chap. 13, *passim;* and for Pym see Conrad Russell, "The Parliamentary Career of John Pym, 1621–9," in Peter Clark, Alan G. R. Smith, and Nicholas Tyacke, eds., *The English Commonwealth*

Edward Coke and Selden, however, strongly opposed these calls for compromise. Coke attacked each of the resolutions in turn, but saved his greatest fire for the fifth. First he objected to the dangerous precedent of allowing an intrinsic prerogative: "His Majesty's prerogative 'intrinsical.' It is a word we find not much in the law. It is meant that intrinsical prerogative is not bounded by any law, or by any law qualified. We must admit this intrinsical prerogative an exempt prerogative, and so all our laws are out. And this intrinsical prerogative is entrusted him by God and then it is due *jure divino* [divine right], and then no law can take it away." This would set the royal prerogative above the law of the land, a move that destroyed the assumptions of "constitutional monarchy governed by the common law." Second, Coke displayed caution about such uncertain phrases as "reason of state" and "a convenient time" which left too much initiative to royal servants: "If we agree to this imprisonment 'for matters of state' and 'a convenient time,' we shall leave Magna Carta and the other statutes and make them fruitless, and do what our ancestors would never do." Again, this would destroy the ancient constitution. Third, accepting such a definition of royal prerogative would create a dangerous new law which would fundamentally alter the distribution of power within the kingdom: "We are now about to declare and we shall now introduce and make a new law, and no king in Christendom claims that law, and it binds the subject where he was never bound. Never yet was any fundamental law shaken but infinite trouble ensued."[71] The proposition of the Lords would give unprecedented powers to the kings of England. Better to confirm old laws than to make new ones which would bind the subject and endanger the nature of the constitution.

Starting out on a more technical tack, Selden distinguished firmly between the resolutions of the Commons which declared the law and the propositions of the Lords which attempted to "explain" the law: "Our resolutions we sent to the Lords were matters of law; and I think, nay I am sure, no man can question the reason of them. But the Lords l[a]ying by the consideration of our propositions, being law, have pro-

---

1547–1640: Essays in Politics and Society Presented to Joel Hurstfield (Leicester, 1979), chap. 8.

71. *Commons 1628*, 3:95.

posed these to explain what is law." Such attempts at explanation, no matter how well intended, muddied the situation; a declaration of the law bore weight in the common law courts, but an explanation did not. In addition, the particular statements presented serious difficulties: "Of the first 3 there is no use; the 4th we have already; and the 5 is not fit to be asked, because it is not fit to be had." Selden attacked each in turn: "Magna Carta has been confirmed 32 or 33 times, and to have it confirmed 34 times I do not know what good it will do." As for the "fundamental propriety" and personal "liberty" of the subject, he retorted: "I never heard it denied but in the pulpit, which is of no weight." A general confirmation of liberties was "not fit to be asked" because "I conceive his Majesty never proceeded but according to law." The fifth proposition drew his strongest fire; it contradicted the earlier resolution of the Commons on discretionary imprisonment and it would "destroy our fundamental liberties," for the wording, with its "reason of state" and "convenient time," allowed "any person" to suffer commitment "at pleasure. By this the cause may be concealed in the breast for a convenient time, and no man is exempted. At this little gap every man's liberty may in time go out."[72] A number of members felt that the first three proposals might contain some useful suggestions, but none dared to oppose the powerful condemnation of the fifth made by Selden and Coke. The two great common lawyers had slowed the initiative seized by the Lords; in the process, however, they had stalled the business of the parliament.

Both sides sought a way out of the impasse. Charles showed his support for the propositions of the Lords with a personal promise to work within the law. In a statement read to the two Houses by the Lord Keeper on April 28, the king confirmed

> that he holds the statute of Magna Carta, and the six other statutes insisted upon for the subject's liberty, to be all in force, and assures you that he will maintain all his subjects in the just freedom of their persons and safety of their estates, and that he will govern according to the laws and statutes of this realm, and that you shall find as much security in his majesty's royal word and promise as in the

72. Ibid., 3:110, 105–6 (the first quotation combines accounts from two diaries), 101, 110, 96. Also see Guy, "Petition of Right," 304–5.

strength of any law you can make, so that hereafter you shall never have cause to complain.

Having given his personal word on the liberties of free subjects, Charles also urged members of the lower House to press ahead with the provision of supply. Sir John Coke, the secretary of state, who had fought battles in the Council on this issue, eagerly accepted the king's promise to govern by the common law and, quoting from the parliamentary speech of James VI and I from 1610, attempted to persuade the lower House to accept the compromise so graciously offered:

> We cannot but remember what his father said, "He is no king, but a tyrant, that governs not by law." But this kingdom is to be governed by the common law, and his Majesty assures us so much; the interpretation is left to the judges and to his great council, and all is to be regulated by the common law. I mean not Magna Carta only, for that Magna Carta was part of the common law and the ancient laws of this kingdom. . . . But his Majesty stopped not there. . . . He assures us our liberties are just: they are not of grace, but of right. Nay, he assures us that he will govern us according to the law of the realm, and that we shall find as much security in his Majesty's promise as in any law we can make.[73]

Secretary Coke, speaking the language of the common law, rejoiced in the royal message.

To one familiar with the normal constitutional discourse of King Charles, the public statement that subjects held their liberties as a matter of right and the promise to rule by the common law looked like a major compromise. In the guise of a concession, however, the king had offered little of substance. To the position already defended by Attorney General Heath, he added only the personal promise of the living monarch. During this whole debate, stretching back to the Five Knights' Case, none of the participants had questioned the force of Magna Carta and the six statutes, nor the willingness of the crown to govern by the law. What both sides disputed was how the king's servants should proceed. On this point the attorneys for the crown and

---

73. *Commons 1628*, 3:125, 125–27. Coke made reference to the speech by James from March 21, 1610.

the lawyers in the Commons had presented rival interpretations of the ancient constitution. These still clashed. Still, in a world of face-to-face politics, this sort of ploy had some chance of success; a personal appeal might have satisfied the sense of grievance felt by many gentlemen.

FROM BILL ON LIBERTIES TO PETITION OF RIGHT

The Commons responded to the king's promise immediately by unanimously voting, upon a motion by Eliot, to frame a bill on "the liberty of the subjects in their persons and estates"; when the committee appointed to carry out this task met that afternoon, Selden arrived to help with the drafting. The next morning, Sir Edward Coke reported out a bill "for our liberties"; debate on this draft bill stretched over several days, and some members, including Coke, pressed for spelling out a charge at the time of imprisonment. On May 1, Sir John Coke interrupted the discussion with another message from the monarch: "His Majesty would know whether we will rest on his royal word or no, declared to us by the Lord Keeper; which if we do, he assures us shall be really performed."[74] Rival loyalties tugged at the knights and burgesses. Caught between King Charles's insistence that the administration of the law had become a matter of trust and their constituents' demand for redress of grievances, the members of parliament at first floundered.

Gaining back some confidence, the Commons began to draft a reply to the king's speeches on May 2. Despite another message that afternoon in which Charles promised once more to abide by the law and threatened to end the session in slightly more than a week, the Commons pressed forward and presented its answer on May 5. When the monarch's reply moved little beyond his earlier messages and threatened the refusal of the royal assent to a bill on the liberties of the subject, another impasse appeared; after much debate and discussion, the Commons abandoned its attempt to uphold its liberties by statute and decided to proceed by petition of right, a collective version of the procedure recommended by Attorney General Heath in the Five Knights' Case. Although Selden believed that this change would pro-

74. Ibid., 3:130, 189; see also 149, 150, 152, 153–54, 155, 159, 165, 166, 167, 168, 172–82. See Flemion, "A Savings to Satisfy All," 38–39.

duce a weaker result ("I think no man doubts that this is of equal force with an act of parliament, for certainly it is not"), he could not oppose the shift from bill to petition in public without angering his patron. Tired of trying to persuade other members to continue to proceed by bill, Coke put the motion to change to a petition.[75]

The Commons quickly assembled a petition for the protection of specific English liberties, but the struggle for its approval by the Lords and the monarch still loomed ahead. In a meeting of a select committee of members from both Houses held on May 8, Sir Edward Coke presented a fair copy of the Petition of Right to delegates of the Lords; on the same day, the lower House sweetened the pot by moving forward on the subsidy. Both the king and the peers replied four days later, Charles with a letter to the Lords in which he stressed "our royal power, lent unto us from God" and claimed that any limitation on the royal prerogative of discretionary imprisonment "would dissolve the very foundation and frame of our monarchy," and the upper House with eight amendments to the text of the petition. The Lord Keeper presented both the letter and the proposed alterations to the Commons in a meeting of the joint conference of both Houses.[76]

The Commons considered these documents on May 14 and decided, after due discussion, not to answer the king's letter, to accept

75. *Commons 1628*, 3:317; see also 189–92, 195–99, 201–5, 210–12, 272. For these events see Guy, "Petition of Right," 305–11; White, *Sir Edward Coke*, 258–64; Elizabeth Read Foster, "Petitions and the Petition of Right," *Journal of British Studies* 14 (1974): 35, 37–38, 40–43; and Michael B. Young, "The Origins of the Petition of Right Reconsidered Further," *Historical Journal* 27 (1984): 449–52. Sir Francis Seymour favored proceeding by petition as early as May 1, and on May 6, when the crucial vote took place, he seconded the motion of Sir Edward Coke to change from a bill to a petition of right. Selden clearly disagreed, but could not directly oppose his patron in public. *Commons 1628*, 3:187, 191, 194, 202, 204, 211, 212, 215, 220, 222, 223, 225, 226, 227, 235, 237, 240–41, 244, 272, 277, 283, 286, 290, 296. Since Seymour strongly advocated a detailed procedure and would not accept the general answers propounded by King Charles as sufficient, the disagreement appears to have been tactical, not strategic.

76. *Commons 1628*, 3:372; see also 325–31, 369, 371–73, 374, 378–79, 379–80, 382; also see *Lords 1628*, 394–97, 399–403, 405–6, 409–13, 421–36, 438–42, 445, 447–48, 451–57, 460–69, 473, 475–77, 479–87, 489–96, 499–500, 507–17, 520–28, 532–33, 536.

portions of the amendments, and to reject all the rest. After considerable prompting by the peers, the Commons finally explained why it refused to answer the letter from Charles I: "first, because it is no parliamentary way, for the King's assent must come after the petition is exhibited; and also that the debate of it would spend time." Technically, of course, this was correct; the monarch could neither give nor refuse consent until after the bill or petition had passed both Houses. Solicitous to save the honor of the king, the peers suggested an additional clause for the petition, which would explain that "We present this our humble petition to your Majesty not only with a care of preserving our own liberties, but with a due regard to leave entire that sovereign power wherewith your Majesty is trusted for the protection, safety, and happiness of your people." The Commons countered by asking how far the upper House agreed with it on the "form and substance of our petition"; when the peers continued to press for their amendments, a series of conferences between select committees from each House helped to thresh out the differences.[77] Although this took some time, the Petition of Right finally received its final reading in both Houses on May 27 and obtained a satisfactory form of royal assent on June 7.

In between came John Pym's speech at the impeachment of Manwaring, one of the most lengthy and resounding affirmations of the ancient constitution in the whole of this parliament. The subcommittee of the committee of religion had put in a good many hours in preparing charges against Manwaring, carefully combing through his book, comparing his citations and quotations from Francisco Suárez with the original, and gathering reports on sermons preached recently. They finally reported on May 5; after further work, Pym reported from the committee on religion to the House on May 14. After some discussion over whether to proceed against Manwaring by attainder or impeachment, Pym noted, "If we go by bill we cannot give our reasons," and Selden agreed, "We cannot fitly go otherwise than by the Lords. This is a temporal crime to have parliaments thus scandaled in parliaments.

77. *Commons 1628,* 3:407, 452, 465; see also 387–401, 404, 406–9, 411–14, 417, 464, 469, 472, 479; see *Lords 1628,* 409–13, 422–23, 424–36, 445, 447–48, 451–57, 475–76, 479–80, 483–84, 486–87, 508, 513, 517. See Flemion, "A Savings to Satisfy All," 40–42.

To go by bill, I do not think it fit. In such cases there was never any bill of attainder."[78] The House charged the former subcommittee, with the addition of Secretary Coke, Sir Robert Poyntz, Sir Edward Rodney, and Selden, to draw up the charge.

After several other discussions in May, the charge was read in the Commons and presented to the Lords at a conference on June 4. Arguing that "by the laws and statutes of this realm the free subjects in England do undoubtedly inherit this right and liberty not to be compelled to contribute any tax or tallage or to make any loans not set or imposed by common consent by act of parliament" and justifying those who refused to lend, the Commons charged Manwaring with "a wicked and malicious intention to seduce and misguide the conscience of the King's most excellent Majesty touching the observation of the laws and customs of this kingdom, to avert his Majesty's mind from calling of parliaments, to alienate his royal heart from his people, and to cause jealousies, sedition, and division in the kingdom."[79] Ironically, Manwaring, who had accused those who refused the loan of sedition, now faced the same charge.

It was only fitting that Pym, the sustaining force in the investigation, should have the glory of the presentation. Sommerville has noted: "Maynwaring's political arguments were largely derived from the works of such theorists as De Dominis, Saravia, Buckeridge and Andrewes. He displayed a wide knowledge of recent absolutist literature. Steeped in the learning of the neo-scholastics, he cared little for the ideology of Coke and his colleagues." Although Pym also displayed some familiarity with natural law theorists, especially Suárez, and should, from Sommerville's interpretation, have attacked the divine from that perspective, the member for Tavistock chose instead to make his presentation to the Lords on the grounds of the ancient constitution. This did not spring from ignorance, for, on May 22, Robert Mason had attacked Manwaring in the House for falsifying Suárez and had quoted a natural law constitutionalist argument from the Spanish Jesuit's *De Legibus*

78. *Commons 1628*, 3:406, 404; see also 408, 409–10, 413. Selden's opposition to attainders did not begin in 1641.

79. Ibid., 4:102; see also 86, 90, 92, 101–3.

to make the point.[80] Natural law, however, did not provide a basis for impeachable offenses; as usual in the governance of early Stuart England, one had to turn to the common law for such purposes.

Arguing that "no alteration of the form of government in a state can be made without danger of ruin," that English "laws did not grow by grant of princes, nor by pragmatic sanction, but are fundamental from the very original of this kingdom and are part of the essential constitution thereof" and that "these laws are not only for the good of the subject, but for the honor and profit of the King himself," Pym built upon Selden's interpretation of the ancient constitution as a mixed monarchy. Arguing that "William the Conqueror swore in person to maintain and observe" these "ancient, original, and essential" laws, Pym also pointed out, in familiar tones, that were they removed "all industry, courage, and valor will fail" and this would diminish the riches of the king as well as those of the people. Presenting the charge in six points which added to those listed above the crimes of "inciting of the King's displeasure against his subjects" and "scandalizing of the law, and seeking to subvert it," Pym proceeded to demonstrate each point with quotations from Manwaring's published sermons. As for those "limitations by which" Manwaring "would seem to qualify his assertions," such as requiring loans only "in time of urgent and pressing necessity" and levying them "in a due proportion," Pym argued that Manwaring "would seem not to leave the power arbitrary; but these limitations leave the judgment arbitrary and the subject remediless; so as they are limitations in show, not in substance." This point gained added force from the example of the people in Normandy who lost their former liberties by the regrant of their laws from the French king with the proviso that taxes and aids might be collected without the consent of the three estates "in cases of urgent necessity."[81] Within the context of similar fears expressed in the debates over the Petition of Right, this point must have sounded an understandable warning.

80. Sommerville, *Politics and Ideology*, 129; *Commons 1628*, 3:528.

81. *Commons 1628*, 4:103, 104, 107; the charges against Manwaring appear on 104 and the demonstrations on 104–7. Selden was named to the committee which drafted the charge on three occasions, and both Coke and Selden had argued in favor of this confirmation of the old laws by William.

In a telling stroke, Pym contrasted the "sentences of authors as speak of kings in general or such kingdoms as are not regulate by any certain law" with the familiar words of King James from his speech of March 21, 1610:

> "But now in this our time we are to distinguish . . . between the state of settled kings and monarchs that do at this time govern in civil kingdoms," etc. " . . . every just king in a settled kingdom is bound to observe that paction made to this people by his laws, in framing his government agreeable thereunto," etc. "And therefore a king governing in a settled kingdom, leaves to be a king, and degenerates into a tyrant, as soon as he leaves off to rule according to his laws," etc. ". . . all kings that are not tyrants or perjured will be glad to bound themselves within the limit of their laws; and they that persuade them to the contrary are vipers and pests, both against them and the commonwealth."

The implications of the last sentence, echoing phrases applied to Manwaring earlier in the speech, were clear. Once again, a member of the parliament of 1628 returned to this crucial passage in James I's speech to bolster a common law interpretation of the constitution. Pym did not accept the theory of "constitutional monarchy created by kings," but even it provided unassailable protection against an absolutist like Manwaring. While Pym noted Manwaring's falsifications of Suárez, he kept even these within a common law context. After reciting seven precedents of disciplinary actions against similar advocates of absolutism, starting in the reign of Edward I and ending with the case of Dr. Cowell, the speech ended with a plea for examination, judgment, and punishment of the offender. On the day after Pym presented this charge to the Lords, impeachment proceedings against the duke of Buckingham began to surface in the Commons.[82]

Throughout the parliamentary session of 1628, men such as Coke, Digges, Eliot, Littleton, Pym, and Selden sought to redress what they saw as the injustices and dangers of the Buckingham regime: first by forcing it to operate within the boundaries of the ancient law on specific, significant points and second by a direct attack upon the favorite,

82. Ibid., 4:108 (the omissions are Pym's); see also 108–9, 109–10, 114–35.

which lies outside of the scope of this essay. The campaign to force the king's servants to follow the common law opened as a renewal of the Five Knights' Case, with its crucial constitutional issues, in the High Court of Parliament. In lengthy presentations to the Lords and especially in the joint conferences of April 7, 16, and 17, the spokesmen of the Commons and the spokesman of the crown presented their rival views on discretionary imprisonment and on the basic framework of the English constitution, this time with the support of considerably more research. In his speech of June 4, Pym used an interpretation of the ancient constitution as the basis for the impeachment of Manwaring for attempting to alienate the king from parliaments, the law, and his people with absolutist arguments. The spokesmen for both sides acted as if they argued for the truth, rather than just an interpretation. Coke and Selden believed that their version of the ancient constitution represented historical reality as established by the most demanding canons of English and continental scholarship, while that put forward by the attorney general both misrepresented the past and endangered the nature of the English monarchy. Heath probably believed just as strongly in his model, justified it primarily on the basis of solid common law tradition, and viewed the arguments of the Commons as derogatory to royal power. Once engaged, each of these legal teams also put together its own case, in part, in reaction to that of the other side. As men who lived on their reputations, they had strong professional reasons for wanting to win such a public contest. These mixed motives may have varnished the truth for which they struggled, but the dispute involved real issues. The stress upon "reason of state" given by Attorney General Heath and Serjeant Ashley not only heralded the importation of a dubious continental principle into the common law, it defended a perspective which gave greater freedom to the crown than that model of "mixed monarchy" upheld by Selden or that of "constitutional monarchy governed by the common law" upheld by Coke. Indeed, on April 16 and 17, Heath deserted the "reason of state" of his presentation in the Five Knights' Case for a more familiar common law defense of "constitutional monarchy created by kings."

Contests over the "ancient constitution" involved much more than political theory; they included many practical, everyday operations of the law. Common lawyers and many other members of both Houses grasped this fact, but they still believed that the king and the principal royal servants remained open to persuasion, that dialogue would carry the day. Early in the session, Selden shared some of this optimism. This spurred him on to greater action, which, in turn, increased his prominence in the House; hence, the prodigious research carried out into statutes and precedents and the care taken in fashioning the arguments presented before the Lords. Selden's discovery of the attempt to enter a judgment drafted by the attorney general in the Rolls of the King's Bench, against all established practice and against the wishes of the justices, must have convinced him even more strongly of the need for restraining royal servants within the limits prescribed by a proper understanding of the law. Members of the lower House clearly found the continual messages by King Charles very perplexing and must have seen the tenacious defense of "constitutional monarchy created by kings" by Attorney General Heath and others as an annoyingly willful persistence in error, not as a failure on the part of the Commons to establish the veracity of its case.[83] The willingness of most members to shift from a bill to a petition of right in order to reach an accommodation affected Selden more adversely than Coke. Having long defended the view that the common law and English constitution consisted of specific laws and procedures established by either custom or statute, Selden resisted the move away from procedure by bill as a grave mistake and refused to expend much energy on the passage of the petition. He more than suspected that such a flimsy device as a petition of right could not keep royal servants within the confines of the ancient constitution. Coke wanted to have even an imperfect official ratification of the law on record rather than none at all. Future events would suggest that both may have made a correct assessment, Selden for the immediate future and Coke for the long run.

If the speeches of James I and Thomas Hedley and the treatise of John Selden spelled out three competing versions of the ancient constitution in 1610, and these had formed the basis for interpreting the nitty-gritty detail disputed in the parliament of 1628 in the attempt

83. For the "constitutionalist" nature of the case put by Selden, Sir Edward Coke, and other common lawyers see J. G. A. Pocock, "The Commons Debates of 1628," *Journal of the History of Ideas* 29 (1978): 332–34.

to reach a constitutional consensus, then no single interpretation had reached a position of hegemony by the end of 1628. Ironically, with the language of "reason of state" and the absolutist natural law discourse of several divines, new and, to common lawyers, dangerous voices entered the domestic debate in 1627. If the literary and art historians have interpreted the discourse of the Caroline court correctly, these "new counsels" became even more powerful in the 1630s. Because the most absolute monarch had to enforce his will primarily through the common law courts in England, "constitutional monarchy created by monarchs" did not pass entirely from the language of leading royal servants.

Of course, in *His Majesties Answer to the XIX Propositions* (London, 1642), even King Charles would be driven back to the interpretation announced in the speech of March 21, 1610, by his father. Taking the high ground of defending a constitution in which the king, the Lords, and the Commons represented a mixture of monarchy, aristocracy, and democracy, this carefully written appeal sought to subvert the Nineteen Propositions as unprecedented and dangerous. Particularly telling was the accusation that the "Cabalists of this businesse" had

> thought fit to remove a troublesome Rub in their way, *The Law;* To this end, (that they might undermine the very foundation of it) a new Power hath been assumed to interpret and declare Laws without Us by extempory Votes, without any Case judicially before either House, (which is in effect the same thing as to make Laws without Us) Orders and Ordinances made onely by both Houses (tending to a pure arbitrary power) were pressed upon the people as Laws, and their obedience required of them.

This reversed the accusation of plotting to undermine the ancient constitution and erect an arbitrary authority, long made against royal servants, and applied it against the leaders of the two Houses. The Militia Ordinance represented just one such attempt to "erect an upstart Authority without us." Professing confidence in "the Loyalty, good affections and integrity of the intentions of that great Bodie," *His Majesties Answer* blamed "the Malignity of Designe (as dangerous to the Lawes of this Kingdom, the Peace of the same, and the Liberties of all Our good Subjects, as to Our Selfe, and Our just Prerogative)" upon the "subtill

Informations, mischievous Practices, and evill Counsels of ambitious turbulent Spirits, disaffected to Gods true Religion, and the Unity of the Professors thereof, Our Honour and Safety, and the publike Peace and prosperity of Our people," spirits "not without a strong influence upon the very actions of both Houses." This echoed the proclamation issued at the dissolution of the session of 1629. The accusation that parliamentary leaders aimed at making this "Kingdom a Republique" and a "new *Utopia* of Religion and Government" complemented warnings of the disastrous consequences of imbalance among the "three estates." In a fruitful combination of conspiracy theory with attacks upon particular demands, telling asides, and an appealing defense of the "ancient, equall, happy, well-poised and never-enough commended Constitution of the Government of this Kingdom," the king's advisers sought to subvert the appeal of the Nineteen Propositions.[84] On the eve of the outbreak of civil war in England, as in the first three decades of the seventeenth century, constitutional debates in England more often pitted rival interpretations of the ancient constitution against each other than theories of absolutism against constitutionalism.

84. *His Majesties Answer to the XIX Propositions* (London, 1642) [E151.25; June 18], 2, 4–5, 8, 17, 17–22. See especially Michael Mendle, *Dangerous Positions: Mixed Government, the Estates of the Realm, and Making of the "Answer to the XIX Propositions"* (University, Ala., 1985) and Corrine Comstock Weston and Janelle Renfrow Greenberg, *Subjects and Sovereigns: The Grand Controversy over Legal Sovereignty in Stuart England* (Cambridge, England, 1981).

4. The Jurisprudence of Liberty: The Ancient Constitution in the Legal Historiography of the Seventeenth and Eighteenth Centuries

INTRODUCTION

During the late spring of 1779 Brigadier General Francis McLean, commanding the British forces at Halifax, established a post of six hundred men on the site of the present town of Castine, Maine. Proclaiming the reinstitution of royal jurisdiction, McLean called for the support of all inhabitants who "are well affected to his Majesty's person, and the ancient constitution under which they formerly flourished, and from the restoration of which they can alone expect relief from the distressed situation they are now in." Later that year, a Massachusetts expedition arrived in Penobscot Bay to reduce the British fort. Countering McLean's proclamation, Brigadier General Solmon Lovell announced the reestablishment of American authority, which, he said, meant rule by the very same ancient constitution that had been McLean's rallying point. "I have thought proper to issue this Proclamation," he explained, "hereby declaring that the allegiance due to the *ancient constitution* obliges to resist to the last extremity the present system of tyranny in the British Government."[1]

The event was isolated—a small scrimmage on the marchland of empire to fix the line between the future province of New Brunswick and the future state of Maine. That both sides appealed to the ancient constitution, however, placed the battle within the mainstream of the

---

1. Proclamation of Brigadier General Francis M'Lean, June 15, 1779, and Proclamation of Brigadier General Solmon Lovell, July 29, 1779, as printed in [John Calef], *The Siege of Penobscot by the Rebels. . . . To which is subjoined a Postscript wherein a short Account of the Country of Penobscot is given* (London, 1781), 26–27, 32.

revolutionary controversy. The ancient constitution had been a central element of the prerevolutionary debate from its beginning with the passage of the Stamp Act to its conclusion with the Declaration of Independence. At one time Patrick Henry was under the mistaken impression that the Virginia Resolves against the Stamp Act, the initial formulation of the American legal case which he drafted, had asserted that without the principle of taxation only by representation "the ancient Constitution cannot subsist."[2] The Declaration of Independence was first published in book form as part of a collection by "Demophilus" entitled *The Genuine Principles of the Ancient Saxon, or English Constitution.*[3] That book was printed in Philadelphia, where the readers of the *Pennsylvania Gazette* had recently been urged to compare the defects of their state's constitution "to the English constitution in its original purity, before the Norman invader had abolished as many of the free customs of the people as he possibly could."[4] What Pennsylvanians should do, "Demophilus" urged, was return to the ancient Saxon constitution. "This Colony, having now but one order of freemen in it; and to the honor of Pennsylvania, but very few slaves, it will need but little argument to convince the bulk of an understanding people, that this ancient and justly admired pattern, the old Saxon form of government, will be the best model, that human wisdom, improved by experience, has left them to copy."[5]

Nothing new or particularly American was being said, yet there were observers in the mother country who seemed to think either that what colonial whigs said was unusual or that they overargued the ancient constitution. "Upon the whole," a writer for London's *Critical Review* complained, "we cannot help thinking that the American advocates

2. "The Resolutions as Recalled by Patrick Henry," in *Prologue to Revolution: Sources and Documents on the Stamp Act Crisis, 1764–1766,* ed. Edmund S. Morgan (Chapel Hill, N.C., 1959), 48.

3. "Demophilus" [George Bryan], *The Genuine Principles of the Ancient Saxon, or English Constitution* (Philadelphia, 1776), 41–46.

4. *Pennsylvania Gazette,* May 15, 1776, p. 2, col. 1. Similarly, on the British constitution: "How different from, and how much superior to, our present form of government, was the Saxon, or old constitution of England" (*Maryland Gazette,* May 2, 1776, p. 2, col. 2).

5. "Demophilus," *Genuine Principles* (cited note 3), 17.

deal too much in . . . references to ancient and prophane history."[6] The point was not well taken. During the eighteenth century the ancient constitution appears to have been more widely cited and defended in Great Britain than in North America. Moreover, there was no dispute about whether the ancient constitution ran in the colonies.[7] "It is curious to remark," the earl of Abingdon noted in 1777 and 1780, "that the Constitution and Form of Government established by our wise Forefathers in America, was precisely, in Principle, the Constitution and Form of Government of the Saxon Heptarchy."[8]

The Americanization of the ancient constitution was an assumed fact. When the question arose in parliament as to whether the appeal for murder lay in the colonies, John Dunning, the Chatham party's lawyer in the Commons, expressed outrage. "I cannot sit silent when it is proposed to be taken away, or suspended with regard to America," he protested. "We must suppose it is an existing right in America. . . . I have heard it reckoned as the remnant of ancient barbarism that ought not to stand. I wish the constitution could be made more palatable to those who have it in their power to destroy it. Gothicism is almost every part of the constitution. Every part of the constitutional history is gothic. Is it to be understood, that we are to have a macaroni constitution in the room of it?"[9] Solicitor General Alexander Wedderburn,

6. *The Critical Review: Or Annals of Literature by a Society of Gentlemen* 20 (1765): 475.

7. John Wilkes said: "I hold Magna Carta to be in full force in America as in Europe" (Edward Royle and James Walvin, *English Radicals and Reformers, 1760–1848* [Lexington, Ky., 1982], 24). For an American contention that the ancient constitution was applicable to the colonies see "The British American, No. V," Williamsburg, June 30, 1774, *American Archives, Fourth Series* (Washington, D.C., 1837), 1:495–98.

8. Willoughby Bertie, earl of Abingdon, *Dedication to the Collective Body of the People of England, in which the Source of our present Political Distractions are pointed out, and a Plan proposed for their Remedy and Redress* (Oxford, 1780), xlii, footnote; Willoughby Bertie, earl of Abingdon, *Thoughts on the Letter of Edmund Burke, Esq; to the Sheriffs of Bristol, on the Affairs of America*, 6th ed. (Oxford, 1777).

9. Speech of John Dunning, Commons Debates, May 4, 1774, *Proceedings and Debates of the British Parliaments Respecting North America, 1754–1783*, ed. R. C. Simmons and P. D. G. Thomas (White Plains, N.Y., 1985), 4:385. See, similarly, speech of John Dunning, Commons Debates, April 29, 1774, ibid., 323.

who thought the appeal "a remnant of ancient barbarism," did not know if it was part of American criminal procedure but with apparent regret admitted that an appeal, with its attendant trial by battle, might still be legal in England and Wales. "The law of England admits of no limitation of time beyond a very distant period indeed," Wedderburn pointed out. "Whatever was the law of England continues to be the law of England."[10] By contrast Edmund Burke rejoiced that neither the appeal of murder nor the trial by battle had been abolished by legislation. "Men have gone upon [the practice] of delivering in their rights to the hands of the state," Burke lamented. "In proportion as they have given up, they have established this kind of government called absolute, or arbitrary in proportion as they have given up [rights]." It was better not to tinker with ancient practices, not even the anachronistic right to appeal by battle. "It is a thing totally agreeable to the old law. If you destroy this, you will destroy the whole system of jurisprudence. This country has left these two together, meaning to keep up government and liberty."[11]

Burke was speaking within the mainstream of eighteenth-century British constitutional thought. Trial by battle "was superstition and barbarism to the last degree,"[12] yet liberty might be imperiled if there was a power in government that could abolish the appeal by mere command. Retaining appeal, even as a dormant anachronism, furthered liberty by preserving liberty's most tenacious support, the authority of custom and the authority of ancient immemoriality. The jurisprudential reason—a major theme to be developed in this essay—was that legislative deviations from the ancient law could be promulgated only if arbitrary authority superior to "law" was constitutional. A more political, less legal explanation was that liberty had been more nearly perfect during ancient than in more recent times, making Gothicism and Saxonism standards for measuring the liberty of existing government institutions. James Otis outlined the theory's most generally accepted historical premises:

10. Speech of Alexander Wedderburn, Commons Debates, May 4, 1774, ibid., 386.

11. Speech of Edmund Burke, Commons Debates, May 4, 1774, ibid.

12. Speech of Edmund Burke, Commons Debates, April 29, 1774, ibid., 324.

Few people have extended their enquiries after the foundation of any of their rights, beyond a charter from the crown. There are others who think when they have got back to old *Magna Charta,* that they are at the beginning of all things. They imagine themselves on the borders of Chaos (and so indeed in some respects they are) and see creation rising out of the unformed mass, or from nothing. Hence, say they, spring all the rights of men and of citizens. — But liberty was better understood, and more fully enjoyed by our ancestors, before the coming in of the first Norman Tyrants than ever after, 'till it was found necessary, for the salvation of the kingdom, to combat the arbitrary and wicked proceedings of the Stuarts.[13]

The same year that Otis wrote, Robert Lowth, bishop of London, making much the same point, pushed the origins of the ancient constitution back to even before the Saxons. "Our Civil Constitution was from the first founded on the liberty of the People," he told the judges and lawyers attending the Durham assizes. That liberty had been "an essential part of the form of government, that universally prevailed among the northern nations, and was transplanted hither with our Saxon ancestors. The people had their acknowledged rights, and the obligation was reciprocal between them and their governors. These were legal kings, not arbitrary tyrants: they were bound and restrained by the laws of the community, framed with the people's participation and consent."[14] Whether the constitution had evolved first among German tribes or later with the Anglo-Saxons after they had conquered the Britons was irrelevant to eighteenth-century constitutional thought. What mattered was that it was the same constitution — then and now. "[T]he present civil constitution of England," Otis concluded, derived "its original" from the Saxons. "This government, like that from

13. James Otis, *The Rights of the British Colonies Asserted and Proved* (Boston, 1764), 31.

14. Robert Lowth, *A Sermon Preached Before the Honourable and Right Reverend Richard, Lord Bishop of Durham, the Honourable Henry Bathurst, One of the Justices of the Court of Common Pleas, and the Honourable Sir Joseph Yates, One of the Justices of the Court of King's Bench; at the Assizes Holden at Durham, August 15, 1764,* 2d ed. (Newcastle, England, 1764), 7–8.

whence they [the Saxons] came, was founded upon principles of the most perfect liberty."[15]

There is no need to rely on provincial lawyers and established clergymen. Scholars and judges also embraced the ancient constitution without qualification. In 1766 Sir William Blackstone, who would serve as Vinerian professor of law at Oxford, member of Parliament, and puisne on the Court of Common Pleas, insisted "that the liberties of Englishmen are not (as some arbitrary writers would represent them) mere infringements of the king's prerogative, extorted from our princes by taking advantage of their weakness; but a restoration of that antient constitution, of which our ancestors had been defrauded by the art and finesse of the Norman lawyers, rather than deprived by force of the Norman arms."[16] As late as a decade before the parliamentary reform act, at least one writer was still defending "the genuine unchangeable English constitution."[17] The operative concept—really a probative concept, as we shall see—was of a timeless constitution of unchanging general principles. As understood in the eighteenth century, this timeless or ancient constitution proved "that our Government was always *Legal;* that the People had their *Rights,* as well as the Kings their *Prerogatives;* and had *Representatives* too, to assert those Rights; that our Kings were not *arbitrary,* nor our Monarchy *absolutely* Hereditary."[18]

The timeless constitution gave English and British lawyers of the seventeenth and eighteenth centuries a jurisprudential instrument with which to maintain the privileges of parliament and the autonomy of the common law courts against the pretensions of prerogativism— that is, as they saw it, the rule of law against arbitrary government. In the 1760s and 1770s, American whigs resorted to the same ancient constitution for the same purpose, turning against parliament the legal theory that had made parliament supreme over the crown. With

15. Bernard Bailyn, *The Ideological Origins of the American Revolution* (Cambridge, Mass., 1967), 80 (quoting James Otis).

16. William Blackstone, *Commentaries on the Laws of England. Book the Second* (Oxford, 1766), 52.

17. John Cartwright, *The English Constitution Produced and Illustrated* (London, 1823), 207.

18. *London Journal,* no. 696, October 28, 1732, p. 1, col. 2.

reluctance they had concluded that parliament rather than the monarchy had become the potential institution for arbitrariness in imperial government.[19] "Our most ardent Desire," the freeholders of Virginia's Hanover County told their representatives in 1774, "is, that we and your latest Posterity may continue to live under the genuine unaltered Constitution of England."[20] They meant the same timeless constitution to which Sir Edward Coke had turned in 1628 and on which parliamentary lawyers had relied in 1641. As another Virginian, Richard Bland, had explained just eight years before, it was "a Fact, as certain as History can make it, that the present civil Constitution of *England* derives its Original from those *Saxons* who, coming over to the Assistance of the *Britons* . . . made themselves Masters of the Kingdom, and established a Form of Government in it similar to that they had been accustomed to live under in their native Country."[21]

But what was the ancient constitution in the eighteenth century? There may be no better discussion than that of the *Craftsman,* the newspaper promoting the politics of viscount Bolingbroke. "From the earliest accounts of time," the *Craftsman* explained, "our ancestors in Germany were a free people, and had a right to assent or dissent to all laws; that right was exercised and preserved under the Saxon and Norman Kings, even to our days."[22] The Saxons, before they had invaded Britannia, had been a free people, living under a constitution of liberty.

When They were settled, according to their Liking, They form'd a Government upon the same Model; That is, their *Leader,* or *General,* was appointed the *chief Magistrate,* though with much less Power

19. John Phillip Reid, "In Legitimate Stirps: The Concept of 'Arbitrary,' the Supremacy of Parliament, and the Coming of the American Revolution," *Hofstra Law Review* 5 (Spring 1977): 459–99.

20. Address of a Meeting of Freeholders of Hanover County to John Syme and Patrick Henry, July 20, 1774, *Revolutionary Virginia: The Road to Independence—Volume I: Forming Thunderclouds and the First Convention, 1763–1774: A Documentary Record,* comp. William J. Van Schreeven, ed. Robert L. Scribner ([Charlottesville], 1973), 140.

21. Richard Bland, *An Inquiry* (1766), reprinted in ibid., 30–31.

22. *Craftsman,* no. 470, July 5, 1735, quoted in Isaac Kramnick, *Bolingbroke and His Circle: The Politics of Nostalgia in the Age of Walpole* (Cambridge, Mass., 1968), 179.

than our *modern Kings;* the *other great Men,* or *Officers of the Army,* held the next Rank in the Commonwealth, like our *Lords;* and the *Body of the People,* who follow'd Them, had a third Share in the Government. These *three Orders* composed what is now called the *Legislature.* . . . This is what We mean by our *ancient Constitution;* and though it hath been often interrupted, or depress'd, by Conquest, Usurpation, and arbitrary Power, the *Stamina* of it have been still preserved, and transmitted down to us thro' all Ages and Changes of Government.[23]

The eighteenth-century ancient constitution bestowed on the fortunate Britons a tenacious spirit of liberty, a spirit molded in the German forests and toughened during Tudor and Stuart constitutional battles, "[a] Spirit of *Liberty*" which, "transmitted down from our *Saxon Ancestors,* and the unknown Ages of our Government, preserved itself through one almost continual Struggle, against the Usurpations of our *Princes,* and the Vices of our *People.*"[24]

Though it must be confess'd that our *old Saxon Constitution* hath undergone many violent Convulsions, since the *Conquest,* I think the whole Series of our History, as far as We can discover it through the Gloom of Antiquity, is one continued Proof that the Foundations of it were never intirely overturn'd; and though various Alterations have been made in the *Form of our Parliaments,* the *Essentials* have been preserved, and the *People* were never totally deprived of their Share in *those Assemblies.*[25]

I. THE LEGAL PERSPECTIVE

Of the contrasting points of view from which we can study the history of liberty, perhaps the one that is overlooked more than any other is the legal perspective. The "ideology of the Ancient Constitution," the premier historian of the ancient constitution has contended, was an "elaborate set of historical arguments by which it was sought to show that the common law, and the constitution as it now stood,

23. *Craftsman* 12, no. 405 (April 6, 1734): 182.
24. *Craftsman* 12, no. 394 (January 19, 1733): 94–95.
25. *Craftsman* 14, no. 467 (June 14, 1735): 20.

had been essentially the same since pre-Conquest times and—if the argument were pressed home—since time immemorial, or at least since an unrecorded beginning in the woods of Germany."[26] One need not quarrel with that conclusion to suggest that another dimension can be added. If we find the ancient constitution a puzzle of historiography because the concept of a timeless, never-changing rule of law seems ahistorical, it may be that we are thinking about historical methodology when it would be more helpful to think about forensic argument.

During the seventeenth and eighteenth centuries, in the American colonies[27] as well as in England and Great Britain, the ancient constitution generally was argued by lawyers and, if not by lawyers, by others more concerned with lawyerly questions than with history qua history. "Every Englishman who thought about the constitution," one historian has explained, "thought it in some degree as a lawyer, and Coke's doctrines merely stated with the force of genius the lawyer's view of history."[28] Our question may well be whether there was a lawyer's view of history. Perhaps it was not the view or theory of history but the use— the lawyer's use of history, or forensic history—that was what gave the ancient constitution significance. After all,

> [t]he doctrine of the ancient constitution . . . was the work of common lawyers, and seems to have been shaped throughout by assumptions concerning the common law of England, deeply implanted in the mind of everyone trained in that study. These assumptions were first, that all the law in England might properly be termed common law; second, that common law was common custom, originating in the usages of the people and declared, interpreted and applied in the courts; third, that all custom was by definition immemorial, that which had been usage and law since time out of mind, so that any

26. J. G. A. Pocock, *Virtue, Commerce, and History: Essays on Political Thought and History, Chiefly in the Eighteenth Century* (New York, 1985), 94.

27. J. G. A. Pocock, *Politics, Language and Time: Essays on Political Thought and History* (New York, 1971), 229.

28. J. G. A. Pocock, "Robert Brady, 1627–1700: A Cambridge Historian of the Restoration," *Cambridge Historical Journal* 10 (1951): 190.

declaration of law . . . was a declaration that its content had been usage since time immemorial.[29]

Although as long ago as the 1640s Sir Roger Twysden pointed out that the historian's law is different from the lawyer's law and, therefore, their history is different,[30] there has been a tendency for us to evaluate forensic history by the canons of the historical method. The common lawyer's view of the past when arguing premises based on the ancient constitution and immemorial law has been described by phrases such as "incorrect,"[31] "not always very accurate,"[32] "pseudo-historical litera-ture,"[33] "propaganda,"[34] and, most frequently, "ahistorical myth"[35] or "mythology."[36] It is not necessary to dwell on these comments. What

29. Pocock, *Politics, Language and Time* (cited note 27), 209. See also Bailyn, *Ideological Origins* (cited note 15), 33; Brian P. Levack, *The Civil Lawyers in England, 1603–1641* (Oxford, 1973), 146; F. Smith Fussner, *The Historical Revolution: English Historical Writing and Thought, 1580–1640* (London, 1962), 318.

30. Sir Roger Twysden, *Certaine Considerations upon the Government of England*, ed. John Mitchell Kemble (London, 1849), 45:23.

31. Stephen A. Siegel, "The Aristotelian Basis of English Law," *New York University Law Review* 56 (1981): 57.

32. Christopher Hill, *Intellectual Origins of the English Revolution* (Oxford, 1965), 178.

33. Isaac Kramnick, "Augustan Politics and English Historiography: The Debate on the English Past, 1730–35," *History and Theory* 6 (1967): 37 (quoting David C. Douglas).

34. Douglass Adair, *Fame and the Founding Fathers*, ed. Trevor Colbourn (New York, 1974), 62 n. 91; David C. Douglas, *English Scholars, 1660–1730*, 2d ed. (London, 1951), 119, 134; Christopher Hill, "The Norman Yoke," in Christopher Hill, *Puritanism and Revolution: Studies in Interpretation of the English Revolution of the 17th Century* (London, 1958), 91.

35. D. W. L. Earl, "Procrustean Feudalism: An Interpretative Dilemma in English Historical Narration, 1700–1725," *Historical Journal* 19 (1976): 33. For other references to "myth" see, J. G. A. Pocock, *The Ancient Constitution and the Feudal Law: A Study of English Historical Thought in the Seventeenth Century; a Reissue with a Retrospect* (Cambridge, England, 1987), 264 (see also 124–25); Pocock, *Politics, Language and Time* (cited note 27), 245; H. T. Dickinson, *Liberty and Property: Political Ideology in Eighteenth-Century Britain* (London, 1977), 141; Fussner, *Historical Revolution* (cited note 29), 28, 31–32; Kramnick, "Augustan Politics" (cited note 33), 38.

36. J. C. Wilsher, "'Power Follows Property'—Social and Economic Interpre-

is important is to realize the extent to which scholars trained in the historical method have been critical of seventeenth- and eighteenth-century practitioners of forensic history. In order to appreciate the extent of the dichotomy between the approaches of the two professions, it is also worth noting that criticisms have not always been consistent. Among other charges that have been made against the practitioners of forensic history, it has been said that they misled "real" historians into accepting their history,[37] and did this even though the history they wrote was history that real historians knew was "bad" history;[38]

-----

tation in British Historical Writing in the Eighteenth and Early Nineteenth Centuries," *Journal of Social History* 16:3 (1983): 8; Donald R. Kelley, "A Rejoinder," *Past & Present* 72 (1976): 145; Peter Laslett, "Book Review," *History* 43 (1958): 143. Recently, even lawyers, who should know better, have called the ancient constitution, or forensic history invoking the Saxon past, a myth. David A. J. Richards, "Interpretation and Historiography," *Southern California Law Review* 58 (1985): 500, 503–4; Thomas C. Grey, "Origins of the Unwritten Constitution: Fundamental Law in American Revolutionary Thought," *Stanford Law Review* 30 (1978): 852, 870.

37. It is said that Butterfield learned that "what he had called whig history was really lawyers' history, justifiably practised by them when thinking about the law in which the latest meaning of an event is the only meaning to matter, and in which new opinion abolishes its predecessor—neither of which is true in historians' history. To a lawyer the doings of the past signify only inasmuch as they persist into and have life in the present. All very fine for them, but this teleological preoccupation, which ruins genuine history, they had imposed on the historians. What Butterfield had been attacking, though it took him some time to find it out, was the readiness with which from the seventeenth century onward historians had accepted the lawyers' interpretation of the history of law, government and constitution" (G. R. Elton, "Herbert Butterfield and the Study of History," *Historical Journal* 27 [1984]: 734–35). See also Donald R. Kelley, "History, English Law and the Renaissance," *Past & Present* 65 (1974): 25; Laslett, "Book Review" (cited note 36), 143; Johann P. Sommerville, "History and Theory: The Norman Conquest in Early Stuart Political Thought," *Political Studies* 34 (1986): 250. "Writers who support the opinions of Edward Coke 'popularized' the theme in such a tendentious manner that it became almost impossible to undertake a study of the Norman Conquest in a proper spirit of historical inquiry" (Douglas, *English Scholars* [cited note 34], 120).

38. Philip Styles, "Politics and Historical Research in the Early Seventeenth Century," in *English Historical Scholarship in the Sixteenth and Seventeenth Centuries,* ed. Levi Fox (Oxford, 1956), 62.

that they "played havoc with history,"[39] perhaps unconsciously,[40] yet did not heed the lessons of historians;[41] that they lacked training in correct history,[42] even though what they wrote, forensic history, was the history they were trained to write.[43]

Unless we are willing to dismiss as "unscholarly" the theories, writings, and values of most seventeenth- and eighteenth-century constitutionalists, it does seem that the use and abuse of the concept of the ancient constitution deserves to be considered from the perspective of those who used and abused it, and not just by the canons of the historical method as practiced by twentieth-century historians.[44] We should stop and ask ourselves what it is that we learn when we are told that by using the term *ancient constitution* Sir William Blackstone was "apparently locating himself within one of the major currents in seventeenth-century historical thought."[45] Blackstone was concerned with *legal*

39. Robert Livingston Schuyler, *Parliament and the British Empire: Some Constitutional Controversies Concerning Imperial Legislative Jurisdiction* (New York, 1929), 3.

40. Harold Hulme, "Charles I and the Constitution," in *Conflict in Stuart England: Essays in Honor of Wallace Notestein,* ed. William Appleton Aiken and Basil Duke Henning ([Hamden, Conn.], 1970), 114.

41. Herbert Butterfield, *George III, Lord North, and the People, 1779–80* (London, 1949), 347.

42. Kelley, "Rejoinder" (cited note 36), 143.

43. Douglas, *English Scholars* (cited note 34), 130; David C. Douglas, *The Norman Conquest and British Historians* (Glasgow, 1946), 5; Forrest McDonald, *Novus Ordo Seclorum: The Intellectual Origins of the Constitution* (Lawrence, Kans., 1985), 11. "Lawyers had played a large part in eroding the foundations of the throne, especially through a fundamental misreading, authoritative in tone, of the history of the common law by men like Coke and Selden (a misreading that was to skew the thinking of Thomas Jefferson and other, lesser men for a long time)" (Robert B. Kirtland, "Keep Your Eye on the Bastards! Or Sobering Reflections on the 150-Year Record of Early Virginia's Attitude Toward Lawyers," *Toledo Law Review* 14 [1983]: 691).

44. It is said that "[t]hroughout the seventeenth and eighteenth centuries, every major piece of either historical or political thinking involved, if it did not consist in, the adoption of an attitude towards the 'ancient constitution'" (J. G. A. Pocock, "The Origins of Study of the Past: A Comparative Approach," *Comparative Studies in Society and History* 4 [1962]: 233).

45. Robert Willman, "Blackstone and the 'Theoretical Perfection' of English Law in the Reign of Charles II," *Historical Journal* 26 (1983): 42.

thought, not historical thought or its "currents." Our perspective of judgment should be Blackstone's, not that of some discipline he was not practicing; nor should we hold him to a standard that he would not have thought relevant had it been explained to him. It does not do to measure usefulness by the historical alone, to say that the "juridical nationalism" of Fortescue and Coke may have been "useful . . . for the rights and privileges of the propertied classes," but "was a serious impediment to any kind of historical understanding."[46] The question should not be whether juridical nationalism was good history but why it was a concept that Fortescue and Coke believed useful, how they intended to utilize it, and whether it did serve or could have performed the role expected of it by its common law practitioners.

Perhaps we have gone too far down a road of professional separation. Is it possible that historians and lawyers can no longer understand one another because they are asking different questions based on different assumptions? It has been said, for example, that we should understand that "the so-called Brady controversy" was a "debate concerning the English legal past taking place during the last years of Charles II's reign."[47] Those who participated in the debate would have been more likely to say that it concerned the English legal *present* as it then existed during the last years of Charles II's reign. Then there is the contention that the common lawyer's way of looking at the past was "traditional" rather than "historical."[48] Admitting that it was not "historical," we might better understand what those lawyers were about if we probed a bit deeper and asked whether their way of looking at the past was more "forensic" than "traditional,"[49] or, if traditional, whether it was traditional within the dynamics of constitutional advocacy, with lawyers making arguments they thought would

46. Kelley, "History, English Law and the Renaissance" (cited note 37), 25.

47. J. G. A. Pocock, *The Myth of John Locke and the Obsession with Liberalism* (Los Angeles, 1980), 3.

48. Pocock, "Origins of Study" (cited note 44), 237.

49. "Many of the constitutional investigations undertaken at this time [1660–1730] were of ephemeral interest, being designed in the first instance to serve the needs of contemporary controversy, but many more although undertaken in the same spirit embodied the result of substantial research" (Douglas, *English Scholars* [cited note 34], 16).

win the case at bar, not explaining what they understood to be the best historical scholarship.

There is one other question to be asked and one further point of precise terminology to be raised. The question is: if seventeenth- and eighteenth-century students of the ancient constitution were not writing history, what were they doing? The answer usually given is politics. The ancient constitution, it is said, was "a political weapon."[50] That answer is certainly correct, but does it go deeply enough? In the context of a constitutional controversy, the adjective *political* may not be as accurate as we would wish.

In 1775 the British ministry, to free troops to fight in America, hired Hanoverian soldiers for garrison duty at Gibraltar and, perhaps, Ireland. A debate over whether the action was constitutional without parliamentary approval erupted in the House of Commons during which Edmund Burke complained that the attorney general, when defending the administration, "had ransacked history, statutes, and journals." Lord North replied by asking "whence the proofs and authorities of a point of law could be better drawn, than from history, statutes, and journals."[51] We would do well to mark North's choice of nouns. Unlike almost all our recent commentators on the ancient constitution, he did not say "point of politics," that is, he did not ask "whence the proofs and authority of a point of politics could be better drawn." To assert that *law* is a more accurate word than *politics* is not to contend that history, statutes, and journals could not be relevant to politics. They are, however, the essence of legal argumentation. That is one reason Lord North's word is more "accurate" than the language of those who use

50. J. G. A. Pocock, "The History of British Political Thought: The Creation of a Center," *Journal of British Studies* 24 (July 1985): 290. Similarly the debate over the origin of parliament has recently been described as "a perennial battleground for political factions seeking charter myths to legitimate their contemporary positions" (Wilsher, "Power Follows Property" [cited note 36], 9). See also Douglas, *English Scholars* (cited note 34), 120; Hill, "The Norman Yoke" (cited note 34), 63; Corinne Comstock Weston, "Legal Sovereignty in the Brady Controversy," *Historical Journal* 15 (1972): 412; Styles, "Politics and Research" (cited note 38), 61.

51. "Parliament," *Scots Magazine* 38 (1776): 15.

political to describe debates about the ancient constitution. However political they may have been, they were even more "legal" or "constitutional."

The distinction may strike some scholars as mere semantics, but we are concerned with the ancient constitution and, more significantly, with how the ancient constitution was used and argued. It was not argued, that is, as will, choice, decision, or policy. It was, rather, argued as precedent, analogy, principle, and forensic history. The ancient constitution in the eighteenth century was not a political program for the sovereign to implement but a constitutional apparatus of forensic advocacy to propagate anew traditional forms of restraint upon the current sovereign.

Nationality may make a difference as to how we see the distinction. A historian who is British could be less disposed than an American to recognize that something which is "constitutional" is not necessarily "political." Consider a Briton who is a historian of the eighteenth century and is writing of the Wilkes election controversy, of the laws discriminating against Catholics, or the unprecedented Stamp Act with which parliament attempted for the first time to tax a geographical group of British subjects none of whom elected representatives to the Commons. That historian might reasonably describe each of them equally as "political." An American historian, by contrast, might more readily think them constitutional if for no other reason than that under the American legal system they posed issues that would be referred to the courts for solution rather than settled in the legislature.

It may be, too, that the distinction is worth pursuing as it could help avoid confusions that have contributed to imprecise or inaccurate history writing. To think, that is, of arguments about the ancient constitution as "legal" or "constitutional" rather than "political" or "historical" should clarify what was said by focusing attention on the forensic reality rather than on the standards of historiography. By way of illustration consider the following paragraph from Sir John Fortescue's *De Laudibus:*

> The Realm of *England* was first inhabited by the *Britons,* afterwards it
> was ruled and civilized under the Government of the *Romans;* then

the *Britons* prevailed again; next, it was possessed by the *Saxons,* who changed the Name of *Briton* into *England.* After the *Saxons,* the *Danes* lorded it over us, and than the *Saxons* prevailed a second Time; at last, the *Normans* came in, whose Descendants obtain the Kingdom to this Day: And, during all that Time, wherein those several Nations and their Kings prevailed, *England* has nevertheless been constantly governed by the same Customs, as it is at present.[52]

Thinking of this statement in terms of history or, perhaps, politics rather than as law, a recent commentator expressed surprise "that Fortescue should have taken this abstract and unhistorical view of law since later on he relates the growth of the English jury system, with remarkable penetration, to the social structure of the country."[53] It may be, rather, that Fortescue is less surprising than consistent. From the perspective of legalism he was, in both instances, on the "liberty" side of constitutionalism against power. By arguing that the ancient constitution remained the same through the invasions of the Romans, Saxons, Danes, and Normans, he was saying that constitutional law—not just in those ancient times but in his own day—was based on the authority of custom and the rule of law and, by implication (although this is an issue for a later period), that it was not the command of a sovereign. By delineating how the constitution had changed to permit the growth of the jury he was supporting the same constitutionalism. Common lawyers thought of the jury as they did the ancient constitution—a timeless, changeless, immemorial protector of liberty. Of course they knew that the jury's function as judge of proof was constantly changing, not only in how it determined facts, but by its encroachment upon other methods of proof through the expansion of writs such as *trespass.* Between the sixteenth and the eighteenth centuries the English and American people as well as the common law bar would come to cherish the jury as their chief institutional defense against arbitrary state prosecution.[54] To evaluate Fortescue's argument as history leads to the conclusion "that Fortescue retained an essentially static view of

---

52. Sir John Fortescue, *De Laudibus Legum Angliae* (London, 1775), 45–47.

53. Styles, "Politics and Research" (cited note 38), 55.

54. John Phillip Reid, *Constitutional History of the American Revolution: The Authority of Rights* (Madison, Wisc., 1986), 47–59.

society."[55] To think of it as constitutional law, however, could lead to the conclusion that Fortescue, like Coke, Selden, and John Adams, espoused a dynamic interpretation of law in which the ancient constitution was an analogy, or precedent, or body of fundamental principles that could be cited to resist and repel whatever new guise arbitrary power might assume.

II. THE ADVOCACY OF LAWYERS

That last conclusion goes against the accepted grain. There is an idea currently rife among scholars that the ancient constitution was not a dynamic device spurring the growth of liberty, but a static shield for preserving the status quo. If this is a misunderstanding, the cause may again be vocabulary. It is a fact, we are told, "that the common lawyers, holding that law was custom, came to believe that the common law, and with it the constitution, had always been exactly what they were now, that they were immemorial."[56] Perhaps the terminology of common lawyers has been taken too literally. At least it does seem that some scholars have given undue weight to the word *immemorial*. The implication has been that lawyers, even as late as Blackstone, should have known better than to have used it.[57] Again it may be that we are

55. Arthur B. Ferguson, "Fortescue and the Renaissance: A Study in Transition," *Studies in the Renaissance* 6 (1959): 189.

56. J. G. A. Pocock, *The Ancient Constitution and the Feudal Law: A Study of English Historical Thought in the Seventeenth Century* (Cambridge, England, 1957), 36. "All the common-lawyers right through the [eighteenth] century . . . believed that the constitution they were so proud of was literally so old as to be without origins: 'immemorial' in the legal sense became eternal in the chronological sense" (Laslett, "Book Review" [cited note 36], 143). See also Pocock, *Politics, Language and Time* (cited note 27), 213; Earl, "Procrustean Feudalism" (cited note 35), 36; Styles, "Politics and Research" (cited note 38), 49–72; Dickinson, *Liberty and Property* (cited note 35), 63.

57. Willman, "Blackstone and 'Theoretical Perfection'" (cited note 45), 42. And for the seventeenth century: "[A] number of practising English lawyers in the period (such as Lord Ellesmere) were perfectly capable of contemplating historical change in the English law, and in a way the real puzzle is why men like Edward Coke did not do so" (Richard Tuck, *Natural Rights Theories: Their Origin and Development* [New York, 1979], 83). See also Pocock, *Ancient Constitution Retrospect* (cited note 35), 273–74.

not asking the most useful question, not why a lawyer like Blackstone was untutored about historical dynamics, but why he ignored what he undoubtedly knew.[58]

Of course common lawyers,[59] even Coke,[60] and certainly constitutionalists arguing in the eighteenth century,[61] knew that changes had occurred in the "immemorial" law throughout Saxon, Norman, English, and British history. There were, to be sure, some writers who seemed to say that the ancient constitution had been unchanged down through the centuries,[62] just as there were others who scorned the en-

---

58. "The ancient feudal constitution contained the origins of English liberties and also of the mechanisms by which, in Montesquieu's analysis, those liberties had been preserved. Properly understood, it was a rational structure which made sense in terms of modern political science. Blackstone appears to be the first writer to have attempted a historical account of the English constitution based upon such a synthesis of Spelman, Hale, and Montesquieu; the result, while not entirely convincing, is a major improvement on what had gone before" (Willman, "Blackstone and 'Theoretical Perfection'" [cited note 45], 44).

59. Kevin Sharpe, *Sir Robert Cotton, 1586–1631: History and Politics in Early Modern England* (Oxford, 1979), 23, 224–25; R. J. Schoeck, "The Elizabethan Society of Antiquaries and Men of Law," *Notes and Queries* 199 (1954): 421.

60. David Yale, "Hobbes and Hale on Law, Legislation and the Sovereign," *Cambridge Law Journal* 31 (1972): 128. See also Kelley, "History, English Law and the Renaissance" (cited note 37), 65, 24ff.

61. [Charles Leslie], *The Constitution, Laws and Government of England, Vindicated in a Letter to the Reverend Mr. William Higden. . . . By a Natural Born Subject* (London, 1709); Anonymous, *The Detector Detected: or, the Danger to which our Constitution now lies Exposed, set in a True and manifest Light* (London, 1743), 7; [John Campbell], *Liberty and Right: Or, an Essay, Historical and Political, on the Constitution and Administration of Great Britain. Part I* (London, 1747), 25; George St. Amand, *An Historical Essay on the Legislative Power of England. Wherein the Origin of Both Houses of Parliament, their Antient Constitution . . . are related in a Chronological Order* (London, 1725), preface (n.p.); Anonymous, *A View of the Internal Policy of Great Britain* (London, 1764), 11–13; [Adam Ferguson], *Remarks on a Pamphlet Lately Published by Dr. Price, Intitled, Observations on the Nature of Civil Liberty, the Principles of Government, and the Justice and Policy of the War with America, &c. in a Letter from a Gentleman in the Country to a Member of Parliament* (London, 1776), 40.

62. [Allan Ramsay], *An Historical Essay on the English Constitution: Or, An impartial Inquiry into the Elective Power of the People, from the first Establishment of the Saxons in this Kingdom. Wherein the Right of Parliament, to Tax our distant Provinces, is explained,*

tire notion of an ancient constitution.[63] But there is little evidence from either side of the Atlantic that members of the bar in general did not appreciate that today's ancient constitution incorporated yesterday's innovations or that today's statutes could become tomorrow's ancient constitution.[64] To acknowledge time, transmission, and change, however, did not require eighteenth-century constitutionalists to abandon the ancient constitution or the concept of immemorial law. Certainly John Fortescue-Aland did not think so when he wrote the preface to a 1714 edition of *De Laudibus*.

> Thus, Sir, we find the Stream of the Laws of *Edward* the Confessor, flowing from a *Saxon* Fountain, and containing the Substance of our present Laws and Liberties, sometimes running freely, sometimes weakly, and sometimes stopped in its Course; but at last, breaking thro' all Obstructions, both mixed and incorporated it self, with the great Charter of our *English* Liberties, whose true Source the *Saxon* Laws are, and are still in being, and still the Fountain of the Common Law. Therefore it was a very just Observation of my Lord *Coke*, who says, that *Magna Charta*, was but a Confirmation, or Restitution of the Common Law of *England;* so the Common Law really is an Extract of the very best of the Laws of the *Saxons*.[65]

---

and justified, upon such constitutional Principles as will afford an equal Security to the Colonists, as to their Brethren at Home (London, 1771), 12–13.

63. William Paley, *The Principles of Moral and Political Philosophy* (London, 1785), 465–66; George Savile, marquis of Halifax, *A Character of King Charles the Second: And Political, Moral and Miscellaneous Thoughts and Reflections* (London, 1750), 68.

64. As John Toland wrote in 1717. J. P. Kenyon, *Revolution Principles: The Politics of Party, 1689–1720* (Cambridge, England, 1977), 197–98. Toland was not a lawyer. For lawyers, both common and Scots, see Francis Plowden, *Jura Anglorum: The Rights of Englishmen* (Dublin, 1792), 129; John Millar, *Observations Concerning the Distinction of Ranks in Society,* 2d ed. (London, 1773), 228–50; George Canning, *A Letter to the Right Honourable Wills Earl of Hillsborough, on the Connection Between Great Britain and her American Colonies* (Dublin, 1768), 24–25; Speech of Lord Mansfield, Lords Debates, February 3, 1766, in John Holliday, *The Life of William Late Earl of Mansfield* (London, 1797), 242–43.

65. John Fortescue-Aland, "Dedication and Preface" to *The Difference Between an Absolute and Limited Monarchy; As it more particularly regards the English Constitution. Being a Treatise written by Sir John Fortescue, Kt. Lord Chief Justice, and Lord High*

Surely we have here a clue of how the eighteenth century conceptualized the ancient constitution: the common law was the "best" of Saxon laws. Not all Saxon laws were incorporated in the current constitution, only those laws that were the "best" had survived. The best laws of the Saxons surviving in the immemorial ancient constitution were laws that in the eighteenth century were identified with "liberty." Liberty was the connecting link across the centuries. It may be that the elements of liberty in Saxon times were the same as the elements of liberty in the eighteenth century. It is, to be sure, more likely that eighteenth-century Britain projected its own liberty concepts back to Anglo-Saxon England and what it looked for it found. Had the question been put to most eighteenth-century common lawyers they would have said that the answer was immaterial. Retention of liberty, viscount Bolingbroke explained, was reason enough for Britons to cling to the mystique of the ancient constitution.

> [O]ur *Constitution* is a System of Government suited to the Genius of our Nation, and even to our Situation. The Experience of many hundred Years hath shewn that by preserving *this Constitution* inviolate, or by drawing it back to the Principles, on which it was originally founded, whenever it shall be made to swerve from them, We may secure to ourselves, and to our latest Posterity, the Possession of that *Liberty,* which We have long enjoy'd. What would We more? What *other Liberty* than This do we seek? And if We seek no other, is not This mark'd out in such Characters as He, that runs, may read? As our *Constitution* therefore ought to be, what it seldom is, the *Rule of Government;* so let us make the Conformity, or Repugnacy of Things to *this Constitution* the Rule, by which We accept them as favourable, or reject them as dangerous to *Liberty.* They, who talk of *Liberty* in *Britain* on any other Principles than Those of the *British Constitution,*

Chancellor of England, under King Henry VI. Faithfully Transcribed from the MS. Copy in the Bodleian Library, and Collated with three other MSS. (London, 1714), xxviii–xxix. See also [James Erskine, Lord Grange], *The Late Excise Scheme Dissected: Or, an Exact Copy of the Late Bill, for Repealing several Subsidies, and an Impost, Now Payable on Tobacco, etc.* (London, 1734), 7. For a recent discussion see Paul Lucas, "On Edmund Burke's Doctrine of Prescription; Or, an Appeal from the New to the Old Lawyers," *Historical Journal* 11 (1968): 56.

talk impertinently at best, and much Charity is requisite to believe no worse of Them.[66]

Bolingbroke's perspective was not unique. During the very last year of the eighteenth century, John Reeves, judge, law writer, legal historian, and political reactionary, was still explaining why the substance of the ancient constitution remained the same even while its premises were constantly changing. Like Bolingbroke, Reeves's measure of continuity was liberty.

> That our Constitution is not precisely the same that it was in the Reign of Ja[mes] I. I am the last man to deny; because it is one of the strongest persuasions I have, about its excellence, that it is capable of, and is continually receiving, improvements, either by the accession of new benefits, or by the attainment of new securities to protect original rights. Many of these have accrued since the time of James I. There was the Petition of Right, which rather secured old Rights than gave new ones; the abolition of the star Chamber was a new benefit; the Habeas Corpus Act was a new benefit; the Bill of Rights was rather a new security to old Rights, except in the circumstance of a protestant King. . . . All these, without enumerating others, were improvements in the Constitution, and nothing can be clearer, than that the Constitution is not now, in all its circumstances, though it is in substance, and in principle, the same that it was heretofore.[67]

That substance was both immemorial and current. It was immemorial because the constitution always supported liberty against arbitrariness, a task requiring only a few general principles, not a detailed code.[68] It was current because the liberty preserved was forever up-to-date.

This notion of immemoriality may not be so easily explained away

66. [Henry Saint John, viscount Bolingbroke], *A Dissertation Upon Parties: In Several Letters to Caleb D'Anvers, Esq.*, 2d ed. (London, 1735), 147–48.

67. [John Reeves], *Thoughts on the English Government. Addressed to the Quiet Good Sense of the People of England. In a Series of Letters. Letter the Second* (London, 1799), 65–66.

68. "[E]ven Coke . . . was far from being the blind idiot that some historians of ideas have tried to make him. In the end, his immemorial law boils down to general principles and maxims, while he knew that the positive law itself was

as Reeves would have thought. It seems to have meant one thing to
eighteenth-century lawyers and quite another to twentieth-century historians of ancient constitutionalism. The lawyers may have been largely
to blame for any misunderstandings. They may not have expressed
themselves as clearly as twentieth-century scholarship expects. In line
with their professional training, eighteenth-century lawyers tended
to explain their understanding of the ancient constitution in lawyer's
terms, suitable perhaps for addressing other lawyers but containing
the seeds of misunderstanding when interpreted from the perspective
of another discipline. An example is analogy, a way of reasoning that
those who do not use it may not look for when seeking understanding. Because analogy was a common lawyer's way of reasoning about
law, analogies drawn to the ancient constitution deserve our attention.
Come now four instances of the technique that, although agreeing
in substance, used different analogies to make the same point. The
first was argued by the magistrate and novelist Henry Fielding. It was
wrong, he contended, to think of "something uniform and permanent,
as if the Constitution of *England* partook rather of the Nature of the
Soil than of the Climate, and was as fixed and constant as the former,
not as changing and variable as the latter."[69] The second was written
by the great Restoration jurist Sir Matthew Hale. He thought the argonauts' ship an analogy more apt than soil and climate.

> So that Use and Custom, and Judicial Decisions and Resolutions,
> and Acts of Parliament, tho' not now extant, might introduce some
> *New* Laws, and alter some *Old,* which we now take to be the very
> Common Law itself. . . . But tho' those particular Variations and
> Accessions have happened in the Laws, yet they being only partial
> and successive, we may with just Reason say, they are the same En-
> glish Laws now, that they were 600 Years since in the general. As the
> Argonauts Ship was the same when it returned home, as it was when
> it went out, tho' in that long Voyage it had successive Amendments,
> and scarce came back with any of its former Materials; and as Titius

capable of change and development" (G. R. Elton, "Review Essay," *History and
Theory* 20 [1981]: 97).

69. Henry Fielding, *An Enquiry into the Causes of the late Increase of Robbers, &c.
With some Proposals for Remedying this Growing Evil* (London, 1751), v.

is the same Man he was 40 Years since, tho' Physicians tell us, That in a Tract of seven Years, the Body has scarce any of the same Material Substance it had before.[70]

In 1725, the analogy of language occurred to George St. Amand of the Inner Temple:

> It may seem an extravagant Position to say, that the present Constitution of our Legislature is built on the same Principles, and has undergone no other Change than what the Alterations of Time have wrought in our Circumstances, made necessary to preserve its Fundamentals; as that in old *Germany* was, if not from the first planting of that Country, at least from the first accounts we have of it, which are sixteen hundred Years old: but as to this, the Constitution may be compar'd with our Language, the present Dialect being so widely different from what it was so many Ages since, 'tis scarce credible that it has receiv'd no other Changes but what such a Length of Time necessarily works in all: And yet, whoever will, gradually ascending, read Books of every Age to the oldest of our *Saxon* Monuments, will not be sensible of the Change. So fares it as to the Constitution in general . . . when the Times and Causes of the several Changes that have happen'd in it, come to be ranged in due Order . . . all appears . . . easy, coherent, and natural.[71]

The final example is an analogy later repeated and made famous by Blackstone—a building. "[I]f the Foundations, the main Pillars, and Corner Stones of this ancient, noble Building are still standing," Fortescue-Aland contended, "tho' it should happen to be fitted up and adorn'd with other Materials now, yet it will bear the Name of the old Fabrick, and properly be accounted the same Identical Building."[72]

The evidence to be developed here is that for lawyers of the seven-

---

70. Matthew Hale, *The History of the Common Law of England,* ed. Charles M. Gray (Chicago, 1971), 40. Selden also wrote of the ancient constitution as an often repaired ship retaining its shape while refitted with new materials. Paul Christianson, "Young John Selden and the Ancient Constitution, ca. 1610–18," *Proceedings of the American Philosophical Society* 128 (1984): 307. For Hale and history see Yale, "Hobbes and Hale" (cited note 60), 127.

71. St. Amand, *Historical Essay* (cited note 61), preface.

72. Fortescue-Aland, "Dedication and Preface" (cited note 65), xiii–xiv.

teenth and eighteenth centuries the ancient constitution was not so much the legal substance of the case being argued and defended as it was an argumentative model of what the English and British constitution in fact was. They used the ancient constitution not to prove something concerning history, but to strengthen the vision they were promoting of current liberty and civil rights. The law they taught was not law locked in a changeless time but immemorial law constantly reaffirmed both by usage and by redefinition.

The last point may be illustrated by considering the arguments of two English barristers who wrote during the period of the American Revolution. Referring to the Saxons as "the persons who formed the embryo of our constitution,"[73] Edward King of Lincoln's Inn summed up the subsequent history of the Saxon constitution as a history of changes that were, from the perspective of liberty, "improvements."

> When I say this, however, I mean not to reflect on times past; as if a tolerable form of government never prevailed 'till these our days: nor to insinuate that the present constitution is so totally different from what was heretofore established, as to be quite void of any support from precedent and prescription. I am persuaded, on the contrary, that the ancient constitution during different periods was *such* as we may reasonably suppose to have been most fit and expedient for the nation at those times; and also *such,* that it is an easy matter to shew how the present form of government regularly, lawfully, and even necessarily, arose from it.[74]

It did so "lawfully" because the ancient constitution was a program for liberty, and as the nation progressed to improvements in liberty it was guided by the law of the ancient constitution. Or, as Edward Wynne said two decades later, "Freedom was always of its very essence; but its freedom has been improved."[75]

73. Edward King, *An Essay on the English Constitution and Government* (London, 1767), 33.

74. "Book Review," *The Critical Review: Or Annals of Literature by a Society of Gentlemen* 22 (1766): 363 (quoting Edward King).

75. Edward Wynne, *Eunomus: or, Dialogues Concerning the Law and Constitution of England. With an Essay on Dialogue,* 2d ed. (London, 1785), 3:327. See also Josiah Tucker, *A Letter to Edmund Burke, Esq; Member of Parliament for the City of Bristol, and*

Richard Wooddeson used a somewhat different measure of "progress" than King when he wrote of "advances towards restoring the pristine laws and constitution" of the Anglo-Saxons.[76] "[T]he English constitution," Wooddeson contended, had "immemorially been in substance much the same" as in 1777, when he first lectured students as Oxford's third Vinerian law professor. Although insisting that the immemorial constitution "remains a venerable fabric, which has well withstood the decays of time, and the ravages of faction," Wooddeson did not mean that it had been unchanged. "[T]he English constitution has immemorially been in substance much the same, or has at least borne a strong resemblance to the present system," he explained,[77] in part because all changes had been by consent of the people, implied by the acceptance of custom. "[C]hanges are gradually and imperceptibly introduced, which, deriving a sanction from time and universal acquiescence, are matured into fundamental laws, or principles of the constitution. . . . Since history and reason alike teach us, that the finished fabric of a well-ordered constitution is to be the work of succeeding generations, and gradually to be improved by progressive experience."[78]

That the Vinerian professor put such stress on a progressive immemorial sameness suggests that the ancient constitution played a larger role in the eighteenth century than has been realized. We might better appreciate that role if our adherence to the canons of the historical method did not make it so difficult for us to take seriously the concept of evolving permanence or to accept the possibility that those who could conceive of a timeless constitution did not have to mean a changeless constitution. Timeless change need not imply changeless

Agent for the Colony of New York, &c. In Answer to His Printed Speech, Said to be Spoken in the House of Commons on the Twenty-Second of March, 1775, 2d ed. (Glocester, England, 1775), 31–32; Anonymous, *A Letter to Doctor Tucker on his Proposal of a Separation Between Great Britain and her American Colonies* (London, 1774), 7; King, *Essay* (cited note 73), 3; Lowth, *A Sermon Preached* (cited note 14), 8.

76. Richard Wooddeson, *Elements of Jurisprudence Treated of in the Preliminary Part of a Course of Lectures on the Laws of England* (Dublin, 1792), 143.

77. Richard Wooddeson, *A Systematical View of the Laws of England; as Treated of in a Course of Vinerian Lectures, Read at Oxford, During a Series of Years, Commencing in Michaelmas Term, 1777* (Dublin, 1792), 1:28.

78. Wooddeson, *Elements of Jurisprudence* (cited note 76), 70.

time. The notion of adaption within the immemorial ancient constitution does not have to be accepted, but it deserves serious attention as a cue to seventeenth- and eighteenth-century constitutional thought. Changing immemoriality was not the eccentric fantasy of lawyers and law professors such as Wooddeson. The thesis of an ever altering timeless law was articulated by many other people besides barristers in the eighteenth century. Samuel Squire, a bishop of the established church, stated the general understanding when he explained why the ancient constitution could add improvements while remaining unchanged. It was that the ancient constitution had always been a constitution of freedom and that the liberty of the Saxons was the liberty of eighteenth-century Great Britain.

> Our ancestors were born free, lived under a free government in their first settlements, brought freedom with them into Britain, and handed it down to us inviolate, at the expence of all that was near and dear to them, their lives and fortunes. . . . Our present constitution cannot so truly be said to have been changed or altered, as improved and perfected by time. Where then was that hereditary indefeasible right of princes; where that omnipotent and uncontroulable power of kings, which men of slavish principles were wont to talk so much of? Our earliest forefathers knew nothing of it, we feel nothing of it at present.[79]

III. USES OF THE ANCIENT CONSTITUTION

The uses of the history of the ancient constitution during the eighteenth century were the uses of forensic history. In addition, ancient-constitution scholarship shared the uses to which most history was put in the eighteenth century. That century was a time when history was used to instruct by example, to instill moral lessons, and to educate the public about government, law, and society.[80] Gilbert

---

79. Samuel Squire, *An Enquiry into the Foundation of the English Constitution; or, An Historical Essay upon the Anglo-Saxon Government Both in Germany and England* (London, 1745), 81–82.

80. "History well wrote is the *easiest* and most *effectual* Teacher of *Moral* Science" (*London Journal*, no. 696, October 28, 1732, p. 1, col. 1). John Jay stated the theme at its simplest: "The history of Great Britain is the one with which we are

Stuart, a Scots advocate, used the ancient constitution to teach people about the then extant British constitution of 1768. To make his case, Stuart limited his evidence to the laws of prehistorical Germany and the laws of Anglo-Saxon England. "If," he explained, "I have made it appear, that the parts which compose our constitution arose more immediately from the forests of Germany, I have answered my intention."[81] John Reeves claimed that the ancient constitution had "written" its own lessons about *current* constitutional law—lessons of law not history. As proof, Reeves traced legal principles back to what he said were their origins. "I thought this the only true way of obtaining, what is called constitutional knowledge;—It was studying the Constitution in the History which itself had written for our Instruction—its own Acts delivered down to us, in its own language."[82]

Instruction for the sake of instruction was seldom enough. Usually the purpose was to get across a practical lesson, such as warning that the norms of the ancient constitution were no longer so well respected as they had been in some known or prehistoric past. Unless the young nobility and gentry "are instructed in what is our Original Constitution," Francis Gregor argued, "what are the Ancient Rights and Privileges thereof, they can never be able to defend it, as they ought, against those who make it their profest Business to cry it down."[83] Arthur Lee

---

in general the best acquainted, and it gives us many useful lessons" ("The Federalist No. 5," in *The Federalist*, ed. Jacob E. Cooke [Middletown, Conn., 1961], 24). See also T. Rutherforth, *Institutes of Natural Law Being the substance of a Course of Lectures on Grotius de Jure Belli et Pacis Read in S. Johns College Cambridge* (Cambridge, England, 1756), 2:110; Martyn P. Thompson, "The History of Fundamental Law in Political Thought from the French Wars of Religion to the American Revolution," *American Historical Review* 91 (1986): 1112.

81. Gilbert Stuart, *An Historical Dissertation Concerning the Antiquity of the English Constitution*, 2d ed. (London, 1770), 290.

82. [Reeves], *Thoughts on English Government* (cited note 67), 8–9.

83. Francis Gregor, "Preface" to Sir John Fortescue, *De Laudibus Legum Angliae*, new ed. (London, 1775), iv. "If Men would apply Themselves more than They generally do to the reading of antient [Roman] History, They would justly be alarm'd at our present Circumstances" (*Craftsman* 12, no. 413 [June 1, 1734]: 229). See also Thomas Herring, *A Sermon Preached before the House of Lords, in the Abbey-Church of Westminster, on Wednesday Jan. 30, 1739–40. Being the Day appointed to be observed as the Day of the Martyrdom of King Charles I* (London, 1740), 23.

cited more recent history when putting the history-as-warning technique to work for the American whig cause during the prerevolutionary controversy. The plan for the crown to pay salaries to colonial judges, Lee contended, alarmed American whigs more than any other grievance, because "[t]he political history of their parent country had taught them the evils their ancestors had experienced from the conduct of Judges so circumstanced."[84]

Another eighteenth-century use of history sometimes emulated by students of the ancient constitution was history-as-pride. In a history of the Gothic constitution, for example, Thomas Rymer surveyed countries such as France and Germany where the ancient constitution once had force and reached the satisfying conclusion that "[i]t is in *England* onely that the ancient, generous, manly Government of *Europe* survives, and continues in its original lustre and perfection."[85]

The most celebrated practitioners of ancient history during the eighteenth century were the American founding fathers. There is a general consensus that they argued "scientific" history at the Constitutional Convention expecting to uncover neutral principles and universal rules applicable to all nations and all ages to guide the future governance of the United States.[86] It is possible that the founding fathers

84. [Arthur Lee], *A Speech, intended to have been Delivered in the House of Commons, In Support of the Petition from the General Congress at Philadelphia* (London, 1775), 13.

85. [Thomas Rymer], *A Prospect of Government in Europe, and Civil Policy. Shewing the Antiquity, Power, Decay of Parliaments* (London, 1681), 66. A hundred years later a survey starting with 1264 concluded: "I have proved, that the constitution, through a series of years, has been arriving at that perfection which it attained at the revolution," ([Francis Basset, Baron Basset of Stratton], *Thoughts on Equal Representation* [London, 1783], 12).

86. "It can be shown, . . . that the use of history in the debates both in the Philadelphia Convention and in the state ratifying conventions is not mere rhetorical-historical window dressing, concealing substantially greedy motives of class and property. The speakers were making a genuinely 'scientific' attempt to discover the 'constant and universal principles' of any republican government in regard to liberty, justice, and stability" (Adair, *Fame and the Founding Fathers* [cited note 34], 97). See also Henry Steele Commager, *Jefferson, Nationalism, and the Enlightenment* (New York, 1975), 127, 144–45, 150, and "America and the Enlightenment," in *The Development of a Revolutionary Mentality* (Washington, D.C., 1972), 27.

at Philadelphia objectively used the science of history according to the historical method,[87] but the conclusion has been too easily assumed. The evidence should be reexamined by asking how the history used at the convention differed from the history of Sir Edward Coke.

There is a second doubt that should be raised. It concerns the assumption that, during the eighteenth century, history and law were related disciplines.[88] It is just not true that in colonial America "[t]o study law was to study its history."[89] History was only marginally necessary for a knowledge of law and not at all needed to practice law. It may have been true that to practice *constitutional* law was to argue forensic history, but that is the type of history historians of the ancient constitution disparage or say is not history. Nor is it correct to think that law led "directly to history,"[90] although again it could be claimed that *constitutional* law led directly to forensic history. The question is not so much how history was used as the nature and methodology of that history. When examined closely it will quite often turn out to involve evidence from the past selected to support an argument rather than an investigation of evidence of the type generally described as "scientific" history. That is, it is forensic history.

Forensic history has been given other names in recent years: "lawyer's history," "law-office history,"[91] and "magisterial historiography."[92] These terms are contumelious labels fastened by its critics onto the style of historical adjudication practiced by the United States Supreme

87. See discussion of James Madison's use of history in Adair, *Fame and the Founding Fathers* (cited note 34), 134ff.

88. "History was the main field of interest. If law is associated with history—and the colonists so regarded it—history emerges as the largest single category" of what was read by eighteenth-century Americans (H. Trevor Colbourn, *The Lamp of Experience: Whig History and the Intellectual Origins of the American Revolution* [Chapel Hill, N.C., 1965], 20).

89. Ibid., 25.

90. Ibid., 84. Somewhat similarly see 25.

91. "By 'law-office' history, I mean the selection of data favorable to the position being advanced without regard or concern for contradictory data or proper evaluation of the relevance of the data proffered" (Alfred H. Kelly, "Clio and the Court: An Illicit Love Affair," *Supreme Court Review* 1965 [1965]: 122 n. 13).

92. Dallin H. Oaks, "Legal History in the High Court—Habeas Corpus," *Michigan Law Review* 64 (1966): 451.

Court in the 1960s. The implications, however, are too negative and too narrowly confined to the historian's professional standards, judging as history a use of the past that is not history but advocacy. Forensic history or lawyer's history could as aptly be termed a form of historical utilitarianism and judged favorably by its adjudicatory aspects rather than unfavorably on its pseudo-historical trappings.

In the eighteenth century the uses of practical or purposeful history were much wider and more scholarly than the lawyer's history associated with brief writing or the historical adjudications of the Warren court. Its reach was often subtle, and one must look carefully or it can be mistaken for history written to explain the past. Sometimes it appears under the guise of the historical method, as in a 1732 London newspaper:

> A Faithful and Judicious History, or, a true Registry of the *Actions* of Men, and the Springs or *probable* Occasions which produced them, is of the greatest Use and Service to Mankind; for, it lays before us, not only our *Actions*, but the *Connection* of those Actions with our *Happiness* or *Misery*, and so is a kind of *visible* or *sensible* Morality; it teaches us by *Facts*, what Philosophers and venerable Sages teach us by *Reason*, with this Difference, That we *see* and *feel* in the One, what we only understand in the Other: We have *Sense* and *Experience* for our Guides, which generally conduct us safer to our Journey's End, than *cool* and *abstract* Reason.[93]

This writer respected history. He wanted, so he said, "Faithful and Judicious History." But he also wanted history to serve a practical purpose, to enlist in the struggle to prevent analytical rationalism from determining the course of eighteenth-century progress. The purpose should not be confused with John Dickinson's famous admonition to the Constitutional Convention. "Experience must be our guide. Reason may mislead us."[94] It is not just, as Dickinson would have it, that history may be a safer or more conservative guide than speculation.

93. *London Journal*, no. 696, October 28, 1732, p. 1, col. 1.
94. Quoted in John P. Roche, "The Convention as a Case Study in Democratic Politics," in *Essays on the Making of the Constitution*, ed. Leonard W. Levy, 2d ed. (New York, 1987), 180.

History should also be the weapon with which the instrumental fends off the analytical.

The distinction to be underlined is utility. The forensic historian, in contrast to the nonforensic historian, searches the past for material applicable to a current issue. The purpose of the advocate, unlike that of the historian, is to use the past for the elucidation of the present, to solve some contemporary problem or, most often, to carry an argument. It is the past put in the service of winning the case at bar.

During the sixteenth, seventeenth, and eighteenth centuries lawyers were not the only persons to put the past to work. It was often called on to support not only law and government but religion as well.[95] Indeed, it was the bishop of St. Davids who contended in 1745 that not just history in general but the ancient constitution in particular could legitimately be used to resolve contemporary political disputes.

> [T]he history of the civil constitution cannot be too carefully studied, or too minutely enquired into, especially in such a country as ours is, divided into parties, and where each party confidently appeals to the antient constitution of the kingdom for the truth of the opinions it maintains, and pretends to make that the measure of its political principles, by which alone it is ready to stand or fall. —Can it then be deemed an useless and an unnecessary undertaking to describe what this ancient constitution of our kingdom was by the incontestable evidence of history, and to delineate that primitive form of government thro' all its several branches, which our Anglo-Saxon ancestors first established in this island?[96]

There were many other pragmatic, political, and constitutional uses to which evidence from the past was put in the seventeenth and eighteenth centuries. It would serve no purpose to delineate them except to note that history was used to propose as well as oppose alterations in the constitution.[97] Of more immediate interest for the topic of this

95. Douglas, *English Scholars* (cited note 34), 19; Sharpe, *Sir Robert Cotton* (cited note 59), 104–5, 248; R. J. Smith, *The Gothic Bequest: Medieval Institutions in British Thought, 1688–1863* (Cambridge, England, 1987), 28–30, 56–57.

96. Squire, *Enquiry into the Foundation* (cited note 79), 3–4.

97. "It is always to be lamented when men are driven to search into the foun-

essay is the most frequent and most significant use that eighteenth-century lawyers and parliamentarians made of the past: to serve their concept of liberty. The past was used for liberty in two ways: to define not the historical but the current meaning of liberty and to defend the contemporary constitutional right to liberty.

As a general matter, Lord Hervey of Ickworth noted in 1734, when opponents of Robert Walpole complained of "the Loss *of Liberty*," they usually talked "of *the Liberty of Old England* in Comparison with, or Opposition to *That* now subsisting in this Country."[98] One of those opponents, viscount Bolingbroke, urged Britons to keep up "the spirit of liberty" by continuing to make that comparison. "Let us justify this Conduct, by persisting in it, and continue to ourselves the peculiar Honour of maintaining the Freedom of our *Gothick Institution of Government,* when so many other Nations, who enjoyed the same, have lost theirs," Bolingbroke wrote.[99] "I need not descend into more Particulars to shew the perpetuity of free Government in *Britain.* Few Men, even in this Age, are so shamefully unacquainted with the History of their Country, as to be ignorant of the principal Events and signal Revolutions, which have happened since the *Norman* Era."[100] After all, Henry Fielding pointed out to the Westminster grand jury, what would the history of England teach but the defense of liberty when that history was itself primarily the story of the English and British people's struggle "to maintain and preserve to themselves and their Posterity, that very Liberty which we now enjoy."[101]

------

dations of the commonwealth. It is certainly necessary to resort to the theory of your government, whenever you propose any alteration in the frame of it, whether that alteration means the revival of some former antiquated and forsaken constitution of state, or the introduction of some new improvement in the commonwealth" (speech of Edmund Burke, Commons Debates, May 8, 1780, *The Parliamentary History of England, From the Earliest Period to the Year 1803* [London, 1814], 21:603–4). See also Pocock, *Virtue, Commerce, and History* (cited note 26), 301–2.

98. [John Hervey, Lord Hervey of Ickworth], *Ancient and Modern Liberty Stated and Compar'd* (London, 1734), 4–5.

99. [Bolingbroke], *A Dissertation Upon Parties* (cited note 66), 102.

100. Ibid., 144.

101. Henry Fielding, *A Charge Delivered to the Grand Jury, at the Sessions of the Peace Held for the City and Liberty of Westminster, etc.* (Dublin, 1749), 16.

Fielding was saying something we no longer comprehend but which would have been readily understood by British people in the seventeenth and eighteenth centuries. To use history to show that liberty had been fought for and had been defended successfully was to make a constitutional point about the English and British people's right to liberty. Those ancestors who struggled for liberty against arbitrary power not only had won it for themselves, by their sacrifice they had purchased it for their descendants. That price paid conferred one of the title deeds by which English constitutional theory before the nineteenth century vested individual citizens with "ownership" of liberty. Civil rights were often purchased by blood.[102]

This concept of the ownership, the possession, the fee-simple to civil rights and to liberty, is essential to understanding the common lawyer's use of forensic history and the seventeenth and eighteenth century's recurrent citation of the ancient constitution. Laity as well as lawyers, Irish as well as English, knew that more was involved than respect for antiquity or finding greater wisdom through the survival of the immemorial over the novel.[103] It was, rather, a matter of authority: the authority for the common law, the authority for the constitution, the authority for liberty. This perspective of authority is a recurring eighteenth-century emphasis that could easily be overlooked if we do not pay close attention to the words that were used. What may pass as rhetorical flourish in the twentieth century could have been the substance of the argument in the eighteenth. Consider, for example, why viscount Molesworth translated Francis Hotman's *Franco-Gallia*. He did so, he explained, to show that during the era of the ancient

102. John Phillip Reid, *The Concept of Liberty in the Age of the American Revolution* (Chicago, 1988), 24. For a more detailed discussion (of the ownership and purchase of civil rights, not just liberty), see Reid, *Constitutional History of the American Revolution* (cited note 54), 96–131 (for purchase by blood, see esp. 127–29).

103. Even though that premise was often stated: "Besides, says the author of the letter on General Warrants, an Act of Parliament newly made, is not so venerable in the eyes of the world, or so secure against future alterations, as the old common law of the land, which has been from time immemorial, the inheritance of every Englishman, and is on account of its antiquity, held, as it were sacred in every man's mind" ([Richard Glover], *Considerations on the Attorney-General's Proposition for a Bill for the Establishment of Peace with America* [London, 1782], 8).

constitution on the Continent, most of Europe had possessed liberty. By 1711, when he wrote, the people of Great Britain alone enjoyed it. "Therefore," Molesworth went on, "a sincere Desire of Instructing the only Possessors of True Liberty in the World, what Right they have to that Liberty, of what great a Value it is, what Misery follows the Loss of it, and how easily, if Care be taken in time, it may be preserved, has induced me to Translate and send Abroad this small Treatise."[104] What we in the twentieth century can easily miss is one clause in Molesworth's statement containing a legal doctrine that ceased to be part of Anglo-American constitutional law in the nineteenth century. He said he was teaching "what Right" the English people had to liberty.

It was the right to current liberty that concerned students of the ancient constitution, not whether the ancient constitution was historical fact or in 1711 still existed just as it had in Gothic Europe. Constitutional law was their discipline of learning, not historiography.

IV. THE AUTHORITY OF THE PAST

We must go back to the basics of an abandoned jurisprudence. It is necessary to be on guard that the nineteenth-century concept of law as the command of the sovereign does not cloud our vision. For most of history English law was not command, but the opposite of command. Law, at least constitutional law, blunted the force of command. Even as late as the age of the American Revolution, the essence of law was that it, law, was "right" as opposed to "power."[105] The theory was of a legality that we have forgotten, and for that reason it would be well to start with the elementary, and the most rudimentary legal principle of ancient constitutionalism was the authority conferred on constitutional law by antiquity. That authority, keep in mind, served liberty primarily by being a restraint on power.

104. [Robert, viscount Molesworth], "Preface" to Francis Hotman, *Franco-Gallia: Or, an Account of the Ancient Free State of France, and Most other Parts of Europe, before the Loss of their Liberties,* trans. Robert, viscount Molesworth (London, 1711), ii–iii.

105. John Phillip Reid, "In the Taught Tradition: The Meaning of Law in Massachusetts-Bay Two-Hundred Years Ago," *Suffolk University Law Review* 14 (Summer 1980): 931–74.

Authority for law was the reason Fortescue-Aland in 1714 still found legal substance in the boast of his ancestor of three generations earlier "that neither the *Roman* nor *Venetian,* which are esteem'd very ancient, can claim so great Antiquity as ours."[106] It was also the legal theory behind a challenge from John Wilkes to Samuel Johnson in 1770. Johnson had defended the constitutionality of Wilkes's expulsion from the House of Commons. "Go back," Wilkes replied, "to the first establishment of representation; trace the claims of the representative body thro' the long records of successive parliaments."[107] Wilkes was doing what members of parliament had always done, what Sir Dudley Digges, for example, did when he spoke for the Commons at its crucial conference with the Lords on April 3, 1628. He was commanded by the Commons, Digges said, "to shew unto your Lordships in general: That the Laws of England were grounded on Reason more ancient than Books, consisting much in unwritten Customs; . . . and so ancient, that from the Saxon dayes, notwithstanding the injuries and ruines of times, they have continued in most parts the same."[108]

It is true that some appeals to mere antiquity were so extravagant that occasional eighteenth-century critics poked fun at the practice;[109] nonetheless we should be impressed with how frequently and intensely appeals were made.[110] Even more to the point is the importance that

106. Fortescue-Aland, "Dedication and Preface" (cited note 65), xv.

107. [John Wilkes], *A Letter to Samuel Johnson, L.L.D.* ([London], 1770), 14–15.

108. Digges quoted in William Prynne, *The First and Second Part of a Seasonable, Legal, and Historicall Vindication, and Chronological Collection of the Good, Old, Fundamentall Liberties, Franchises, Rights, Laws of all English Freemen. . . . Collected, recommended to the whole English Nation, as the best Legacy he can leave Them* (London, 1655), 18.

109. "The Word Parliament made such a terrible sound as wou'd Intimidate a Person of small Resolution and Courage, and make him forego the Argument even thro' Fear. A Stranger to the Controversy wou'd Imagine, that Parliaments were as Ancient at least, as the Flood, and that a House of Commons was preser'd in *Noah's* Ark" (Mathias Earbery, *The Old English Constitution Vindicated, and Set in a True Light* [London, 1717], i).

110. See, e.g., William Prynne, *The Second Part of a Seasonable Legal and Historical Vindication, and Chronological Collection of the Good old Fundamental Liberties. . . .*

the eighteenth century attached to the mere attribute of being ancient. An example is provided by Francis Gregor's boast that Fortescue had proved "that the *Common Law* is the most rational, as well as the most antient in Europe."[111] Today it is difficult to tell if Gregor took greater pride in the common law's rationality or its antiquity. It may come as a surprise, but most of his contemporaries would have put more stock in antiquity.[112]

What was the attraction of the past? While answering that question it would be well not to be misled by platitudes such as that of the seventeenth-century constitutionalist Edward Cook suggesting that age made the law "the more venerable, and gave an addition of honour to it,"[113] or that of Lord Keeper Finch, who spoke of an English constitution "made Glorious by Antiquity."[114] Nor should we be taken in by the supposition of recent scholars that "history could legitimize certain institutions"[115] or that time, experience, and usage were argued to "legitimate" actions.[116] That last idea is close to seventeenth- and eighteenth-century constitutional theory. It was, however, custom not

---

(London, 1655), 3–14. The appeal was frequently made in grand-jury charges. Maurice Shelton, *A Charge Given to the Grand-Jury, at the General Quarter-Sessions of the Peace, Holden at St. Edmunds-Bury for the Liberty thereof; In the County of Suffolk: On the 11th of October, An. Dom. 1725* (London, 1726), 17.

111. Gregor, "Preface" to Fortescue, *De Laudibus Legum Angliae* (cited note 83), v.

112. There is little merit to the suggestion that in the early seventeenth century "the antiquity of a system of positive law was proof of its conformity to the eternal Law of Reason" (Styles, "Politics and Research" [cited note 38], 54).

113. [Edward Cook], *Argumentum Anti-Normannicum: or an Argument Proving, From Ancient Histories and Records, that William, Duke of Normandy Made no absolute Conquest of England, by the Sword; in the sense of our Modern Writers* (London, 1682), xviii.

114. Speech of Lord Keeper Finch, November 3, 1640, printed in John Rushworth, *Historical Collections: The Third Part; in Two Volumes* (London, 1692), 1:13.

115. Reed Browning, *Political and Constitutional Ideas of the Court Whigs* (Baton Rouge, La., 1982), 38. Nor is it very meaningful to conclude that change was "generally suspected . . . because change did threaten the character of the state" (J. R. Pole, *The Gift of Government: Political Responsibility from the English Restoration to American Independence* [Athens, Ga., 1983], 4). What change threatened was not the character of the state but the authority of law.

116. Pocock, *Politics, Language and Time* (cited note 27), 82.

history that was the legitimatizing agent. The problem is with the word *legitimate*. Time did more than make a rule of law legitimate.[117] It was time that converted a rule from a standard of conduct into coercive law. As Maurice Shelton charged the Suffolk County grand jury at Bury St. Edmunds in 1726, "After an Use and Practice of our Laws, time out of mind, then they are taken to be the Common Law of *England,* and not before; nothing but Time immemorial making any thing Part of our Constitution."[118]

That charge at Bury St. Edmunds explained the jurisprudential significance of time, of antiquity, and of the law's appeal to the past. That appeal was not just a mustering of evidence proving what was law. It was one of the processes that vested law with its power to command obedience. Shelton did not exaggerate when he said "nothing but Time immemorial making any thing Part of our constitution," for he did not mean "Time immemorial" as twentieth-century scholars have assumed but as it was understood at law. Moreover, when he said "nothing but Time" he probably was not saying that custom was the only authority for constitutional law. Most other authorities for constitutional law— the original contract, ownership, sacrifice of ancestors, and sometimes even nature—depended on the same evidence—custom and the passage of time—for proof.

We must not forget the problem of the meaning of legal time or immemoriality in constitutional law, but for the moment we are concerned with the question of authority and why the ancient constitution was almost exclusively a matter of law, seldom of historiography. Of course there were observers in the eighteenth century who brought up the issue of historical dynamics, complaining that constitutionalists defended the "English" constitution not on grounds of fitness or utility, but by the authority of custom alone. "One would suppose," the *Critical Review* objected, "they thought it was to be defended on no other

117. Although legal arguments were given strength by time. "[T]here is no legal argument which hath such force in our courts of law, as those which are drawn from the words of antient writs" ([Daines Barrington], *Observations on the Statutes, Chiefly the more Ancient from Magna Charta to the Twenty-first of James First, ch. XXVII. With an Appendix; Being a Proposal for new modelling the Statutes* [London, 1766], 78).

118. Shelton, *Charge to the Grand-Jury* (cited note 110), 21.

principles, than those of its having been established in nearly the same form wherein it now exists, for ages immemorial. A fact which some have with great labour and difficulty endeavoured to render probable; but of which there is much reason to suspect the truth."[119] Even though we in the twentieth century agree with the argument's historical theory, we should hesitate before embracing its jurisprudential implications, at least for the seventeenth and eighteenth centuries. From the perspective of those times, the *Critical Review* was not raising neutral objections, but wading in on one side of the current debate about the nature of the constitution—the side of arbitrary power or anti-constitutionalism. The other side—the side that won in seventeenth-century England, lost in the eighteenth century, and then won again in America at Yorktown—located right in the rule of law rather than in the command of the sovereign. And the authority for law was in the past, in the ancient constitution, as George Lawson said when going back to the Saxon kings and to Edward the Confessor's time to find evidence of authority. "What these power[s] of these [Saxon] Parliaments, and of these Kings were, is the great Question," he explained. "For that once known, the Constitution will be evident."[120] He did not mean the Confessor's constitution. He meant the constitution of 1689.

In order to illustrate the ancient constitution as authority for law, our investigation can be limited to one issue: the jurisdiction of the houses of parliament. Francis Hargrave was explaining constitutional authority when he discussed a dispute between the Lords and the Commons over the Lords's jurisdiction in civil cases. That dispute was settled, Hargrave pointed out, "under the supposition of a *primitive* and *inherent* right in the lords, attached to their order by the law and constitution of the kingdom."[121] The controversy had occurred during the reign of Charles II, over a century before Hargrave wrote. John

119. "Book Review," *The Critical Review: Or Annals of Literature by a Society of Gentlemen* 22 (1766): 362–63.

120. George Lawson, *Politica Sacra & Civilis: Or, a Model of Civil and Ecclesiastical Government*, 2d ed. (London, 1689), 148.

121. Francis Hargrave, "Preface" to Sir Matthew Hale, *The Jurisdiction of the Lords House, or Parliament, Considered According to Antient Records* (London, 1796), iv–v.

Somers, future lord chancellor of England, was offering a solution to a constitutional crisis of his own time, the 1680s, when he devoted thirteen pages to instances of early Saxon "parliaments" electing kings or deciding the succession to the throne. It was evidence proving a point of constitutional law: "That it hath been the constant opinion of all Ages that the Parliament of *England* had an unquestionable power to limit, restrain and qualify the Succession as they pleased, and that in all Ages they have put their power in practice."[122]

Sir Robert Atkyns, a contemporary of Somers's who served as a judge on the court of Common Pleas and lord chief baron of the Exchequer court, was explicit when explaining why the House of Commons enjoyed powers and privileges by inherent right and not by grace and grant of the crown. "I shall clearly prove," he contended, "that these Powers and Priviledges were indeed their ancient Right and Inheritance. Which they cannot be unless that House, or the Commons by their Representative, have been ever from the beginning of the Government a part and member of the Parliament." He then "proved" the Commons had been part of parliament since the beginning of relevant time by marshaling the selective evidence of forensic history. Lord Coke, for example, was quoted for the evidence that tenants on the ancient demesne had always had a privilege "[n]ot to contribute to the Wages of the Knights of the Shire."

How the Priviledge must be as Ancient as their Tenure and Service, for their Priviledge comes by reason of their Service, and their Service is known by all to be before the Conquest, in the time of *Edward* the Confessor, and in the time of the Conquerour. And it is expressly said by this learned and Reverend Judge [Coke], That these Tenants, in the Ancient Demesn[e], claimed this by Prescription; and it could not be so, if the Wages of the Knights of the Shire had begun within the Memory of Man, or of any Record. Therefore it clearly follows, That Knights of the Shire to serve in Parliament, and the paying Wages to them for the Service, has been Time out

122. [John Somers, Baron Somers], *A Brief History of the Succession of the Crown of England, &c. Collected out of the Records, and the most Authentick Historians* (London, 1680), 13.

of Mind, and did not begin 49 H[enry] 3 for that is within Time of memory in a Legal Sence.[123]

Reading this argument, today's critics of ancient-constitution history will readily conclude that it is nonsense, unsupported by historical evidence. But Judge Atkyns said he was calling on the evidence of history in a "Legal Sence." He said nothing of being interested in the evidence of history in a historical sense. Atkyns used the Saxon constitution not to prove a historical point but, as he said, "clearly [to] prove" as a matter of constitutional law in 1689 that the House of Commons possessed its powers and privileges by inherent right, not by royal grant.

Three decades earlier, William Prynne had encountered a similar *legal* controversy and had enlisted the same constitutional proof—evidence from the ancient constitution—to establish the constitutional authority of the other house of parliament, the Lords.[124] The House of Commons had proclaimed itself "the only *Supream Judges and Judicature of the Realm,* paramount [to] our *Kings, Lords, Laws, Liberties, Great Charters,* and all other *Courts of Justice,* having an absolute, arbitrary, unlimited power, to act, vote and determine what they please, without appeal or consult."[125] The Lords, the Commons voted, was not an inherently equal branch of parliament because its members sat "only by Patent, by the *Kings will, Tenure or descent;* not by the Peoples free Election . . . ; That they represent themselves only not the Commons [the people]; and are the Sons only of Conquest, of Usurpation; (brought in by the Conquerour,) not of Choice and Election."[126]

123. Sir Robert Atkyns, *The Power, Jurisdiction and Priviledge of Parliament and the Antiquity of the House of Commons Asserted* (London, 1689), 17–18.

124. In another work, Prynne proved English fundamental laws and rights "in a *Chronologicall way*" by surveying "the ancient Britons, Saxons, Danes, Normans, and English Kings, till our present times; plentifully, undeniably evidencing, declaring, vindicating, asserting, establishing, perpetuating these Fundamentall, Hereditary Rights, Liberties, Priviledges, Franchises, Customes, Lawes" (*Second Part of a Seasonable, Legal, and Historical Vindication* [cited note 110], 1).

125. William Prynne, *A Plea for the Lords, and House of Peers: Or, a full, necessary, seasonable, enlarged Vindication, of the just, antient hereditary Right of the Lords, Peers, and Barons of this Realm to sit, vote, judge, in all the Parliaments of England* (London, 1658), "To the Reader," [11].

126. Ibid., 5.

"To this I answer," Prynne wrote, turning directly to the authority of the ancient constitution, "That our *Lords, Dukes, Earls, Barons, Nobles* (yea *Archbishops, Bishops, Abbots, Priors* too who held by Barony) sate antiently in all our General National Councels and Parliamentary Assemblies, *many hundreds of years before the Conquest,* both in the *Britons* and *Saxons* reigns, by right of the Peerage and Tenures, as now they doe."[127] It was a matter of right established by law, and law in this case was found in the custom of the realm. Public officials, be they "Kings, Magistrates, Judges, Ministers, Peers, or Members of Parliament," need not be elected if they hold their positions by other valid customary procedures; procedures that vested their offices with "a general implicit or tacit consent." This constitutional principle is "especially" valid "when the antient Laws of the Land, continuing still in full force, and the custom of the Kingdom time out of mind, requires no such ceremonie of the peoples particular election or call."[128] In England "the *antient Laws,* Statutes, *and Customs of the Kingdom* conferred jurisdiction on the Lords differently than on the representatives of the common people. The Lords enjoyed parliamentary privileges *"without any election of the people,"* but members of the Commons were elected. If, however, custom had been otherwise, and the king from time out of mind had appointed the knights and burgesses to parliament, then they would sit in the Commons constitutionally by royal pleasure and they would not need to be elected, because crown appointment would be "a Law and usage" sanctioned by the consent of popular acquiescence.[129]

That the Commons's tenure by election was from time out of mind, that is immemorial, did not mean it was so ancient it had no known origin. The Lords's jurisdiction rested on that degree of immemorality,

127. Ibid.

128. Ibid., 14–15.

129. "[I]f the Laws and Customs of the Realm were, that the King himself might call two Knights, Citizens and Burgesses to Parliament, such as himself should nominate in his Writ out of every County, City and Borough, without the Freeholders, Citizens, and Burgesses election of them, by a common agreement and consent to such a Law and usage made by their Ancestors, and submitted and consented to for some ages without repeal, this Law and Custom were sufficient to make such Knights, Citizens and Burgesses lawfull Members of Parliament, obliging their posterity whiles unrepealed" (ibid., 15).

not that of the House of Commons. Its beginning could be traced to the reign of Henry III. The ancient constitution stretched back only as far as relevant time.

> By, and in the very primitive constitution of our *English Parlia-ments,* for many hundred years together there were no Knights nor Burgesses at all, but only *the King and his Nobles:* after which, when elected Knights gestes were first sent to Parliament about 49 H. 3 it was granted by the Kings grace, and unanimously agreed by the kingdoms, peoples general consents, that our Parliaments should always be constituted and made up, not by Knights and Burgesses only, . . . but likewise *of the King* . . . and of the Lords . . . who ought of right to sit, vote, make Laws, and give Judgement in Parliament by vertue of their Peerage, Baronies, Offices, without any election of the people.[130]

The Commons's jurisdiction came from royal command, popular consent, and usage unbroken for the duration of relevant time out of mind. The authority of this jurisdiction vested the Commons with constitutional security from interference by the king,[131] but did not vest it with superiority over the Lords, whose constitutional tenure ran to even more anciently relevant time. As there had never been a time when the Lords were not part of parliament, their right was of greater immemoriality. They held by immemorial custom and by consent that was at least implied if not expressed. "This right of theirs is confirmed by *prescription* and *custom,* from the very first beginning of Parliaments in this kingdom till this present, there being no president to be found in History or Record of any Parliament held in this Island since it was a kingdom, without the King . . . or without *Lords and Peers.*"[132] The legal conclusion was not that the Lords had a higher, more constitutional jurisdiction than the Commons, but that if the Commons had a right to sit in parliament, the Lords could not be denied co-jurisdiction, as the legal authority upon which their right depended, though no

130. Ibid., 18–19.

131. For a recent discussion of this point of law see William M. Lamont, *Mar-ginal Prynne, 1600–1669* (London, 1963), 179–80.

132. Prynne, *Plea for Lords* (cited note 125), 19.

greater than that of the Commons, was more constitutionally demon-
strable:

> Their sitting, voting, judging therefore in Great Councils, Parlia-
> ments, being so antient, clear and unquestionable ever since their
> first beginnings til[l] now; and the sitting of Knights, Citizens, Bur-
> gesses by the peoples election, in our antientest Great Councils,
> Parliaments, not so clearly evident by *History or Records* as theirs: we
> must needs acknowledge, subscribe to this their Right and Title; or
> else deny the Knights, Citizens, Burgesses rights to sit, vote in our
> Great Councils, Parliaments, rather than theirs, who have not so an-
> tient nor clear a Title or right as they by many hundreds of years.[133]

Summarizing the authority for the Lords's jurisdiction (and *not* the extent of that jurisdiction), Prynne cited four sources, one of which most
interestingly was the consent of all previous Houses of Commons.

> This Right and Privilege of theirs is vested legally in them by the
> very *Common Law* and *Custom* of the Realm, which binds all men; By
> the unanimous consent of all our Ancestors, and all the Commons
> of *England* from age to age assembled in Parliament, since they sat
> in any Parliaments; who alwaies consented to, desired, and never
> opposed the Lords sitting, voting, power or Judicature in Parlia-
> ment; and by *Magna Charta*.[134]

The legal doctrine must be obvious. Although the past in the form
of constitutional custom was researched for proof of the source of law
and as evidence of law, it was primarily cited as authority for law. Custom, which was not history, was the authority making law binding on
government as well as upon subjects. It still was considered law's authority by Allan Ramsay as late as the age of the American Revolution,[135] when he questioned the "power" of parliament to have pro-

133. Ibid., 21.
134. Ibid.
135. In the year of the Declaration of Independence it was asserted that there
was a popular legislative power above parliament that still potentially existed:
"Our ancestors formerly assembled and resolved upon their laws and their measures in their collective capacity: their princes and their leaders were as evidently
commissioned in the execution of them, as one private person is by another:

mulgated the Septennial Act of 1716, destroying "the annual elective power of the people."

> [T]his annual elective power, the first principle of our constitution, is a right of inheritance, which was brought into England by our Saxon forefathers, at the first establishment of the Saxon mode of government, in this island; and which the people, hold by the ancient, common law of the land. And which they had enjoyed, from generation to generation, for twelve-hundred years, before the reign of William the third. And therefore this elective power of the people, may be truly called, their constitutional right of inheritance. An inheritance that can no more be taken from them, or restrained, justly, than any estate, in land, can be taken from the right owner.[136]

Think of the implications of Ramsay's thesis: writing in London in 1771 he was arguing that the ancient constitution was a higher authority than command of the sovereign parliament.

V. THE THEORY OF THE PAST

It is necessary to be precise. We are discussing law, not history, and the issue is why the authority of law to command obedience could be established by appealing to the past. It is not quite accurate to say that English law, "being customary, relied for authority on the presumption of its own continuity."[137] It was not continuity but consent that vested authority, and the legal doctrine dominating seventeenth- and eighteenth-century customary law was not presumption but pre-

------

the power then reverted to the body and on occasion issued from it again. This was the first origin of our form of government; where we are to seek, where we shall find and by which we shall comprehend its real, original nature and essence. Whatever changes or variations have through necessity and the mutability of things since been made or happened in its outward form and circumstances, these have all referred and related to its primitive inherent principle" ([Matthew Robinson-Morris, second Baron Rokeby], *A Further Examination of our Present American Measures and of the Reasons and the Principles on which they are founded* [Bath, 1776], 100).

136. [Ramsay], *Historical Essay* (cited note 62), 144.

137. Pocock, "Origins of Study" (cited note 44), 237.

scription. "Every Priviledge is by Prescription," Judge Robert Atkyns stated in 1689. "[I]t is held, That a man cannot prescribe to an Incident or Appendant, nor indeed to any Power or Authority where the Principal Thing hath not had a perpetual continuance." Atkyns overstated the principle, however, when he added, "[W]here the beginning of a thing is known, there can be nothing belonging to it by Prescription."[138] Time and unchallenged exercise of the right or the property prescribed were necessary to prove prescription, not immemoriality alone. Edmund Burke was closer to the mark when he wrote, "Prescription is the most solid of all titles, not only to property, but, which is to secure that property, to government."[139]

The doctrine of prescription told people that they owned a privilege or had, by time, acquired a right. The doctrine of consent was different. It had more to do with explaining why time vested a rule of conduct with the coercive force of law. With legislation, consent was established by direct vote or representation. With custom, the proof of consent was time. Consent to law, Oxford's Vinerian law professor Richard Wooddeson told his students in the 1770s, could be proved by "long and uniform custom [which] bestows a sanction, as evidence of universal approbation and acquiescence."[140]

The theory of consent played two roles in seventeenth- and eighteenth-century constitutional law. First, it reenforced the individual citizen's civil and property rights by adding a theoretical justification for the rule of prescription.[141] Second, it strengthened public

138. Atkyns, *Power, Jurisdiction and Privilege* (cited note 123), 17. Edmund Burke also overstated the principle when he claimed, "Our Constitution is a prescriptive constitution; it is a constitution whose sole authority is that it has existed time out of mind" (H. T. Dickinson, "The Eighteenth-Century Debate on the Sovereignty of Parliament," *Transactions of the Royal Historical Society,* 5th Series, 26 [1976]: 199).

139. Quoted in Pocock, *Politics, Language and Time* (cited note 27), 226. In the eighteenth century a fundamental civil right was the right to government. Reid, *Constitutional History of the American Revolution* (cited note 54), 39–46.

140. Wooddeson, *Elements of Jurisprudence* (cited note 76), 46.

141. In the eighteenth century, "[m]en of property . . . knew that much English law was based on custom, precedent and prescription rather than on the deliberate, conscious decisions of an absolute monarch or a sovereign legislature. They also knew that many property rights were based on possession and

liberty by providing a popular basis for the privileges the British government possessed and, by implication, restraining its power, including the power of parliament to promulgate coercive legislation.

> However the historical fact may be of a social contract, government ought to be, and is generally *considered* as founded on consent, tacit or express, on a real, or *quasi,* compact. This theory is a material basis of political rights; and as a theoretical point is not difficult to be maintained. For what gives any legislature a right to act, where no express consent can be shewn? what, but immemorial usage? and what is the intrinsic force of immemorial usage, in establishing this fundamental or any other law, but that it is evidence of common acquiescence and consent? Not that such consent is subsequently revocable, at the will even of all the subjects of the state, for that would be making a part of the community equal in power to the whole originally, and superior to the rulers thereof after their establishment.[142]

If we say that the implied consent of custom, not history, vested unwritten law with its authority, we must not forget that custom was also law. "General customs, which are the universal rule of the whole kingdom," John Adams observed in 1773, "form the common law in its stricter and more usual signification." A striking instance of the doctrine was England's "four superior courts of record, the chancery, the king's bench, the common pleas, and the exchequer." Their authority to bind individuals to judgment had not been promulgated "in any written statute or ordinance" but depended "merely upon immemorial usage, that is, upon common law," for its support.[143]

We should be especially impressed by what John Adams said about the binding force of custom when we consider that the issue he was

---

long prescriptive right rather than on legal documents. Thus, in both the field of common law and the sphere of property rights, it was recognized that an appeal to prescription could make good a lack of documentary legal evidence" (Dickinson, "Eighteenth-Century Debate" [cited note 138], 197).

142. Wooddeson, *Elements of Jurisprudence* (cited note 76), 35–36.

143. John Adams in *Boston Gazette,* February 1, 1773, reprinted in *The Works of John Adams, Second President of the United States: With a Life of the Author, Notes and Illustrations,* ed. Charles Francis Adams, 10 vols. (Boston, 1850–1856), 3:540.

discussing was judicial tenure. The rule that custom was law that had to be obeyed restrained him from arguing for the constitutional principle we know he favored. As an American whig, Adams wanted judges independent of the royal prerogative, serving securely for life at good behavior. Colonial judges, however, did not have tenure for life, and the reason was not just royal charter or gubernatorial instructions, but that immemorial English custom ordained that they serve at pleasure. "[T]he office of chancellor of England," Adams quoted an English barrister arguing in a common law court, "could not be granted to any one for life. And why? Because it never was so granted. *Custom and nothing else prevails, and governs in all those cases.*" Adams had to agree. "[C]ustom was the criterion, and that alone," he admitted. "So that, if the king should constitute a baron of the exchequer during pleasure, he would have an estate for life in his office, or the grant would be void. Why? Because the custom had so settled it. If the king should constitute a judge of the king's bench, or common bench [Common Pleas], during good behavior, he would have only an estate at the will of the grantor. Why? Because the custom hath determined it so. And that custom could not be annulled or altered but by act of parliament."[144]

The certainty that custom gave to nonstatutory constitutional law in the seventeenth and eighteenth centuries is further illustrated by a quotation Adams dismissed; a quotation he might have cited to argue that judges should have life tenure. "If," another barrister had told an English court, "any judicial or ministerial office be granted to any man to hold, so long as he behaves himself well in the office, that is an estate for life, unless he lose it for misbehavior." Adams agreed only if

144. John Adams in *Boston Gazette*, January 18, 1773, reprinted in *Works*, 3:526–28. Adams's lesson, that custom made law, is one that some twentieth-century historians have indicated is not worth keeping in mind, causing them to make misleading statements. For example, it was said of the dispute during the reign of James I concerning the antiquity of the House of Commons: "The statements of the anti-royalist party contain frequent references to the antiquity of the House. And nothing can have served better than this assumption to convince men that the privileges of Parliament were not of royal grace but of inherent right" (Herbert Butterfield, *The Englishman and His History* [Cambridge, England, 1944], 47). Butterfield's history is correct, but the implication misses the mark of accuracy. The evidence of antiquity was argued not to "convince" but to *prove* the constitutionality of the privilege.

the granted position was "an office that by custom, that is, immemorial usage, or common law, . . . or by an express act of parliament, . . . has been granted in that manner, but not otherwise."[145] Here in stark outline was the basic constitutional function of custom as authority. It did not purport this or that form of government so much as government by the rule of law or law that was a restraint on arbitrary power. It was a barrier against the will and pleasure of governmental capriciousness. In English and British constitutionalism it was primarily a barrier against the will and pleasure of the crown. Much as an American whig might wish that high-court judges served at life tenure, that tenure, to be constitutional, would have had to have been based on custom or colonial statute; it could not be ordained by the discretion of the royal prerogative.

It will not do to make much of a prerogative threat in the eighteenth century. Few voices were then raised on behalf of royal sovereignty over law, and although almost every constitutionalist who wrote of the dangers of arbitrary government wrote that the danger was prerogativism, it is impossible to tell how many believed that threat was real.[146] The jurisprudents of custom may have used the crown as their straw man, but their true fear was unrestrained power and their objective was preservation of the rule of law.[147] Still, they make it seem that

145. Adams in *Boston Gazette,* February 1, 1773, reprinted in *Works,* 3:546.

146. But see Earbery, *Old Constitution Vindicated* (cited note 109), xii, 6–7. Whigs, of course, still made much of the royalist claims of passive obedience preached in James II's reign. John Withers, *The Whigs Vindicated, the Objections that are commonly brought against them Answer'd, and the Present Ministry Prov'd to be the best Friends to the Church, the Monarchy, the Lasting Peace, and real Welfare of England,* 6th ed. (London, 1715), 5.

147. A recent historian, writing of the "prejudice" and "[t]he chauvinism of common lawyers," has suggested that in the seventeenth century "the enemies at the gates, of course, were those twin menaces, civil and canon law," which common lawyers believed was the law of arbitrary tyranny (Kelley, "History, English Law and the Renaissance" [cited note 37], 37–38). Whether true or not for the seventeenth century, Kelley's statement is not correct for the eighteenth, when common lawyers were not concerned with civil law but theorized that it and canon law were rendered harmless by merging into immemorial custom. "Many of our present ecclesiastical laws are undoubtedly of foreign extraction, and some are entirely of English origin. But now they all alike depend, as to their

the king was the threat, and one reason, as indicated by John Shute Barrington, a barrister of the Inner Temple and first viscount Barrington, was the legacy of the ancient constitution which had originally been designed to keep royal power in its place.

> All that we learn of our *Saxon* Ancestors from History, is, that, before their Coming here, Things of great Consequence were determin'd by all the Freemen, and the lesser by the principal Persons; and when upon their Coming here, they had such a standing Officer as a King, his Power was so limited, that he could do nothing without the Consent of the one or the other . . . ; and the greatest of the *Saxon* Kings acknowledge[d], that they owe[d] their Crown to the Election of the Nobles and People.[148]

Barrington was putting the ancient constitution to its most basic eighteenth-century use—to craft the bulwarks of constitutional restraint. The chairman of the Suffolk County quarter sessions was also thinking of restraint when he recounted to the grand jury instances from the history of the ancient Britons as well as the Saxons demonstrating that government power had anciently been limited. The same limitations, he was saying, held in 1726.[149] Thirteen years later, William Petyt's *Jus Parliamentarium* was published by an editor hoping to spread the word of restraint and ancient constitutionalism. Petyt, he explained, possessed an

---

general binding authority, on the same foundations as the whole body of our English laws, immemorial custom, and express act of parliament" (Wooddeson, *Elements of Jurisprudence* [cited note 76], 155–56).

148. [John Shute Barrington, first viscount Barrington], *The Revolution and Anti-Revolution Principles Stated and Compar'd, the Constitution Explain'd and Vindicated, and the Justice and Necessity of Excluding the Pretender, Maintain'd against the Book Entituled, Hereditary Right of the Crown of England Asserted,* 2d ed. (London, 1714), 68.

149. Shelton, *Charge to the Grand-Jury* (cited note 110), 10–11. The Westminster grand jury was reminded that "the Patriarchal Scheme, and the Doctrines of indefeisible, unalienable Hereditary Right are of mere modern Invention. . . . So that you see, the Title of his present Majesty King GEORGE is unquestionable, and most agreeable to our Ancient Constitution and Laws" (charge of April 24, 1728, *Sir John Gonson's Five Charges to Several Grand Juries . . .* , 4th ed. [London, n.d.], 20).

uncommon Penetration into the Knowledge of our ancient Records and legal Antiquities; more particularly those which give a true Idea of the Frame and Constitution of this limited Monarchy: A Government which consists in the Execution of Laws dictated by Reason and Experience, and receiving their binding Force from the Consent of the People governed; not flowing from, or depending upon the misinformed Judgment, or capricious Will of One, or a few.[150]

Whether or not he thought he was publishing a study of history, Petyt's editor certainly thought he was publishing a study of constitutional authority.

In the hands of some lawyers the jurisprudence of constitutional custom was a theory of authority that not only checked power, it never served power. Custom was authority for liberty only, it was not authority for arbitrariness or even, perhaps, for ordinary government power. William Jones, fellow of University College, Oxford, and later a judge of the high court at Calcutta, explained the theory in 1768. "In questions of private right, precedents are law," Jones contended. "But in questions that regard the Constitution, they lose a principal part of their force, *what has been,* is by no means to be considered as the invariable rule for *what should be.*"[151]

> In many cases, rights at first imperfect and infirm acquire strength from age, they are confirmed by the exercise of them; but it is not so with the powers of government; they derive their force from their intrinsic merit alone; originally bad, no prescription, no usage, however inveterate, can protect them. The rights of the individual, of the church, of the crown may have their respective limitations, but against those of the Constitution "no time can run."[152]

"Respect for the sentiments of our ancestors," Jones argued, should be a criterion for "maintaining the original rights of mankind," it should

---

150. William Petyt, *Jus Parliamentarium: or, the Ancient Power, Jurisdiction, Rights and Liberties, of the Most High Court of Parliament, Revived and Asserted* (London, 1739), preface.

151. [William Jones], *The Constitutional Criterion: By a Member of the University of Cambridge* (London, 1768), 2–3.

152. Ibid., 3–4.

not be "employed in confirming the usurpations against them."[153] Or, as James Burgh contended, the past could not be authority for rules of arbitrary power. "The longer grievances have continued, the more reason for redressing them."[154]

Jones's jurisprudence was extremist and, although commanding some respect among constitutional theorists, was devoid of practical application. It is revealing for our purposes, however, for it illustrates one of the salient aspects of eighteenth-century ancient constitutionalism: its usefulness to opponents of arbitrary power.

Due perhaps to our emphasis on the historical method rather than on common law argumentation, the ancient constitution's role in combating medieval arbitrariness—and, of course, as a defense of liberty as liberty was defined in the seventeenth and eighteenth centuries—has not always been credited by recent scholars. The ancient constitution, it was suggested in 1965, "was supposed to be immemorial, and its merit consisted in the antiquity of its usage rather than in any rationalization of its principles."[155] Seventeenth- and eighteenth-century constitutional jurisprudes would have been puzzled by that statement. They would have agreed, of course, that the reasonableness of the ancient constitution was not in the principles it contained. Its rationalization or reasonableness was in the authority that the ancient constitution bestowed on principles which the party utilizing and citing the ancient constitution was defending or espousing. The "merit" of the ancient constitution was not in the antiquity of its usage but in the degree of security from governmental whim and caprice that antiquity provided current, existing civil rights. We would be unwise to underestimate the significance of security. In the customary jurisprudence of an unwritten constitution there is no element more essential to liberty than security against arbitrariness.

But what was the concept of arbitrariness in the seventeenth and

153. Ibid., 3.

154. J. Burgh, *Political Disquisitions; or, An Enquiry into public Errors, Defects, and Abuses. Illustrated by, and established upon Facts and Remarks, extracted from a Variety of Authors, Ancient and Modern* (Philadelphia, 1775), 3:271.

155. J. G. A. Pocock, "Machiavelli, Harrington and English Political Ideologies in the Eighteenth Century," *William and Mary Quarterly* 22 (1965): 572; Pocock, *Politics, Language and Time* (cited note 27), 133.

eighteenth centuries? To understand the answer to that question it is necessary to rid ourselves of twentieth-century thoughts about arbitrariness having something to do with despotism, tyranny, or cruel government. It may today, but that was not the legal definition in the eighteenth century. Then it was not the harshness of power, the brutality of power, or the certainty of the exercise of power that made government arbitrary. It was, rather, the possession of power unchecked.[156] Tyrannical power was abuse of power; arbitrary power was power without restraint.

In eighteenth-century parlance, arbitrary was the difference between liberty and slavery, right and power, constitutional and unconstitutional. To the eighteenth-century legal mind, knowing what was arbitrary delineated the concept of the rule of law. "For it is certain," Jared Eliot reminded Connecticut's lawmakers in 1738, "*That to the Constitution of every Government, Absolute Sovereignty must lodge somewhere.* So that according to this Maxim, Every Government must be Arbitrary and Despotick. The difference seems to be here; Arbitrary Despotick Government, is, When this Sovereign Power is directed by the Passions, Ignorance & Lust of them that Rule. And a Legal Government, is, When this Arbitrary & Sovereign Power puts it self under Restraints, and lays it self under Limitations."[157] It was, viscount Bolingbroke agreed, a matter of power and not of the type and structure of government. Whether power was vested in a single monarch, in "the *principal Persons of the Community,* or in the *whole Body of the People,*" was immaterial. What matters is whether power is without control. "Such Governments are Governments of *arbitrary Will,*" he concluded.[158]

Just as the eighteenth-century concept of arbitrariness should not be confused with cruelness or terror, for it could be benevolent, mild, and materially beneficial, so it should not be confounded with abso-

156. Reid, "In Legitimate Stirps" (cited note 19).

157. Jared Eliot, *Give Cesar his Due. Or, the Obligation that Subjects are under to their Civil Rulers, As was shewed in a Sermon Preach'd before the General Assembly of the Colony of Connecticut at Hartford, May the 11th, 1738. The Day for the Election of the Honourable the Governour, the Deputy-Governour, and the Worshipful Assistants* (New London, Conn., 1738), 36 n.

158. [Bolingbroke], *A Dissertation Upon Parties* (cited note 66), 159.

luteness. "[E]ven *absolute Power*," John Locke pointed out, "where it is necessary, is *not Arbitrary* by being absolute, but is still limited by that reason, and confined to those ends, which required it in some Cases to be absolute," such as martial discipline which vests an army officer with power to order a trooper to die but cannot "command that Soldier to give him one penny of his Money."[159] Law was the distinction. If the officer acted within the parameters of law, his absolute orders were not arbitrary. That element—law—was all-important to eighteenth-century constitutional thought. For "court whigs," Reed Browning has pointed out—and also, it should be added, for most other educated Britons and Americans—there were "but two types of government: arbitrary and lawful,"[160] or as John Arbuthnot explained in 1733, "what is not legal is arbitrary."[161]

Law is one of three legal concepts by which the eighteenth century measured arbitrariness. The other two were liberty and constitutionalism. Arbitrary power was the antithesis of liberty and the opposite of constitutionalism.[162] These points and counterpoints were concisely summarized by George Campbell, preaching in Aberdeen, Scotland, on the fast day commemorating the American rebellion.

> [W]hen men are governed by established laws which they know, or may know, if they will, and are not liable to be punished by their governors, unless when they transgress those laws, we say they are under a *legal government*. When the contrary takes place, and men are liable to be harrassed at the pleasure of their superiors, tho' guilty of no transgression of a known rule, we say properly they are under *arbitrary power*. These are the only distinctions I know between *free* and *slavish*, *legal* and *arbitrary*, as applied to governments.[163]

159. John Locke, *Two Treatises of Government: A Critical Edition with an Introduction and Apparatus Criticus*, ed. Peter Laslett, 2d ed. (Cambridge, England, 1967), book 2, sec. 139.

160. Browning, *Political and Constitutional Ideas* (cited note 115), 196.

161. [John] Arbuthnot, *The Freeholder's Political Cathechism: Written by Dr. Arbuthnot* ([London], 1769), 9.

162. Reid, *Concept of Liberty* (cited note 102), 55–67, 74–83.

163. George Campbell, *The Nature, Extent, and Importance, of the Duty of Allegiance: A Sermon Preached at Aberdeen, December 12, 1776, Being the Fast Day Appointed*

Or, as Connecticut's Jared Eliot added, a government under the restraint of law "is what we call a Legal Limited & well Constituted Government. Under such a Government only there is true Liberty."[164]

Arbitrariness and people's fear of arbitrary power were why the ancient constitution and immemorial law were tools of constitutional advocacy during the seventeenth and eighteenth centuries. The authority of custom was then the most viable alternative to rule by the will and pleasure of sovereign command. Immemorial law was not argued to block judicial judgments or (except in rare instances such as by American whigs during the prerevolutionary controversy) to restrict parliamentary legislation. The ancient constitution was a standard of reference for seventeenth-century antiprerogativists and for eighteenth-century constitutionalists opposed to arbitrary power. They argued the evidence of ancient constitutionalism when seeking either to prove the authority of a legal principle or to preserve liberty's security through the rule of law.[165] What seventeenth- and eighteenth-century constitutionalists sought from the ancient-constitution advo-

---

by the King, on Account of the Rebellion in America (Aberdeen, Scotland, 1777), 24–25. This sermon got Campbell into trouble with the authorities, and he thought it advisable to publish a second edition, which is available in many more research libraries than the first. In it the passage quoted is altered in wording but not in meaning. George Campbell, *The Nature, Extent, and Importance, of the Duty of Allegiance: A Sermon, Preached at Aberdeen, December 12, 1776, Being the Fast Day Appointed by the King, on Account of the Rebellion in America*, 2d ed. (Aberdeen, Scotland, 1778), 41–42, 43.

164. Eliot, *Give Cesar his Due* (cited note 157), 36 n.

165. It has been suggested that during the early seventeenth century, the ancient constitution was not a doctrine opposed "to the royal sovereignty or even prerogative" (Pocock, *Ancient Constitution Retrospect* [cited note 35], 270). The issue may be whether it opposed arbitrary prerogativism and not prerogative power exercised by law. It should be recognized, however, that exponents of prerogativism could speak as if championing the rule of law through immutable ancient liberties. The earl of Strafford is quoted as saying on behalf of the Petition of Right in 1628: "We must vindicate—what? New things? No; our ancient lawful and vital liberties, by reinforcing the ancient laws made by our ancestors, by setting such a stamp on them as no licentious spirit shall dare hereafter to enter upon them" (Gerald M. Straka, "Sixteen Eighty-eight as the Year One: Eighteenth Century Attitudes Towards the Glorious Revolution," *Studies in Eighteenth-Century Culture* 1 [1971]: 149–50).

cacy and the concept of immemoriality was the security of governance by law.

VI. THE AUTHORITY OF CONSENT

It has recently been suggested that "the attraction which the concept of the ancient constitution possessed for lawyers and parliamentarians probably resided less in whatever ultimate principle provided its base, than in its value as a purely negative argument." The explanation is that "a truly immemorial constitution could not be subject to a sovereign: since a king could not be known to have founded it originally, the king now reigning could not claim to revoke rights rooted in some ancestor's will."[166] That theory was the essence of seventeenth-century constitutionalism, and at that time the "argument" was not thought negative. It was, rather, positive constitutional doctrine as likely to create and define rights as to defend them or maintain the status quo.

A seventeenth- and eighteenth-century constitutionalist usually did not argue immemorial law negatively by saying, for example, that the crown was forbidden to command some result, such as to abolish jury trial, because jury trial was immemorial and had never been ordained by the will and decision of a known sovereign, a predecessor of the present king. That seventeenth- or eighteenth-century constitutionalist would have been more likely to argue that the people had a right to trial by jury because it had existed by immemorial custom from time out of mind. The right to trial by jury, like any other right attributed to the ancient constitution, was positive, it was real, material, tactile, concrete, and existed independently of creation, will, or pleasure. Law was thought of and spoken of as a separate entity, the conceptualization of the abstract into the tangible in a way that we no longer comprehend. When Sir Edward Coke said that "no man ought to be wiser than the law,"[167] he was thinking of an autonomous reality that humans could manipulate but was altered only by internal evolution.

We cannot say that the autonomy of law was a concept believed in by those who espoused it. At worst its validity had to be accepted, be-

---

166. Pocock, *Ancient Constitution* (cited note 56), 51.
167. Quoted in Fussner, *Historical Revolution* (cited note 29), 135.

cause the concept of an autonomous law was essential for constitutional government as constitutionalism was then conceived. The law, which was the seventeenth and eighteenth centuries' custodian of civil rights, had to be independent of sovereign command or liberty would have been no more secure than any ordinary revocable grant.

"Are not the Liberties of the People settled upon as sure a Foundation from the Concessions of our Princes?" an anonymous writer asked in 1734. "Are they not indeed upon a surer Foundation than Original Contract; since these Concessions are to be seen, and the *Original Contract* not to be seen?"[168] For constitutionalists of customary restraints the answer was unreservedly "no." Rights that were grants rather than entrenched in timeless custom were rights without security, the same as being not rights at all. Liberty depended on the supremacy of law over power. "[I]f ever you set the King above Laws," the grand jury of Chester was instructed during the 1690s, "then it must necessarily follow, that the King derives his *Title* to the Crown of *England* not from the *Laws* of *England,* but from something else."[169] That something else was what seventeenth- and eighteenth-century constitutionalists could not concede, or there would have been no English constitutionalism. Not only did individual rights have to come from "law" rather than the king's grace, so did the king. For students of the ancient constitution the legal formula had to be "That *the Law makes the King.*" That was how in 1694 William Atwood, sometime chief justice of New York, stated what was probably the most fundamental legal doctrine for seventeenth-century constitutionalists.[170] "The Office of the King," Samuel Johnson added that same year, "depends wholly upon the Law

168. Anonymous, *A Defence of English History, Against the Misrepresentations of M. de Rapin Thoyras, in his History of England, Now Publishing Weekly* (London, 1734), 11.

169. "Grand Jury Charge," Henry Booth, earl of Warrington, *The Works of the Right Honourable Henry late L[ord] Delamer, and Earl of Warrington* (London, 1694), 649 (see also 655, 388).

170. [William Atwood], *The Antiquity and Justice of an Oath of Abjuration. In Answer to a Treatise Entituled The Case of an Oath of Abjuration Considered* (London, 1694), 83. See also Anonymous, *An Enquiry into the Nature and Obligation of Legal Rights. With Respect to the Popular Pleas of the Late K. James's Remaining Right to the Crown* (London, 1693), 16; [Barrington], *Revolution and Anti-Revolution Principles* (cited note 148), 55; Pocock, *Ancient Constitution* (cited note 56), 16.

both in its making and in its being."[171] "This High Office and Dominion was given him by Law, and all his Powers which are very Great, and give him an Opportunity of doing a world of Good, are all stated by Law; for else how should we know they are his? and they are butted and bounded by Law, or else they might be pretended to be Infinite. We find it thus in the first Constitution of this Monarchy."[172]

The law that made the king was the ancient constitutional autonomous law, not the legislation of parliament, for, although parliament could alter, amend, and reorganize that law, it, like the king, was the product of the same law and received its authority from that law. Just as the king was king because the law of the ancient constitution made him king, so parliament was parliament due to the same law.[173] The concept of sovereign, demiurgic law was explained in 1610 by Thomas Hedley, long before there were notions of either parliamentary supremacy over the king or parliamentary sovereignty over the law.

> But then you will say, the parliament, which is nothing else in effect but the mutual consent of the king and people, is that which gives matter and form and all complements to the common law. No, nor that neither, for the parliament hath his power and authority from the common law, and not the common law from the parliament. And therefore the common law is of more force and strength than the parliament. . . . But from logic to law, the king by his prerogative may dispense with a statute law, so he cannot with the common law. Also, the common law doth bind, and lead or direct the descent

171. Samuel Johnson, *Notes Upon the Phoenix Edition of the Pastoral Letter. Part I* (London, 1694), 57.

172. Ibid., 22. "And again all Englishmen that have any tolerable knowledg[e] of the Constitution are sensible, that the Office of the King depends wholly upon the Law both in its making and in its being, that a King as he is Impowered by Law must act by Law; and therefore they must needs know at first sight, that a King whose Authority is Antecedent to the Law, Independent of the Law, and Superiour to the Law . . . is an invented and studied King, whom the English law knows not" (ibid., 57–58). See also Anonymous, *Enquiry into the Nature* (cited note 170), 3, 13.

173. "The great *Security* of the Prince consists in this, That the *same Medium* which secures the Peoples *Rights*, secures his *Prerogative*" (*London Journal*, no. 722, April 28, 1733, p. 1, col. 2).

and right of the crown. But whether a statute law may do so or no, it hath been doubted. But you will say the parliament hath often altered and corrected the common law in divers points and may, if it will, utterly abrogate it, and establish a new law, therefore more eminent. I answer set a dwarf on a tall man's shoulders, and the dwarf may see farther than the tall man, yet that proves him not to be of a better stature than the other. The parliament may find some defects in the common law and amend them (for what is perfect under the sun), yet the wisest parliament that ever was could never have made such an excellent law as the common law is. But that the parliament may abrogate the whole law, I deny, for that were includedly to take away the power of the parliament itself, which power it hath by the common law.[174]

It will be said that Hedley's theory of sovereign law was superannuated by the time of the American Revolution, which occurred eight decades after the Glorious Revolution when parliament did what he said it could not do, change the descent and right of the crown. But, in fact, the Glorious Revolution changed perceptions about autonomous law much less than has been assumed. How else do we explain the shocked reactions of so many contemporaries to Blackstone's discovery that by the 1760s parliament had become omnipotent? If Blackstone was right, the earl of Abingdon protested, the ancient constitution was a dead letter and to "that *arbitrary Power,* against the Introduction of which, *separately,* we have been contending from the Saxon Era to the Era of George III, *conjunctively,* we must now submit; though attended, in this Form, by a State of Slavery, tenfold more oppressive, than any other Form could possibly inflict."[175] *Slavery* was also the word that American

174. Speech of Thomas Hedley, Commons Debates, June 28, 1610, in *Proceedings in Parliament 1610,* ed. Elizabeth Read Foster (New Haven, Conn., 1966), 2:173–74.

175. Bertie, *Thoughts on the Letter of Edmund Burke* (cited note 8), li. For the strongest reaction to Blackstone, by an Irish barrister, see [Charles Francis Sheridan], *Observations on the Doctrine laid down by Sir William Blackstone, Respecting the extent of the Power of the British Parliament, Particularly with relation to Ireland. In a letter to Sir William Blackstone, with a Postscript Addressed to Lord North* (Dublin, 1779).

whigs used when they discovered that parliament and not the "law" was to be their rule.[176]

Except for *arbitrary* there was no word that practitioners of ancient-constitution jurisprudence put to such frequent use as *slavery*. Slavery and its opposite concept, liberty, need close scrutiny for they reveal much about why we should not be thinking of history and historiography; they tell why the legal concept of custom, not the historical method, was what guided the selective research and the selective polemics of ancient constitutionalists. In the seventeenth and eighteenth centuries forensic historians used the ancient constitution for three purposes: proof of authority, establishment of consent, and avoidance of slavery. If we were to sum these up in one concept it would be said that the object of seventeenth- and eighteenth-century ancient constitutional advocacy was to preserve the contemporary version of liberty through the rule of law.

This is not the place to discuss the theory of legal and constitutional custom. The concept of custom should not be treated as it is treated here, as a side aspect of ancient-constitution jurisprudence. It was, in fact, more important to the development of Anglo-American liberty than was the ancient constitution, and deserves a separate symposium. The best we can do, if we must treat custom briefly, is to object to those historians of the ancient constitution who insist that the "philosophy of custom" was "a view of institutions as based purely upon immemorial usage and experience, with no conscious beginnings and nothing more to justify an institution than the presumption that, being immemorial, it must on innumerable occasions have proved satisfactory."[177] We must resist arguments that confound historical "immemorial" with legal "immemorial."[178] Legal custom was less a presumption

---

176. Reid, *Concept of Liberty* (cited note 102), 91–97. Among the radicals of Britain the new law of parliamentary sovereignty was resisted long after it was law and the old law was still appealed to. "*Trial by Jury*, as an element of the *Constitution*, was, consequently, *antecedent* to all *Law*, and *superior* to all *Law*, as no law can abolish it. It was even centuries anterior to Lawyers by profession" (Cartwright, *The English Constitution* [cited note 17], 138).

177. Pocock, "Machiavelli" (cited note 155), 571–72.

178. True, some practitioners of ancient constitutionalism used the word *his-*

of satisfaction with institutions that had no beginnings and was more like Sir Matthew Hale's argonauts' ship, a constant flow of change, a process of preservation rather than experimentation, of securing liberty through reinvigoration of the rule of law.[179]

The concept of custom should also be kept in mind when considering the ramifications of the authority of the past. The principle that concerns us is the authority *for* law not the authority of history. History in the seventeenth and eighteenth centuries did not bestow coercive authority, although practitioners of forensic history sometimes assumed that it did. If we wish to be exact, we should associate authority or "power"[180] with custom rather than history. Custom was one of law's authorities.

Custom was almost as important to existing law for consent implied as for authority conferred. Immemorial usage was "evidence of common acquiescence and consent," Vinerian law professor Wooddeson emphasized. "Laws ratified by custom, are generally the most ancient, and esteemed highly sacred, having been approved by the experience of ages."[181] Judge Atkyns explained the doctrine of implied consent by invoking a remarkable instance of the timeless concept of law, one that

---

tory but, as with Bolingbroke in the following sentence, the appeal was generally to custom: "When I say *that Parliaments were intirely built on the same general Principles, as well as directed to the same Purposes, as they still are,* I shall be justfy'd by the whole Tenor of our *History,* and of our *Law*" (*A Dissertation Upon Parties* [cited note 66], 198). See also Sommerville, "History and Theory" (cited note 37), 254.

179. Custom "quietly passes over obsolete laws, which sink into oblivion, and die peacefully, but the law itself remains young, always in the belief that it is old. Yet it is not old; rather it is a perpetual grafting of new on to old law, a fresh stream of contemporary law springing out of the creative wells of the subconscious" (Fritz Kern, *Kingship and Law in the Middle Ages,* trans. S. B. Chrimes [Oxford, 1970], 179). See also M. T. Clanchy, "Remembering the Past and the Good Old Law," *History,* new series 55 (1970): 172.

180. "Power" was Chief Justice Hale's word: "Usage and Custom generally receiv'd, do *Obtinere vim Legis.* . . . This is that which directs Discents, has settled some ancient Ceremonies and Solemnities in Conveyances, Wills and Deeds, and in many more Particulars" (Hale, *History of Common Law* [cited note 70], 44).

181. Wooddeson, *Elements of Jurisprudence* (cited note 76), 35, 47. It was not a matter of how well an institution worked, but of public approval of its force and operation.

was repeated so often we must assume that it made sense to common lawyers of the late seventeenth century. "We our selves of the present Age," he wrote, "chose our Common Law, and consented to the most ancient Acts of Parliament, for we lived in our Ancestors a 1000 Years ago, and those Ancestors are still living in us."[182] Before protesting this idea, reflect that Atkyns was speaking of legal consent, not of a physical fact. You may say he was employing a legal fiction, but you would be wrong. As was said in 1769 of the "*ancient and approved laws*" of "the British, Roman, Danish, Saxon and Norman times," "if they had not been liked by these people, they would have been altered."[183] The consent is implied or constructive, not actual and direct.

The principle of implied consent was not intended to strengthen the authority of law qua custom by giving it a popular base, but to strengthen customary law or ancient constitutionalism against the onslaughts of other types of law such as prerogative law, Star Chamber law, or civil law. The argument that common law and custom were laws popularly consented to would later anger Thomas Jefferson and Jeremy Bentham, but in the seventeenth and eighteenth centuries it was a contention that reenforced the jurisprudential pretensions of constitutionalism and customary liberty.

Resistance to prerogative law, however, was not the chief jurisprudential function performed in the seventeenth and eighteenth centuries by the concept of an autonomous law based on the authority of custom and popular consent implied from acquiescence in the ancient constitution. Its prime function, rather, was to fend off law by will and pleasure, whether that law was based on paternalism, nationalism,

---

182. Sir Robert Atkyns, *An Enquiry into the Power of Dispensing with Penal Statutes* (London, 1689), 6. Fortescue-Aland also meant the fiction of implied consent when he wrote: "Besides, the Laws themselves gain Strength and Authority by the Antiquity of their Profession. The longer any Laws continue in Use and Practice, the stronger and more forcible is the Argument for their Goodness and Excellence" ("Dedication and Preface" [cited note 65], xv).

183. [Samuel Johnson], *A History and Defence of Magna Charta* (London, 1769), 3–4 (quoting Fortescue). For the contrary contention that this was historical proof, see Quentin Skinner, "History and Ideology in the English Revolution," *Historical Journal* 8 (1965): 174.

divine right, reason, efficiency, or nature. This was a losing battle, of course, at least after about 1740 because the law that it opposed was the law that had the future before it, the law that would dominate the nineteenth century in the form of parliamentary sovereignty. The contest as seen in the seventeenth century was summed up by William Prynne when he boasted that one of his forensic-history books concerned "My *Antiquity triumphing over Novelty.*"[184] It was a telling forensic strategy. A proponent of customary constitutionalism could oppose any constitutional innovation or reform by insisting that constitutional custom was grounded on something more secure than political choice, on, for example, as Edmund Burke insisted when opposing extension of parliamentary representation, "the peculiar circumstances . . . and . . . habitudes of the people."[185]

As long as you had no quarrel with the status quo, customary constitutionalism provided a higher sense of security and, therefore, a more certain degree of secured liberty, than did prerogative, parliamentary, or democratic discretion. The artificial reason of immemorial custom was perceived as safer, certainly less risky, than the analytical or natural reason of even the wisest men.[186] Philosophical reason could not make better law according to ancient constitutionalists as they knew that the best law came from timeless change through centuries of experience,

---

184. Prynne, *Plea for Lords* (cited note 125), 5.

185. Quoted in Pocock, *Politics, Language and Time* (cited note 27), 227.

186. "The artifice [of artificial reason] is simply the law: there are cases for which a lawyer can draw a solution from positive legal sources. Such a legal solution will be better than the solution an ideally wise person would reach with only natural reason to depend on. That is true because the law is a collective product, a repository of many wise men's thinking about related problems over a long stretch of time. The value of a correct legal solution will sometimes not be evident to a critic whose cognitive and moral acuity, however distinguished, are only his. It is permissible to toy a bit with language here and say that what seems reasonable to one person, or one age, will not typically be as rational as the law, whose rationality is not fully visible in any single perspective. When one has laid hold of this truth and presumed in favor of the law's rationality, one will of course begin to see it" (Charles Gray, "Reason, Authority, and Imagination: The Jurisprudence of Sir Edward Coke," in *Culture and Politics from Puritanism to the Enlightenment,* ed. Perez Zagorin [Berkeley, Calif., 1980], 31).

popular consent, and uncountable judicial and human decisions.[187] American whigs believed that they well knew the difference for they had experienced it. They had wanted to remain in the British Empire governed by the customary ways of the eighteenth-century imperial constitution. They had watched from afar as the logic of sovereignty persuaded the ruling faction in Great Britain that despite tradition, experience, and a hundred and fifty years of constitutional custom, parliament had both the right and the power to legislate directly for the colonies. American whigs resorted to civil war rather than risk the constitutional insecurity of a law of absolute legislative command that would brook no restraints from the ancient constitution.[188]

The threat of sovereign discretion was not an American fear alone in the last half of the eighteenth century. A surprisingly large number of people in the mother country were apprehensive that the old safety of customary liberty was fast losing ground to the capricious rationality of law by legislative command. The bishop of Worcester was concerned enough in 1760 to warn that any enquiry about the British constitution was "a question of FACT; that must be tried by authorities and precedents only; and decided at last by the evidence of historical testimony, not by the conclusions of philosophy or political specula-tion."[189] That was the traditional theory of constitutionalism, the old methodology that William Dowdeswell outlined when he argued that even the House of Commons, if acting as a court of judicature, did not have the legal right to be arbitrary. It should, rather, be controlled by

187. Pocock, *Politics, Language and Time* (cited note 27), 214–15; Pocock, *Ancient Constitution* (cited note 56), 173.

188. Thus it was reasoned that parliament had the authority to legislate for and to tax the colonies because, even if the right had never before been exercised, "it is essential to government, founded in justice and equity, and in the law of nature and nations" (Alexander Carlyle, *The Justice and Necessity of the War with our American Colonies Examined. A Sermon Preached at Inveresk, December 12, 1776, Being the Fast-Day Appointed by the King, on account of the American Rebellion* [Edinburgh, 1777], 10).

189. [Richard Hurd], *Moral and Political Dialogues Between Divers Eminent Persons of the Past and Present Age; With Critical and Explanatory Notes*, 2d ed. (London, 1760), 224.

taught, nondiscretionary, common law standards of decision, the most important of which was usage.

> When this usage is collected from *antient, uniform, and uninterrupted* practice of Parliament, we have the custom of Parliament; and that *custom* is the *law of Parliament.*

> These restraints therefore do not stand solely on the decision of the House, or the judgment of a court having competent jurisdiction in the case: they are much better founded in the *previous usage,* and the *repeated acquiescence* of those who are affected by them. They are also similar to the like restraints at common-law, except in those very few instances in which the clear undisputed usage of Parliament, not deduced from one, but established by many precedents and the general tenor of parliamentary proceedings, may have, for very good reasons not adopted, the practice of other courts. So that an incapacity at common-law to be elected into the House of Commons stands in need of the following conditions. It must be similar to the like incapacity established and declared at common-law in similar cases; it must not be repugnant to common-sense; nor contradicted by the usage of Parliament.[190]

There was, of course, a more basic principle at stake than common law methodology. Eighteenth-century constitutionalists clung to the old constitutionalism of rights buttressed by appeal to the past rather than the new constitutionalism of rights established by appeal to abstract principles because they did not want to lose governance by the rule of law. As late as 1823 the polemicist who is remembered as the "dean of the radical reformers"[191] demonstrated how comfortably and effortlessly eighteenth-century radicalism had been able to assume a guise of antiquity as he urged Britain to return to the old constitutionalism that by then existed only in the United States. What the old breed of constitutionalists had been opposed to, John Cartwright explained, was "a Constitution which can be twisted and moulded into any form,

190. [William Dowdeswell], *The Sentiments of an English Freeholder, on the Late Decision of the Middlesex Election* (London, 1769), 8.

191. J. R. Dinwiddy, *Christopher Wyvill and Reform, 1790–1820* (York, England, 1971), 2.

to agree exactly with the whims, the caprices, and the despotic views of the Ministers for the time being."[192] In other words, the old breed of constitutionalists—which included the ancient constitutionalists—had been opposed to the constitutionalism that would become the rule of the British constitution of the nineteenth and twentieth centuries.

VII. ADVOCACY OF THE PAST

There have been two main arguments made up to this point. First, the ancient constitution was not primarily an institutional framework for a broad model of government such as mixed monarchy. It was a defense of governance by the rule of law. Second, the purpose of the ancient constitution was advocacy, not history.[193] The next question is whether practitioners of ancient-constitution advocacy in the seventeenth and eighteenth centuries intended to argue forensic history rather than impartially to investigate the past. The evidence leaves little doubt that they understood they were pleading a constitutional cause.

Our evidence starts with the generation after Coke and Selden, which means that it starts with Nathaniel Bacon. Puritan, zealous parliamentarian, and member of the Long Parliament for Cambridge University, Bacon made no bones about the cause for which he was writing: "A Private Debate concerning the right of an *English King* to Arbitrary rule over *English Subjects,* as Successor to the *Norman Conquerour,* (so called) first occasioned this Discourse," he explained in the "advertisement" of his first "history." With that purpose, he had "necessarily fall'n upon the *Antiquity* and *Uniformity* of the *Government* of this *Nation.*"[194] Bacon included an appendix in another book entitled "A Vindication of the ancient way of Parliaments in England." He wrote it, he explained, "be-

---

192. Cartwright, *The English Constitution* (cited note 17), 164 n. 7.

193. It is not suggested that there have not been historians who have pointed out that "history" was a weapon in the struggle over sovereignty: Weston, "Legal Sovereignty" (cited note 50), 417; M. P. Thompson, "The Idea of Conquest in the Controversies over the 1688 Revolution," *Journal of the History of Ideas* 38 (1977): 37–38; Styles, "Politics and Research" (cited note 38), 54.

194. Nathaniel Bacon, *An Historical and Political Discourse of the Laws & Government of England, from the First Times to the End of the Reign of Queen Elizabeth* (London, 1689), "Advertisement" to "First Part" (n.p.).

cause some mens Pens of late have ranged into a denial of the *Commons* ancient Right in the *Legislative* powers; and others, even to annul the Right both of *Lords* and *Commons* therein, resolving all such power into that one principle of a King, *Quicquid libet, licet,* so making the breach much wider than at the beginning."[195]

Bacon used the forensic history of ancient constitutionalism to question the Stuart concept of monarchy.[196] People on the other side of the controversy, not liking what he was doing, took steps against Bacon's books, as explained by the printer of a fourth edition of his history, published the year after James II was driven into exile by the Glorious Revolution.

> This *Book* at its first *Publishing,* which was shortly after the Death of *King Charles the First,* had the ill fortune to be coldly received in the world, by reason of the Circumstances of those times; but after *K. Charles the Second* was possest of the *Crown,* and endeavoured to advance the *Prerogative* beyond its just bounds, the *Book* began to be much enquired after, and lookt into by many *Learned Men* who were not willing to part easily with their *Birth-Rights,* so that in a short time it became very scarce, and was sold at a great rate; this occasion'd the private Reprinting of it in the year 1672, which as soon as the Government perceived, they Prosecuted both the *Publisher* and the *Book* so violently, that many hundreds of the Books were seized and burnt; that, and the great want of the *Book* since occasioned the Reprinting of it (without any *Alterations* or *Omissions*) in the year 1682, when the Press was at liberty by reason of the ceasing of the Act for Printing, but the *Prerogative* then getting above the

195. [Nathaniel Bacon], *The Continuation of the Historical & Political Discourse of the Laws & Government of England, Until the end of the Reign of Queen Elizabeth* (London, 1682), 179. The "Mens Pens" were royalist "histories" that rejected Cokeian constitutional law, claiming that the crown created parliament at its pleasure. Earl, "Procrustean Feudalism" (cited note 35), 35.

196. He said "of the *Saxon* Commonwealth": "Afar off it seems a Monarchy, but in approach discovers more of a Democracy," and "It was a beautiful composure, mutually dependent in every part from the Crown to the Clown; the Magistrates being all choice men, and the King the choicest of the chosen: election being the birth of esteem, and that of merit" (Bacon, *Discourse* [cited note 194], 69, 70).

Law, it met with a new Persecution, and the *Publisher* was Indicted for the Reprinting of it.[197]

During the Restoration, Edward Cook anonymously published a book that has in recent years been criticized as bad history. It may have been bad, but it is by no means certain that Cook intended it to be history. Surely his title suggests that it was not history, or, if history, it was, at best, forensic history: *Argumentum Anti-Normannicum: or an Argument Proving, from Ancient Histories and Records, that William, Duke of Normandy Made no absolute Conquest of England, by the Sword; in the sense of our Modern Writers.*[198] The question Cook was disputing, to be discussed below, was the most bitterly argued point of constitutional law during the seventeenth century. Just a few years earlier Peter Heylyn, a Laudian theologian, had enlisted on the other side of that debate, when he stated as the operative doctrine of English constitutional law that "the power of *making Laws* . . . is properly and legally in the King alone." And "for the proof thereof," he claimed, all he had to do was show that William of Normandy had become king of England by conquest following a war in which the Anglo-Saxons who opposed him were defeated. "When the *Norman* Conqueror first came in, as he wonne the Kingdom by the sword, so did he govern it by his power: His *Sword* was then the *Scepter,* and his *will* the *Law.* There was no need on his part, of an Act of Parliament; much less of calling all the *Estates* together, to know of them after what form, and by what Laws they would be governed."[199]

The stakes for this history seemed incredibly high for those participating in the debate—the governance of England and of Great Britain. If Heylyn's "history," and with it the constitutional law it supported,

197. John Starkey, "Advertisement" to ibid. (n.p.).

198. Edward Cook, *Argumentum Anti-Normannicum: or an Argument Proving, from Ancient Histories and Records, that William, Duke of Normandy Made no absolute Conquest of England, by the Sword; in the sense of our Modern Writers* (London, 1682).

199. Peter Heylyn, *The Stumbling-Block of Disobedience and Rebellion, Cunningly laid by Calvin in the Subjects way, Discovered, Censured, and Removed* (London, 1658), 267. "And so this strand of systematic and unashamed absolutist theorizing spanned the Interregnum years, a decade before gaining its final articulation by Hobbes, a generation before gaining its full historical dress from Dr. Brady" (Skinner, "History and Ideology" [cited note 183], 169).

was to prevail, James Tyrrell warned, "all the Liberties and Priviledges we now enjoy, being at first derived from the Concessions of Kings (and those in great part wrested from them by Force) their successors may, whenever they shall think it conducing to the greater safety of the Kingdom (of which they are to be the sole Judges), resume them."[200] It was that use of forensic history, to prove the constitutionality of royal legislation, that led Sir Robert Atkyns to attack as "Innovating Writers" those "historians" who, by dating the House of Commons from the reign of Henry III, "would destroy Foundations, and remove our Ancient Land-marks, and the Ancient and Just Limits and Boundaries of Power and Authority."[201] It may be indicative of how serious this brand of forensic history could be that Atkyns did not publish until the year after the Glorious Revolution.

William Prynne, whose work as a historian has been questioned by the historiographers of ancient constitutionalism, also spelled out the fact that it was current constitutional liberty that motivated his research. He was, Prynne wrote, explaining and defining rights immutable "against those *traiterous* late published Pamphlets, which professedly deny it, and endeavour, a *totall abrogation* of all *former Lawes,* to set up a *New modell* and *Body* of the *law,* to rule us for the future, according

200. Quoted in Earl, "Procrustean Feudalism" (cited note 35), 38. Earl says Tyrrell was commenting on royalist history, but it is evident he was commenting on constitutional law.

201. Atkyns, *Power, Jurisdiction and Priviledge* (cited note 123), 14. In litigation Atkyns argued: "I shall clearly prove, that these [House of Commons] Powers and Privileges were indeed their ancient Right and Inheritance. Which they cannot be, unless that House, or the Commons by their Representative, have been ever from the beginning of the Government a part and member of the Parliament" (Sir Robert Atkyns, *Parliamentary and Political Tracts* [London, 1734], 31). Atkyns was arguing for the defense in the prosecution of Sir William Williams. Surprisingly, as counsel he even assumed the burden of historical proof: "To support the power and privilege of the House of Commons, as being an essential part of the parliament; it is absolutely necessary to make it out against these innovators, that the House of Commons have ever been a part of the parliament, and that they were long before 49 H. 3. Or otherwise they are but precarious in their power and privileges, and enjoy them but of grace" (Rex v. Williams, 13 *State Trials* 1369, 1392 [1684–95]).

to their pleasures." Prynne was not objecting to any particular laws but to a way of looking at law, a definition of authority—law as command. He was defending, the title of his book said, "the Good, Old, Fundamentall Liberties, Franchises, Rights Laws, of all English Freemen."[202]

During the 1650s, the years of the Long Parliament and Oliver Cromwell, a rival school of jurisprudence had become more vocal, rejecting the good old law and claiming "*That to plead for these and other fundamental laws and liberties, as unalterable,* (though the only Bulwarks & Badges of our Freedome) is nothing else, *but to enslave the Nation.*" What that new legalism could mean, Prynne warned, was that "people do not only lose their Liberty, *but* are brought under such a kinde of Tyranny, out of which (AS BEING WORSE THAN THE EGYPTIAN BONDAGE) there is no hope of deliverance." He was rallying his readers against the new theorists of rational nationalism, including the Levellers, "who," Prynne asserted, "shall endeavour by force, fraud, or flattery to compell or perswade them, to sell, resign, betray, or give up these their *Ancestrall* Priviledges, Inheritances, Birthrights to them."[203]

To turn back those whom he called enemies of "our *Hereditary, fundamentall laws, liberties, rights, franchises,*" which were "their own, and

202. Prynne, *First and Second Part of a Seasonable, Legal, and Historicall Vindication* (cited note 108), 9. In the "Epistle" of the work discussed earlier, in which he defended forensically the inherent jurisdiction of the House of Lords, Prynne stated he was the Lords's "advocate." The "seditious *Design*" of the Commons to legislate without concurrence of the upper House "has ingaged me (the unablest of many) out of my great affection to *Royalty and the real Nobility,* and a deep sence of the present and tottering *condition* of our *Kingdom, Parliament* (the very *pillars* and *foundation* whereof are now not only *shaken,* but almost *quite subverted*) voluntarily, without any Fee at all, to become your Honors *Advocate,* to plead your Cause, and vindicate your undoubted hereditary right of *sitting, voting, judging in our Parliaments*" (Prynne, *Plea for Lords* [cited note 125], "Epistle" at [2]).

203. Prynne, *First and Second Part of a Seasonable, Legal, and Historicall Vindication* (cited note 108), 3, 7. In the introduction of an earlier work Prynne wrote: "*I here present thee with* Truth Triumphing over Falsehood, Antiquity over Novelty; *to settle both the Judgement and Practice, in these unset[t]led* times, *wherein the very* Foundation *of* Parliaments, States, Churches, Governments, *are shaken and subverted*" (*Truth Triumphing over Fals[e]hood, Antiquity over Novelty* [London, 1645], "The Epistle to the Reader" at [1]).

every other *English Freemans* best *inheritance* and *security*,"[204] Prynne adapted the most effective jurisprudential weapon at his command, the ancient constitution. Marshaling his evidence in a totally timeless context,[205] he sought the principles of restraint—principles he wanted established as inherent in the constitution of Cromwellian England— by claiming that before the Roman conquest "the *British* Kings were obliged to governe their subjects justly, and righteously, according to the established Lawes of those times, which secured their Liberties, Properties, Goods, Lives against all violence and arbitrary Tyranny, Rapines, Taxes,"[206] and that centuries later, the "English *Saxons* from the first Settlement of their Kingdomes and Monarchies, had no Soveraign Power at all to make, alter, or repeal Lawes, impose Taxes . . . but onely by common consent in General Parliamentary Councils, much lesse to imprison, condemn, exile, out-law any mans person, or to deprive him of his Life, Lands, Goods, Franchises, against the Law."[207]

Government by the rule of law was the dogma of Atkyns, Prynne, and the other seventeenth-century constitutionalists of limitations. That creed was summed up at the end of the first decade of the next

204. Prynne, *First and Second Part of a Seasonable, Legal, and Historicall Vindication* (cited note 108), 5.

205. "I shall in a *Chronological* way tender you a large *Historical Catalogue of National, Parliamental, civil and military* Contests, Votes, Declarations, Remonstrances, Oathes, Vows, Protestations, Covenants, Engagements, Excommunications, Confirmations, Evidences, Statutes, Charters, Writs, Records, Judgments and Authorities in all ages, undeniably evidencing, declaring, vindicating, establishing, perpetuating these *Fundamental Hereditary Rights, Liberties, Priviledges, Franchises, Customs, Laws,* and abundantly manifesting the extraordinary *care, industry, zeal, courage, wisdome, vigilancy of our Ancestours,* to defend, preserve, and perpetuate them to posterity, without the least *violation* or *diminution*" (ibid., 8 [see also at 7]).

206. Prynne, *Second Part of a Seasonable, Legal, and Historical Vindication* (cited note 110), 13–14. On taxes in ancient British times: "[I]t is clear, That Taxes and Tribute not granted and assented to in Parliament, though imposed by a *Conquering Invader,* binde not the *Nation*" (ibid., 17).

207. Ibid., 49. On taxes in Saxon times: "[T]he ancient *English Saxon Kings* at and from their primitive Establishment in this Realm, had no power nor prerogative in them to impose any publick Taxes . . . on their people without their Common Consents and Grants in their Great Councils of the Realm" (ibid., 64–65).

century when a writer cast it in terms of grades of supremacy with restraint higher than command—the autonomy of sovereign law over the
discretion of prerogative power. "Whenever the Crown," it was said, "in
any Cases, issues any Grants or Commissions contrary to Law, they are
void; which shews the Superiority of the Law over the Regal Power. And
that Power cannot extend it self in any Instances beyond the Bounds
of the Common or Statute-Laws, in which 'tis solely founded."[208] This
positioning of autonomous law was not confined to royal command.
By implication it applied to all command that in time would come to
be identified with the concept of sovereignty in British constitutional
law. It expressed a formula from the past, not the rule of the future,
yet as long as it remained a viable explanation of British constitutional
theory, the forensic history of ancient constitutionalism was a major
factor shaping the contours of constitutional debate—which does not
mean it had much influence in determining the result.

Throughout the eighteenth century the British constitution was in
a remarkable state of contrariety—not a state of transition, it is always
in such a state, but a state of polarity. Constitutional theory in Great
Britain was torn between competing constitutional doctrines which,
without tearing the nation into impotency, existed side by side, each
supported by tenable, familiar, aggressive legal theories. Indeed, the
eighteenth century can be called an epoch of two constitutions in
both Great Britain and the American colonies, with the mother country eventually falling under one constitution and the American states
consciously selecting the other. If we wish to summarize the development in two sentences, we might say that the British who opposed the
American version of the constitution were "looking ahead," away from
the ancient constitution, to government by consent, to a constitution
of parliamentary command, in which government was entrusted with
arbitrary power and civil rights were grants from the sovereign. The
Americans were "looking backward," not to government by consent
but to government by the rule of law, to a sovereign that did not grant

208. Anonymous, *The Divine Rights of the British Nation and Constitution Vindicated. In Remarks on the Several Papers Publish'd against the Reverend Mr. Hoadly's Considerations upon the Bishop of Exeter's Sermons* (London, 1710), 60.

rights but was limited by rights, a sovereign that was, like liberty, created by law, the guardian of liberty. Perhaps they were not looking back to the ancient constitution, but they were looking back to the constitution of Sir Edward Coke, to the constitution that had triumphed over Charles I and James II.

Ranged in opposition to the constitution of supreme, immutable autonomous law in the eighteenth century was a school of legal theorists who, in the seventeenth and eighteenth centuries, were thought of as "anticonstitutionalists." In more recent time they have been called absolutists, modernists, Filmerians, Bodinians, Austinians, or rationalists. For the moment—that is for most of the eighteenth century—parliamentarians, satisfied with having established supremacy over the crown, had not sensed the potential of sovereignty over law and the extreme ground among the jurisprudes of arbitrary power was held by a small minority of royalists. The constitution they wanted was summed up by the claim that "Parliaments owe their Being to him [the king], but he his own to Birth-Right."[209] This was a theory of constitutional law that could be stated as a straight principle of pragmatic jurisprudence but sometimes was advanced in the dress of history, usually in the form of an attack on ancient constitutionalism. The chief exponent of this school of law in the period covered here was Robert Brady, who wrote several studies of contemporary constitutional theory which he cast in historical contexts.

In the twentieth century Brady has become somewhat of a historian's folk hero, the lonely prophet of a darker, less enlightened age, who had the vision and the intelligence to be the good historian courageously but in vain exposing the misconceptions and misrepresentations of those bad historians, the ancient constitutionalists. He has been described as "a pioneer in modern historiography,"[210] the "most advanced historian of his day,"[211] the seventeenth-century scholar who helped expose "the politically disastrous consequences of anachro-

209. Ibid., 81 (quoting a critic of the legal theories of Bishop Benjamin Hoadly).

210. Pocock, *Ancient Constitution Retrospect* (cited note 35), 351.

211. Smith, *Gothic Bequest* (cited note 95), 17.

nistic thinking,"[212] and who wrote "with a rigorous devotion both to scholarship and the interests of the royalist cause."[213]

Probably no one disputes that Brady was a better historian than his opponents, the adherents to ancient constitutionalism. To the extent that he was he probably should also be called a better forensic historian—or a better historian who wrote forensic history—for he was no less an advocate than the ancient constitutionalists, a fact about which he openly boasted. "I have written these *Tracts*," Brady said, explaining the history he published, "to *undeceive* the People, and to shew them, That really they were not *possessed* of *these Peices* [*sic*] of *Soveraignty* and *Empire* antiently, nor of such share in the Government, as these *Unquiet, Tumultuous* Men endeavour to make them believe they had, and still ought to have."[214]

What separated Brady from the seventeenth- and eighteenth-century lawyers who wrote history, aside from the fact that he wrote to oppose them, was that he had less reason than they to depart from what are today recognized as the canons of historical methodology. In most other respects he was like them. He was writing on one side of the current constitutional controversy, he was a royalist bent on demythifying the ancient constitution,[215] and he was just as ready to select and manipulate historical facts as any of the forensic historians whose writings have been more sharply criticized in the twentieth century.[216] In-

212. Pocock, "Origins of Study" (cited note 44), 234. See "Editor's Introduction" to Viscount Bolingbroke, *Political Writings,* ed. Isaac Kramnick (New York: 1970), xlii; Kramnick, *Bolingbroke and His Circle* (cited note 22), 128.

213. Kramnick, "Augustan Politics" (cited note 33), 37. Brady is said to have "raised out of the morass of a pseudo-historical argument the first serious study of the Norman Conquest." Styles, "Politics and Research" (cited note 38), 72. See also Dickinson, "Eighteenth-Century Debate" (cited note 138), 191.

214. Robert Brady, *An Introduction to the Old English History, Comprehended in three several Tracts* (London, 1684), "Epistle" (n.p.).

215. "No omnipotent Parliament and elective crown could threaten the Stuarts when the idea of the ancient constitution was proved to be so erroneous" (Kramnick, "Augustan Politics" [cited note 33], 37). See also Kramnick, *Bolingbroke and His Circle* (cited note 22), 128–29.

216. See, e.g., [Robert Brady], *The Great Point of Succession Discussed. With a Full and Particular answer to a late Pamphlet, Intituled, A Brief History of Succession, &c.*

deed, Brady made no bones about the forensic and polemical purpose of his "history." It was the advancement of a constitutional theory that had never been dominant in English constitutionalism, a legal theory that repudiated not just the ancient constitution, but the principle of limited government, the doctrine of mixed monarchy, the rule of law, and the authority of custom.

> *First,* That not only all Government, but particularly Monarchy does owe its immediat[e] Foundation and Constitution to God Almighty.
>
> *Secondly,* That by the Law of God, Nature and Nations the Crown ought to descend according to Priority of Birth, and Proximity of Blood.
>
> *Thirdly,* That if an Act of Parliament were obtained to exclude his R. H. [the duke of York, it] would be unjust, unlawful, and *ipso facto* void, as contrary both to the Law of God and Nature; and the known Fundamental Laws of the Land.[217]

There was no need to rely on the logic of patriarchy. History going back to Roman times, if cleared of ancient constitutionalism, demonstrated "*That all the* Liberties *and* Priviledges *the People can pretend to, were the* Grants *and* Concessions *of the* Kings *of this Nation, and were Derived from the Crown.*"[218] Brady was attempting much more than what a twentieth-century admirer has termed enhancing "the power of the crown by situating it in a context of incessant change."[219] He was less

---

(London, 1681), 2–25. "Every bit as rigid in his own way as the whig historians, Brady likewise was guilty of present-mindedness and hence anachronism in his account of the English past though his skilful and rigorous use of Spelman's *Glossary* made this less obvious in his case. In sum, Brady's examination of early English history was always subservient to the larger cause of placing a legal sovereignty based on the sword in the Stuart kingship" (Weston, "Legal Sovereignty" [cited note 50], 431). See also Corinne Comstock Weston and Janelle Renfrow Greenberg, *Subjects and Sovereigns: The Grand Controversy over Legal Sovereignty in Stuart England* (Cambridge, England, 1981), 196–97.

217. [Brady], *Great Point of Succession* (cited note 216), 25–26.

218. Robert Brady, *A Complete History of England, from the First Entrance of the Romans under the Conduct of Julius Caesar, Unto the End of the Reign of King Henry III* (London, 1685), "Preface" (n.p.).

219. Pocock, *Ancient Constitution Retrospect* (cited note 35), 353.

interested in historical dynamics than royal absolutism. Brady's foren-sic history was driven by the legal theory that, as Isaac Kramnick sug-gests, "[n]o omnipotent Parliament and elective Crown could threaten the Stuarts if the claim that the ancient constitution had accorded power to Parliament was erroneous."[220]

It may be wondered why Brady's history has earned such praise from recent historians who have otherwise been so sharply critical of forensic history when practiced by constitutionalists. He was not much honored before this century. His own contemporaries, in both the seventeenth and the eighteenth centuries, had rather strong things to say about both his work and his advocacy. In 1725, George St. Amand referred to Brady as "the very learned Advocate for Slavery," and three years later, in a charge to the Westminster grand jury, he was called one of the "Advocates for Arbitrary Power."[221] In the year of the battle of Lexington, the Scots lawyer Gilbert Stuart described Brady as "a writer who is known to have disgraced excellent talents, by . . . giving a varnish to tyranny,"[222] and even as late as 1796 Francis Hargrave still thought it worthwhile to remind readers that Brady was "arbitrary" and to refer to him as "the learned but bigoted Dr. Brady."[223] These men in the eighteenth century were still fighting the controversy that New York's future chief justice William Atwood had joined in 1681 when he summed up Brady's argument by stressing conclusions that today are apparently considered to have been the discoveries of good history, but which Atwood and his contemporaries thought blatant forensic politics.

> For according to him [Brady] the Tenents *in Capite* were the only *Members* of the Great Council before 49 *H.* 3. and if others were

220. Kramnick, "Editor's Introduction" to Bolingbroke, *Political Writings* (cited note 212), xlii.

221. St. Amand, *Historical Essay* (cited note 61), 89; charge of October 9, 1728, *Sir John Gonson's Five Charges* (cited note 149), 107.

222. Gilbert Stuart, "A Discourse Concerning the Laws and Government of England," in Francis Stoughton Sullivan, *Lectures on the Constitution and Laws of England: With a Commentary on Magna Charta, and Illustrations of Many of the English Statutes. To which Authorities are added, and a Discourse prefixed, concerning the Laws and Government of England by Gilbert Stuart, LL.D.*, 2d ed. (London, 1776), xix (n.).

223. Hargrave, "Preface" to Hale, *Jurisdiction* (cited note 121), lxxxiii, lxxix.

after, 'twas by Usurping upon the Rights of Tenents *in Capite*, who, and not others, when the *new Government was set up, began to be Represented* by *two Knights for every County, out of their own number*, and they *at first*, that is then, *Elected* their own Representatives; and yet these Tenents *in Capite* might be set aside if the King and his Council pleased, nor was any power given to others to chuse till 10 *H.* 6. *c.* 2 which gave no new power, and the Lords depend upon the Kings pleasure.[224]

More than a century after Atwood published this comment John Reeves explained "the Cause of [Atwood's] warmth." It was, of course, the constitutional issues that were at stake. Brady's opponents used the ancient constitution against him because "it would set the Privileges and Pretensions of the Commons upon a higher footing, if they could be proved to be of very remote Antiquity; and that so late a period, as that of Henry III. and Edward I. and the rebellious proceedings that were the immediate Cause of their being summoned to Parliament, gave them a very low origin in point of time, and something very like usurpation in point of Title."[225] The "warmth," therefore, was caused by a dispute about legislative jurisdiction.[226] As Atwood's contemporary Judge Robert Atkyns pointed out, to accept the evidence that the representatives of the Commons were first called to parliament by Henry III could mean in law that "all the Power and Priviledge the House of Commons claims, is not by Prescription, but that they depend upon the King's Royal Will and Pleasure, and had their Original

224. [William Atwood], *Additions Answering the Omissions of our Reverend Author* (London, 1681), 37–38. For Atwood on Brady, see Weston, "Legal Sovereignty" (cited note 50), 412–13.

225. [Reeves], *Thoughts on English Government* (cited note 67), 117–18.

226. Thus Brady contended that not only was the House of Lords anciently summoned at the king's discretion, it was also discretionary as to which members were summoned. To which Atwood pointed out: "[*T*]*he making this to have been* the Constitution of the House of Lords, *and maintained in* Practice ever since, *is as much as to say, the* Rights *of that Order of men, are not set*[*t*]*led at this day*" ([William Atwood], *Jus Anglorum ab Antiquo; or, A Confutation of an Impotent Libel against the Government by King, Lords, and Commons. Under pretence of Answering Mr.* PETYT, *and the author of Jani Anglorum Facies Nova. With a Speech according to the Answerer's Principles, made for the Parliament at Oxford* [London, 1681], "Preface" at [18]).

by his meer Concession, and not by Ancient Inherent Right, nor Original Constitution, and therefore may be resumed at Pleasure."[227] If not Brady and his friends, at least everyone who supported the Commons said the controversy concerned parliamentary autonomy and that it was purely forensic. "As on Mr. *Petyts,* and my side," Atwood wrote, "the *design* can be no other, than to shew how deeply rooted the Parliamentary Rights are; So the Doctors [Brady's] in opposition to ours, must be to shew the contrary, (a *design* worthy of a Member of Parliament) and 'tis a Question whether he yields these Rights to be more than *precarious.*"[228]

It is a wonder how we in the twentieth century have come to think that these controversies were solely concerned with disputes about history. In the seventeenth and eighteenth centuries it was not lawyers alone who knew they turned on other matters than the canons of historiography. Just consider the attitude of a clergyman, Samuel Johnson, commenting on a *History* by another clergyman, Abednego Seller. "[W]hen I had discover'd of what Stamp the Historian was," Johnson observed, meaning that Seller was a Jacobite or what Johnson termed "a King *James's* Man," "I needed no great sagacity to understand the Design and Drift of the History. It is this plainly, to thrust out the present Government, by leaving no Room for it, and by telling us that the late Tyranny was Sacred and Irresistible."[229]

Everyone also understood that no matter the premises of the debate, whether about the origins of a house of parliament or the an-

---

227. Atkyns, *Power, Jurisdiction and Priviledge* (cited note 123), 14.

228. [Atwood], *Additions Answering Omissions* (cited note 224), 37. Atwood also said of a book by Brady "against Mr. *Petyt* and my Self" that it "not only treats us with Pedantick Scorn . . . but it seems, to trample on the best Constitution, our Government it self, under Colour of its being *New* in the 49th of Hen. 3" (*Jus Anglorum* [cited note 226], "Preface" at [1]). It has, nevertheless, been suggested that the argument involved "the Whig interpretation of English history" (James Moore, "A Comment on Pocock," in *Theories of Property: Aristotle to the Present,* ed. Anthony Parel and Thomas Flanagan [Waterloo, Ontario, 1979], 174).

229. Samuel Johnson, *Reflections on the History of Passive Obedience* (London, 1689), 1; Samuel Johnson, *An Answer to the History of Passive Obedience, just not reprinted under the Title of A Defence of Dr. Sacheverel* (London, 1709), 1. He was criticizing [Abednego Seller], *The History of Passive Obedience Since the Reformation* (Amsterdam, 1689).

tiquity of the constitution, there was one fundamental issue at stake: whether the magistrate was the creature of the law or the law the command of the magistrate.[230] The law would remain safely superior over the magistrate only as long as it was perceived older and not of his creation. "To support the Power and Priviledge of the House of Commons, as being an essential part of the Parliament," Atkyns insisted, "it is absolutely necessary to make it out against these Innovators, that the House of Commons have ever been a part of the Parliament, and that they were long before 49 *H.* 3." Otherwise, he warned, "they are but precarious in their power and priviledges, and enjoy them but of Grace."[231]

The dispute continued into the eighteenth century. Isaac Kramnick has pointed out that, contrary to general impression, Brady did not wait until the nineteenth century for vindication, that he had some disciples in the eighteenth.[232] But a distinction must be made between disciples of his better history and those of his new law. Most eighteenth-century writers citing him seem to have embraced his conclusions of law, writing against the ancient constitution[233] and the "myth" of

230. Thus the editor of one of Petyt's books noted that during the reign of Charles II "Then it was that the Body of Mercenaries undertook to maintain several extraordinary Points; they would prove, That the Laws are the King's Laws; that from him they receive their binding Force; that Parliaments owe their very Essence to the Royal Favours; that they are only for Counsel; that they are not very ancient; that the Commons were not anciently a constituent Part of Parliament" (Petyt, *Jus Parliamentarium* [cited note 150], "Preface").

231. Atkyns, *Power, Jurisdiction and Priviledge* (cited note 123), 17. Atkyns's jurisprudence was quite extreme for he put a heavy burden of proof on his own side of the controversy. To prove "the transcendent Power of the High Court of Parliament," he said that he had to maintain "[t]hat the House of Commons was originally and from the first Constitution of the Nation, the Representative of one of the three Estates of the Realm, and a part of the Parliament" (ibid., 13). Of course, the burden was less than we might think as it consisted of forensic, not "historical," proof. See also note 201, above.

232. Isaac Kramnick, "Editor's Introduction" to Viscount Bolingbroke, *Historical Writings* (Chicago, 1972), xliii. "But Nemesis awaited Brady. The Revolution robbed him of place, and, for over two hundred years, of recognition of his true stature" (Smith, *Gothic Bequest* [cited note 95], 8).

233. "The ancient Constitution of *England* was as arbitrary as any on the Con-

Magna Carta.[234] They appear, in other words, to have been more interested in questioning the authority of customary constitutionalism than in pursuing scientific history. It was a rare person in the eighteenth century who thought it possible to accept Brady's history and reject his law.[235] To take his history wholeheartedly, one almost had to accept his constitutionalism—at least until the nineteenth century.[236]

Constitutionalist reaction to Brady continued into the age of the American Revolution, even into the last decade of the century. Arbitrary government was still the fear, and the legacy of the ancient constitution remained so strong that well into the 1770s unlimited power, or law as command of the sovereign, described as new constitutional theory that had only recently "sprung up amidst the decaying Forms of *Gothick Policy.*"[237] As late as the year of the Stamp Act, when parliament decided to impose the "new" law of command on the colonies, Brady's history was labeled "insufficient."[238] On both sides of the Atlantic in the 1760s the forensic habit of arguing historically lingered on, as did the concept of immemoriality as a shelter for immutable civil rights.[239]

---

tinent." Anonymous, *The Ancient and Modern Constitution of Government Stated and Compared. And also Some Remarks on the Controversy Concerning the Dependence of Members of Parliament on the Crown* (London, 1734), 7.

234. Anonymous, *Defence of English History* (cited note 168), 13–14.

235. "For tho' I agree with *Brady* in many of his *Facts,* and think them *undoubted Records* and *True Testimonies;* yet I agree with him *in none of his political Principles,* nor *in the Use* he designed to make of *his facts*" (*Daily Gazetteer,* no. 6, July 5, 1735, p. 1, col. 2).

236. As, for example, John Reeves, who reacted so strongly against the French Revolution and, as a result, embraced Brady so wholeheartedly he was prosecuted by the Commons for saying the king was supreme in British law. See [Reeves], *Thoughts on English Government* (cited note 67), 117.

237. Anonymous, *The Spirit and Principles of the Whigs and Jacobites Compared. Being the Substance of a Discourse delivered to an Audience of Gentlemen at Edinburgh, December 22, 1745* (London, 1746), 29.

238. Anthony Ellys, *Tracts on the Liberty, Spiritual and Temporal, of Subjects in England. Addressed to J. N. Esq; at Aix-la-Chapelle. Part II* (London, 1765), 195.

239. [Joseph Galloway], *A Letter to the People of Pennsylvania* (1760), reprinted in Bernard Bailyn, *Pamphlets of the American Revolution, 1750–1776* (Cambridge, Mass., 1965), 1:260–62; [Sir John Sinclair], *Considerations on Proceedings by Infor-*

Perhaps the most telling indication of the significance for the eighteenth century of the jurisprudence associated with the ancient constitution was the fact that there were in Great Britain several prosecutions (and much talk of other prosecutions) against people who published pamphlets doubting either the antiquity of the House of Commons or parliament's coordination with the crown.[240] British officials willing to go to the trouble of seeking indictments in these situations thought something serious was at stake, a perception that has not always been appreciated in the twentieth century. Discussing the House of Commons's expulsion, fining, and imprisoning during Elizabeth's reign of a member for writing that the House was the new person in the trinity of king, Lords, and Commons, Sir John Ernest Neale in 1953 observed, "To the precedent-quoting, wishful-thinking House of Commons of Elizabethan times, whose fantastic notions about the antiquity and powers of Parliament were the prop of their adolescent egoism, it was lese-majesty."[241]

Egoism was not at stake. Constitutionalism was, and constitutionalism was such a fragile growth that it needed constant vigilance. When James II was on the throne, Brady's opponents had felt it wise to remain silent.[242] Later it was thought necessary to silence Brady's disciples to preserve the constitutional settlement and the Protestant

---

mation and Attachment. Addressed to the Members of the House of Commons. By a Barrister at Law, 2d ed. (London, 1768), 6–9.

240. For discussion of some see Kenyon, *Revolution Principles* (cited note 64), 158, and Pocock, *Ancient Constitution Retrospect* (cited note 35), 303.

241. J. E. Neale, *Elizabeth I and Her Parliaments, 1559–1581* (London, 1953), 1:407. Neale also described the incident as "Deviationist history castigated by authority: another curious example of the likeness of those days to ours!" (408–9). Another historian has suggested that the reason the Commons prosecuted this case was its "enhanced prestige" (Kramnick, "Augustan Politics" [cited note 33], 35).

242. "This scurvy Pedigree of the Commons in Parliament, drawn up by Dr. *Brady,* was so well liked by the Loyal Clergy . . . that Mr. *Petyt* found the Tide so strong against him, as not to venture on a Reply" (Samuel Johnson, *An Argument Proving, That the Abrogation of King James by the People of England from the Regal Throne, and the Promotion of the Prince of Orange, one of the Royal Family, to the Throne of the Kingdom in his stead, was according to the Constitution of the English Government, and Prescribed by it,* 4th ed. [London, 1692], 4).

succession.[243] One hundred and ten years after Brady published his *Complete History of England,* parliament spent part of at least four days debating what was described as a "Libel on the British Constitution." The offensive book had been written by John Reeves, who espoused not only Brady's history but, more importantly, his constitutional law as well. Reeves's book, the earl of Albemarle complained, contained "doctrines directly hostile to the spirit of our constitution, and tending to alienate from the minds of the people their affection for it." Reeves was accused of propagating five constitutional principles: "1. That the king alone makes laws. 2. That the other branches of the legislature are derived from the king. 3. That our liberties were grants from the king. 4. That the only object of the Revolution was to secure us a Protestant king. And 5. That the verdict of juries went for nothing."[244]

In the ensuing parliamentary debate, the libel came down to a matter of John Reeves against the ancient constitution, and ancient constitutionalism prevailed. At issue was the mixed limited constitution of 1795, but discussion turned on forensic history, which meant, of course, that even the Saxons were relevant. One member of the Commons, a serjeant-at-law, protested that he could never "admit that it was historically correct, that the monarchy of this country was at any time antecedent to its constitution."[245] It was probably immaterial whether the fact could be proved historically. It could not be admitted constitutionally. "To assert that the Lords and Commons derived all their functions from the crown was most unconstitutional doctrine," John Courtenay insisted. "Not under the Saxon or even the Norman line had any such doctrine prevailed; during the latter period, the English always claimed the rights they enjoyed under the Saxon government, though they were not always successful in their claims."[246] Courtenay

243. Helen E. Witmer, *The Property Qualifications of Members of Parliament* (New York, 1943), 28.

244. Speech of the earl of Albemarle, Lords Debates, December 2, 1795, *The Parliamentary History of England, From the Earliest Period to the Year 1803* (London, 1818), 32:681–83.

245. Speech of Serjeant Adair, Commons Debates, November 23, 1795, ibid., 32:625.

246. Speech of John Courtenay, Commons Debates, November 26, 1795, ibid., 32:645.

did not have to offer historical proof, for he was talking of law and the proof was in the existing constitution. The House of Commons voted an address to the king that the attorney general be directed to prosecute John Reeves.[247]

It would be better for our knowledge of seventeenth- and eighteenth-century liberty if intellectual historians would give some thought to the purpose of forensic history. To ignore eighteenth-century constitutionalism is to make certain that we do not understand it. At the very least it should be considered that potentially there was an ultimate sovereignty vested in the king, who could commit no illegal act. Today we know that this potential sovereignty was harmless theory, but the eighteenth century did not enjoy our perspective and for many people then it seemed constitutionally vital to have a counter theory of limitations upon the king's power. The constitutional imperative, therefore, arose not due to the inherent merits of ancient constitutionalism but from fear of the alternative—a fear Dr. Brady had said was groundless.

> In the name of God let the English People enjoy all their *Just, Due, Legal Rights, Liberties* and *Privileges,* and let them never be *disturbed* in the present Establishment of more Freedom to them, than all the Subjects in the World do enjoy . . . ; Let them enjoy every thing whereto the KING or His *Antecessors* have given their *Consent,* and that hath been *Allowed* and *Owned* by *Usage* and *Practice* many *Centuries* of Years, and found *Agreeable* to the *Interest* of *Prince* and *People.*[248]

Brady's law makes sense in twentieth-century Great Britain, for (if you substitute *state* or *parliament* or *cabinet* for *king*) it is twentieth-century British law. It made little sense, except to a monarchist, in the seventeenth and eighteenth centuries when liberty rested on customary grounds. Brady, Judge Atwood objected, was asking the English to trust sovereign will and pleasure, unchecked even by theoretical limits.

> Perhaps 'twill be said I injure this *good man* in imputing to him a *design* in relation to the present Government; Since he owns that the *most excellent great Council* [Parliament] . . . received *its perfection from*

247. Proceedings of December 15, 1795, ibid., 32:681.
248. Brady, *Introduction to the Old English History* (cited note 214), "Epistle" (n.p.).

the Kings Authority, and time. But 'tis obvious that *its Perfection,* must be meant [must mean] of such *its Perfection,* as his Book allows, and he would make *evident,* but what is that? That Lords should . . . be Summon'd to Parliament, or past by, at the King's pleasure, and that if the King pleas'd he might Summon *one Knight for a County, one Citizen for a City, one Burgess for a Burgh, and those nam'd to the Sheriff.*[249]

Atwood was not saying that prerogative discretion of such extremes was inevitable if Brady's constitutional theory became law. What he and other constitutionalists said was that if the forensic history of ancient constitutionalism were repudiated there would be no theoretical defenses against prerogativism,[250] or, to use a twentieth-century expression, the security of mixed monarchy would "lose all credibility."[251] That was why the Irish law professor Francis Stoughton Sullivan, as late as the year of the Declaration of Independence, urged in the second edition of his *Lectures* that students study the ancient constitution and the Gothic forms of government.

> From hence only shall we be able to determine whether the monarchy of England, as is pretended, was originally and rightfully an absolute royalty, controuled and checked by the virtue of the prince

---

249. [Atwood], *Additions Answering Omissions* (cited note 224), 41. Atwood went on to contend that representation did not receive its "Perfection" from the king, but "that *its Perfection* were such as we say it has at this day, *viz.* for Lords to come of Right in their own Persons, and that the Commons should send Representatives of their free Choice" (ibid., 42).

250. Similar to Atwood, but a century later, consider the attack of another barrister on the anticonstitutionalist historical argument of Josiah Tucker: "The intention of these misrepresentations is sufficiently apparent. They evidently tend to invalidate the existence of political and indeed of civil liberty beneath the feudal government, except in the instance of the Barons. To reduce the husbandmen and the tradesmen to a state of villenage. To deny the existence of the rights we at present enjoy, till they are wrung from the crown by the arms of its vassals, and disseminated by similar usurpations of the commons. And finally, by these insidious deductions to strengthen the author's attack upon the privileges we fell, and the constitution we revere" ([James Ibbetson], *A Dissertation on the National Assemblies Under the Saxon and Norman Governments* [London, 1781], 36).

251. Weston, "Legal Sovereignty" (cited note 50), 416. For another good discussion, see Thompson, "Idea of Conquest" (cited note 193), 38 n. 26.

alone, and whether the privileges of the subjects, which we are so proud of, were usurpations on the royal authority, the fruits of prosperous rebellion, or at best the concessions of gracious princes to a dutiful people. . . . The question is of a matter of fact; for on the decision of the fact, how the constitution of England antiently stood, the question of the right solely depends.[252]

Sullivan stated what is today an incredible theory of law. We must, therefore, be impressed that we do not find it in some extreme polemical tract of ancient constitutionalism, but in lectures intended to teach law students the common law. On both sides of the Irish Sea during the American Revolution the two university professors entrusted with the task of teaching the common law of England were, in fact, teaching the ancient constitution of Sir John Fortescue, Sir Edward Coke, and Sir Matthew Hale. Reject Brady and follow William Petyt, Richard Wooddeson instructed his Oxford students, adding with a confidence that only a common lawyer could place in forensic history "that among the [ancient] Britons there existed legislative assemblies of the democratical kind."[253] Sullivan told his students in Dublin to study the constitution of *contemporary* Great Britain by going back in time, to as far as the Roman Empire and the forests of prehistoric Germany.

> This research will be of use, not only to understand our present constitution, which is derived from thence, but to make us admire and esteem it, when we compare it with that which was its original, and observe the many improvements it has undergone. From hence, likewise, may be determined that famous question, whether our kings were originally absolute, and all our privileges only concessions of theirs; or whether the chief of them are not originally inherent rights, and coeval with the monarchy; not, indeed, in all the subjects, for that, in old times, was not the case, but in all that were *freemen,* and, as all are such now, do consequently belong to all.[254]

Sullivan's history may be nonsense to twentieth-century intellectuals, but it was the very essence of eighteenth-century constitutionalism,

252. Sullivan, *Lectures* (cited note 222), 16.
253. Wooddeson, *A Systematical View* (cited note 77), 1:6.
254. Sullivan, *Lectures* (cited note 222), 170.

and, in the eighteenth century, customary constitutionalism was the only pillar strong enough to support liberty.

VIII. FORENSIC TECHNIQUES OF ANCIENT CONSTITUTIONALISM

Arguments should not be misconstrued. The claim made here is not that advocates of the ancient constitution understood law better than their opponents or that they always argued correct legal principles. Constitutional law was much more uncertain during the seventeenth and even the eighteenth century than it would be in Great Britain after 1850 or in the United States after 1803. In England and the colonies the law of Selden, Coke, Somers, Bolingbroke, and James Otis was at least as doubtful as the law of James I, Strafford, Jeffries, Walpole, and Thomas Hutchinson.[255] What is contended is that exponents of ancient constitutionalism were generally arguing for restraint on government power and did not want government acting capriciously toward life or property. And the reason was not because thinking of the past led them to champion restraint but because the ancient constitution was a convenient, pragmatic, contemporary, and forensic way of arguing restraint by those already converted to that side of the constitutional paradox.

If we accept the premise that students of the ancient constitution in the seventeenth and eighteenth centuries were arguing the contemporary constitution, not history, we will better understand what they were saying and why they said things in certain "unhistorical" ways. It was not just common lawyers but everyone arguing against arbitrary power in those centuries who tended to look at the past from what recent critics have termed an ahistorical standpoint. Of course the learned, accepted method of thought about the common law makes the perspective even more pronounced. Even today, a lawyer trained in common law methodology thinks that a judge who rules on a question in litigation is stating the law as it has always been. If the judge

255. Coke especially. See W. S. Holdsworth, "The Influence of Coke on the Development of English Law," in *Essays in Legal History Read before the International Congress of Historical Studies Held in London in 1913*, ed. Paul Vinogradoff (London, 1913), 306.

reverses a previous decision and states a new rule in its place, lawyers are aware that the law has changed, but the new rule is thought of by lawyers less as being new than as having always been *potentially* the law on that particular matter. What to a historian is now the "old" rule, to the lawyer is the "erroneous" rule. A long line of precedents that has been overruled is not, to the lawyer, the former law as it would be to the historian, but incorrect law, discarded law, or not law at all.[256] What separates the lawyer's view of the past from the historian's is the reality for the lawyer of that potential. Because the lawyer knows the new rule has always potentially been valid, it had always been the correct interpretation waiting to be promulgated.

Most of the techniques of arguing ancient constitutionalism outlined here are the techniques of forensic history in general—the marshaling of facts supporting only one side of a litigation, for example. There was, by contrast, one aspect of ancient-constitution forensic history not prevalent in most forensic history, a characteristic that ancient-constitution history shared with whig history: the division of the past between heroes and villains. "[W]e find nothing in our Common *Histories* of these Times, but the *Brave Feats* performed by the *English* for their Fundamental Rights and Liberties," Robert Brady complained of ancient constitutionalism. "Nothing in *Sir Edward Coke*[,] *Mr. Selden, Mr. P*[r]*yn*[*ne*], and all late Writers when they *chop* upon these Times, and mention any thing relating to them, but the *Magnanimity* of the *English* in Appearing for their *Birth-rights,* and the great *Privileges* they had formerly injoyed."[257]

Brady understated the complaint. Ancient constitutionalists not only saw the past of Saxon or English freedom in heroic terms, they were apt to judge the existence and extent of liberty by their taught perceptions of historical times without bothering with empirical data. Why should "a modern lawyer" be interested whether feudalism was introduced by the Saxons or the Normans, a barrister, James Ibbetson, asked in 1777. He had an answer typical of eighteenth-century ancient constitutionalists.

256. J. W. Gough, *Fundamental Law in English Constitutional History* (Oxford, 1955), 6.

257. Brady, *Complete History of England* (cited note 218), "Preface" (n.p.).

If we attribute to the Normans the introduction of the Beneficium or feud, with its necessary consequences, as well as its oppressive deductions; we must regard it as an innovation upon the common law, the arbitrary imposition of a tyrant inimical to the liberties of the suspected subjects of his acquired territory.

If we derive the feudal constitution from the Saxons, it assumes a milder form; we connect it with a government that tended to promote the liberty of the subject, and to preserve it from infringement; with the names of Alfred and of Edward, and with the laws that have made those names venerable.[258]

Put another way: to find that an institution had Norman origins was to reveal it as an engine of arbitrary power. To find an institution had Saxon origins was to discover that it had been developed by liberty to serve a free people.

The tactic also worked the other way. A supporter of the constitution of power could strengthen the case for government authority by attributing institutions to the Normans. That was why Ibbetson was critical of writers whom he thought supported the authority of arbitrary power, especially when they pushed the origins of institutions and laws no further back in time than the Norman era. "The Dean, in attempting to debase the rights of the people," Ibbetson wrote of Josiah Tucker, "has exaggerated the oppressions of the feudal aristocracy. He has endeavoured to demonstrate that the military tenants were the only freemen of the realm, and that the charters of the Boroughs originated at the late period from the indulgent avarice of the Norman monarchs."[259] Joseph Towers also criticized Tucker, accusing him of slanting history to fit his definition of law, in other words, of writing forensic history.

The zeal with which the Dean of Glocester [Tucker] is animated . . . to oppose the principles of the assertors of the common rights of mankind, leads him to give an account of the condition and manners of our ancestors in the greatest degree humiliating and degrading. He feels no desire to maintain the honour of his country:

258. [James Ibbetson], *A Dissertation on the Folclande and Bocland of the Saxons* (London, 1777), 8–9.

259. [Ibbetson], *Dissertation on the National Assemblies* (cited note 250), 33.

but, to support his own political reveries, would represent the majority of the people of England as the descendants of the lowest and meanest slaves."[260]

Facts or what historians call truth were less important than the perceived truths of the ancient constitution and the needs of the current constitution. The ancestors of contemporary Britons could not have been slaves because, if they had been slaves, they could not have left a legacy of freedom. And they had to have bequeathed freedom if freedom was the constitutional inheritance of contemporary Britons.

A second technique of ancient-constitution history was selectiveness. Brady complained of this tactic, referring to one of Petyt's arguments, for example, as "grounded upon some parts of three several Records in the Fifteenth of King *John,* which he hath again picked out to serve his purpose, and impose upon his Readers."[261] Although forensic historians from Coke to sitting justices on the United States Supreme Court always have used only those bits of the past that supported their legal position, the methodology has for some reason been found singularly irritating by professional historians. "The Americans' blending of empiricism and rationalism," Gordon Wood has complained of colonial whig arguments during the revolutionary controversy, "lent a permissiveness to their use of history that makes it seem to us superficial and desultory; indeed they often appear to be simply selecting from the past examples to buttress generalizations deduced by pure reason. Since it was the constant and universal principles applicable to solving immediate problems that they were really after, there was always the danger in the delicate balance between historical experience and self-evident truth that the rational needs of the present would overpower

260. Joseph Towers, *A Vindication of the Political Principles of Mr. Locke: In Answer to the Objections of the Rev. Dr. Tucker, Dean of Glocester* (London, 1782), 55.

261. Brady, *Introduction to the Old English History* (cited note 214), 39. Interestingly, the technique was used by both sides and so, too, the complaint. In 1718 a defender of the ancient constitution charged that Matthias Earbery (who argued that Saxon and Norman kings possessed absolute power) "only transcribes what he thinks makes for him, and leaves out whatever makes against his Opinion" (Anonymous, *The Old Constitution and Present Establishment in Church and State Honestly Asserted* [London, 1718], 52). The work criticized was Earbery, *Old Constitution Vindicated* (cited note 109).

the veracity of the past."[262] Wood prejudiced his case when referring to "their use of history." He assumed that it was history without asking if it was what he meant by history. We, however, should ask why the veracity of the past should be a consideration in an argument that admittedly was concerned with "immediate problems," not problems of history but problems of eighteenth-century constitutional law and constitutional liberty. The American whigs, like other forensic historians, did not turn to constitutional history or to legal records with open minds. They could not and did not expect to base their case upon what the past had in fact been, for had they looked with a historian's open mind they would have found conflicting authorities and they would have had to deal with precedents hostile to their argument. Practical people facing practical problems, they took from the past what they needed or found useful.

It is quite another matter that forensic historians sometimes manipulated data or changed historical facts. Altering the record or rereading the past were techniques used by forensic historians defending parliamentary autonomy in the seventeenth century,[263] and they are still employed by American courts today. Much of the history with which the federal judiciary has found new "rights" for native Americans under the resurrected and reinterpreted Intercourse Act is pure invention.

A more frequent and certainly more lawyerlike technique employed by practitioners of ancient constitutionalism was to assume that a desired principle of law was part of the ancient constitution and to shift onto the other side the burden of proving otherwise. "The standing

262. Gordon S. Wood, *The Creation of the American Republic, 1776–1787* (Chapel Hill, N.C., 1969), 8–9. Even a historian who claims to believe that the founding fathers seriously searched history for guidance has complained: "The colonists were selective in their use of whig history. They seized and made their own, specific concepts and ideas only. They took seventeenth-century historical arguments against the Stuarts and directed these arguments against the eighteenth-century Parliament" (Colbourn, *Lamp of Experience* [cited note 88], 189). The whigs took seventeenth-century *constitutional* arguments against the arbitrariness of the Stuarts and directed these *constitutional* arguments against the arbitrariness of imperial legislation.

263. Sharpe, *Sir Robert Cotton* (cited note 59), 44.

body of our Laws is a clear proof that the power of our Kings is limited: How come we by Municipal Laws, if we must submit to their will?" the earl of Warrington asked. "But if it shall be answer'd me that this Government was the work of some King, and that he directed the form of our Constitution: I do in the first place desire to know who that King was, and in what Age he lived." Pressing the burden further should opponents of the ancient constitution find their English Justinian, Warrington formulated a presumption of fact that the other side had the burden of disproving. As it was obvious that any king who could have formed such a constitution "was extremely Wise and Just," the presumption was "[t]hat that King did believe that it was not so just and reasonable to govern by his Will, as by those rules which the Law has prescribed, that is, that it was more reasonable that the Law should controul his Will, rather than that his Will should over-rule the Law."[264] Like any competent common lawyer, Warrington was trying to put his side of the constitutional debate into a "no-lose" position. If his burden had been imposed the case could have been won. After all, what the other side had to prove was that the English Justinian knew of the tenets of the ancient constitution and deliberately rejected them, leaving Warrington with the argument that if the king knew of the ancient constitution he admitted its existence and his rejection was illegal.

A final technique of the forensic history of ancient constitutionalism worth noting because it was so frequently employed was to make the principles of the ancient constitution a standard of official or legal conduct. *Junius* did this with vindictiveness against Lord Mansfield, accusing the chief justice of King's Bench of violating both the substance and the spirit of the ancient constitution.

264. Warrington, "A Speech against the Assertion of Arbitrary Power, and the Non-Swearers," in *Works* (cited note 169), 389. And, of course, the other side also argued for the burden of proof. Thus a writer who contended that, before Norman times, kings ruled without the Commons wrote of ancient constitutionalists: "I say, these Men must either prove the Commons were in Parliament before *Henry I*st, or they must grant that an House of Commons, Antiently was not essential to a Parliament, and that the House of Lords was such without them" (Earbery, *Old Constitution Vindicated* [cited note 109], ii).

I see, through your whole life, one uniform plan to enlarge the Power of the Crown, at the expence of the Liberty of the subject. To this object, your thoughts, words, and actions have been constantly directed. In contempt or ignorance of the Common Law of England, you have made it your study to introduce into the Court where you preside, maxims of jurisprudence unknown to Englishmen. The Roman Code, the Law of Nations, and the Opinion of Foreign Civilians, are your perpetual theme;—but who ever heard you mention Magna Charta or the Bill of Rights with approbation or respect? By such treacherous acts, the noble simplicity and spirit of our Saxon Laws were first corrupted. The Norman Conquest was not complete, until Norman Lawyers had introduced their Laws, and reduced Slavery to a System.—This one leading principle directs your interpretation of the Laws.[265]

This tactic, evaluating actions by the tenets of the ancient constitution, was particularly effective against Mansfield. He was a Scot, and it was part of the popular English prejudice against Scots in the 1770s that they had never been governed by the ancient constitution and, therefore, could not be trusted to defend liberty or be expected to understand the rule of law.

As *Junius* demonstrated, a tactic of ancient-constitution practitioners was to portray deviations from the standards of liberty as deviations from the ancient constitution. Instances of "liberty" standards in the second half of the eighteenth century were the right of some freeholders to representation and the constitutional autonomy of the House of Commons, both of which were legacies of the ancient constitution. "Parliaments, in some shape," Blackstone at least twice argued, "are of as high antiquity as the Saxon government in this island; and have subsisted, in their present form, at least five hundred years."[266] This principle of the ancient constitution was so self-evident that Richard

265. *Junius,* "To the Right Hon. Lord M[ansfield]," *The Gentleman's Magazine and Historical Chronicle* 40 (1770): 516.

266. William Blackstone, *Tracts, Chiefly Relating to the Antiquities and Laws of England,* 3d ed. (Oxford, 1771), 20, and *An Analysis of the Laws of England,* 6th ed. (Oxford, 1771), 11.

Wooddeson, Blackstone's second successor as Vinerian law professor, dismissed as a precedent without constitutional standing the fact that Edward II had not called the Commons to parliament and had treated the Lords "merely as counsellors."

> This, however, being in exclusion of the lords of parliament, as well as of the commons, and happening when the powers of the nobles was at the highest, can hardly be thought an intended invasion of the rights of the legislature. Whatever similar instances, if any, can be produced, may justly be looked upon as violations of right, and infringements of the constitution. I am speaking of a legislative power in our kings, independent even of the lords' concurrence, which no age ever recognized.[267]

Wooddeson may have been forced to this argument because, by the 1770s, when he wrote, the notion that the House of Commons was coeval with the ancient constitution had long been under historical criticism and its exponents were beginning to retreat. For ancient constitutionalists, however, the evidence of history was no barrier. If, on one hand, you were a law professor like Wooddeson, you could use the law of the ancient constitution to deny the facts of history: the House of Commons had to have been part of the Saxon government, or there could have been no ancient constitution; there was an ancient constitution, therefore the Commons could not have originated in Plantagenet times. If, on the other hand, you were too historically minded to deny that the Commons was of recent origin or, unlike Wooddeson, felt compelled to admit there was no historical evidence of its antiquity, there was, nevertheless, another tactic of forensic history for vesting representation with antiquity. This was to assume that the eighteenth-century British constitution could not have been a constitution of freedom if its ancestor, the English constitution of earlier times, had not also been a constitution of freedom, and project back onto antiquity the structural apparatus of constitutional liberty then existing in the eighteenth century. Edward Wynne, writing in the 1780s, described this technique as "corresponding with the abstract reason of things."

267. Wooddeson, *A Systematical View* (cited note 77), 1:18–19.

The true antiquity of the Representation of the Commons is a point, as I take it, entirely unfathomable. There is very little evidence at all about the matter, that goes very far back; and most of that is so ambiguous, as to furnish no clear decisive conclusion. But whatever the mode of this representation originally was, or tho' it might long continue to be different from what it has since been, it is very difficult to dispute its existence: because it corresponds with the abstract reason of things in the idea of a free Government; it results from the origin of Government as founded on consent, and that of our own in particular, not an absolute but a limited Monarchy. The Body of the People must, therefore, always have had some right to share the legislative power; it cannot be supposed this right could ever be entirely given up, but only delegated to others, entrusted to act for them.[268]

Wynne's argument is not as simpleminded as it may seem on its first reading. On the contrary, it is a sterling example of what surely was the most attractive probative feature of the ancient constitution for those arguing it forensically, its pliability. The ancient constitution could be nearly anything you wanted or needed it to be. When the earl of Carysfort wanted it to be democratic, he just looked for the evidence and, as he expected, found it. "In the early times of our history," Carysfort pointed out, "we find the strongest evidence of the Democratic spirit of our Constitution. The Sheriffs who had the charge of the counties, the execution of justice, and the preservation of the peace, were elected by the freeholders, so were the Conservators of the Peace. . . . The consent of the people is, by our best Lawyers, considered as a term equivalent to authority of Parliament."[269]

There was little on the liberty side of constitutional law that could not be supported by ancient-constitution scholarship. After all, as Wynne pointed out, "[h]istory . . . will not only explain subsequent laws, but will supply the silence of law itself."[270] Judge Robert Atkyns,

268. Wynne, *Eunomus* (cited note 75), 3:61–62.

269. John Joshua Proby, earl of Carysfort, *A Letter from the Right Honourable Lord Carysfort, to the Huntingdonshire Committee* (London, 1780), 5.

270. Wynne, *Eunomus* (cited note 75), 1:60.

sitting in the court of Exchequer Chamber, found the silence of non-existent evidence forensically handy when counsel cited the histories of Sir Robert Cotton and William Prynne to prove that the House of Commons did not exist before the reign of Henry III. "*But we must not be* govern'd by Historians in matters of Law," Atkyns wrote, "and therefore, notwithstanding this Observation of Sir *Robert Cotton*'s and Mr. *Prynne*'s, we must presume, that the House of Commons and Elections of Knights of the Shire, are as antient as the common Law, and have been time immemorial, because we find no written Law that does first begin any such Institution."[271] Atkyns's audacity must be marked. Even Hugo Black would have been hard pressed to top him. The House of Commons had to be coeval with the common law because there was no written law creating it. He was not, of course, asking for an act of parliament creating parliament. That would have been unreasonable. But it was not unreasonable to conclude that the absence of a modern law was proof of ancient law. In truth, the technique is not that unusual today. The first Intercourse Act, federal judges have deducted, must have covered Indian nations wholly within state jurisdiction such as the Passamaquoddy and the Oneida or else the act would have said they were not covered.

Gilbert Stuart, the Scots advocate, used a similar technique to defend the same point of constitutional law that Atkyns defended, when citing an ancient tract which Coke and other writers had used to prove "the high antiquity of the *commons*."

> It is to be acknowledged, however, that Mr. Selden has demonstrated that this tract could not possibly be of the age of the Confessor, from its employing terms which were not in use till long after. But this does not wholly derogate from its force as to the point in question. For, allowing it to have been written in the reign of Edward III. the period which, with great probability, some writers have assigned it, it yet proves that the sense of that period was full and strong with regard to the antiquity of the constitution, as consisting of king, lords and *commons;* a circumstance which must have great weight in opposition to those, who would make us believe, that our consti-

271. Atkyns, *Parliamentary and Political Tracts* (cited note 201), 150.

tution, as so formed, was unknown till the times of Henry III. and Edward I.[272]

Acknowledged forgeries of the past which had been concocted to document the ancient constitution are good evidence in the present for proving the ancient constitution because they are evidence either of what the forgers believed or of what they wanted the courts of their day to believe.

IX. FORENSIC TECHNIQUES OF TIMELESS CONSTITUTIONALISM

The ancient constitution must not be thought mainly a model of liberty that existed in the golden age of antiquity when a warrior people cherished freedom and knew how to preserve it. The forensic value of the ancient constitution was not in its past perfection but in its present timelessness. The ancient constitution was a model, true enough, but it was also a means of constitutional renaissance, resuscitation, and redemption, made all the more relevant because it was not a constitution that had existed only in the distant past, but one that still existed, now, in the present.

Strikingly, in addition to its pliability, the most potent forensic attribute of ancient constitutionalism was its timelessness. It was a concept that entailed most of the anachronisms for which ancient-constitution polemics have been criticized by recent historiographers. Richard Goodenough, discussing the American rebellion in the year of the Declaration of Independence, summed up the constitutionality of a doctrine for which Americans were fighting, the doctrine of consent, by insisting, "[I]t is prior to all written Records; it is antecedent to all Statutes; it is co-eval with, and essential to the very Existence, of this Constitution."[273] If the historical thesis strikes us as unlearned, we

272. Stuart, "Discourse Concerning Laws and Government" (cited note 222), vii–viii n. 8.

273. [Richard Goodenough], *The Constitutional Advocate: By which, from the Evidence of History, and of Records, and from the Principles of the British Government, Every Reader may form His own Judgement concerning the Justice and Policy of the present War with America. Addressed to the People at Large, And humbly submitted to the Considerations of their Representatives* (London, 1776), 27.

would do well to first recall its purpose: it provided a debating point that could be assumed, sometimes without even being proved.[274] When ancient-constitution conclusions had to be proved, the "proof" was established by being obvious, by being desired, or by being fitted into the generally accepted principles of eighteenth-century British constitutionalism.

Six years before Goodenough's pamphlet, John Missing had lectured no less a legal expert than Lord Mansfield, the chief justice of England, on the rights of Britons to petition the throne by observing, "[T]he Common Law is more ancient, than that [*sic*] any Histories, Law-Books or Records can assist us to trace it; but though Histories, Law-Books and Records fail us, there is a Mode, my Lord, of discovering its Origin, and if this should lead us very far back into Antiquity, yet by a due Use of Common Sense, we shall run no Hazard . . . ; for, my Lord, if we ever so little exert our rational Faculties, we shall see, this Part of it at least, to be the Law of Nature, which is, the Law of God." After all, it was obvious to Missing and should have been to Mansfield that "[t]he Right to complain when injured, is the Right of Human Nature, it is the main End of Peoples submitting to Government; it is the Origin of all Human Laws, and all Courts of Justice are established only to hear and redress Grievances; so that your Lordship sees this is no NOVEL Institution, it is as old as human Nature itself, and the immediate Law of God."[275]

274. That was the simplest technique. During the Wilkes election controversy a pamphleteer asked when the House of Commons had obtained jurisdiction to decide the qualifications of members, and answered: "That they gained it at the same time, and by the same means that they gained their right of impeaching the greatest personages in the land; at the same time, and by the same means, that they acquired the right they exercise with regard to money bills, and other undoubted privileges. In short, their jurisdiction in this respect, which is confirmed by immemorial usage, is as ancient as the *Common Law,* and must be so deemed, for no written law can be produced which shews the commencement of the institution: It is coeval with the constitution, and without such a jurisdiction the House of Commons, as has been shewn, could not exist as an independent body" ([Jeremiah Dyson], *The Case of the Late Election for the County of Middlesex, Considered on the Principles of the Constitution, and the Authorities of Law* [London, 1769], 41).

275. John Missing, *A Letter to the Right Honourable William Lord Mansfield, Lord Chief Justice of the Court of King's Bench: Proving that the Subjects of England, lawfully*

The timelessness of the ancient constitution was a matter of common sense as much as it was of knowing the contours of current liberty, for some things did not change, such as the fact that people had always lived under law and government. Many premises of the ancient constitution were self-evident. After all, as William Dugdale had noted the previous century, "the *Common Law*, is, out of question, no less antient than the beginning of differences betwixt man and man, after the first Peopling of this Land; *it being no other than pure and tryed Reason; . . . or the absolute perfection of Reason,* as Sir *Edward Coke* affirmeth, adding, *that the ground thereof is beyond the memory or Register of any beginning.*"[276] Not just twentieth-century historians but eighteenth-century opponents of ancient constitutionalism were on notice not to ask for historical certainty. The ancient constitution was shaped by subjective not objective proof.

The timelessness of the ancient constitution was developed more in response to polemical needs than anything else. Timelessness made it possible for an advocate of certain principles or institutions, the House of Commons for example, to place those principles or institutions in the context of continual constitutionality no matter if they had been overturned or were inoperative.[277] Even long-standing constitutional

---

assembled to Petition their King, or to Elect or Instruct their Representatives, are intitled to Freedom of Debate; and that all Suits and Prosecutions for exerting that Right, are Unconstitutional and Illegal (London, 1770), 10–11.

276. William Dugdale, *Origines Juridiciales, or Historical Memorials of the English Laws, Courts of Justice, Forms of Tryal, Punishment in Cases Criminal, Law-Writers, Law-Books, Grants and Settlements of Estates, Degree of Serjeant, Innes of Court and Chancery,* 2d ed. (London, 1671), 3, col. 1.

277. Algernon Sidney noted that Filmer "is not ashamed to cite Bracton, who, of all our antient law-writers, is most opposite to his maxims. He lived, says he, in Henry the third's time, since parliaments were instituted: as if there had been a time when England had wanted them; or the establishment of our liberty had been made by the Normans, who, if we will believe our author, came in by force of arms, and oppressed us. But we have already proved the essence of parliaments to be as antient as our nation, and that there was no time, in which there were not such councils or assemblies of the people as had the power of the whole, and made or unmade such laws as best pleased themselves. We have indeed a French word from a people that came from France, but the power was always in ourselves; and the Norman kings were obliged to swear they would govern according to the laws that had been made by those assemblies. It imports little,

custom could not supersede the timeless validity of a fundamental doctrine of the ancient constitution. Consider the grounds on which, at the very late date of 1783, the crown's right to create peers at discretion was questioned. In the reign of Henry VII, it was charged, "a power was *usurped* by the Crown of conferring titles of dignity at pleasure; which *incroachment*, not being opposed by the *Commons*, has been continued to this day, contrary to the ancient law and constitution of the kingdom."[278] The choice of the word *incroachment* is what interests us. The practice was an "incroachment" against the timeless constitution even as late as 1783. The fact that three hundred years had passed since the "usurpation" had first been introduced did not matter. The usurpation had not become law either because the crown had no prescriptive rights against the ancient constitution, or because time did not run against immutable principles no matter what occurred.

For purposes of argument, to gain polemical advantage, one needed only to postulate a timeless continuity,[279] and practices to which you objected became subversions of the ancient constitution as it still existed *in fact* as well as in theory.[280] Or even when there were changes in constitutional government that could not be denied—substantial departures from past constitutional practice such as the loss by the clergy of self-taxation or the loss by the House of Lords of jurisdiction over judicial appeals—they could often be dismissed as matters of mere form, changes in detail, not fundamental alterations. "If you ask whether these things are not an Altering or Breach of the *Constitution*,"

---

whether Bracton lived before or after they came among us" (*Discourses Concerning Government*, in *The Works of Algeron Sydney*, new ed. [London, 1772], 312).

278. [William Wenman Seward], *The Rights of the People Asserted, and the Necessity of a More Equal Representation in Parliament Stated and Proved* (Dublin, 1783), 37.

279. "Keep in mind that our object is, to ascertain how it was, or must have been, according to the Constitution at its *origin*. It is only by ascending to that point, we can know what it *now is;* because, whatever it originally was it continues to be; no change ever having been made, notwithstanding the numerous changes which have occurred in the *practice* of governing" (Cartwright, *The English Constitution* [cited note 17], 207–8).

280. So it could be said that in the 1640s a faction in the House of Commons "took the whole *Government* into their own Hands, and Created themselves a *Commonwealth*, thus totally subverting the *Constitution*" ([Leslie], *Constitution, Laws and Government of England* [cited note 61], 8).

Charles Leslie explained. "I think not. For while the *Fountain Constitution* stands Secure, any various Runnings of the *Rivulets* are no Breach of the *Constitution*."[281] What mattered was the essence and the general principles of the constitution. It was that essence and a few "first principles" that were timeless, not particular rules or changing customs. With that timelessness, the ancient constitution was always available as a standard when arguments were made for correcting the rivulets of erroneous details.

In the early years of the reign of George III there was a reaction among some constitutionalists to the role that ministers had begun to play in the formulation of government policy. Saying that the office of "minister" was "entirely unknown to our Constitution," one pamphleteer argued for its abolition. "To demonstrate the Inconsistency of this Office, with the Principles of the Constitution, it will be sufficient to shew the Nature of it, and trace it to it's Original in other Governments, from which it appears to have been 'very improperly borrowed,' among us."[282] We must not be puzzled as to what the author meant by "constitution" and "constitutional." He was using good late eighteenth-century constitutional words when he said that an office filled by an appointee of the king and recognized by parliamentary legislation was not known to the constitution. Of course, his constitution was not the constitution of Lord Mansfield or the current attorney general. We might say that the constitution he cited was not so much the ancient constitution as the timeless constitution, but that would be a distinction without a forensic difference, as the appeal was still to what today's historians call a mythical constitution. What is important about the concept of timelessness is the forensic technique that timelessness kindled. By arguing for constitutional change by appealing to antiquity, it utilized the idea of timeless first principles that existed independently of changes in specific details, even changes in substance. In fact, the concept of timeless first principles gave shape to the two most prominent techniques of forensic history in the seventeenth and eighteenth centuries—the regenerative ancient constitu-

---

281. Ibid., 17.

282. Anonymous, *Political Disquisitions Proper for Public Consideration in the Present State of Affairs in a Letter to a Noble Duke* (London, 1763), 3.

tion and the ancient constitution continually being "restored to its first principles."

There was a way of speaking and of arguing that dominated public discussion about the British constitution in the eighteenth century. It used words and phrases such as "restore," "return to," "original purity of the constitution," and "the first principles."[283] These expressions provided a reference for arguing constitutional law that came directly out of ancient-constitution thinking. That thinking in turn was the product of the eighteenth-century notion that the history of the ancient constitution was a tale of continual degradation and renewal. The Saxon constitution, Allan Ramsay pointed out, had flourished for six hundred years, "till it was overwhelmed, and destroyed, by William . . . and lay buried under a load of tyranny, for one hundred and forty seven years. When again it arose like a phenix from its own ashes, in the reign of Henry the third."[284] Or, as viscount Bolingbroke suggested, discussing the same period of post-Norman regeneration, William may have been arbitrary but even under the worse tyranny the law of the ancient constitution, no matter how weakened and battered, always rebounded as the law of liberty. The Normans

> introduced many illegal Practices, and some foreign Principles of Policy, contrary to the Spirit, and Letter too, of the *antient Constitution;* and . . . *these* [Norman] *Kings* and the *Lords abused their Power over the Freemen, by Extortion and Oppression, as Lords over Tenants.* But it will remain true that neither *Kings,* nor *Lords,* nor both together, *could prevail over Them, or gain their Consent to give their Right, or the Law, up to the King's Beck. But still the* Law *remain'd Arbiter both of* King *and* People, *and the* Parliament *supreme Expounder and Judge both of it and Them.* Tho' the Branches were lopped, and the Tree lost its Beauty for a Time, yet the Root remain'd untouch'd, was set in a good Soil, and had taken strong Hold in it; so that Care and Culture, and Time were indeed required, and our Ancestors were forced to water it, if I may use such an Expression, with their Blood; but with this

283. W. Paley, *An Essay upon the British Constitution: Being the Seventh Chapter of the Sixth Book of the Principles of Moral and Political Philosophy* (London, 1792), 3. And see text to note 302 below.

284. [Ramsay], *Historical Essay* (cited note 62), 10.

Care, and Culture, and Time, and Blood, it shot again with greater Strength than ever, that We might sit quiet and happy under the Shade of it; for if the same Form was not exactly restored in every Part, a Tree of the same Kind, and as beautiful, and as luxuriant as the former, grew up from the same root.[285]

The rebirth in post-Norman times had been complete. The ancient constitution had been regenerated to new strength, but otherwise unchanged in every material way. And as late as 1771, "though much impaired, maimed, and disfigured, it hath stood the admiration of many ages; and still remains the most noble, and ancient monument of Gothick antiquity."[286]

Ramsay and Bolingbroke were not just writing history. They were practicing the most utilized polemical device of eighteenth-century law and politics. "[T]he model of the British constitution," a reviewer explained in the year that the Stamp Act was promulgated, "has again and again preserved its existence, when the morals and principles of the people were sunk to the lowest degree of vice, ignorance, and slavery, both civil and religious. This model prevailed against the impetuous Tudors, as well as the despotic Stuarts; and by the excellent checks it contains (whatever may be the fate of families or factions) it must survive all its enemies."[287]

As was discussed above, the purpose of the model can be easily misunderstood. It has the appearance of serving the conservative or the reactionary, but in truth it lent itself to almost any constitutional theory except, as a general rule, the justification of power.[288] If thought is given to the question, it should be evident that the concept of a self-

285. [Bolingbroke], *A Dissertation Upon Parties* (cited note 66), 194–95.

286. [Ramsay], *Historical Essay* (cited note 62), 10.

287. "Book Review," *The Critical Review: Or Annals of Literature by a Society of Gentlemen* 19 (1765): 208. See also Burgh, *Political Disquisitions* (cited note 154), 1:171.

288. "Those eighteenth-century Englishmen who were dissatisfied with their constitution and wanted to reform it typically presented their proposed reforms as involving a return to the constitution's original principles—a doctrine not characteristic of opposition thought under the first four Stuarts and involving attitudes rather fundamentalist than prescriptive, rather reactionary than conservative" (Pocock, *Politics, Language and Time* [cited note 27], 133).

restoring, self-healing, regenerative constitution could be more useful to radical reformers than to political or constitutional conservatives defending the status quo.

Due to the turn that ancient constitutionalism gave to eighteenth-century political controversy, in debates between the British administration and its opponents it was the government's side that was most likely to eschew arguments of the past and rely instead upon abstract constitutional reasoning or upon principles of expediency.[289] An example occurred during the debate in the House of Commons over repeal of the Stamp Act. As reported in a contemporary "history," the ministry defended parliament's constitutional authority to tax the North American colonies but admitted that the tax was politically inexpedient.

> The constitution of this country, said they, has been always fluctuating, always gaining or losing: even the representation of the Commons was not till the reign of Henry the seventh reduced to any fixed system. What does it avail then to recur to ancient records, when the constitution is no longer the same; when no body can ascertain its state at the times, which are quoted, and when there are even in the great charter things, which are no more constitutional? Such misplaced industry is as idle as all that mass of learning and dissertation collected from natural lawyers, such as Locke, Selden, Puffendorff and other speculative men under whose arguments and refinements the subject has been almost buried. Beyond the era of Edward the first, or king John, the Mode of taxation is involved through the uncertainty of history in doubt and obscurity. Some of the writs upon record were conformable, some contrary, to law. . . . Can any just conclusion be drawn from such discordant, such opposite precedents?[290]

289. As was also true for the "prerogative" side in the seventeenth century. E. Evans, "Of the Antiquity of Parliaments in England: Some Elizabethan and Early Stuart Opinions," *History* 23 (1938): 221.

290. [Robert Macfarlane], *The History of the Reign of George the Third, King of Great-Britain, &c. to the Conclusion of the Session of Parliament, Ending in May, 1770* (London, 1770), 235–36. The argument was directed against the technique being discussed, of "restoring the constitution to first principles." The criticism

Speakers on the other side of the Stamp Act debate—the pro-American side led by William Pitt and Lord Camden—apparently not only argued the relevancy of the past, they recalled how the timeless constitution regenerated itself by "recovering" legal rights.

> We acknowledge, said they, that the constitution has been always in a fluctuating state, and that the earlier periods of our history are not without obscurity. But does it hence follow that we are to form do [no] analogical reasonings upon them? Because we know not the whole, must we make no use of what we know? Had our ancestors argued in this manner, and built their arguments upon the actual state of the constitution, they would have crouched beneath the rod of tyranny, when it happened to be shook over them, and would never have made a single effort to recover their just rights. . . . Let the actual situation of affairs be ever so bad, we must not look up to our forefathers for precedents, because the struggles between privilege and prerogative prevented them from being regular and uniform. What then! are there no general maxims, no principles congenial to the constitution to guide our researches in this region, which you represent as obscure and perplexed? What is become of

---

was well understood at the time: "There are many sorts of abuses and grievances crept into the administration of government, which politicians tell us, are no way to be corrected, but by going back to the first principles on which our system is erected. But where are these to be found? Perhaps in some mouldy records which are no longer legible, and if they were, would still be subject to be misinterpreted and wrested to the worst purposes by mercenary lawyers, who are ever ready to make their advantage of antiquated and ambiguous expressions. *Magna Charta* itself could not stand before the sort of law delivered by the judges of Charles I. in the case of *ship money*, or the decisions of Jefferies in the two following reigns" ("Hanseaticus," *St. James's Chronicle*, August 26, 1766, rpt. in *A Collection of Letters and Essays in Favour of Public Liberty, First Published in the News-Papers in the Years 1764, 65, 66, 67, 68, 69, and 1770. In Three Volumes* [London, 1774], 2:44–45). "Speculative Politicians talk as lightly and fluently of *reverting to first principles*, as if it required no more trouble than to rectify a piece of clock-work that was out of order. History, on the contrary, informs us, that this cannot be effected but by civil war, and that the event, in general, is not reformation but TYRANNY" ([William Vincent], *A Letter to the Reverend Dr. Richard Watson, King's Professor of Divinity in the University of Cambridge* [London, 1780], 14).

that unalienable right of a British subject, which secures him from being taxed, or judged but by the common consent of his peers? This is the first, the vital principle of our liberty.[291]

It was to provide a forensic technique for making that "effort to recover" that the timeless, regenerative, ancient constitution served its most notable eighteenth-century function. What may seem paradoxical inconsistencies to the uninformed were tools of the trade for the forensic historian of ancient constitutionalism. Innovations were argued on grounds of preserving the ancient constitution,[292] and restoration was argued to hide the introduction of constitutional novelties.[293] Joseph Galloway used this technique to press the constitutional contention that Pennsylvania judges, like their common law counterparts in England, should have tenure *quam diu se bene gesserint*. English judges had enjoyed that tenure since the Glorious Revolution. The Bill of Rights, however, had not been extended to the colonies where judges sat *durante bene placito*. Galloway knew that the English rule had been an innovation in 1689 and would be an innovation if introduced into Pennsylvania. Appreciating that drastic changes in the constitution were always suspect and might encounter resistance for that reason alone, Galloway followed the path of least constitutional resistance. He made his case for the innovation of tenure at good behavior by transmuting it into the restoration of a lost but still extant constitutional right.

291. [Macfarlane], *History of George III* (cited note 290), 239.

292. "It is nowadays a commonplace that no constitution can be static. . . . But if this is obvious now, it has not always been so. Constitutional disputes have often taken the form of a controversy as to what a particular constitution already was, when the real issue was whether or not it should be altered. In England, particularly, reform has again and again been represented by its partisans not as innovation but as maintenance or restoration" (Mark A. Thomson, *A Constitutional History of England, 1642 to 1801* [London, 1938], 3).

293. "The idea of an ancient and an immemorial constitution . . . was designed to lend the respectability of antiquity to constitutional practices and attitudes which had far more innovation in them than their proponents cared to admit" (Robert Ashton, "Tradition and Innovation and the Great Rebellion," in *Three British Revolutions: 1641, 1688, 1776*, ed. J. G. A. Pocock [Princeton, N.J., 1980], 213).

Here it is worthy your Information, *first,* that the Rights and Liberties claimed and declared by the Bill of Rights, that second Magna Charta, and the Act of Settlement created no Innovation of the ancient Constitution. The Parliament had no Design to change but only to restore the ancient Laws and Customs of the Realm, which were the true and indubitable Rights and Liberties of the People of *England.* This appears as well from the Bill of Rights, and the Resolves which preceded the Act of Settlement, as from the Act itself. From whence it follows, that this Right of the People to have their Judges indifferent Men, and independent of the Crown, is not of a late Date, but Part of the antient Constitution of your government and inseparably inherent in the Persons of every freeborn *Englishman;* and that the granting Commissions to the Judges *during Pleasure,* was then esteemed by the Parliament, and truly *was,* an arbitrary and illegal Violation of the People[']s antient Liberties.[294]

Galloway was doing much more than saying that the "ancient constitution" ran in the American colonies or that a right vested in "freeborn Englishmen" by the ancient constitution was "inherent" in freeborn Americans, even though they had never enjoyed that right. The ancient constitution had a validity and a force that not only superseded time and centuries of practice, it superseded space and applied equally to the new world as to the old. He was also adapting to the colonies the most familiar, effective, and stunning of the forensic techniques of ancient constitutionalism. It is a technique, incidentally, still popular among United States Supreme Court justices, a use of "history" that in its twentieth-century American context has been described "as a precedent-breaking device,"[295] based on a "Marxist-type perversion of the relation between truth and utility" that assumes "history can be written to serve the interests of libertarian idealism,"[296] or can be manipulated to supply "an apparent rationale for politically in-

---

294. [Joseph Galloway], *A Letter to the People of Pennsylvania; Occasioned by the Assembly's passing that Important Act, for Constituting Judges of the Supream Courts and Common-Pleas, During Good Behaviour* (Philadelphia, 1760), 25–26.

295. Kelley, "Clio and the Court" (cited note 91), 155.

296. Ibid., 157.

spired activism that can be indulged in the name of constitutional continuity."[297]

In the eighteenth century the operative verb for this forensic tactic was *restore*. Ancient constitutionalists were "Restoring the Constitution"[298] or, better still, restoring "the genuine Constitution"[299] or "our true Constitution."[300] The purpose of parliamentary reform, for example, was described as "the restoration of the people to their fundamental rights."[301] A critic of ancient constitutionalism summed up the vocabulary when complaining "of those who speak of the 'principles of the constitution,' of bringing back the constitution to its 'first principles,' of restoring it to its 'original purity,' or [']primitive model.'"[302]

The back-to-first-principles technique of ancient-constitution forensic argument was employed by people from all sides of the political spectrum during the eighteenth century. James Burgh, who was an ex-

297. Ibid., 131.

298. Burgh, *Political Disquisitions* (cited note 154), 3:428–29. Of course, it was a technique that used what purported to be history to disguise reform, and was indulged in even by individuals, such as John Locke, who were not historically minded. "[T]he set[t]lement of the nation upon sure ground of peace and security . . . can noe way soe well be don[e] as by restoreing our ancient government, the best possibly that ever was if taken and put together all of a piece in its originall constitution" (letter from John Locke to Edward Clarke, January 28/February 8, 1689, in *The Correspondence of John Locke*, ed. E. S. De Beer, 8 vols. [Oxford, 1976–1989], 3:545 [letter 1102]).

299. Cartwright, *The English Constitution* (cited note 17), 172.

300. Ibid., 177.

301. Thomas Day, *Two Speeches of Thomas Day, Esq. at the General Meetings of the Counties of Cambridge and Essex, Held March 25, and April 25, 1780* (n.p., 1780), 17. The process of "restoration" was often thought of as a positive, ongoing constitutional duty. "In a free government, when care is not taken from time to time to bring back the constitution to its first principles, in proportion as the epoch of its origin becomes remote, the people lose sight of their rights, they soon forget them in part, and afterwards retain no notion of them" ([J. P. Marat], *The Chains of Slavery. A Work Wherein the Clandestine and Villainous Attempts of Princes to Ruin Liberty are Pointed Out, and the Dreadful Scenes of Despotism Disclosed. To which is prefixed, An Address to the Electors of Great Britain, in order to draw their timely Attention to the Choice of Proper Representatives in the next Parliament* [London, 1774], 185).

302. Paley, *Principles of Moral and Political Philosophy* (cited note 63), 465.

treme democrat, though not of the Tom Paine type, urged his fellow Britons not to "be discouraged from using the proper means for restoring the constitution."[303] When he was denied the seat in the Commons to which the freeholders of Middlesex had elected him, John Wilkes followed an eighteenth-century political ritual by demanding the "restoration of the constitution."[304] When, by contrast, parliament in 1701 had enacted legislation excluding certain "placemen" from membership, William Pudsey had hailed the legislation as going "a great way towards the restoring our Constitution to it's primitive Virtue and Sincerity."[305] Later, in 1744, the issue of placemen was again in agitation, and a bill "for double taxing" incomes on pensions and "places" was before the House of Commons. "[I]n order to preserve a free government," Edward Southwell told the House, quoting Machiavel, "it often becomes necessary to bring it back to its first principles; which is a maxim the friends of liberty will always take care to observe, and, we may expect, that it will be as constantly opposed by ministers, who always have been, and always will be, grasping at arbitrary power."[306] The administration, opposing the bill, tried to reverse the argument about arbitrary power by claiming that double taxing was not a practice known to liberty; it was "the practice of arbitrary governments, or of princes that were aiming at arbitrary power."[307] Southwell did not back down. Double taxation was arbitrary, he admitted, but a little arbitrariness could be tolerated for the greater good of restoring the Saxon constitution to its ancient purity.

303. Burgh, *Political Disquisitions* (cited note 154), 3:308.

304. Letter from John Wilkes to Fletcher Norton, April 20, 1773, *The Gentleman's Magazine and Historical Chronicle* 43 (1773): 201 (not quoting the letter directly).

305. William P[udse]y, *The Constitution and Laws of England Consider'd* (London, 1701), 51.

306. Speech of Edward Southwell, Commons Debates, December 8, 1744, *The Parliamentary History of England, From the Earliest Period to the Year 1803* (London, 1812), 13:1039. That comment enjoyed other moments. E.g., "Machiavel," it was said, "asserted, that no government can be lasting which is not frequently reduced to its first principles." *A Second Address to the Public from the Society for Constitutional Information* (n.p., n.d.), 6 (Huntington Library rare book #305198); Smith, *Gothic Bequest* (cited note 95), 85.

307. Speech of Southwell, December 8, 1744, *Parliamentary History*, 13:1045.

Upon this principle, Sir, let us examine the motion now before us, in order to see whether it is not returning a step back to our ancient constitution; and, I am sure, no man, who has read the histories of this nation, will say, that our ancestors the Saxons ever thought of inviting men to serve the public by great salaries or pensions: on the contrary, we know, that all those offices that are of true Saxon originals, such as sheriffs, parish offices, and most of our offices in cities and boroughs, are attended with an expence, instead of being of any advantage to the officer. At least, if they now make any advantage of them, it is by some innovation unknown to our ancestors, and such a one as they would never have allowed to be introduced.[308]

Southwell and other opponents of corruption by pensions and places used the ancient constitution hoping to "restore" balance to the British government. That is, they hoped to "restore" more representative, responsible government by strengthening the independence of the House of Commons. It is interesting to compare that purpose to Carter Braxton's use of the same technique for an opposite end: to "restore" government to constitutional responsibility by keeping it independent of democratic caprice. Advising Virginians in 1776 on how to frame their new government, and fearful that the colonies were likely to vest all authority in their elective legislatures, Braxton wanted Americans to think of the virtues of the ancient constitution of balances and limitations rather than to rationalize a new scheme based on notions of equality or the sovereignty of the common people. The crown, Braxton admitted, had driven Americans to rebellion not only by its policies but by using the corruption of pensions and places to undermine the restraints on its prerogatives which the constitution had vested in the two other branches of parliament. As a result, Virginians were "prone to condemn the whole" British constitution even though only "a part"—corruption—"is objectionable." It was wiser and safer to turn to the tried and the tested than to risk experimentation.[309] "[C]ertainly it would in the present case be more wise to con-

308. Ibid., 13:1039–40.
309. "However necessary it may be to shake off the authority of arbitrary British dictators, we ought nevertheless to adopt and perfect that system, which England has suffered to be so grossly abused, and the experience of ages has

sider, whether if the constitution was brought back to its original state, and its present imperfections remedied, it would not afford more happiness than any other."[310] The best government, then, was government responsible to the constitution itself, not one responsible to fickle public opinion.

Braxton was combating what he called "popular governments." By contrast, the last significant use of the ancient constitution in eighteenth-century Great Britain was by people who wanted to "restore" popular influence to the House of Commons by "restoring" annual or, at least, triennial elections. When John Sawbridge introduced into the House of Commons "his annual motion" to "restore" yearly elections, he was praised by the *London Magazine* for his zeal in "bringing government back to the original institutions by which it gained permanency and strength."[311] That argument was an instance of ancient-constitution advocacy at its best. Annual elections would have introduced a radical change to eighteenth-century British government—unless, of course, you viewed the question not from the

----

taught us to venerate. This, like almost every thing else, is perhaps liable to objections; and probably the difficulty of adapting a limited monarchy will be largely insisted on. Admit this objection to have weight, and that we cannot in every instance assimilate a government to that, yet no good reason can be assigned, why the same *principle* or spirit may not in a great measure be preserved" ([Carter Braxton], *An Address to the Convention of the Colony and Ancient Dominion of Virginia; on the Subject of Government in general, and recommending a particular Form to their Consideration* [Philadelphia, 1776], 13; the words quoted in the text are from 11).

310. Ibid., 11. James Burgh also thought the restored ancient constitution would afford "happiness" when he told Britons: "The present form of government by king, lords and commons, if it could be restored to its true spirit and efficiency, might be made to yield all the liberty, and all the happiness of which the great and good people are capable in this world" (Colin Bonwick, *English Radicals and the American Revolution* [Chapel Hill, N.C., 1977], 22).

311. "Parliamentary History," *The London Magazine or Gentleman's Monthly Intelligencer* 45 (1776): 403. That same year it was contended that if the ministry restored triennial parliaments it would "heal the Breach, by restoring the Constitution" ([James Stewart], *A Letter to the Rev. Dr. Price, F.R.S. Wherein his Observations on the Nature of Civil Liberty, the Principles of Government, &c. Are Candidly Examined; His Fundamental Principles refuted, and the Fallacy of his Reasoning from these Principles detected* [London, 1776], 18).

perspective of the eighteenth century but from the perspective of the ancient constitution.

A generation after Sawbridge had died, Granville Sharp continued the fight for annual elections by invoking the ancient constitution in what by the 1790s had become a classic, perhaps dated argument:

> [A] more equal representation of the Commons in annual Parliaments (*i.e.,* ELECTED "every year once, or more often if need be") *is not only an* ANCIENT, *but even an* INDISPENSABLE, *right of the people.* That this ancient constitution is *indispensable* the many fatal effects of deviating from it have rendered sufficiently obvious; and therefore no *remedy* can be more efficacious, and constitutionally natural, than a *revival* of that *primitive and fundamental right,* according to the rule of Law, that, "*as often as any thing is doubtful or* CORRUPTED, *we should* RECUR *to first Principles.*"[312]

When people protested "*that the whole constitution must be new-modelled*" if there were to be annual elections, Sharp replied that it was not a re-modeling but a restoring that he was after. "[W]e are far from desiring that '*the constitution may be new-modelled*;' we only pray, that the unjust *usurpations,* (made without the consent of the people), the *corruptions, and other such abuses,* may be taken away and reformed: and then the ancient constitution of *annual* elections, and '*more often if need be,*' will recover its full vigour without any other alteration."[313] Of course, Allan Ramsay added, it was not an innovation to "weed, from our constitution, all modern heterogeneous matter, that hath poisoned its principles, and established a tyranny upon the ruins of our ancient laws, and liberties."[314]

Innovation could always be softened by being clothed in the dress of ancient constitutionalism. The strategy was to avoid the suggestion of

312. [Granville Sharp], *The Legal Means of Political Reformation, Proposed in Two Small Tracts, viz. The First on "Equitable Representation," and the Legal Means of obtaining it (1777). The Second on "Annual Parliaments, the ancient and most Salutary Right of the People" (1774),* 8th ed. (London, 1797), 3–4.

313. Granville Sharp, *A Defence of the Ancient, Legal, and Constitutional, Right of the People, to elect Representatives for every Session of Parliament; viz. Not only "every Year once," but also "More often if Need be"* (London, 1780), 15–16.

314. [Ramsay], *Historical Essay* (cited note 62), 153.

altering this institution or introducing that doctrine. The forensic tactic, rather, was "preservation" of the purpose and the spirit of the ancient constitution. The Society for Constitutional Information was an organization of reformers primarily interested in "restoring" popular elections for members of the House of Commons. "Let the ingenuous and uncorrupted part of our countrymen," the Society urged Britons in the early 1780s, "decide which are the real friends of the constitution, and which the introducers of innovation; those who would preserve it in its original vigour, or those who, with a seeming reverence for the forms, would annihilate the spirit."[315]

In the polemics of a constitutional debate, the phraseology was in the language of a forensic vocabulary. The constitutional values were values familiar to us, true enough, "rights," "popular," "freedom," and the like. But the operative words were eighteenth-century, ancient-constitution words, "restore," "original purity," and "preserve." They were not the words of the nineteenth-century constitution of command: "reform," "change," or "decree." "May what you have already gained," Thomas Day told the Society for Constitutional Information at one of its county meetings for 1780, "be only a prelude to that complete redress, which can alone restore the power and freedom of this nation, by restoring the Constitution to its original purity."[316]

X. DO LAWYERS CARE?

We are not quite done with the historiography of the ancient constitution. There are two lingering questions that should be addressed, even though they may never be answered to the satisfaction of most scholars. The first is whether twentieth-century historians of the ancient constitution really believe that history was so controlling of people in the seventeenth and eighteenth centuries that it not only provided the context of argument but dictated the outcome of events. The second is whether the lawyers and other practitioners of ancient

315. *Second Address to the Public* (cited note 306), 14.

316. Day, *Two Speeches* (cited note 301), 11. Almost a century earlier, Samuel Johnson said of William III: "[I]t is our peculiar Happiness in this Reign, that we live under a Prince who had no other Business here, but to restore the Constitution; which, as his Declaration speaks, was wholly overturned in the former Reigns" (*An Argument Proving* [cited note 242], 3).

constitutionalism cared whether the facts that they argued from the past were historical or provable and, indeed, whether it is likely they gave the matter much thought.

Strong claims have been made in recent years for the authority of history in the seventeenth century. The most obvious is that history shaped thought. "The ideology of the Ancient Constitution," one argument maintains, "can be accounted for by means of a purely structural explanation: all English law was common law, common law was custom, custom rested on the presumption of immemoriality; property, social structure, and government existed as defined by the law and were therefore presumed to be immemorial."[317] Less obvious are assertions of how history shaped events. If only the opponents of Coke, Selden, and the ancient constitution had been able to invest "the civil law, the martial law, or the . . . feudal law with histories of their own," it has been surmised, then they and not the common lawyers might have determined the course of constitutional development. The reason, apparently, is that had these other laws possessed histories of their own they might "have shaped the governance of England."[318] The fact of the matter is that the opponents of Coke and Selden could have come up with these histories, but what would have been the point? They were not arguing for civil law or martial law, but prerogative law, and

317. J. G. A. Pocock, *The Machiavellian Moment: Florentine Political Thought and the Atlantic Republican Tradition* (Princeton, N.J., 1975), 340–41. Seventeenth-century history also is said to have shaped thought by contributing to the ignorance of the lawyers: "The unitary legal system in England, the prestige of the law and the lawyers, the intimate relationship between views of law and legal history and political realities combined to keep Englishmen wilfully ignorant of the past of their own society" (Laslett, "Book Review" [cited note 36], 143). Even more remarkable is an explanation as to why common lawyers had continued their "constitutionalist" opposition to civil law and to arbitrary power long after better *scholarship* led French lawyers to abandon ancient constitutionalism: "One of the underlying reasons for this was the curious reluctance of the English to consider historical perspective or context. Their tendency was rather to move directly from the most abstract principles of natural law to the most technical practices of English courts without any reference to contracts or parallels with continental jurisprudence" (Kelley, "History, English Law and the Renaissance" [cited note 37], 27).

318. Pocock, *Ancient Constitution Retrospect* (cited note 35), 302.

prerogative law had just as much "history" as common law or ancient-constitution law. It was not their histories that were in controversy but their jurisprudence. Both sides argued "history" not so much when the past seemed relevant but when the past seemed arguable—when they thought the past-as-precedent could be argued to carry the point of law for which they were contending. That is why the advocates for law by royal command found their "history" in the Tudor century and "the constitutionalists were forced into" what has been called "a kind of historical obscurantism—compelled to attribute their liberties to more and more remote and mythical periods in the effort to prove them independent of the will of the king."[319] But were the two sides exploring history, or, because already committed to a theory of government, did they turn to the epochs that supported their theory by precedents, analogies, and appeals to custom? Was it "two different views of history"[320] or two different views of constitutionalism that were at stake? Perhaps what the material of this essay comes down to is whether, as is often assumed, "[t]he past was looked to . . . to solve the

319. Pocock, *Ancient Constitution* (cited note 56), 17. "The pattern in the early seventeenth century is a recurrent one: we find the common lawyers and the parliamentary Opposition appealing to a remote against a more recent past, as the Whig Reformers were to do two centuries later and as the Barons, so far as our evidence goes, had done, centuries before" (Styles, "Politics and Research" [cited note 38], 53).

320. "It was the Crown lawyers, defending Impositions or Proclamations or Arbitrary Imprisonment, who were the more likely to invoke the practices of the sixteenth century. The distinction involved is between two different views of history, or rather between two different aspects of it. If history is a manual of statecraft, it follows that it repeats itself. Human nature remains the same, but situations recur, so that the experience of the past can be applied to the problems of the present. But the appeal to antiquity is concerned with institutions rather than with policy and allows no element of change. Now the political conflicts of the early seventeenth century, so far as they were not complicated by religion, were centered on institutions; on the breakdown of a medieval system of government. They were largely conceived in historical and legal terms and it was in this field that the great scholars of the time were primarily interested. We must therefore examine a little the prevailing conceptions of English history and see how much there was in them of genuine historical judgement" (Styles, "Politics and Research" [cited note 38], 53–54).

problems of the present,"[321] or whether, as has been suggested here, the past was looked to for selective incidents which were cited not as historical evidence but as constitutional authority in the form of legal precedents or legal analogies to argue issues of current law, politics, or religion.

There is no need to defend forensic history. There is not even need for historians to understand it, although they might save themselves much puzzlement if they made the effort. One problem may be that too much is owed to Sir Edward Coke, and, as Christopher Hill pointed out, regrettably he was not an intellectual. Like so many other practitioners of forensic history he was merely a lawyer.[322] But then it may be a mistake to look to the intellectual. Forensic history in the seventeenth and eighteenth centuries was not an intellectual pursuit. It was a pragmatic, professional, and above all constitutional pursuit, with a pragmatic, professional, and above all constitutional purpose. It relieved the lawyer, judge, or legislator of the burden of resolving gravid legal issues aided only by the limited insight of one mind and one age.[323]

One could stress the pragmatic and point out that the legal issues being resolved were English legal and constitutional issues. What were required were English solutions, that is, English legal judgments, and legal or constitutional judgments are not the same as moral judgments or even political judgments. How better to arrive at those judgments, it might be argued, than by English experience, even if that experience is selected by a picking and choosing of supporting evidence. Even if the evidence compiled of the past is not a historian's "true" picture of the past, it may be a legally relevant picture of what, for the issue at bar, is the legally relevant part of the English experience.

There was another purpose to forensic history, a constitutional purpose that in the twentieth century has come to be called "the search

321. Christopher Brooks and Kevin Sharp, "History, English Law and the Renaissance," *Past & Present* 72 (1976): 142.

322. "Coke can hardly be left out of an inquiry into the intellectual origins of the English Revolution, yet he presents difficulties. He was a lawyer, not an intellectual" (Hill, *Intellectual Origins* [cited note 32], 227).

323. Gray, "Reason, Authority, and Imagination" (cited note 186), 35.

for neutral principles." That we, today, believe that no principles can be applied neutrally does not mean that the common lawyers of the seventeenth and eighteenth centuries had received that insight. The common lawyer's use of forensic history was part of the legal imagination of those centuries and was essential to what people in those centuries thought was the rule of law. Even selective, polemical forensic history can have the appearance, no matter that it does not have the reality, of freeing constitutional and judicial decision from the caprice of being based on the policy of the day rather than on impersonal, objective principle. And it does so by elucidating standards of law (or the rule of law) much like the common law's "artificial reasoning" that was at the heart of Coke's legal philosophy. Forensic history brought to the process of decision-making both a canon of relevance and a measure of "rightness," by steering decision from the dictates of mere power.

Right would prevail over naked power or mere reason if the law were autonomous from will and pleasure, and law was autonomous to the extent that people had trust in the neutrality of its methodology of arriving at decision. Aside from the procedure of the common law writ system and the tradition of a relatively independent judiciary, there was little in English or British law to blunt the will and pleasure of arbitrary decision except the mechanics of balance in the tripartite British constitution and the entrenchment of rights in the prescription of a neutral past. Rights to property were secured by being answerable only to certain forms of action, extending over the years from the possessory assizes to the more recent writ of *ejectment*. Liberty was secured by analogizing its "ownership" to property and arguing the ancient constitution not just as a constitution of liberty but as a source of "first principles" that always were neutral because they were timeless and their origins were divorced from any discoverable politics.

Acceptance was the most important aspect of constitutional neutrality. The English in the seventeenth century and the British and Americans in the eighteenth century, to a high percentage, accepted as a fundamental given of liberty that the abstraction of "law" could be trusted where personal decision could not. Common lawyers made concerted efforts to persuade people of the law's equal protection. Sir Edward Coke, for example, had not been solving contemporary

problems "by the recovery of an ancient heritage," as has sometimes
been suggested,[324] when telling the English that their material property in their goods and their intangible property in liberty and country
were secured by the neutrality of the ancient patrimony that was their
shared inheritance. The right to be secured in both their property in
private possessions and their property in liberty belonged to all English citizens equally because they owned that right and every other
civil right individually. That was the lesson Lord Coke wanted to teach.
It was, he explained, partly a matter of instruction, a matter of people
learning that what they had—rights as well as chattels—they owned
because they also owned the right to live under the common law and
could depend on the "learned & faithfull Councellors" of the law.

> There is no Subject of this Realme, but being truely instructed by
> good and playne euidence of his auncient and vndoubted patri-
> mony & byrth-right, (though hee hath for some time by ignorance,
> false perswasion, or vaine feare, bene deceiued or dispossessed) but
> will consult with learned and faythful Councellors for the recouerie
> of the same: The autient & excellent Lawes of England are the birth-
> right and the most antient and best inheritance that the subjects of
> this realme haue, for by them he inioyeth not onely his inheritance
> and goods in peace & quietnes[s], but his life and his most deare
> Countrey in safety.[325]

"I know," Coke added, "that at this day al[l] Kingdomes and States
are gouerned by Lawes, & that the particular & approued custome of
euery natio[n], is the most vsuall binding & assured Law."[326]

We may wonder how much of this Coke believed. We cannot doubt
that he believed English laws "excellent," the best in the world, but

324. William J. Bouwsma, "Lawyers and Early Modern Culture," *American Historical Review* 78 (1973): 327.

325. *The Fift[h] Part of the Reports of Sr. Edward Coke Knight, the Kings Attorney
Generall: Of diuers Resolutions and Iudgements giuen vpon great deliberation in matters
of great importance & consequence by the reuerend Iudges and Sages of the Law; together
with the reasons and causes of their Resolutions and Iudgements* (London, 1605), "To the
Reader" at [2–3].

326. Ibid., [4].

did he really believe they were immemorially "auncient"? The guess of the historiographers of ancient constitutionalism has been that Coke believed he was writing history and that he intended to write history, not law. It must be surmised that this is a guess because there is no indication they asked themselves if Coke was interested in history. The conclusion seems to have been assumed. Yet there is a legitimate question whether any of the forensic historians discussed here believed that the history they wrote provided a historically accurate rather than a constitutional picture of the past.

The question can be limited to lawyers, as it has been the lawyers, not nonlawyer forensic historians of the seventeenth and eighteenth centuries, whom the better historians of our day have accused of not knowing what they were about. And if we are concentrating on lawyers, there is yet another way — in regard to lawyers — to put the question we have been asking. It may be thought that that question is whether the lawyers, who certainly knew that they were practicing forensic history, also thought that their history of the ancient constitution was history by the historical method. That, however, is not the question we need answered. The significant question is, "Did lawyers care?"

Perhaps we should not answer the question with regard to Coke. It is possible that Coke believed everything he wrote about British, German, Saxon, Norman, and English history. It is also possible that he did not care a fig whether there had or had not been a historical provable ancient constitution. It is hard to disagree with Donald R. Kelley's conclusion that "Coke was not interested in 'history' at all."[327] Although we cannot say that Coke wanted English citizens to believe that there had been, in actual fact, an ancient constitution, we can be certain why he wanted them to accept at least the fiction of ancient

327. Kelley, "History, English Law and the Renaissance" (cited note 37), 33. Which does not mean one would agree with Kelley's explanation for that conclusion: "It is true that Coke himself did not hesitate to make use of historical writings, but this was merely because as a lawyer he believed the more arguments the better — there was no telling, he remarked, what might persuade some people. But it was not in history that one learned about the law; on the contrary it was in the study of law that one found 'the faithful and true Histories of all Successive Times'" (32).

constitutionalism. The jurisprudence of ancient constitutionalism—whether the ancient constitution was fact or fiction—was the jurisprudence of limited, mixed government, the jurisprudence of what Coke understood to be liberty.

As for the practitioners of ancient constitutionalism in the two centuries after Coke and Selden, we can be no more certain, but it is safer to venture a guess. For those lawyers of the seventeenth and eighteenth centuries the questions may not be whether they thought they were writing scientific history or whether they cared if their history was according to the historical method. The more revealing question is, why should they have cared?

Although it is not permissible to suggest that the historiographers of the ancient constitution could have been mistaken, it may be permissible to point out that there are questions that they appear to have overlooked. For it does seem that they forgot to ask what lawyers are and they forgot to consider what lawyers do. It is irrevocable error to miss the fact that lawyers are advocates and assume they are something else. The general assumption seems to have been that when they are not writing amateur history they do work akin to that of political theorists.[328] Lawyers are not political theorists and political theory is not law, at least not common law.

We can forget custom, even though custom had more to do than did history with how the ancient constitution was argued in the seventeenth and eighteenth centuries. We may concentrate on history and ask again the question asked and answered before, whether ancient-constitution advocacy was history. If historiographers are correct that there is such a thing as "true" history, then there is also something quite its opposite, history that is "true only in a brief."[329] The same could be said for most "history" appearing in judicial opinions.

328. "We might suggest that lawyers merely endorsed ideas which had first been formulated by others, and themselves contributed nothing to political thinking. There is much truth in this, but there was one political idea which lawyers—including Coke, Hedley and [Sir John] Davies—made peculiarly their own. This was the idea that ancient and rational customs should not, or could not be abrogated" (Sommerville, "History and Theory" [cited note 37], 260).

329. "Evarts not being a historian but a lawyer, it must be called 'lawyer's history' when he said [when arguing the *Tenement Cigar Case* before the United

In *Commonwealth* v. *Chapman* in 1847, Chief Justice Lemuel Shaw observed that from the time of the first settlement of Salem and Boston to the Declaration of Independence, the people living in the colony of Massachusetts Bay "were governed and protected by the laws of England, so far as those laws were applicable to their state and condition."[330] The next lawyer appearing before Shaw's court for whom *Chapman* was squarely and favorably on point might know that colonial Massachusetts law was only partly English law, that it contained much local custom and included some rules adapted from the law merchant. That lawyer would not be advised to write a "correct history." Better for the purpose of winning the case at bar to copy the words of Chief Justice Shaw or just to cite *Commonwealth* v. *Chapman*.[331]

To return to the question being asked: if Shaw thought the history he was stating useful for the law that he wished to promulgate, did he have much reason to be troubled about proving historical accuracy? Mr. Justice Joseph Story had stated a similar historical conclusion some years before. "The common law of England," he wrote in a United States Supreme Court decision, "is not to be taken in all respects to be that of America. Our ancestors brought with them its general principles, and claimed it as their birthright; but they brought with them and adopted only that portion which was applicable to their situation."[332] Story was pronouncing a rule of jurisprudence useful to federal judges willing to exercise judicial power—the purpose he had in mind. He was inviting judges to pick and choose among English common law precedents and decisions, adopting doctrines that would advance commercial growth and rejecting rules like the law of waste that might retard it. It is pos-

---

States Supreme Court], 'Ethical and political writers speak but one language on the nature of these fundamental rights and their security against rightful interference by government.' Such a statement can be true only in a brief" (Benjamin Rollins Twiss, *Lawyers and the Constitution: How Laissez Faire Came to the Supreme Court* [Princeton, N.J., 1942], 104).

330. *Commonwealth* v. *Chapman*, 13 *Metcalf* (*Mass.*) *Reports* 68, 73 (1847).

331. "'Lawyer's history,' . . . proceeds, generally speaking, on the assumption that anything said in a judicial decision which it is convenient to treat as authentic fact *is* authentic fact, whatever a competent historical scholar might have to say about the matter" (Twiss, *Lawyers and the Constitution* [cited note 329], 147).

332. *Van Ness* v. *Pacard*, 2 *Peters* (*U.S.*) 137, 144 (1829).

sible—barely possible—that Story believed that the principle he promulgated was based on sound history provable by the canons of the historical method. It is more likely that the historical soundness of the rule had little bearing on why he adopted it. The rule was desirable as law, and for that reason alone it probably made sense as history.

Today a judge writing a decision in, let us suppose, a native American land case, does not say to his law clerk, "What rule does history support?" Rather, the judge tells her, "We're going to adopt such-and-such rule. Find me some history to support it." It will not matter to the judge or his colleagues on the court the quality of the historical evidence that she finds. If the question at bar concerns the validity of a Plains Indians treaty, an authoritative pronouncement by Francis Paul Prucha will be all to the good. If the only "history" that supports the desired result is a quotation out of a book commissioned by the plaintiff Indian nation, a book that tells only the Indians' side of events from the Indians' prejudices, published locally in Pierre, South Dakota, and not known or respected by any scholar of native American history, it will not matter. What does matter is that there is a published statement to be quoted and the judges have no reason not to quote it. They use it, after all, not as a piece of historical evidence, but as authority.

Today's judge in the native American land case is no different than Sir Edward Coke, William Prynne, or Robert Atkyns. Undoubtedly they all wanted their history to be scientific history because they wanted to persuade. But with questions of law there are other means of persuasion than the scholarship of another discipline. When a case was being argued, if it took forensic history to win, then forensic history would do. Bad history can produce good law as readily as can scientific history. Justice Hugo Black based the "incorporation doctrine" of the Fourteenth Amendment on what he possibly thought was a careful reading of the past. It was not careful at all according to Leonard W. Levy. It was, rather, selectively forensic. "Black did not merely misread history nor wishfully attribute to it a factual content that it did not possess; he mangled and manipulated it by artfully selecting facts from one side only, by generalizing from grossly inadequate 'proof,' by ignoring confusion and even contradictions in the minds of some of his key historical protagonists, and by assuming that silence on the part of their opponents signified acquiescence."[333] Had Levy talked to Black and had he convinced him that forensic history is not history, we may imagine Black would have been mildly interested. "What is important," he might have replied, "is that it is now undisputable law that the states of the union must adhere to the principles of the Bill of Rights in the same way that the federal government must." By the same token, if J. G. A. Pocock were able to communicate with Sir Edward Coke, we may suppose that Coke might express surprise that history has come to doubt the perfection of Saxon law and might offer some complicated explanation, having more to do with constitutional law than with history, about what he thought ancient constitutionalism should stand for. It is, however, unlikely that his answer would be much different in meaning than if he said, "So what? The ancient constitution may have been bad history but Charles I and James II learned that it was good law."

Justice Black's "incorporation doctrine" was based on what he claimed was the "original intention" of the framers of the Fourteenth Amendment. There are parallels linking ancient constitutionalism in the seventeenth and eighteenth centuries with today's doctrine of "original intent." Robert Brady's 1684 political complaint that the theory of "*Ancient Right* and *Privileges*" taught people "to prescribe against the Government for many Things they *miscal[l]* Fundamental Rights"[334] was not that much different from the historian of 1988 calling for real history to "bury" the doctrine of original intent, "that badly battered theory of Constitutional interpretation."[335] Both ancient constitutionalism and original intentism came under criticism in their own days for reasons that were not likely to persuade their practitioners.

Critics of original intentism, like recent critics of ancient constitu-

333. Leonard W. Levy, "Introduction" to Charles Fairman and Stanley Morrison, *The Fourteenth Amendment and the Bill of Rights: The Incorporation Theory* (New York, 1970), xii–xiii.

334. Brady, *Introduction to the Old English History* (cited note 214), "Epistle" (n.p.).

335. Christopher Collier, "The Historians Versus the Lawyers: James Madison, James Hutson, and the Doctrine of Original Intent," *Pennsylvania Magazine of History and Biography* 112 (January 1988): 140.

tionalism, confuse forensic history with academic history and concentrate on irrelevancies such as the unreliability of the record.[336] Also like critics of ancient constitutionalism, they seem to have slight regard for the rule of law.

The principle of the rule of law is the striking connection between the ancient constitution and the doctrine of original intent. Both ancient constitutionalism and original intentism may be "bad" history, but both, if used with the discipline of the common law method, can be restraints on the will and pleasure of arbitrary decision, whether royal, legislative, or (especially in the case of original intent) judicial. "Original intent, sensibly defined, provides a limited Constitution that properly applies to new situations," Robert Palmer pointed out in 1987. "Original intent analysis, however, will not yield a constitutional law that is equivalent to that now practiced, nor will it yield a constitutional law that is demonstrably superior in handling social needs or maximizing individual liberties. . . . The only sure consequence of original intent analysis is that it would require less judicial discretion and consequently more frequent resort to the people in the amendment process."[337] The same jurisprudential end was served by the cor-

336. One historian writing in a legal periodical said that he would "be satisfied if lawyers, judges, historians, and legal scholars are reminded, as they periodically need to be, that the mere fact that a record is in print does not make it reliable" (James H. Hutson, "The Creation of the Constitution: The Integrity of the Documentary Record," *Texas Law Review* 65 [November 1986]: 39).

337. Robert C. Palmer, "Liberties as Constitutional Provisions 1776–1791," in William E. Nelson and Robert C. Palmer, *Liberty and Community: Constitution and Rights in the Early American Republic* (New York, 1987), 146. "For those who fear the risks of expansive judicial interpretation of open-ended constitutional provisions, obedience to the commands of history provides a way of narrowing, albeit not completely, the options open to the conscientious judge. Here history is used to control not exclusively or even primarily because an historical view of intent is special, but because it is a pragmatic device for cabining the discretion of judges. . . . Reference to historical intent as a method for limiting judicial discretion might still be thought to be more legitimate or perhaps more constraining than some of these other techniques, but it is the constraint and not the legitimacy that under this view justifies taking original intent as command" (Frederick Schauer, "The Varied Uses of Constitutional History," in Nelson and Palmer, *Constitution*, 7).

rect use of ancient constitutionalism. When advocates and legislators in the eighteenth century made an attempt to tie decision and policy to the accepted, taught, time-honored tenets of the ancient constitution, they were saying that judgment should be guided and that law, not discretion, should rule. To use the ancient constitution in argument or in judgment could persuade an individual that impartial justice had been done or persuade a generation that a principled decision had been reached.

We need not be convinced. The historians will continue to carry the day, for historiography is their preserve and lawyers are always fair game. And yet, is history so narrow that there is no other measure than the norms of professional historiography? Something worth remembering happened in the England where those uneducated lawyers clung tenaciously to ancient constitutionalism during the seventeenth and eighteenth centuries; something setting that country and its constitutional tradition of rule by law apart from the continent of Europe.[338] It is a wonder for historians to consider that those common lawyers were the only lawyers of Europe to keep viable the ancient constitution, if not as a source of liberty, at least as a restraining

---

338. It is good to keep in mind that the triumph of history among Continental lawyers, so often held up to prove the comparative intellectual barrenness of the common law mind, coincided with the defeat of constitutionalism. "In France historians and lawyers had quietly disposed of many of their cherished professional beliefs—that the 'Salic law' and the Parlement of Paris were derived from the early Franks, for example, and that their laws were older than those of the Romans. The English, on the other hand, clung even more tenaciously to their myths, and they continued to rest their case upon the aboriginal character and prehistorical origin of common law. The fact that between Fortescue and Coke lay over a century of exploration into European legal and institutional history, much of it by professional jurists, did not seem to matter. On the contrary, as J. G. A. Pocock has said, 'Between 1550 and 1600 there occurred a great hardening and consolidation of common-law thought.' It is something of a paradox that this should have happened precisely when the continent was enjoying a golden age of legal and historical scholarship and when a kind of 'historical revolution' was beginning in England itself" (Kelley, "History, English Law and Renaissance" [cited note 37], 30). The hardening of common-law thought is less a paradox to the legally minded, for this was the period of hardening of common-law constitutional resistance to arbitrary government.

force on arbitrary government. A historical issue deserving attention is why these narrow-minded, ahistorical English lawyers were the only lawyers in Europe during the seventeenth and eighteenth centuries to have any idea what it might be like to live under the rule of law.

Epilogue: Diverse Viewpoints on Ancient Constitutionalism

I

The theme of the Windsor Castle Conference with which this book originated—"Magna Carta and Ancient Constitution"—brings automatically to mind J. G. A. Pocock's much discussed study of the ancient constitution and its bearing on Stuart politics and thought. Few would deny that the compliment in the choice of theme is richly deserved. For recognition is general that his *Ancient Constitution and the Feudal Law* opened up a new way of looking at the Petition of Right and the Bill of Rights, documents of the first importance in the history of political liberty in the western world.[1]

Yet it is doubtful that Pocock's conception of the ancient constitution faithfully mirrors that of Stuart Englishmen who asserted ancient rights and liberties. For one thing, Christopher Hill, as long ago as 1958, noticed in Tudor England a growing interest in the Saxon past and wrote of a legend of Saxon freedom in the seventeenth century. He even refers to a theory that "stressed the unbroken continuity of common law, which had carried Anglo-Saxon liberty into post-conquest England."[2] I, too, think the ancient constitution is best described as a Saxon constitution, and in what follows I explain my reasons for thinking so as a necessary preliminary to commenting on the foregoing essays.[3] My focus is on Pocock's interpretation of the legal

1. This research was supported in part by a grant from the Faculty Research Award Program of the City University of New York.

2. Christopher Hill, *Puritanism and Revolution* (London, 1958; first published in Mercury Books, 1962), 60, more generally 57–67.

3. I first expressed this view in a paper prepared for a seminar on the ancient constitution (April 3–4, 1986). This seminar was part of a larger program on political thought in a series offered by the Folger Institute Center for the History of British Political Thought. The subject is more fully developed in my "England: Ancient Constitution and Common Law," in *The Cambridge History of*

terms *immemorial* and *time before memory*, from which his most striking generalizations flow.

II

Pocock's description runs on these lines. Stuart historians, known as legal antiquaries, wrote of an immemorial constitution and law shaped by Sir Edward Coke's prefaces to his *Reports* (1600–1615) and his *Institutes of the Laws of England* (1628–1644). The *Reports* supplied law cases for students of common law, while the *Institutes* served as a great legal textbook, their popularity enhanced by the high prestige of an author who was speaker of the Elizabethan House of Commons and then successively chief justice of the Common Pleas and King's Bench before becoming a prominent parliamentary leader in the 1620s. Pocock writes of Coke's pursuing "the precedents of existing institutions into the distant past" and his identifying parliament's liberties and the whole constitution with an ancient law "of no known origin" that had "suffered no change in the course of history." As a result proponents of this fundamental constitution thought in terms of an ancient constitution "which owed its being to no man."[4]

Another descriptive passage states graphically that "common lawyers, holding that law was custom, came to believe that the common law, and with it the constitution, had always been exactly what they were now, *that they were immemorial: not merely that they were very old, or that they were the work of remote and mythical legislators, but that they were immemorial in the precise legal sense of dating from time beyond memory—beyond in this case, the earliest historical record that could be found* [italics added]." This is "the doctrine or myth of the ancient constitution, which bulked so large in the political thought of the seventeenth century." The myth was extraordinarily useful to whoever supported rights and liberties. If these were based on an immemorial constitution, they rested on as firm a legal foundation as the royal prerogative. Moreover, as Pocock

---

Political Thought, 1450–1700, ed. J. H. Burns with the assistance of Mark Goldie (Cambridge, England, 1991), 374–411.

4. J. G. A. Pocock, "Robert Brady, 1627–1700: A Cambridge Historian of the Restoration," *Cambridge Historical Journal* 10:2 (1951): 189. See also his *The Ancient Constitution and the Feudal Law: A Study of English Historical Thought in the Seventeenth Century* (Cambridge, England, 1957), 41.

points out, if rights and liberties were not created by earlier kings, their successors could not legally withdraw them.[5]

Although common law reasoning imparted a distinctive flavor to the doctrine of the ancient constitution, there is no reason to think that legal antiquaries lacked interest in the statutes of a legislating parliament. Indeed, their concept of an ancient constitution from the first included this kind of parliament. This was true of Coke, the great champion of common law, who was very fond of two medieval treatises: the *Modus tenendi Parliamentum,* published in 1572, and the *Mirror of Justices,* which circulated in manuscript in Tudor England and was printed in French in 1642. An English edition appeared in 1646. If taken at face value, the *Modus* provided powerful evidence of such a parliament under Edward the Confessor (d. 1066); and the *Mirror* stated that Alfred the Great had ordained as perpetual usage—a term deemed significant by the common law mind—that parliaments be held twice a year. While speaker of the House of Commons in 1592–1593, Coke brought the *Modus* to its attention, and in the influential preface to his *Ninth Reports* he wrote of the *Mirror* as a learned and ancient treatise.[6]

Nor did legal antiquaries including Coke doubt the superiority of statutes to common law or of parliament to common law courts. All things being equal they would have preferred to rely on ancient statutes in asserting ancient rights and privileges, but the choice was not theirs to make. The parliament rolls where these should have been recorded were not to be found and were believed lost. There was no assumption that they might not have existed. Lacking the essential parliament rolls to establish that early laws were indeed the product of a legislating parliament, the legal antiquaries had no alternative

5. Pocock, *Ancient Constitution,* 36, 37, 51–52, and "Robert Brady," 189.

6. The *Modus* is discussed in Nicholas Pronay and John Taylor, *Parliamentary Texts of the Later Middle Ages* (Oxford, 1980), 51, 56, and *passim;* but see especially p. 80 for the proem. Also pertinent is E. Evans, "Of the Antiquity of Parliaments in England," *History* 23 (December 1938): 207–9. *The Mirror of Justices,* ed. W. J. Whittaker, intro. F. W. Maitland (London, 1895), 8. See also *The Reports of Sir Edward Coke, Knt., in English, In Thirteen Parts Complete . . . ,* revised and edited by George Wilson, Serjeant At Law, 7 vols. (London, 1776–1777), preface to the *Ninth Reports,* i–ii, vii, ix.

except to search historical materials such as medieval chronicles and annals as well as later statutes for signs of pertinent ancient customs that formed part of common law.[7]

To attain this status these customs had to meet certain tests; only if this occurred, could the term *immemorial* be rightfully applied to them. The authoritative statement is in the *First Part of the Institutes* (1628), often referred to as "Coke on Littleton," where it is explained that customs attain force of law by title of prescription. This common law principle became conspicuous in Stuart discourse when it was applied to ancient customs embodying rights and liberties. If these customs were to be allowed by the common law, they must be in accord with reason and God's will expressed in the Scriptures. But other criteria were more prominent in political argument. Before customs could be deemed prescriptive, and hence immemorial, they had to have existed before (or beyond) time of memory without written record to the contrary. Stuart polemicists used the date of Richard I's coronation, September 3, 1189, to divide time before memory from time of memory. They considered that in a legal sense whatever was before 1189, so far as customs were concerned, was before time of memory; whatever was since Richard I's coronation was said to be within time of memory. Littleton, writing in the fifteenth century, reported that some found a title of prescription at common law "where a custom, or usage, or other thing, hath been used for time whereof mind of man runneth not to the contrary (*a tempore cujus contraria memoria hominum non existit*)," that is, before time of memory. To be deemed prescriptive customs must also have been exercised regularly and constantly without protest before and after 1189; usage must have been long, continued, and peace-

7. In this connection see the valuable statement in William Prynne's "Preface to the Reader," *An Exact Abridgement of the Records in the Tower of London* (London, 1657), n.p. Prynne recommended turning, in particular, to the medieval historians Matthew of Paris, Matthew Westminster, William of Malmesbury, Henry of Huntingdon, Roger de Hoveden, Simon Dunelmensis, Ralph Diceto, Ralph Cistrensis, and Thomas of Walsingham and to the chronicle attributed to John Brompton, which was especially associated with laws attributed to Edward the Confessor. See also Stowe 543, F73b in the British Library. This is No. 13: "The opinions of Mr. Selden and Mr. Prynne, concerning the deplorable loss of our ancient parliamentary records."

able without the interruption, for example, of a Norman conquest. If these conditions were met, a customary usage was established that demonstrated tacit consent and the rights and liberties involved were allowed by the common law.[8]

To Coke's authority should be added that of Lord Chief Justice Matthew Hale (d. 1676), the most eminent lawyer and judge of his age. He was, successively, justice of the Common Pleas, lord chief baron of the Exchequer, and chief justice of King's Bench. Writing about statutes made before 1189 in his posthumously published *History of the Common Law* (1713), he distinguished precisely between time of memory and time before or beyond memory, stating

> that according to a juridical account and legal signification, *time within memory* is the time of limitation in a writ of right, which by the statute of Westminster I cap. 38. was settled, and reduced to the beginning of the reign of King Richard I. or *Ex prima Coronatione Regis Richard Primi,* who began his reign the 6th of July 1189, and was crown'd the 3d of September following: so that whatsoever was before that time is *before* time of memory; and what is since that time, is, in a legal sense, said to be *within* or since time of memory.[9]

Likewise pertinent is the further comment that statutes made before the beginning of Richard I's reign that had not been since altered or repealed were "now accounted . . . part of the common law; and in truth" were "not now pleadable as acts of parliament (*because what is before time of memory is supposed without a beginning or at least such a beginning as the law takes notice of* [italics added]." They obtained their strength "*by mere immemorial usage or custom* [italics added]."[10]

If the term *immemorial* conveys no more than the simple fact that the constitution, to be termed ancient, must have originated before 1189 and if reference to its having no beginning, and hence no human maker, was legal parlance, it follows that the ancient constitution was in

8. Sir Edward Coke, *The First Part of the Institutes of the Laws of England* (1628), lib. 2, cap. 10, sec. 170. See also Sir Matthew Hale, *The History of the Common Law of England,* ed. Charles M. Gray (Chicago, 1971), 17–18.

9. Hale, *History of the Common Law,* 3–4.

10. Ibid., 4.

all probability a Saxon constitution, established either before or after the Saxons entered England. Under these circumstances it was said to be as old as the name of England; under its auspices ancient rights and liberties would be viewed as just as legal as under Pocock's ancient constitution. Witness the remarks of James Tyrrell, a Whig polemicist commenting on an "immemorial" House of Commons: "Who ever supposed that the commons claimed a right by prescription ever since the creation, or ever since the first peopling of this island? . . . Any body may see that this word *ever* is to be understood according to the nature of the subject in hand, *viz.* from the first institution of the *Saxon* government in this island."[11] To legal antiquaries the presence of the word *ever* in a medieval statute referring to the House of Commons afforded solid proof that it was part of parliament before 1189. Thus the statute 2 H.V, no. 10 received mention in parliamentary debates and political tracts for just this reason: it established that the House of Commons was legally "immemorial."[12]

Finally, it should be noted that Coke, lacking any knowledge of political feudalism, considered Magna Carta a reaffirmation of ancient customs and laws that had protected Saxon liberties before the Norman conquest. Like many others he followed the medieval historian Matthew Paris in asserting that Magna Carta's main provisions were derived from the Confessor's laws and those of Henry I, whose coronation charter (1100) contained his pledge to restore these laws after the previous reign's abuses. To Hale, the Confessor's laws were such that the English were "very zealous" for them as "being the great rule and standard of their rights and liberties."[13]

11. James Tyrrell, *Bibliotheca Politica*, 2d ed. (London, 1727), 420, 421, 425, 426. This was published initially at the Revolution (1689). See also Sir Roger Twysden, *Certaine Considerations upon the Government of England*, ed. John Mitchell Kemble (London, 1849), 119, 120, thought to have been written in the 1650s.

12. Twysden, *Certaine Considerations*, 126–27. William Hakewill in *Commons Journal* 1 (December 17, 1621): 667. See too E. Nicholas, *Proceedings and Debates of the House of Commons, in 1620 and 1621* (Oxford, 1776), ii, 346; William Petyt, "A Discourse," *Ancient Right of the Commons of England Asserted* (London, 1680), 39–49; Anthony Ellis, *Tracts on the Liberty Spiritual and Temporal of Protestants in England* (London, 1767), pt. 1, 463. Ellis was working from Tyrrell and Petyt.

13. Preface to the *Eighth Reports*, in *Reports*, ed. Wilson, x; Hale, *History of the Common Law*, 5.

III

It is, then, of singular interest that J. C. Holt in his "Ancient Constitution in Medieval England," and in publications centering on Magna Carta, tells of an earlier movement in which the Confessor's laws were likewise treated as the great standard of rights and liberties. Not only did this movement culminate in King John's grant of Magna Carta to his barons in June 1215. It was distinctive as well because the authors of the rebellion claimed to be restoring ancient customs that were part of a golden past (before the Angevins) and to be acting in the Confessor's name. Holt assigns to this medieval ancient constitutionalism an important influence on Stuart England when he writes that the legal antiquaries revived Magna Carta and "above all, in truly medieval style, proceeded to apply the great tradition to their own particular circumstances." This renaissance, as he calls it, was due to the work of officials of the crown, notably William Lambarde and Coke. Referring to the intellectual origins of the civil war, he wonders whether these were in fact so different from the medieval movement that he has described.[14] In a published work he is even more precise. Granting the dissimilarities between the two movements, Holt concludes that the argument about the relationship of royal power to law was "closely similar in each case, all the more so in that the antiquarians of the second occasion drew on the antiquarians of the first in mounting their case against . . . the royal prerogative and what their predecessors described more plainly as the will of the king, which carried with it the . . . charge of tyranny."[15]

A word about the Confessor, the penultimate Saxon king before the Norman conquest. A member of the house of Wessex that united the kingdoms of the heptarchy into England and hence a descendant of Alfred the Great, who saved England from the Danes, he is usually adjudged an indifferent king in the secular sphere though well remembered as builder of Westminster Abbey and the only English king to be canonized for his piety. He came to be seen as the epitome of Saxon liberties. Though he was no legislator, even Coke referred approvingly to Holy Edward's laws, the source of Coke's knowledge of Saxon law.

14. Holt, herein, 51–59.

15. J. C. Holt, *Magna Carta and Medieval Government* (London, 1985), 17.

These laws had an influence on Coke comparable to Sir John Fortescue's *De Laudibus,* a highly influential treatise that Ellis Sandoz has ably analyzed in his introduction to this volume. Readers will find much of interest in it; for, unquestionably, Sir John Fortescue—the doyen of late medieval political theorists—advanced political ideas that anticipated the ancient constitutionalism of the Stuart century. In Sandoz's discussion, the role of common lawyers and the dominant position of common law loom large—as does a new concept of the common welfare accepted by king and parliament. He sees at the heart of England's ancient constitution an emphasis on "securing through the consent of the realm laws protecting the immemorial liberty of free men, serving the well-being of the whole community, and assuring a balance between parliament and king that will foster effective no less than just rule." But despite the comprehensiveness of Sandoz's discussion, it may be queried whether a place might not have been found, in the interest of a well-balanced account, for a discussion of the ideas on law-making expressed by the Elizabethan statesman Sir Thomas Smith and later by Coke in his *Institutes* (1628–1644). After all, Smith asserted the high power of parliament, and Coke not only distinguished between new and old law but also maintained the supremacy of statutes over common law.

The time has come, however, to resume this commentary on the Confessor's laws. For almost four centuries, from Edward II's coronation oath (1308) to the Glorious Revolution (1688–1689), monarchs promised to keep the Confessor's laws. In the result the coronation oath came to be seen as the original contract on which the Saxon constitution was founded; so, too, did Magna Carta, which confirmed those laws. By the time the pertinent language entered the coronation oath, notes F. W. Maitland, the Confessor had "become a myth—a saint and hero of a golden age, of a good old time."[16]

The barons in 1215 also invoked the name of Henry I, son of the Conqueror. Sometimes referred to as the "lion of justice," he was said

16. F. W. Maitland, *Constitutional History of England* (Cambridge, England, 1961), 100. Recognition of the high symbolic importance of the Confessor's law in Stuart political thought moved forward in a major way with the publication of Janelle Greenberg's pioneering "The Confessor's Laws and the Radical Face of the Ancient Constitution," *English Historical Review* 104:412 (July 1989): 611–37.

repeatedly in Tudor and Stuart chronicles to have founded the first parliament in which the Commons appeared. According to Holt, the political movement of 1215 began with the demand for the confirmation and reissue of Henry's coronation charter. Westminster, Lambeth, and the royal treasury contributed early versions, from which the authors of the rebellion worked. At the same time historico-legal research produced two texts drawn from the first half of the twelfth century: the *Leges Edwardi Confessoris* and the *Leges Henrici Primi*, a blend of Anglo-Saxon and Frankish law. Additional materials were interpolated in the body of the *Leges Edwardi Confessoris*, notably about judgment by peers and baronial advice, which anticipated the program of 1215. These collections of laws were associated with the coronation oath, in which successive kings promised to uphold the Confessor's laws. Here was a political movement with a political program. Holt writes: "The coronation oath, the charter of Henry I, the laws of Henry I and Edward the Confessor, were not an accidental association; they were all expressions of ancient law which was now being used as a standard whereby Angevin government could be weighed, criticized, and corrected." In the result the barons took over the Confessor as "the source of good and ancient law," and Holt adds that the men of 1215 had their own views about the Confessor and Henry I. The first was "a canonized saint, a worker of miracles [he allegedly touched for the king's evil]"; and Henry I, the lion of justice, was "the keeper of the bees and the guardian of the flocks."[17]

Holt also suggests possible corridors through which medieval ancient constitutionalism reached Stuart England. One of them was provided by a legend recorded after 1220 in annals at St. Augustine's, Canterbury. These told of an encounter at Swanscombe Down between William the Conqueror and the men of Kent, led by Stigand, archbishop of Canterbury, and Aethelsige, abbot of St. Augustine's, that resulted in the preservation of ancestral laws and customs in Kent, even though the rest of England was enslaved. The point was nonetheless clear: ancient law was good law and Saxon law. The legend reappeared in Lambarde's much-reprinted *Perambulation of Kent* (1576) and Holinshed's *Chronicle* (1577), Holt notes; and he could have cited

17. Holt, herein, 68–71.

as well chronicles associated with Richard Grafton (1568), John Speed (1611), and Samuel Daniel (1621).[18]

Even more to the point was the publication in late Tudor England of the Confessor's laws. Once more Lambarde is a principal. In 1568 he published his *Archaionomia,* the London text of *Leges Edwardi Confessoris;* and it is significant that Coke's library contained both the *Perambulation* and *Archaionomia,* the latter, as earlier noted, the main source of his knowledge of Saxon law.[19] The Confessor's laws were clearly accessible in Stuart England. Two editions of *Archaionomia* appeared in 1644, one of them edited by the respected legal antiquary Sir Roger Twysden, with Henry I's laws appended. And then there was John Selden's edition of Eadmer's annals, published in 1623. Eadmer was a monk of Canterbury and chaplain to Archbishop Anselm in Norman England and a contemporary of the events he described. Selden's edition of Eadmer's annals contains not only the Confessor's laws but also the anonymous Lichfield chronicle and the chronicle of Ingulphus of Croyland, two of Coke's major sources in the preface to his *Eighth Reports.* The Lichfield chronicle tells how the Conqueror in the fourth year of his reign summoned twelve of the most discreet and wise men in every shire to declare, as Coke put it, "the integrity of their laws . . . without varying from the truth." To Coke these were the Confessor's laws, which became the first Magna Carta.[20] And "Ingulphus," which was known only in the nineteenth century to be a forgery, tells of the Conqueror's making provision for their inviolate observance. Ingulphus claimed to have carried a copy of the confirmed laws back to his monastery.[21] In this connection Coke also made use of Roger de Hoveden's chronicle, and it was often cited in this context.[22]

This is not the place to discuss at length the flow of medieval politi-

---

18. Ibid., 71–72. Richard Grafton, *An Abridgement of the Chronicles of England* (1562), ii, 2; John Speed, *The History of Great Britain under the conquests of the Romans, Saxons, Danes and Normans* (1611), i, 416; Samuel Daniel, *The Collection of the Historie of England* (1617), 39.

19. Holt, herein, 72–73.

20. Coke, preface to the *Eighth Reports,* in *Reports,* ed. Wilson, iv–v.

21. Ibid., v; *Ingulph's Chronicle of the Abbey of Croyland,* trans. Henry T. Riley (London, 1854), 175.

22. Preface to the *Eighth Reports,* in *Reports,* ed. Wilson, vii.

cal literature into Tudor England in the generation before Coke wrote the highly influential historical prefaces to his *Reports*. Put simply, the volume of such literature was due to the advent of the printing press and to the interest in printing manuscripts displayed by such influential Elizabethan leaders as Matthew Parker, archbishop of Canterbury, Lord Burghley, and Sir Francis Walsingham. All of them were interested in establishing the continuity of Elizabethan institutions as a key to the stability of the Elizabethan state and church settlement.

Thanks to the researches of May McKisak, F. J. Levy, and Antonia Gransden, much is known about Parker's role in particular. He was the first Englishman to organize the printing of a series of important medieval historical texts, doing so in the period from 1567 to 1574. Chief among them was Matthew Paris's *Greater Chronicle*, a prime historical source for Magna Carta and King John's reign, printed in 1571 and reprinted in 1589 and again in 1640. Relying on Paris's account, Parker also wrote a book on Stephen Langton, who allegedly supplied the barons with Henry I's coronation charter. Parker is equally memorable as founder of the Society of Antiquaries, with some forty members, that met from 1572 to 1604 and again in 1614. Lambarde belonged, and it is now known that there was a direct link between his publication of *Archaionomia* and Burghley.[23]

Another notable figure in this context was the very learned Sir Henry Savile, Elizabeth's Greek tutor and warden of Wadham College. He, too, moved in high political circles. He was the associate of Burghley and Walsingham, and James I later knighted him. His *Rerum Scriptures* (1596, 1601) contained a host of medieval chronicles, including Ingulphus. By the end of the sixteenth century, thanks to Parker and Savile, in particular, there had been a great influx of medieval politi-

---

23. Lambarde carried out the venture under the supervision of Laurence Nowell, Burghley's protégé. F. J. Levy, *Tudor Historical Thought* (San Marino, Calif., 1967), 136, 141. See also David Douglas, *English Scholars, 1660–1713*, 2d ed. (London, 1951), 69. That the publication of *Archaionomia* was deemed eventful also appears from Parker's commendation in the preface to Asser's biography of Alfred the Great, which he printed. May McKisak, *Medieval History in the Tudor Age* (Oxford, 1971), 79. See also Philip Styles in *English Historical Scholarship in the Sixteenth and Seventeenth Centuries*, ed. Levi Fox (London, 1956), 51, and Samuel L. Kliger in *The Goths in England* (Cambridge, Mass., 1952), 21–25.

cal literature concerned with the events that Holt describes. Witness the appearance of such medieval chronicles as Matthew Paris's *Greater Chronicle* and also those associated with Eadmer, Florence of Worcester, William of Malmesbury, Henry of Huntingdon, Roger de Hoveden, and Ingulphus.[24] Any doubt that this development is related to the prosperous course of ancient constitutionalism in the Stuart century is removed by even a casual look at the authorities cited in Coke's historical prefaces. That Stuart polemicists put the prefaces to good use in their tracts appears from William Prynne's enormously influential *Soveraigne Power of Parliaments* (1643) and his very revealing *Third Part of a Seasonable, Legal and Historical Vindication* (1655); Bulstrode Whitelocke's *Notes uppon the Kings Writ*, not published until 1766 but written in the late 1650s; and William Petyt's *Ancient Right of the Commons of England Asserted* (1680). The evidence is overwhelming that medieval political literature centering on the origins of Magna Carta and its relationship in the contemporary view to Saxon England had a secure place in Stuart political thought.

In short, Holt has identified a major new source of ancient constitutionalism, and his findings, though he does not draw the conclusion explicitly, point to an accepted view by the seventeenth century that the ancient constitution was a Saxon constitution with the Confessor as its founding father and patron saint. At the same time Holt's analysis supports Pocock's theory that ancient constitutionalism was more than the response of the moment in Stuart politics. Viewed as resulting from an encounter between a common law mind-set and a medieval constitution, it did have deep roots in the past, as Pocock suggests. On the other hand, Holt's association of medieval political literature, or elements of it, with Coke and Lambarde has the effect of downgrading Pocock's idea that the historical views of Stuart Englishmen were largely shaped by the existence of only one important law system in their history, that of common law.[25]

24. Antonia Gransden, *Historical Writing in England, c. 1307 to the Early Sixteenth Century* (New York, 1928), ii, 479; Douglas, *English Scholars*, 164–67.

25. Pocock, *Ancient Constitution*, 30, 58–59. For comment revealing that Pocock's idea is now controversial, see R. J. Smith, *The Gothic Bequest: Medieval Institutions in British Thought, 1688–1863* (Cambridge, 1987), 4.

According to Pocock, it was not until legal antiquaries became aware of the existence after 1066 of a rival system of feudal law, which interacted with Saxon law, that it was possible for them to see that the common law had grown up under varying influences and at different times. Not only was feudalism not "discovered" until the latter part of the seventeenth century, Pocock considers that in late Tudor England there was "a great hardening and consolidation of common-law thought," which explain the tone of Coke's historical writings. Pointing out that the common law interpretation was probably "the result of deep-seated and unconscious habits of mind," he expressed the view in 1957 that a detailed study of Tudor common law thought was needed to learn how and when that interpretation arose.[26]

Christopher Brooks's "The Place of Magna Carta and the Ancient Constitution in Sixteenth-Century English Legal Thought" is such a study, and his findings are negative. He accepts Pocock's depiction of Coke's ideas as accurate and admits the effectiveness of the "ancient constitution" in early Stuart political controversy but draws back from the proposition that ancient constitutionalism "had always been the major constituent of English legal thought" and "part of a longer tradition within English law." Nor does he discern in Tudor England a common law mentality on the order of that assigned by Pocock to Stuart England, although he thinks the picture somewhat different by the 1590s.[27]

Brooks's analysis draws on a wide variety of sources: the writings of Sir John Fortescue, Christopher St. Germain, and Thomas Starkey and also materials from legal textbooks, tracts, lectures at Inns of Court, and the like. From his examination he concludes that the legal mind of Tudor England was essentially an inheritance from Aristotelianism, as formulated by medieval schoolmen, and Rome's legal literature, as transmitted by Renaissance humanism. Nor does he find any "systematically thought-out view that customs were valid simply because long usage had proved their utility and justness."[28] Moreover, Tudor society, concerned about social, economic, and political upheaval, was

26. Pocock, *Ancient Constitution*, 31–32.
27. Brooks, herein, 97–100, 103–4.
28. Ibid., 97.

preoccupied with law and order rather than libertarian ideals. In this climate of opinion Magna Carta was viewed not so much as a charter of liberties as a statute to correct defects in common law. Finally, Brooks considers that Coke took up the language of ancient constitutionalism in response to the polemics of the Jesuit controversialist Robert Parsons, who at the time was causing a flutter at the Stuart court. In sum, the legal mind of this period is best described as part of a broader Renaissance tradition with Continental overtones, and Coke's political reflections were not the outcome of a tradition of legal thought in Tudor England.[29]

There is, however, a resource not mentioned by Brooks that might have yielded more promising results. The working libraries of lawyers often contained the *Modus* and, more rarely, the *Mirror of Justices.* Both were pillars of ancient constitutionalism and as such highly esteemed by Coke. Moreover, if the *Mirror* was less likely to be found in these libraries, it is known that it was being handed around in manuscript among lawyers. The Society of Antiquaries put the *Modus* to good use; one of its members, Francis Tate, supplied the manuscript from which the *Mirror* was published. Lambarde, also a member, reported in his *Archeion* (1635)—apparently completed by 1591—that the *Modus* was to be seen in many hands.[30] His testimony is of great interest because he was quoted on ancient constitutionalism in the late seventeenth century as often as Coke; and their names were often coupled as authorities for its principles.

Yet Brooks's findings are important and his research admirable. On balance these eliminate from further consideration Pocock's suggestion that a study of the Tudor legal mind might turn up decisive evidence of a long-standing tradition of ancient constitutionalism that flowered in Stuart England. But Pocock's subtitle, *A Study of English Historical Thought in the Seventeenth Century,* points to another quarter that would bear investigation in this context. If Brooks closed off one possibility, why not examine the newly printed medieval literature to which Holt called attention? To be sure, common law assumptions had

29. Ibid., 102, 78–114, *passim.*

30. Maitland, "Introduction" to *The Mirror of Justices,* xi. See also Pronay and Taylor, *Parliamentary Texts,* 18–21, 57, 57, n. 163.

played a conspicuous role in bringing about ancient constitutionalism; but so, too, had the medieval historical materials in which legal antiquaries sought evidence for an immemorial constitution. In closing one door, Brooks opens another; in this sense his paper complements Holt's. In their respective ways, one negatively, the other positively, they point to the ancient constitution as a Saxon constitution and to the possibility of a lengthy political tradition that explains the nature of Coke's response to Parsons.

Although Paul Christianson's "Ancient Constitutions in the Age of Sir Edward Coke and John Selden" contains little pertaining to Holt's and Brooks's papers, there is at one stage of his discussion an important section on Selden that fits the mold. What Christianson sets out to do is to construct several models of the ancient constitution based on materials drawn from 1610. He then tests these by reference to the parliamentary debates on the Petition of Right. It should be stated that his intention seems to be one of supplementing Pocock's model but not supplanting it. Christianson's first model comes from James I's much discussed speech of March 21, which is described here as the source of a "constitutional monarchy created by kings." Although one typically thinks of ancient constitutionalism in relation to anticourt elements, Christianson seems not to think this point requires comment, and he proceeds to explain that James as king in England was very different from the monarch who in Scotland expressed his ideas in the *Trew Law of Free Monarchies* (1598). That tract has been described as "a powerfully argued justification of divine right which drew on Scottish history as well as the Old Testament to prove its case." And the same writer, noting that it was "informed by both relentless logic and a high sense of awesome responsibility," concluded that it "contained the awful warning that 'the kings . . . in Scotland were before any estates . . . before any parliaments were holden, or laws made . . . and so it follows of necessity, that the kings were the authors & makers of the laws, and not the laws of the king."[31]

The second model is in a parliamentary speech of Thomas Hed-

31. Jenny Wormald, reviewing *Minor Prose Works of James VI and I*, ed. James Craigie, in *English Historical Review* 103:407 (April 1988): 423–24. See also Christianson, herein, 120–25.

ley, making, for the time in which it was made, an unusually sweeping claim for "the absoluteness of the common law."[32] He asserted, according to Christianson, a "constitutional monarchy governed by the
common law." The third model is one of "mixed monarchy," meaning
a parliamentary monarchy on the lines enunciated in Sir James Whitelocke's famous speech of 1610. The latter had advanced extremely high
claims for the king in parliament. Christianson attributes to Selden
the same doctrine of parliamentary sovereignty, employing the following language: "In contrast to King James and Thomas Hedley, Selden
fashioned an image of the ancient constitution as a mixed monarchy in
which kings, clergy, nobles, and freemen had shared sovereignty from
the very beginning."[33]

Although Christianson's enterprise and skill in constructing three
new models of the ancient constitution command admiration, it is very
difficult to introduce three models satisfactorily without more explanation than is provided here. For example, it is not altogether clear
that James's speech, taken by itself, will bear the weight that has been
placed upon it. A listener could be forgiven for thinking that he was
being reintroduced to the *Trew Law* as the king began. Thus James
spoke of kings being justly called gods because of their great power
and adduced as one sign of this great power that kings were makers of
law. According to James, laws were "properly made by the king only;
but at the rogation of the people"—a description that commended
itself to that notable champion of high royal power, Sir Robert Filmer.
Further, kings could make and unmake their subjects and were ac-
countable only to God.

But as the king proceeded, the tone of his speech moderated. Distinguishing between the original state of kings and that of settled monarchies, James stated that every just king in a settled kingdom made a
compact with his people when he made laws. Unless he ruled in accordance with them, he degenerated into a tyrant. To Christianson, these

---

32. Margaret Judson, *Crisis of the Constitution: An Essay in Constitutional and Political Thought in England, 1603–1645* (New York, 1964), 233. Pocock in his *The
Ancient Constitution and the Feudal Law: A Study of English Historical Thought in the
Seventeenth Century; a Reissue with a Retrospect* (Cambridge, England, 1987), 270ff.,
has also given Hedley much attention.

33. Christianson, herein, 132.

words meant that James had made a creative leap forward in which he subverted the standard constitutional version of power derived from the people. In the result he appropriated "the strengths of constitutional government (stability and the consent of the community of the realm), and still maintained the creative initiatives of monarchs." Finally, Christianson asserts that Charles I in his *Answer to the Nineteen Propositions* (June 1642)—which I have urged elsewhere introduced a new era of political definition—was "driven back to the interpretation [of the kingship] announced in . . . 1610 by his father."[34]

Also to be considered in this connection are Francis Oakley's comments. He, too, notes the change of tone as the speech proceeds, and like Christianson he thinks the king at times conciliatory. But he also calls attention to James's insistence that the laws were *his* laws, and he thinks it likely that the king's intention was "to soften for his audience the somewhat uncompromising contours of an otherwise distressingly absolutistic effusion."[35]

The second model comes from Hedley's speech on impositions in 1610. In it he declared that parliament had its "power and authority from the common law, and not the common law from the parliament." This was evidenced by parliament's inability to change the laws of succession, bind future parliaments, or abrogate the whole of the common law. But, significantly, parliament could amend that law. This meant, Christianson concludes, that in Hedley's view "common law reigned supreme in the ancient constitution" and, more specifically, "assigned all powers and privileges within the realm." Yet the mere fact that parliament could amend the common law gives one pause, suggesting as it does that common law was not in fact supreme. Another discordant note comes from the statement that in Hedley's opinion one parliament could not bind another—a proposition generally identified with a theory of parliamentary sovereignty. In any case, one would like to

---

34. I am using the text of James's speech as it appears in Francis Oakley, *Omnipotence, Covenant, & Order* (Ithaca, N.Y., 1984), 96–97, 104. The reference to Filmer comes from *Patriarcha and Other Political Works,* ed. Peter Laslett (Oxford, 1949), 119. Christianson, herein, 122, 182–84. Corinne Comstock Weston and Janelle Renfrow Greenberg, *Subjects and Sovereigns: The Grand Controversy over Legal Sovereignty in Stuart England* (Cambridge, England, 1981), 35ff.

35. Oakley, *Omnipotence,* 118.

know more about his outlook compared with such contemporaries as William Hakewill, who, like Hedley, opposed impositions. Hakewill, who has been lauded as "the best historian in the commons," had no doubt that if a statute were involved, it carried all before it. There is much reason for thinking that this, too, was Coke's position, though Christianson states otherwise.[36]

The third model is that of "mixed monarchy," a term used here to denote the sovereignty of the king in parliament. It would have been helpful if Christianson had explained more fully his choice of terminology. One is left wondering if Selden himself used it and if so in what context. For the term was used in a general fashion before 1642 but took on a fixed, technical meaning after Charles I's *Answer* became public. That is, after 1642 it had implications much further reaching than Christianson's usage suggests.[37] Putting this subject aside, it should be said that his further comments on Selden and "mixed monarchy" are of very considerable interest in light of what has been stated in this commentary about a Saxon constitution.

Selden is described as having found the first and lasting framework of the ancient constitution in the Saxon invasion which established the kingship, parliament, and Germanic customs in England. This was the situation when the Norman conquest intervened; but Selden, though tempted by his newly acquired knowledge of feudal tenure, drew back from any sweeping change in 1066, deciding in fact that the Conqueror's laws were so much like those of the Confessor that the Saxon constitution had been preserved. In the following centuries feudal and Saxon laws blended to produce a "mixed monarchy" presided over by the three estates of king, lords, and commons, a view of the constitution very different, it is stated here, from Coke's and Sir

---

36. Christianson, herein, 128–32, 139. For Coke's view, see *First Institutes,* lib. 2, cap. 10, sec. 170; for Hakewill's, *The Libertie of the Subject* (London, 1641), 98–99. This is Hakewill's speech on impositions, which the House of Commons of the Long Parliament ordered to be published along with Prynne's *Soveraigne Power of Parliaments* and the last three volumes of Coke's *Institutes.* It is perhaps significant that it did not choose to honor Hedley in this way. See also Conrad Russell on Hakewill in *Parliaments and English Politics, 1621–1629* (Oxford, 1979), 141, n. 3.

37. Weston and Greenberg, *Subjects and Sovereigns,* chap. 3.

John Davies's, the latter also prominent in Pocock's discussion.[38] In an earlier work, profitably read in conjunction with this essay, Christianson points out that Selden's main conclusions regarding continuity at the conquest were reached by way of the Lichfield chronicle and Hoveden's chronicle, both of which shed light on the Confessor's laws.[39] Coke, too, made use of these materials, as earlier noted.

Christianson's paper concludes with a substantial analytical section on the debates of 1628, in which he finds Selden upholding "mixed monarchy," Coke assuming a position more like Hedley's, and Attorney General Heath, though he flirted with an argument based on reason of state, returning ultimately to James I's "constitutional monarchy created by kings."[40] Though Christianson does not say so, Selden by the 1650s, disillusioned by parliamentarian versions of Charles I's *Answer,* redefined the three estates to exclude the king, an action scuttling one of the most vital parts of the mixed monarchy that Christianson has described.[41] On the other hand Selden may have believed in the sovereignty of the king in parliament as early as 1610, but if so more detail about his outlook in this respect would have been welcome. The problem is that very few Englishmen seem to have thought in terms of a full-fledged theory of parliamentary sovereignty before the civil war concentrated their minds on the issue.

In his "Jurisprudence of Liberty: The Ancient Constitution in the Legal Historiography of the Seventeenth and Eighteenth Centuries" John Phillip Reid undertook the formidable task of discussing ancient constitutionalism over two centuries, a task the more difficult because of the attention he gives to the American colonies. Dealing at great length with the subject before him, he has among other things reminded historians that they do not possess a monopoly of wisdom in appraising the goals and activities of the legal antiquaries of Stuart England.

Reid's analysis is distinctive because he is aware of the relationship between the common law principle of prescription and the ancient

38. Christianson, herein, 132–43.

39. Paul Christianson, "Young John Selden and the Ancient Constitution, ca. 1610–1618," *Proceedings of the American Philosophical Society* 128:4 (1984): 306.

40. Christianson, herein, 151–81.

41. Weston and Greenberg, *Subjects and Sovereigns,* 5.

constitution. This is the only essay to make the connection, and it is a vital one. That relationship provides the frame of reference for much of what he has to say. According to Reid, contemporaries viewed the ancient constitution as "a timeless constitution of unchanging general principles" because they thought in terms of prescription. Although he makes no mention of the importance of "1189" in determining the legality of ancient rights and liberties, he places a high value on customary usage because it demonstrated consent on the part of the community over a long period of time and this consent was vital to political liberty. Accordingly, the ancient constitution, which appears from Reid's evidence to be a Saxon constitution, was of cardinal importance in the history of liberty, and he writes admiringly of the ancient constitution for just this reason.[42]

The ancient constitution performed an indispensable service in his view in both the seventeenth and eighteenth centuries. In the seventeenth century it protected English rights and liberties against the crown; in the eighteenth it performed a similar function for the colonies who were threatened with arbitrary government by a sovereign parliament at Westminster. The theory of parliamentary sovereignty, which Reid finds inimical to liberty and the rule of law, is viewed here as a latecomer to the scene, becoming the ruling principle of the English constitutional system only in the nineteenth century.[43]

In Reid's opinion the preferable method of studying these centuries is by way of "forensic history" rather than the historical methods of modern scholars. Finding the ancient constitution to be "almost exclusively a matter of law, seldom of historiography," he recommends the adoption of a legal perspective that would enable the historian to see that the protagonists of the ancient constitution, as well as the opponents, were essentially filing briefs on behalf of the causes to which they were devoted, their interest in history extending only to its utility in presenting their case. Following out this line of reasoning and inspired by the values described above, Reid has little patience with twentieth-century historians who have lavished praise on Dr. Robert Brady. Whatever his virtues as a historian, the most important fact

42. Reid, herein, 228–34.
43. Ibid., 244–49.

about him was that he was the enemy of political liberty and the advocate of arbitrary government.[44]

In preparing their tracts Stuart advocates of ancient constitutionalism worked, as Reid rightly states, from the common law principle of prescription. It was central in the seventeenth-century political literature that he is discussing. Unfortunately, however, apparently lacking an awareness of the role of 1189 in common law reasoning at this time, Reid is in no position to deal adequately with the issue that defines their argument. This appears from his references to Sir Robert Atkyns—a Stuart judge and Whig polemicist active in the Brady controversy of the 1680s. Reid describes Atkyns as attacking as "Innovating Writers" those historians who by dating the House of Commons from Henry III's reign "would destroy Foundations, and remove . . . Ancient Landmarks, and the Ancient and Just Limitations and Boundaries of Power and Authority" but fails to clarify Atkyns's objection to this dating. The point is that high Tory writers were in the habit of placing the beginnings of the first House of Commons in 1265 (49 H.III) because it was the year of the earliest extant writ of summons to that House. That is, it was founded within time of legal memory, and this meant that the Commons had no legal base independent of the crown. It followed, accordingly, that the king could summon, prorogue, and dissolve that House at will, indeed, not even summon it at all—a conclusion dismaying to ancient constitutionalists who favored frequent parliaments.[45]

Reid's argument is flawed in other ways. For instance, he does not realize that Prynne, disillusioned by the outcome of the civil war, switched sides and became a crypto-royalist. Rewarded at the Restoration with the position of keeper of the tower records, he was one of the innovating writers whom Atkyns condemned.[46] Nor does Reid point

44. Ibid., 256–69. There is a great deal on Brady in this paper, but the indicated pages give an example of Reid's criticism.

45. Ibid., 252, 259–63. Atkyns—relying on Coke's *First Institutes*, lib. 2, cap. 10, sec. 170—makes it manifest in his *An Enquiry into the Power of Dispensing with Penal Statutes* (London, 1689), 21, that he considered legal memory to begin in Richard I's reign. Reid uses at one point Ellis's *Tracts on Liberty*, as they were called; and Ellis takes unequivocally the same position. The pertinent page is in pt. 1, 461. See note 12 above. Ellis was much read in the American colonies.

46. Weston and Greenberg, *Subjects and Sovereigns*, chap. 5, esp. 126, 131.

out that the doctrine of parliamentary sovereignty, "arbitrary" in colonial eyes, would not have seemed this way in England, where it had a much longer history than he allows. Nor does he think in terms of an ancient constitution in which a sovereign parliament figures, though this could easily be the case in the right set of circumstances, given the place of the *Modus* in Stuart political thought during most of the century. Nor, finally, is it at all clear that the ancient constitutionalism that Christianson associates with Selden or with William Petyt, the major Whig polemicist in the Brady controversy, amounted to no more than a legal brief with historical sources used as authorities.

Compared with Selden, whose scholarly credentials are widely praised, Petyt, as a practicing lawyer with a substantial practice, comes closer to Reid's description. He did think of Brady as an enemy of liberty, and he turned to the English past in search of a defense against Brady's thoroughgoing assault on Cokean historiography. Yet Petyt was also a devoted antiquarian who spent much of his life in search of the primary source materials from which history is written. At the Revolution he became keeper of the tower records. One of the legal counsel that advised the Lords on the use of the words *original contract* in writing the Bill of Rights, he couched his response in historical terms,[47] and his personal library was full of the medieval political literature mentioned above. To cite but a few examples, he had the medieval histories associated with Matthew Paris, Matthew of Westminster, Florence of Worcester, Hoveden, Lambarde (*Archeion, Archaionomia, Perambulation of Kent*), Ingulphus, and a chronicle that has been wrongly attributed to John of Brompton. He also had Selden's *Jani Anglorum, History of Tithes,* and *Notes on Fortescue.*[48] A personal library of this dimension hardly suggests a common lawyer in search of historical authorities for a brief.

On the other hand, Reid makes an important contribution in recognizing that the common law principle of prescription provides the appropriate point of departure in the study of ancient constitutional-

47. Ibid., 256.

48. *Catalogue of Manuscripts in the Library of the Honourable Society of the Inner Temple,* ed. J. Conway Davies (London, 1972). See in particular the listings under MS 512, volume M. Also see note 7 above.

ism, especially for the seventeenth century; and he has accumulated substantial data, drawn primarily from English sources, for the proposition that the ancient constitution was commonly seen as a Saxon constitution. Moreover, there is need to remind historians, carried away by the revisionism currently underway in early Stuart history, that principles and ideology were at work in the struggles between the Stuart kings and their subjects. J. H. Hexter certainly thinks so.[49] Nor can Reid be faulted for reminding twentieth-century scholars that the Stuart historians so influential in shaping ancient constitutionalism were usually common lawyers who applied common law reasoning to historical literature. But whether Reid's zeal for "forensic history" will play as well is a judgment best left to readers of his paper. Finally, it may be doubted that his view of Brady as a historian will go unchallenged.

IV

These carefully prepared essays will quickly move into the stream of comment on ancient constitutionalism generated by Pocock's seminal study. On some points they will supplement his analysis or supplant it, but at the least they will raise serious questions. Witness, for example, Holt's exposition of a medieval ancient constitution centering on the Confessor's laws and his suggestions about the manner in which that constitution reached Stuart England. And Brooks's findings are valuable in relationship not only to Pocock's study but also to Holt's, clearing the way for a new focus on the rising tide of medieval political literature in late Tudor England before Coke began his historical prefaces. Then there is Christianson's innovative attempt to create three models of the ancient constitution that invite comparison with Pocock's conception. To these should be added Reid's adversarial account of the ancient constitution and his advocacy of forensic history. Finally, all four authors, though they wrote within Pocock's parameters, adduce evidence for an ancient Saxon constitution with historical origins. This aspect of the essays has provided a unifying

---

49. See, for example, *Parliament and Liberty from the Reign of Elizabeth to the English Civil War*, ed. J. H. Hexter (Stanford, 1992).

thread in discussing their contents and will need to be considered in future analyses of Pocock's image of the ancient constitution.

There is a larger picture here that can be briefly sketched. First of all, it seems clear that the ancient constitutionalism that Pocock introduced to the scholarly world has a broader range than has hitherto been thought. It runs, so these papers suggest, from the baronial rebellion in the name of the Confessor's laws to Reid's ancient Saxon constitution of the eighteenth century, which was influential in both England and America. This sweep of time encompasses Fortescue's contribution to the stock of political ideas. His *De Laudibus* contains his celebrated account of England as a mixed government, termed here a *dominium politicum et regale,* and a spirited assertion of the rule of law, both sources of American constitutionalism. By the time that the doctrine of the ancient constitution penetrated colonial America, new elements had created a more complex picture. The first of these was the outpouring of medieval political literature under the impact of the printing press and with the encouragement of political figures high in the ruling circles of Elizabethan England. Another was the development of political pamphleteering on a large scale in Stuart England. In the course of the seventeenth century political literature took on a life of its own under the influence in particular of Charles I's *Answer* and the Brady controversy in the decade before the Glorious Revolution; transformed by the struggle between the Stuart kings and their subjects, it provided a noticeable political impulse in colonial America. From this source colonial leaders received a veritable storehouse of political ideas and practices, focusing on the original contract, the rule of law and government by consent, Magna Carta as a reaffirmation of Saxon liberties including trial by jury and the principle of no taxation without representation, the relationship between king and parliament, and the like.[50]

For this last point, the curious should turn to the wealth of evidence

---

50. An eighteenth-century tract that carried the ideological message of Stuart England to colonial America is Roger Acherley's *Britannic Constitution,* 2d ed. (London, 1759). He argued from prescription and associated the idea of an original contract with both the Confessor's laws and Charles I's *Answer.* See in particular 140ff., 168, 497.

in Trevor Colbourn's *Lamp of Experience* (1965), which tells so much about the ancient Saxon constitution in colonial intellectual life. One need only to examine his list of books in public and private colonial libraries and compare their contents with what is now known about Stuart polemical literature to recognize the extent of the interaction between England and colonial America in this respect. Little wonder, given these circumstances, that the Declaration of Independence, so Reid states, was first published in book form in a collection entitled *The Genuine Principles of the Ancient Saxon, or English Constitution* (1776).[51] Its contents were largely drawn from Obadiah Hulme's *Historical Essay on the English Constitution* (1771), which, Colbourn notes, "rounded out the colonists' picture of their Saxon ancestors," who had founded their government, in Hulme's words "upon the common rights of mankind."[52] To Bernard Bailyn, the *Historical Essay* represented the historical understanding that underlay American constitutionalism on the eve of independence.[53] And, it might be added, in the years before the founding fathers gathered at Philadelphia preparatory to writing the Constitution to which the American Bill of Rights would soon be added.

51. Reid, herein, 186.

52. H. Trevor Colbourn, *The Lamp of Experience: Whig History and the Intellectual Origins of the American Revolution* (Chapel Hill, N.C., 1965), 30–31. See also Bernard Bailyn, *The Ideological Origins of the American Revolution* (Cambridge, Mass., 1967), 81–83 n. 26, 183–84. Hill, *Puritanism and Revolution*, 94–99.

53. Bailyn, *Ideological Origins*, 184.

Appendix:
Text and Translation of Magna Carta

There follows the text in Latin and in English translation of Magna Carta of 1225, the third Great Charter of Henry III. This is the definitive version that received statutory confirmation by Edward I in 1297, thereby entering the *Statutes of the Realm* as the first English statute. Thus, it is the Great Charter ultimately relied upon by Sir Edward Coke, John Selden, and the other great common lawyers of the seventeenth century. By then, according to Coke, it had been confirmed at least thirty-two times.

THE GREAT CHARTER OF HENRY III
(Third Revision, Issued February 11, 1225)

Henricus Dei gratia rex Anglie, dominus Hibernie, dux Normannie, Aquitanie, et comes Andegavie, archiepiscopis, episcopis, abbatibus, *prioribus,* comitibus, baronibus, vicecomitibus, prepositis, ministris et omnibus ballivis et fidelibus suis *presentem cartam inspecturis,* salutem. Sciatis quod nos, intuitu Dei et pro salute anime nostre et *animarum* antecessorum et successorum nostrorum, ad exaltationem sancte ecclesie et emendationem regni nostri, *spontanea et bona voluntate nostra, dedimus et concessimus archiepiscopis, episcopis, abbatibus, prioribus, comitibus, baronibus et omnibus de regno nostro has libertates subscriptas tenendas in regno nostro Anglie in perpetuum.*

1 (1). In primis *concessimus* Deo et hac presenti carta nostra *confirmavimus* pro nobis et heredibus nostris in perpetuum quod anglicana ecclesia libera sit, et habeat *omnia* jura sua integra et libertates suas

The text given here is that of *Statutes of the Realm* (London: Record Commission, 1810–1828), 1:22–25, as reprinted in Faith Thompson, *Magna Carta: Its Role in the Making of the English Constitution, 1300–1629* (Minneapolis, 1948), 377–82. Italicized words indicate those passages not found in the original 1215 Magna Carta of King John which were introduced in 1216, 1217, or 1225; numbers in parentheses refer to articles in the 1215 document.

illesas. Concessimus etiam omnibus liberis hominibus regni nostri pro nobis et heredibus nostris in perpetuum omnes libertates subscriptas, habendas et tenendas eis et heredibus suis de nobis et heredibus nostris *in perpetuum.*

2 (2). Si quis comitum vel baronum nostrorum sive aliorum tenencium de nobis in capite per servicium militare mortuus fuerit, et, cum decesserit, heres *ejus* plene etatis fuerit et relevium debeat, habeat hereditatem suam per antiquum relevium, scilicet heres vel heredes comitis de baronia comitis integra per centum libras, heres vel heredes baronis de baronia integra per centum libras, heres vel heredes militis de feodo militis integro per centum solidos ad plus; et qui minus debuerit minus det secundum antiquam consuetudinem feodorum.

3 (3). Si autem heres alicujus talium fuerit infra etatem, *dominus ejus non habeat custodiam ejus nec terre sue antequam homagium ejus ceperit; et, postquam talis heres* fuerit in custodia, cum ad etatem pervenerit, *scilicet viginti et unius anni,* habeat hereditatem suam sine relevio et sine fine, *ita tamen quod, si ipse, dum infra etatem fuerit, fiat miles, nichilominus terra remaneat in custodia dominorum suorum usque ad terminum predictum.*

4 (4). Custos terre hujusmodi heredis qui infra etatem fuerit non capiat de terra heredis nisi rationabiles exitus et rationabiles consuetudines et rationabilia servicia, et hoc sine destructione et vasto hominum vel rerum; et si nos commiserimus custodiam alicujus talis terre vicecomiti vel alicui alii qui de exitibus *terre* illius nobis debeat respondere, et ille destructionem de custodia fecerit vel vastum, nos ab illo capiemus emendam, et terra committetur duobus legalibus et discretis hominibus de feodo illo qui de exitibus nobis respondeant vel ei cui eos assignaverimus; et si dederimus vel vendiderimus alicui custodiam alicujus talis terre, et ille destructionem inde fecerit vel vastum, amittat ipsam custodiam et tradatur duobus legalibus et discretis hominibus de feodo illo qui similiter nobis respondeant, sicut predictum est.

5 (5). Custos autem, quamdiu custodiam terre habuerit, sustentet domos, parcos, vivaria, stagna, molendina et cetera ad terram illam pertinencia de exitibus terre ejusdem, et reddat heredi, cum ad plenam etatem pervenerit, terram suam totam instauratam de carucis *et omnibus aliis rebus, ad minus secundum quod illam recepit. Hec omnia observentur de custodiis archiepiscopatuum, episcopatuum, abbatiarum, prioratuum,*

ecclesiarum et dignitatum vacancium que ad nos pertinent, excepto quod hujus-
modi custodie vendi non debent.

6 (6). Heredes maritentur absque disparagatione.

7 (7). Vidua post mortem mariti sui statim et sine difficultate *ali-*
qua habeat maritagium suum et hereditatem suam, nec aliquid det pro
dote sua vel pro maritagio suo vel pro hereditate sua, quam heredi-
tatum maritus suus et ipsa tenuerunt die obitus ipsius mariti, et maneat
in capitali mesagio mariti sui per quadranginta dies post obitum ipsius
mariti sui, infra quos assignetur ei dos sua, *nisi prius et fuerit assignata,*
vel nisi domus illa sit castrum; et si de castro recesserit, statim provideatur ei
domus competens in qua possit honeste morari, quousque doe sua ei assignetur
secundum quod predictum est, et habeat rationabile estoverium suum interim de
communi. Assignetur autem ei pro dote sua tercia pars tocius terre mariti sui que
sua fuit in vita sua, nisi de minori dotata fuerit ad hostium ecclesie.

(8). Nulla vidua distringatur ad se maritandam, dum vivere voluerit
sine marito, ita tamen quod securitatem faciet quod se non maritabit
sine assensu nostro, si de nobis tenuerit, vel sine assensu domini sui, si
de aliquo tenuerit.

8 (9). Nos vero vel ballivi nostri non seisiemus terram aliquam nec
redditum pro debito aliquo quamdiu catalla debitoris *presencia* suffi-
ciant ad debitum reddendum *et ipse debitor paratus sit inde satisfacere;* nec
plegii ipsius debitoris distringantur quamdiu ipse capitalis debitor
sufficiat ad solutionem debiti; et, si capitalis debitor defecerit in solu-
tione debiti, non habens unde reddat *aut reddere rolit cum possit,* plegii
respondeant pro debito; et, si voluerint, habeant terras et redditus
debitoris quousque sit eis satisfactum de debito quod ante pro eo sol-
verunt, nisi capitalis debitor monstraverit se inde esse quietum versus
eosdem plegios.

9 (13). Civitas Londonie habeat omnes antiquas libertates et liberas
consuetudines suas. Preterea volumus et concedimus quod omnes alie
civitates, et burgi, et ville, *et barones de quinque portubus,* et *omnes* portus,
habeant omnes libertates et liberas consuetudines suas.

10 (16). Nullus distringatur ad faciendum majus servicium de feodo
militis nec de alio libero tenemento quam inde debetur.

11 (17). Communia placita non sequantur curiam nostram, set
teneantur in aliquo loco certo.

12 (18). Recognitiones de nova disseisina *et* de morte antecessoris non capiantur nisi in suis comitatibus, et hoc modo: nos, vel si extra regnum fuerimus, capitalis justiciarius noster, mittemus justiciarios per unumquemque comitatum *semel in anno,* qui cum militibus comitatuum capiant in comitatibus assisas predictas. *Et ea que in illo adventu suo in comitatu per justiciarios predictos ad dictas assisas capiendas missos terminari non possunt, per eosdem terminentur alibi in itinere suo; et ea que per eosem propter difficultatem aliquorum articulorum terminari non possunt, referantur ad justiciarios, nostros de banco, et ibi terminentur.*

13. *Assise de ultima presentatione semper capiantur coram justiciariis nostris de banco et ibi terminentur.*

14 (20). Liber homo non amercietur pro parvo delicto nisi secundum modum *ipsius* delicti, et pro magno delicto, secundum magnitudinem delicti, salvo contenemento suo; et mercator eodem modo salva mercandisa sua; et villanus *alterius quam noster* eodem modo amercietur salvo wainagio suo, si inciderit in misericordiam nostram; et nulla predictarum misericordiarum ponatur nisi per sacramentum proborum *et legalium* hominum de visneto.

(21). Comites et barones non amercientur nisi per pares suos, et non nisi secundum modum delicti.

(22). *Nulla ecclesiastica persona* amercietur *secundum quantitatem beneficii sui ecclesiastici, set secundum laicum tenementum suum, et secundum quantitatem delicti.*

15 (23). Nec villa, nec homo, distringatur facere pontes ad riparias nisi que ex antiquo et de jure facere debet.

16. *Nulla riparia decetero defendatur, nisi ille que fuerunt in defenso tempore regis Henrici avi nostri, per eadem loca et eosdem terminos sicut esse consueverunt tempore suo.*

17 (24). Nullus vicecomes, constabularius, coronatores vel alii ballivi nostri teneant placita corone nostre.

18 (26). Si aliquis tenens de nobis laicum feodum moriatur, et vicecomes vel ballivus noster ostendat litteras nostras patentes de summonitione nostra de debito quod defunctus nobis debuit, liceat vicecomiti vel ballivo nostro attachiare et inbreviare catalla defuncti inventa in laico feodo ad valenciam illius debiti per visum legalium hominum, ita tamen quod nichil inde amoveatur donec persolvatur nobis debitum quod clarum fuerit, et residuum relinquatur executoribus ad facien-

dum testamentum defuncti; et si nichil nobis debeatur ab ipso, omnia catalla cedant defuncto, salvis uxori ipsius et pueris suis rationabilibus partibus suis.

19 (28). Nullus constabularius vel ejus ballivus capiat blada vel alia catalla alicujus *qui non sit de villa ubi castrum situm est,* nisi statim inde reddat denarios aut respectum inde habere possit de voluntate venditoris; *si autem de villa ipsa fuerit, infra quadraginta dies precium reddat.*

20 (29). Nullus constabularius distringat aliquem militem ad dandum denarios pro custodia castri, si *ipse eam* facere voluerit in propria persona sua, vel per alium probum hominem, si ipse eam facere non possit propter rationabilem causam, et, si nos duxerimus eum vel miserimus in exercitum, erit quietus de custodia secundum quantitatem temporis quo per nos fuerit in exercitu *de feodo pro quo fecit servicium in exercitu.*

21 (30). Nullus vicecomes, vel ballivus noster, vel alius capiat equos vel carettas alicujus pro cariagio faciendo, nisi *reddat liberationem antiquitus statutam, scilicet pro caretta ad duos equos decem denarios per diem, et pro caretta ad tres equos quatuordecim denarios per diem. Nulla caretta dominica alicujus ecclesiastice persone vel militis vel alicujus domine capiatur per ballivos predictos.*

(31). Nec nos nec ballivi nostri *nec alii* capiemus alienum boscum ad castra vel alia agenda nostra, nisi per voluntatem illius cujus boscus ille fuerit.

22 (32). Nos non tenebimus terras eorum qui convicti fuerint de felonia, nisi per unum annum et unum diem; et tunc reddantur terre dominis feodorum.

23 (33). Omnes kidelli decetero deponantur penitus per Tamisiam et Medeweiam et per totam Angliam, nisi per costeram maris.

24 (34). Breve quod vocatur Precipe decetero non fiat alicui de aliquo tenamento, unde liber homo *perdat* curiam suam.

25 (35). Una mensura vini sit per totum regnum nostrum, et una mensura cervisie, et una mensura bladi, scilicet quarterium London, et una latitudo pannorum tinctorum et russettorum et haubergettorum, scilicet due ulne infra listas; de ponderibus *vero* sit ut de mensuris.

26 (36). Nichil detur de cetero pro brevi inquisitionis *ab eo qui inquisitionem petit* de vita vel membris, set gratis concedatur et non negetur.

27 (37). Si aliquis teneat de nobis per feodifirmam vel soccagium,

vel per burgagium, et de alio terram teneat per servicium militare, nos non habebimus custodiam heredis nec terre sue que est de feodo alterius, occasione illius feodifirme, vel soccagii, vel burgagii, nec habebimus custodiam illius feodifirme vel soccagii vel burgagii, nisi ipsa feodifirma debeat servicium militare. Nos non habebimus custodiam heredis *nec* terre alicujus quam tenet de alio per servicium militare, occasione alicujus parve serjanterie quam tenet de nobis per servicium reddendi nobis cultellos, vel sagittas, vel hujusmodi.

28 (38). Nullus ballivus ponat decetero aliquem ad legem *manifestam vel ad juramentum* simplici loquela sua, sine testibus fidelibus ad hoc inductis.

29 (39). Nullus liber homo *decetero* capiatur vel imprisonetur aut disseisiatur *de aliquo libero tenemento suo vel libertatibus vel liberis consuetudinibus suis,* aut utlagetur, aut exuletur aut aliquo *alio* modo destruatur, nec super eum ibimus, nec super eum mittemus, nisi per legale judicium parium suorum, vel per legem terre.

(40). Nulli vendemus, nulli negabimus aut differemus rectum vel justiciam.

30 (41). Omnes mercatores, *nisi publice antea prohibiti fuerint,* habeant salvum et securum exire de Anglia, et venire in Angliam, et morari, et ire per Angliam tam per terram quam per aquam ad emendum *vel* vendendum sine omnibus toltis malis per antiquas et rectas consuetudines, preterquam in tempore gwerre, et si sint de terra contra nos gwerrina; et si tales inveniantur in terra nostra in principio gwerre, attachientur sine dampno corporum vel rerum, donec sciatur a nobis vel *a* capitali justiciario nostro quomodo mercatores terre nostre tractentur, qui tunc invenientur in terra contra nos gwerrina; et, si nostri salvi sint ibi, alii salvi sint in terra nostra.

31 (43). Si quis tenuerit de aliqua escaeta, sicut de honore Wallingefordie, Bolonie, Notingeham, Lancastrie, vel de aliis que sunt in manu nostra, et sint baronie, et obierit, heres ejus non det aliud relevium nec fiat nobis aliud servicium quam faceret baroni, si *ipsa* esset in manu baronis; et nos eodem modo eam tenebimus quo baro eam tenuit, *nec nos, occasione talis baronie vel escaete, habebimus aliquam escaetam vel custodiam aliquorum hominum nostrorum, nisi alibi tenuerit de nobis in capite ille qui tenuit baroniam vel escaetam.*

32. *Nullus liber homo decetero det amplius alicui vel vendat de terra sua quam ut de residuo terre sue possit sufficienter fieri domino feodi servicium ei debitum quod pertinet ad feodum illud.*

33 (46). Omnes *patroni abbatiarum* qui habent cartas regum Anglie *de advocatione,* vel antiquam tenuram *vel possessionem,* habeant earum custodiam cum vacaverint, sicut habere debent, *et sicut supra declaratum est.*

34 (54). Nullus capiatur vel imprisonetur propter appellum femine de morte alterius quam viri sui.

35. *Nullus comitatus decetero teneatur, nisi de mense in mensem; et, ubi major terminus esse solebat, major sit. Nec aliquis vicecomes vel ballivus faciat turnum suum per hundredum nisi bis in anno et non nisi in loco debito et consueto, videlicet semel post Pascha et iterum post festum sancti Michaelis. Et visus de franco plegio tunc fiat ad illum terminum sancti Michalis sine occasione, ita scilicet quod quilibet habeat libertates suas quas habuit et habere consuevit tempore regis Henrici avi nostri, vel quas postea perquisivit. Fiat autem visus de franco plegio sic, videlicet quod pax nostra teneatur, et quod tethinga integra sit sicut esse consuevit, et quod vicecomes non querat occasiones, et quod contintus sit eo quod vicecomes habere consuevit de visu suo faciendo tempore regis Henrici avi nostri.*

36. *Non liceat alicui decetero dare terram suam alicui domui religiose, ita quod eam resumat tenendam de eadem domo, nec liceat alicui domui religiose terram alicujus sic accipere quod tradat illam ei a quo ipsam recepit tenendam. Si quis autem de cetero terram suam alicui domui religiose sic dederit, et super hoc convincatur, donum suum penitus cassetur, et terra illa domino suo illius feodi incurratur.*

37. *Scutagium decetero capiatur sicut capi solebat tempore regis Henrici avi nostri. Et salve sint archiepiscopis, episcopis, abbatibus, prioribus, templariis, hospitalariis, comitibus, baronibus et omnibus aliis tam ecclesiasticis quam secularibus personis libertates et libere consuetudines quas prius habuerunt.*

(60). Omnes autem istas consuetudines predictas et libertates quas concessimus in regno nostro tenendas quantum ad nos pertinet erga nostros, omnes de regno nostro tam clerici quam laici observent quantum ad se pertinet erga suos. *Pro hac autem concessione et donatione libertatum istarum et aliarum libertatum contentarum in carta nostra de libertatibus foreste, archiepiscopi, episcopi, abbates, priores, comites, barones, milites, libere tenentes, et omnes de regno nostro dederunt nobis quintam decimam partem omnium mobilium suorum. Concessimus etiam eisdem pro nobis et heredibus nostris quod nec nos nec heredes nostri aliquid perquiremus per quod libertates in hac carta contente infringantur vel infirmentur; et, si de aliquo aliquid contra hoc perquisitum fuerit, nichil valeat et pro nullo habeatur.*

His testibus domino Stephano Cantuariensi archiepiscopo, Eustachio Lundoniensi, Jocelino Bathoniensi, Petro Wintoniensi, Hugoni Lincolniensi, Ricardo Sarrisberiensi, Benedicto Roffensi, Willelmo Wigorniensi, Johanne Eliensi, Hugone Herefordiensi, Radulpho Cicestriensi, Willelmo Exoniensi episcopis, abbate sancti Albani, abbate sancti Edmundi, abbate de Bello, abbate sancti Augustini Cantuariensis, abbate de Evashamia, abbate de Westmonasterio, abbate de Burgo sancti Petri, abbate Radingensi, abbate Abbendoniensi, abbate de Maumeburia, abbate de Winchecomba, abbate de Hida, abbate de Certeseia, abbate de Sireburnia, abbate de Cerne, abbate de Abbotebiria, abbate de Middletonia, abbate de Seleby, abbate de Wyteby, abbate de Cirencestria, Huberto de Burgo justiciario, Ranulfo comite Cestrie et Lincolnie, Willelmo comite Sarrisberie, Willelmo comite Warennie, Gilberto de Clara comite Gloucestrie et Hertfordie, Willelmo de Ferrariis comite Derbeie, Willelmo de Mandevilla comite Essexie, Hugone Le Bigod comite Norfolcie, Willelmo comite Aubemarle, Hunfrido comite Herefordie, Johanne constabulario Cestrie, Roberto de Ros, Roberto filio Walteri, Roberto de Veteri ponte, Willielmo Brigwerre, Ricardo de Munfichet, Petro filio Herberti, Matheo filio Herberti, Willielmo de Albiniaco, Roberto Gresley, Reginaldo de Brahus, Johanne de Munemutha, Johanne filio Alani, Hugone de Mortuomari, Waltero de Bellocampo, Willielmo de sancto Johanne, Petro de Malalacu, Briano de Insula, Thoma de Muletonia, Ricardo de Argentein., Gaulfrido de Nevilla, Willielmo Mauduit, Johanne de Baalun.

Datum apud Westmonasterium undecimo die februarii anno regni nostri nono.

THE THIRD GREAT CHARTER OF
KING HENRY THE THIRD;
Granted A.D. *1224–25,*

*In the Ninth Year of His Reign. Translated from the Original,
Preserved in the Archives of Durham Cathedral.*

Henry, by the Grace Of God, King of England, Lord of Ireland, Duke of Normandy and Aquitaine, and Count of Anjou, to the Archbishops, Bishops, Abbots, Priors, Earls, Barons, Sheriffs, Governors, Officers, and all Bailiffs, and his faithful subjects, who see this present Charter,—Greeting. Know ye, that in the presence of God, and for the salvation of our own soul, and of the souls of our ancestors, and of our successors, to the exaltation of the Holy Church, and the amendment of our kingdom, that we *spontaneously and of our own free will, do give and grant to the Archbishops, the Bishops, Abbots, Priors, Earls, Barons, and all of our kingdom,*—these under-written liberties to be held in our realm of England for ever.—(I.) In the first place we grant unto God, and by this our present Charter we have confirmed for us, and for our heirs for ever, that the English Church shall be free, and shall have her whole rights and her liberties inviolable. We have also granted to all the free-men of our kingdom, for us and for our heirs for ever, all the under-written liberties to be *had and* held by them and by their heirs, of us and of our heirs.—(II.) If any of our Earls or Barons, or others who hold of us in chief by Military Service, shall die, and at his death his heir shall be of full age, and shall owe a relief, he shall have his inheritance by the ancient relief; that is to say, the heir or heirs of an Earl, a whole Earl's Barony for one hundred pounds: the heir or heirs of a Baron, a whole Barony, for one hundred pounds; the heir or heirs of a Knight, a whole Knight's Fee, for one hundred shillings at the most: and he who owes less, shall give less, according to the ancient customs of fees.—(III.) But if the heir of any such be under age, his Lord shall not have the Wardship of him nor of his land, before he

Source: Richard Thomson, *An Historical Essay on the Magna Charta of King John: To which are added, the Great Charter in Latin and English; The Charters of Liberties and Confirmations, Granted by Henry III. and Edward I.; The Original Charter of the Forests; and Various Authentic Instruments Connected with Them; etc.* (London, 1829), 131–44.

shall have received his homage, and afterward such heir shall be in ward; and when he shall come to age, that is to say, to twenty and one years, he shall have his inheritance without relief and without fine: yet so, that if he be made a Knight, whilst he is under age, his lands shall nevertheless remain in custody of his Lords, until the term aforesaid. — (IV.) The warden of the land of such heir who shall be under age, shall not take from the lands of the heir any but reasonable issues, and reasonable customs, and reasonable services, and that without destruction and waste of the men or goods. And if we commit the custody of any such lands to a Sheriff, or to any other person who is bound to us for the issues of them, and he shall make destruction or waste upon the ward-lands, we will recover damages from him, and the lands shall be committed to two lawful and discreet men of the same fee, who shall answer for the issues to us, or to him to whom we have assigned them: and if we shall give or sell to any one the custody of any such lands, and he shall make destruction or waste upon them, he shall lose the custody; and it shall be committed to two lawful and discreet men of the same fee, who shall answer to us in like manner as it is said before. — (V.) But the warden, as long as he hath the custody of the lands, shall keep up and maintain the houses, parks, warrens, ponds, mills, and other things belonging to them, out of their issues; and shall restore to the heir, when he comes of full age, his whole estate, provided with carriages and all other things at the least as such as he received it. All these things shall be observed in the custodies of vacant Archbishoprics, Bishoprics, Abbies, Priories, Churches, and Dignities, which appertain to us; excepting that these wardships are not to be sold. — (VI.) Heirs shall be married without disparagement. — (VII.) A widow, after the death of her husband, shall immediately, and without difficulty, have her freedom of marriage and her inheritance; nor shall she give any thing for her dower, or for her freedom of marriage, or for her inheritance, which her husband and she held at the day of his death; and she may remain in the principal messuage of her husband, for forty days after husband's death, within which time her dower shall be assigned; unless it shall have been assigned before, or excepting his house shall be a Castle; and if she depart from the Castle, there shall be provided for her a complete house in which she may decently dwell, until her dower shall be assigned to her as aforesaid: and she shall have her reasonable Estover within a common term. And for her dower, shall be assigned to her the third part of all the lands of her husband, which were his during his life, except she were endowed with less at the church door.—No widow shall be distrained to marry herself, whilst she is willing to live without a husband; but yet she shall give security that she will not marry herself, without our consent, if she hold of us, or without the consent of her lord if she hold of another.—(VIII.) We nor our Bailiffs, will not seize any land or rent for any debt, whilst the chattels of the debtor present sufficient for the payment of the debt, and the debtor shall be ready to make satisfaction: nor shall the sureties of the debtor be distrained, whilst the principal debtor is able to pay the debt; and if the principal debtor fail in payment of the debt, not having wherewith to discharge it, or will not discharge it when he is able, then the sureties shall answer for the debt; and if they be willing, they shall have the lands and rents of the debtor, until satisfaction be made to them for the debt which they had before paid for him, unless the principal debtor can shew himself acquitted thereof against the said sureties.—(IX.) The City of London shall have all its ancient liberties, and its free customs, as well by land as by water.—Furthermore, we will and grant that all other Cities, and Burghs, and Towns, and the Barons of the Cinque Ports, and all Ports, should have all their liberties and free customs.—(X.) None shall be distrained to do more service for a Knight's-Fee, nor for any other free tenement, than what is due from thence.—(XI.) Common Pleas shall not follow our court, but shall be held in any certain place.—(XII.) Trials upon the Writs of Novel Disseisin and of Mort d'Ancestre, shall not be taken but in their proper counties, and in this manner:—We, or our Chief Justiciary, if we should be out of the kingdom, will send Justiciaries into every county, once in the year; who, with the knights of each county, shall hold in the county, the aforesaid assizes.—And those things, which at the coming of the aforesaid Justiciaries being sent to take the said assizes, cannot be determined, shall be ended by them in some other place in their circuit; and those things which for difficulty of some of the articles cannot be determined by them, shall be determined by our Justiciaries of the Bench, and there shall be ended.—(XIII.) Assizes of Last Presentation shall always be taken before our Justiciaries of the Bench, and there shall be determined.—(XIV.) A Free-man shall not be amerced for a small offence, but only according to the degree of the offence; and for a great delinquency, according to the magnitude of the delinquency, saving his contentment: and a Merchant in the same manner, saving his merchandise, and a villain, if he belong to another, shall be amerced after the same manner, saving to him his Wainage, if he shall fall into our mercy; and none of the aforesaid amerciaments shall be assessed, but by the oath of honest and lawful men of the vicinage. — Earls and Barons shall not be amerced but by their Peers, and that only according to the degree of their delinquency. — No Ecclesiastical person shall be amerced according to the quantity of his ecclesiastical benefice, but according to the quantity of his lay-fee, and the extent of his crime. — (XV.) Neither a town nor any person shall be distrained to build bridges or embankments, excepting those which anciently, and of right, are bound to do it. — (XVI.) No embankments shall from henceforth be defended, but such as were in defence in the time of King Henry our grandfather; by the same places, and the same bounds as they were accustomed to be in his time. — (XVII.) No Sheriff, Constable, Coroners, nor other of our Bailiffs, shall hold pleas of our crown. — (XVIII.) If any one holding of us a lay-fee die, and the Sheriff or our Bailiff shall shew our letters-patent of summons concerning the debt, which the defunct owed to us, it shall be lawful for the Sheriff, or for our Bailiff to attach and register all the goods and chattels of the defunct found on that lay-fee, to the amount of that debt by the view of lawful men. So that nothing shall be removed from thence until our debt be paid to us; and the rest shall be left to the executors to fulfil the will of the defunct; and if nothing be owing to us by him, all the chattels shall fall to the defunct, saving to his wife and children their reasonable shares. — (XIX.) No Constable, nor his Bailiff, shall take the corn or other goods of any one, who is not of that town where his Castle is, without instantly paying money for them, unless he can obtain a respite from the free will of the seller; but if he be of that town wherein the Castle is, he shall give him the price within forty days. — (XX.) No Constable shall distrain any Knight to give him money for Castle-guard, if he be willing to perform it in his own person, or by another able man, if he cannot perform it himself, for a reasonable cause: and if we do lead or send him into the army, he shall be excused from Castle-guard, according to the time that he shall be with us in the army, on account of the fee for which he hath done service in the host.—(XXI.) No Sheriff nor Bailiff of ours, nor of any other person, shall take the horses or carts of any, for the purpose of carriage, without paying according to the rate anciently appointed; that is to say, for a cart with two horses, ten-pence by the day, and for a cart with three horses, fourteen-pence by the day.—No demesne cart of any ecclesiastical person, or knight, or of any lord, shall be taken by the aforesaid Bailiffs.—Neither we, nor our Bailiffs, nor those of another, shall take another man's wood, for our Castles or for other uses, unless by the consent of him to whom the wood belongs.—(XXII.) We will not retain the lands of those who have been convicted of felony, excepting for one year and one day, and then they shall be given up to the Lords of the fees.—(XXIII.) All Kydells (weirs) for the future, shall be quite removed out of the Thames and the Medway, and through all England, excepting upon the sea coast.—(XXIV.) The Writ which is called Præcipe, for the future shall not be granted to any one of any tenement, by which a Free-man loses his court.—(XXV.) There shall be one Measure of Wine throughout all our kingdom, and one Measure of Ale, and one Measure of Corn, namely, the Quarter of London; and one breadth of Dyed Cloth, of Russets, and of Halberjects, namely, Two Ells within the lists. Also it shall be the same with Weights as with Measures.—(XXVI.) Nothing shall for the future be given or taken for a Writ of Inquisition, nor taken of him that prayeth Inquisition of life or limb; but it shall be given without charge, and not denied.—(XXVII.) If any hold of us by Fee-Farm, or Socage, or Burgage, and hold land of another by Military Service, we will not have the custody of the heir, nor of his lands, which are of the fee of another, on account of that Fee-Farm, or Socage, or Burgage; nor will we have the custody of the Fee-Farm, Socage, or Burgage, unless the Fee-Farm owe Military Service. We will not have the custody of the heir, nor of the lands of any one, which he holds of another by Military Service, on account of any Petty-Sergeantry which he holds of us, by the service of giving us daggers, or arrows, or the like.—(XXVIII.) No Bailiff, for the future, shall put any man to his open law, nor to an oath, upon his own simple affirmation, without faithful witnesses produced for that purpose.—(XXIX.) No Free-man shall be taken, or imprisoned, or dispossessed, of his free tenement, or liberties, or free customs, or be outlawed, or exiled, or in anyway destroyed; nor will we condemn him, nor will we commit him to prison, excepting by the legal judgment of his peers, or by the laws of the land. —To none will we sell, to none will we deny, to none will we delay right or justice. —(XXX.) All Merchants, unless they have before been publicly prohibited, shall have safety and security in going out of England, and in coming into England, and in staying and in travelling through England, as well by land as by water, to buy and sell, without any unjust exactions, according to ancient and right customs, excepting in the time of war, and if they be of a country at war against us: and if such are found in our land at the beginning of a war, they shall be apprehended, without injury of their bodies or goods, until it be known to us, or to our Chief Justiciary, how the Merchants of our country are treated who are found in the country at war against us: and if ours be in safety there, the others shall be in safety in our land. —(XXXI.) If any hold of any Escheat, as of the Honour of Wallingford, Boulogne, Nottingham, Lancaster, or of other Escheats which are in our hand, and are Baronies, and shall die, his heir shall not give any other relief, nor do any other service to us, than he should have done to the Baron, if those lands had been in the hands of the Baron; and we will bold it in the same manner that the Baron held it. Neither will we have, by occasion of any Barony or Escheat, any Escheat, or the custody of any of our men, unless he who held the Barony or Escheat, held otherwise of us in chief. —(XXXII.) No Free-man shall, from henceforth, give or sell any more of his land, but so that of the residue of his lands, the Lord of the fee may have the service due to him which belongeth to the fee. —(XXXIII.) All Patrons of Abbies, which are held by Charters of Advowson from the Kings of England, or by ancient tenure or possession of the same, shall have the custody of them when they become vacant, as they ought to have, and such as it hath been declared above. —(XXXIV.) No man shall be apprehended or imprisoned on the appeal of a woman, for the death of any other man than her husband. —(XXXV.) No County Court shall, from henceforth, be holden but from month to month; and where a greater term hath been used, it shall be greater. Neither shall any Sheriff or his Bailiff, keep his turn in the hundred but twice in the year; and no where but in due and accustomed place; that is to say, once after Easter, and again after the Feast of Saint Michael. And the view of Frank-pledge, shall be likewise at Saint Michael's term, without occasion; so that every man may have his liberties, which he had and was accustomed to have, in the time of King Henry our grandfather, or which he hath since procured him. Also the view of Frank-pledge shall be so done, that our peace may be kept, and that the tything may be wholly kept, as it hath been accustomed; and that the Sheriff seek no occasions, and that he be content with so much as the Sheriff was wont to have for his view-making, in the time of King Henry our grandfather.—(XXXVI.) It shall not from henceforth, be lawful for any to give his lands to any Religious House, and to take the same land again to hold of the same House. Nor shall it be lawful to any House of Religion to take the lands of any, and to lease the same to him from whom they were received. Therefore, if any from henceforth do give his land to any Religious House, and thereupon be convict, his gift shall be utterly void, and the land shall accrue to the Lord of the fee.—(XXXVII.) Scutage from henceforth shall be taken as it was accustomed to be taken in the time of King Henry our grandfather.—Saving to the Archbishops, Bishops, Abbots, Priors, Templars, Hospitallers, Earls, Barons, and all others, as well ecclesiastical as secular persons, the liberties and free customs which they have formerly had.—Also all those customs and liberties aforesaid, which we have granted to be held in our kingdom, for so much of it as belongs to us, all our subjects, as well clergy as laity, shall observe towards their tenants as far as concerns them. *And for this our grant and gift of these Liberties, and of the others contained in our Charter of Liberties of our Forest, the Archbishops, Bishops, Abbots, Priors, Earls, Barons, Knights, Free Tenants, and all others of our Kingdom, have given unto us the fifteenth part of all their moveables. And we have granted to them for us and our heirs, that neither we nor our heirs shall procure or do any thing, whereby the Liberties in this Charter contained shall be infringed or broken; and if any thing shall be procured by any person contrary to the premises, it shall be had of no force nor effect. These being witnesses, the Lord Stephen Archbishop of Canterbury, Roger of London, Joceline of Bath, Peter of Winchester, Hugh of Lincoln, Richard of Salisbury, Benedict of Rochester, William of Worcester, John of Ely, Hugh of Hereford, Ralph of Chichester, William of Exeter, for the Bishops: the Abbot of Saint Edmund's, the Abbot of Saint Alban's, the Abbot of Battle Abbey, the Abbot of Saint Augustine's Canterbury, the Abbot of Evesham, the Abbot of Westminster, the Abbot of Peterborough, the Abbot of Reading, the Abbot of Abingdon, the Abbot of Malmsbury, the Abbot of Winchcomb, the Abbot of Hyde, the Abbot of Chertsey, the Abbot of Sherburn, the Abbot of Cerne, the Abbot of Abbotsbury, the Abbot of Middleton, the Abbot of Selby, the Abbot of Whitby, the Abbot of Cirencester, Hubert de Burgh, the King's Justiciary, Randolph Earl of Chester and Lincoln, William Earl of Salisbury, William Earl of Warren, Gilbert de Clare, Earl of Gloucester and Hertford, William de Ferrers, Earl of Derby, William de Mandeville, Earl of Essex, Hugh le Bigod, Earl of Norfolk, William Earl of Albemarle, Humphrey Earl of Hereford, John Constable of Chester, Robert de Ros, Robert Fitz Walter, Robert de Vipont, William de Brewer, Richard de Montfichet, Peter Fitz Herbert, Matthew Fitz Herbert, William de Albiniac, Robert Gresley, Reginald de Bruce, John de Monmouth, John Fitz Alan, Hugh de Mortimer, Walter de Beauchamp, William de Saint John, Peter de Mauley, Brian de Lisle, Thomas de Muleton, Richard de Argentine, Walter de Neville, William Mauduit, John de Baalun. — Given at Westminster, the Eleventh day of February, in the Ninth Year of our Reign.*

Notes on Contributors

CHRISTOPHER W. BROOKS studied at Princeton and Johns Hopkins before receiving his D.Phil. from Oxford University. He has held fellowships at the Huntington Library and at the National Humanities Center and is a Lecturer in History at the University of Durham. He is the author of *Pettyfoggers and Vipers of the Commonwealth: The "Lower Branch" of the Legal Profession in Early Modern England* and is currently working on a book about law, society, and politics in England from 1485 to 1660.

PAUL CHRISTIANSON studied at St. Olaf College and the University of Minnesota, where he received his Ph.D. He is Professor of History at Queens University, Ontario, is a Fellow of the Royal Historical Society, and has held fellowships at the Huntington Library. His publications include *Reformers and Babylon: English Apocalyptic Visions from the Reformation to the Eve of the Civil War*. His study of John Selden has so far resulted in publication of "John Selden, the Five Knights' Case, and Discretionary Imprisonment in Early Stuart England," "Royal and Parliamentary Voices on the Ancient Constitution, c. 1604–1621," and "Young John Selden and the Ancient Constitution, ca. 1610–18."

J. C. HOLT holds his D.Phil. from Oxford and until 1988 when he retired was Professor of Medieval History and Master of Fitzwilliam College in Cambridge University. He has served as President of the Royal Historical Society, and he is a Fellow of the British Academy and a Corresponding Fellow of the Medieval Academy of America. His books include *Magna Carta* (1965; 2d ed., 1992) and *Magna Carta and Medieval Government*. He recently became Sir James Holt, having been knighted in 1990 by Her Majesty Queen Elizabeth II.

JOHN PHILLIP REID was educated at Georgetown University, the Harvard Law School, the University of New Hampshire, and New York University School of Law, where he received his LL.M. and J.S.D. and where he is Professor of Legal History. He has held fellowships with the Guggenheim Foundation and the Huntington Library. His recent books include *The Constitutional History of the American Revolution* (3 vols.); *The Concept of Liberty in the Age of the American Revolution;* and *The Concept of Representation in the Age of the American Revolution.*

ELLIS SANDOZ studied at Louisiana State University, Georgetown University, the University of Heidelberg, and the Ludwig Maximillian University in Munich, where he completed the *Dr.oec.publ.* He is Professor of Political Science and Director of the Eric Voegelin Institute for American Renaissance Studies at Louisiana State University. He has been a Fellow of the Huntington Library, a 40th Anniversary Fulbright Distinguished American Scholar, and a member of the National Council on the Humanities. His recent books include *A Government of Laws: Political Theory, Religion, and the American Founding; Political Sermons of the American Founding Era, 1730–1805;* and *Eric Voegelin's Significance for the Modern Mind.*

CORINNE COMSTOCK WESTON studied at the University of Maine and received her Ph.D. from Columbia University. She is Professor Emeritus of History at Herbert H. Lehman College of the City University of New York and served also as a member of the Ph.D. Faculty of CUNY. She is an American Fellow of the Royal Historical Society and has served on the National Screening Committee for the Fulbright-Hays Program and as a reader for the National Endowment for the Humanities. Her publications include *English Constitutional Theory and the House of Lords, 1556–1832;* with Janelle Greenberg, *Subjects and Sovereigns: The Grand Controversy over Legal Sovereignty in Stuart England;* "The Theory of Mixed Monarchy under Charles I and After"; and "England: Ancient Constitution and Common Law."

Index

The typeface used for this book is ITC New Baskerville, which was created for the International Typeface Corporation and is based on the types of the English type founder and printer John Baskerville (1706–75). Baskerville is the quintessential transitional face: it retains the bracketed and oblique serifs of old-style faces such as Caslon and Garamond, but in its increased lowercase height, lighter color, and enhanced contrast between thick and thin strokes, it presages modern faces.

The display type is set in Didot.

This book is printed on paper that is acid-free and meets the requirements of the American National Standard for Permanence of Paper for Printed Library Materials, z39.48-1992. ♾

Book design by Rich Hendel, Chapel Hill, North Carolina
Typography by Tseng Information Systems, Inc., Durham, North Carolina
Printed by Worzalla Publishing Company, Stevens Point, Wisconsin, and bound by Dekker Bookbinding, Grand Rapids, Michigan